THE MANNER IS ORDINARY

The Manner Is Ordinary

BY JOHN LaFARGE, S.J.

➤➤❯❮❮❮

Harcourt, Brace and Company
New York

Library of Congress Catalog Card Number: 54-5250

Imprimi Potest: John J. McMahon, S.J., Provincial, New York Province

Nihil Obstat: John M. A. Fearns, S.T.D., Censor Librorum

Imprimatur: ✠ FRANCIS CARDINAL SPELLMAN, Archbishop of New York

Mariae assumptae et pro peccatoribus roganti
d.d.d.
scriptor

CONTENTS

ILLUSTRATIONS

(between pages 152-53)

A LaFarge family group, Glen Cove, New York, 1861-62.

The author's parents.

The author as a child, at age 15, and as a young priest in 1905.

Parish meeting at St. James, St. Mary's City, Maryland, and the first pupils of St. Alphonsus School.

A weekly forum meeting at the Catholic Interracial Center, New York.

The Editorial Board of *America*.

The Catholic Interracial Forum, Charleston, West Virginia, 1951.

The annual retreat of the Catholic Laymen's Union, July, 1953.

ACKNOWLEDGMENTS

This story, for better or worse, would never have been written save for the persuasive arguments of *America*'s Literary Editor, the Reverend Harold C. Gardiner, S.J., aided and abetted by Miss Anne Ford, and my own Superiors. Nor could the manuscript have taken manageable shape in so short a time without the lavish help of the chief editor of my publisher's staff, and of the Reverend Edward A. Conway, S.J., of the *America* staff. Father Robert C. Hartnett, S.J., *America*'s present Editor-in-Chief, greatly aided my work through various practical facilities. I was immensely assisted, as usual, by the diligent co-operation of my secretary, Mr. William H. Dodd. I am indebted to Mr. George K. Hunton, secretary of the Catholic Interracial Council, for help and suggestions concerning Chapters XIII and XX. Many interesting items concerning the beginnings of the Slav colony in Maryland were supplied by Mr. John Balta, of St. Mary's City.

Important details about my earlier years and the family background were furnished or confirmed for me by my sister Miss Margaret LaFarge, who also kindly placed at my disposal many letters, photographs, and other documents in her possession. Very helpful, too, were the unpublished memoirs of the LaFarge and Perry families compiled by my late sister Frances (Mrs. Edward H. Childs). To her daughter, Dr. Frances Sergeant Childs, as well as to my nephews, L. Bancel LaFarge, Henry A. LaFarge, and Edward H. LaFarge, and to Miss Sarah Redwood Lee of Washington, D. C., I am indebted for photographs and other documents, as well as to Mr. Lamont Moore, of New Haven, who arranged for my use of the collection of my father's letters in the manuscript division of the Yale University Library. Dr. Edward E. Best, Captain M. V. Boutté, and Mr. M. A. Thomas, charter members of the Catholic Laymen's Union and the Catholic Interracial Council, were most helpful in supplying information.

Mrs. Ward Thoron and Miss Aileen Tone graciously supplied information concerning the latter days of Henry Adams, and other kind friends offered welcome suggestions and advice. I wish also to express my thanks to Mr. Leon Edel, the author, and his publisher, the J. B. Lippincott Company, for the quotation from *Henry James, The Untried Years: 1843-1870,* as well as to Houghton Mifflin Company for the quotation from Mabel LaFarge's *Letters to a Niece;* and to the New American Library's *New World Writing* for the quotation from Margaret Mead's "Sex and Censorship in Contemporary Society."

I have taken the liberty of adding, in appendix form, several matters which might have interrupted the narrative if placed in the body of the text, but which I felt should be a matter of record.

JOHN LAFARGE, S.J.

PARS HIEMALIS

Every week of the year the priest reads to himself the 150 Psalms of David which, in the monastic Orders, the monks chant in choir. These are distributed into a certain quota for each day and alternate with selected passages of Scripture and prayers suitable for the season of the year or for some sacred personage or event honored in the church calendar. This daily "office" was a few centuries ago gathered into one book, the Breviary, which is divided into Winter, Spring, Summer and Autumn parts; or, in Latin, Pars Hiemalis, Pars Verna, Pars Aestiva, Pars Autumnalis.

Following, as he does, this perpetual sequence of prayer and praise, the priest sees all life interwoven with seasonal significance. The Breviary recalls each year the immense story of God's dealings with mankind: how He created man and saved him from his own misdeeds, how He raises him up and glorifies him in union with the risen and glorified Christ. So, too, the four volumes recall the unfolding of one's own life; for each of us is called, in a way, to recapitulate some part of the history of all humanity.

Winter is the season of Advent; of Jesus' coming into this world; of birth and life with parents and family intimacy; of youth's schooling, friendships, rewards and failures. It is the season when the future growth lies hidden. It seems fitting that the Winter volume begin one's life story.

CHAPTER ONE

Father As I Knew Him

➤➤ ◄◄

In 1891, when I was a boy of eleven, Father returned from his trip to the South Seas with Henry Adams. I went down to Long Wharf in Newport to meet him and we drove up to our house on Sunnyside Place, the old Grant cottage, in a Long Wharf cab. I was charmed to see that Father was a real person, who wore an impressive black beard. I was glad to know that I really had a father in fact, since my picture of him before that time had been quite indefinite.

Father was then fifty-six; he was near forty-five years old when I was born. It hardly occurred to me that one could have a father who was not an old man. Since I was the last of nine children, I was never part of my father's early life at home, and had never known him as directly and personally as had my two older brothers, Grant and Bancel. It was Bancel in many ways who took Father's place as a parent, playing the role with me that a young father might assume with his children.

I had no recollection of Father at all in my very early childhood, and during my sixth and seventh years he was away on his first trip to Japan with Adams. After his return, he was busy in New York with the tremendous painting of the Ascension, in the Episcopal Church of the Ascension on Fifth Avenue. His occasional visits to Newport were few and usually hurried, the longest being the summer he engaged a studio there on Corné Street.

The reason for Father's absence from home was simple enough. He was so hampered by the enormous amount of

3

decorative work he was doing, in murals and stained glass, that it seemed impossible for him to transfer his activities away from the city. He had tried living in Newport several times in earlier years, and if each time he found it "impossible," he blamed this to some extent on the climate. But in point of fact, he needed contact with his patrons, with such stained glass manufacturers as Calvin and Wright on Washington Square, and he needed to see personally to all the incidentals of an immensely productive artistic activity.

As for the other possibility, that of moving his household to New York, neither he nor my mother had ever reached any feasible plan, though they talked of it from time to time after his return from the South Seas in 1892. It was only in the autumn of 1895 that my mother finally closed the house in Newport and came to New York, where we all lived together, for the first time in my own life, under one roof. That year we rented the capacious Richard Watson Gilder house at 55 Clinton Place, now Eighth Street, and the next winter took an equally capacious red brick mansion at 22 East Tenth.

Before these years in New York, Father existed for me only as the great ancestor, the mysterious source of the Japanese drawings and paintings with which our home was filled. It was only natural that I had no very clear impression of him personally: he was simply someone who came and went quite unpredictably, a person who when at home must never be disturbed. My feelings toward him were a mixture of fear, of fascination, and of regret.

My fear was of his irascibility, though not for what he might do to me, since Father was not a physically violent or truculent person; it was rather a fear of what he might do to himself. "Mr. LaFarge he get mad as hell," was the remark of one of his Japanese studio helpers. Father himself wrote to Henry Adams in 1887: "My temper is frightful and the world is stuffed with sawdust." He also remarked that my brother Grant was the only person he knew with a worse temper than his own. Even in these early years I was conscious that Father was capable of creating a great deal of trouble in his own life by losing his peace of mind.

Father's standard defense against certain knocks and blows of life was to say, "I am an ill man." None of us knew exactly how ill he really was and how far he had dramatized his own physical condition as a sort of protection against the wickedness and impossibility of the world around him. He had, it is true, been through a very severe illness in the years 1866 and 1867, six and seven years after his marriage. At that time he contracted some form of lead poisoning which he said partly paralyzed his hands. He undoubtedly suffered a great deal from a sort of general malaise. He often alluded to the fact that he struggled against the obstacle of sickness and that for him it was, in fact, an incentive to greater effort. Yet his illness did not prevent his undertaking a series of long and arduous journeys to the East, to the South Pacific, and to Europe, as well as to other parts of this country, living for months under conditions of great privation and continued physical exertion.

Despite his restlessness and his difficult temperament, there was nothing mysterious about Father. Many-sided as was his career, it followed a logical pattern: overladen and vexatious, much in conflict with the affairs of daily life, but perfectly intelligible. His faults were human, such as might attach to anybody with a similar temperament who was convinced of a similar task and was placed in a similar position. The wonder is that he kept as good as he was. Father had no particular love for the abnormal, the unusual and occult, or the spiritualistic; he was only interested in strange manifestations of psychology when they displayed something that was essentially human. At the same time, he had a terrific sense of the complexity of human existence, the enormous number of fine shadings and gradations in human life. He was not particularly mystical, but his mind was definitely contemplative.

He embodied this contemplative spirit in the best known of all his works, the great mural altarpiece of the Ascension of Our Lord. Bishop Donald W. Aldrich, formerly rector of the

Ascension Church, speaking to me of the effect the painting exercised upon the mind of the public, said that by day or by night, all through the year, a stream of visitors would sit and gaze at the painting, as if losing themselves in it, as the artist had lost himself in the sublime mystery that it represented.

Yet it is somehow consistent with Father's active, inquiring mind that immediately after he received the commission for this painting in 1886, he astonished his friends and the church's trustees by packing up and departing with Henry Adams for Japan. There was definite method in his madness. His idea in going to Japan was to study with sketches the Japanese landscape, the mountains, streams and atmosphere which were the background of the contemplative paintings of the Japanese and Chinese artists. This, instead of the bare hills of Judea, was to be the background of his painting of the Ascension.

I think his contemplative attitude was increased or emphasized by contrast with surroundings in which he did his work, the '90s and the first decade of the twentieth century. Efficiency was then enthroned, people felt unlimited optimism, believed in progress, and there was a sense of patent material accomplishment. Part of the fascination Father's conversation exercised as he sat year after year in his favorite seat at the Century Club in New York City was the contrast of his continually inquiring spirit with the intensely smug and efficiency-minded world around him. His admirers frequently remarked that LaFarge was a continual searcher, a questioner. That is true, yet his questioning was based on the conviction that he had reached certain truths and that there *were* answers to the questions. Innumerable queries tormented him to the end, and yet there was always somewhere an answer, he seems to have realized, which led to a greater answer, until all answers would be fused in the Supreme Answer, which is God.

As a child I did not understand or appreciate the conversational gifts that made him famous, yet everything Father did was intensely interesting. He was interesting to see; his person was always absolutely neat, and scrupulously adapted to whatever he was undertaking to do. He had his own kind of pen, his own kind of paper, his own distinctive way of doing everything; every gesture of his body seemed to relate to the ultimate ends of his life and work. Father in a benign mood was as fascinating as Father in an irascible one was alarming.

He was interested in everything that concerned man and mankind; yet not in the spirit of the mere sentimental humanitarian, in fact, he was curiously unsentimental. His dry, humorous cynicism was in accordance with ancestral traditions. He was concerned in somewhat eighteenth-century fashion with all varieties of human beings, near and far, different races and types of men, their ways, their habits, their songs, their dances, their customs, and their wars, their psychology, the peculiarities of old and young, men and women—particularly the strange things that women do to you when you are trying to get through your work as an artist.

As might be imagined, he cared for all the arts—except that, curiously enough, he had no ear for music. I asked him once what music he liked best and he said, "John, the music that makes the least sound." As for public matters, he was fairly indifferent to political issues, though, after a visit to Chicago, he preferred Teddy Roosevelt to John P. Altgeld.

In the range of his talents, as of his interests, he was—as was often said—the type of a Renaissance man, a remote sort of parallel to Leonardo da Vinci and men of that age. I always felt mixed emotions over his triumphs in the field of decorative art, in which he came more and more to concentrate, because I felt that his separation from home and family would not have been necessary if he had not devoted himself so thoroughly to mural work and stained glass. If he had stuck to his easel, to the work of his studio, I felt, he would have been closer to us and we would have remained united. Yet Father's title to fame, such as it is, rests largely on his work of decoration. One of the many eulogies pronounced at his death in 1910 was based on this phase of his activities:

One of the greatest artists this country has produced, a universal genius who belongs to all time, has released his hold upon the brush which limned the beauties of earth. He translated medieval moods: he vied with the pre-Raphaelites of the Japanese; he revived the lost art of artifices in stained glass and placed his work with theirs in the venerable cathedrals in France; he drank deep of the romance of the isles of the Southern Seas, yet through protean changes he retained his own individuality and enriched and glorified the art of the land of his activity.

All this may or may not be true, but still as a boy I used to look longingly at his early illustrations of Browning, his portraits of my mother and my brother Grant, his sketches of Newport in oil, and his charming painting of Paradise Valley, "The Green Map," with its solitary white lamb resting on a carpet of briary verdure. I deeply regretted that those days were gone forever, that they had never been a part of my own life and that all I knew was a parent lost in work which removed him from my own personal knowledge and contact.

One of the things I remember best about my father was his deep respect and reverence for his mother, née Louisa Binsse, who had married a Welshman, Thomas Jones, after my grandfather's death.

Like all the Binsses, Bonne Maman, as we called Grandmother, was fond of litigation. They were said to have been natural litigants from the very beginning. The oldest Binsse, the first ascertainable in history and my earliest traceable paternal ancestor, was a man called Patrick Binns who emigrated from Limerick in Ireland to Nantes in Brittany, where he added the name of Saint-Victor. The Binsses showed some of the Irish traits; they were inclined to be quarrelsome, yet people liked them because they were also extremely charitable. They had a tradition of dissent, talkativeness, and charity which appeared in one generation after another. Bonne Maman's brother, Louis François Binsse, was active in Catholic charities in his day and was a trustee of St. Patrick's Cathedral; her nephew, Louis B. Binsse, known as "the saint of

Sixteenth Street," was one of the pioneers in the St. Vincent de Paul Society in New York.

In my childhood Bonne Maman resided at 5 West Thirty-third Street, where I made the acquaintance of her two old faithful domestics, Ann Ward and Ann Hogan. Both Anns came to my grandmother as young colleens just out of Ireland, remaining with her—Ann Ward sixty years and Ann Hogan some forty-five years—to their deaths. Ann Hogan was a large jovial type; Ann Ward was a sad-faced, thin, deprecatory little person whose favorite expression was "Sweet Peter!" Yet it was Ann Hogan who, as a member of the Third Order of St. Francis, kept her coffin in her room; every night between one and two she would arise from her bed, don her Franciscan habit, lie down in the coffin and meditate for an hour on death quite peacefully and naturally. Both of them made a deep impression on me by their piety and their complete devotion and unselfishness. They must have suffered some pretty anxious times dealing with the temperament of all the LaFarges and Binsses.

I did not see much of Father's brothers or sisters except of his youngest sister Aimée, who was twenty years older than myself, and only two years older than my oldest brother Grant. Aunt Aimée lived to the advanced age of eighty-six years. She was intensely devoted to her husband, the late George L. Heins, who was a partner of my brother Grant in the firm of Heins and LaFarge and with him was one of the original architects of the Cathedral of St. John the Divine. Emily, Father's oldest sister, married John H. Lawrence of New York, a well-known banker, and after his death went to Paris where she spent the rest of her life. She had three daughters; Agnes, the older one, married a Frenchman, the Count de Merlemont, whose home I visited in 1938. The Merlemonts were descendants of the family of de Rancé, the founder of the Trappists. The second daughter, Margaretta, married John Chase of New York, and the third, Aimée, married Ian Douglas Campbell, heir to the Dukedom of Argyle. Though her son, Ian, was brought up a Presbyterian, she herself was given a Catholic burial. Of Father's brothers, the only one I ever saw was Louis, who emigrated to the West Coast and founded the whole branch of the West Coast LaFarges with whom we always remained in affectionate relationship.

My grandmother LaFarge's father, Louis François Binsse de Saint-Victor, came to this country in the 1790s from Santo Domingo where he had been a planter along with his brother Maximilien.* Louis François decided to try his fortunes in New York and there he married another refugee from France, Victorine Bancel de Confoulens, whose father kept a little school for the émigrés. The brother Maximilien went back to Paris and was somewhat of an artist, poet and litterateur in his own right. His son Paul de Saint-Victor, who had dropped the Binsse, as he did himself, is well known in French literature. We always remained in correspondence with Paul de Saint-Victor. When my father went to Paris in 1856 he stayed with his uncle Maximilien and there became acquainted with the outstanding personages in French art and literature.

Once you start tracing relatives and their forebears, there seems to be no end to it; at least these names may give some idea of the background of my father's life. He was not given to talking about his family or his connections with them. Father was an American first, last, and always. He loved France, he loved things French, and he had a French type of mind. Yet he also was convinced that American art and literature and the American Church must stand on their own. I never felt that he was anything else but an American, and I think the contacts he made abroad helped him to appreciate the greatness of this country.

At the same time, his reverence for what was truly good and beautiful at home made him doubly appreciative of all that was worth respecting in the very distant lands to which he

---

* A wealth of information on persons and ideas of this period is to be found in *French Refugee Life in the United States, 1790-1800,* by my niece, Dr. Frances S. Childs (Johns Hopkins, 1940).

traveled, a trait that explains certain of his attitudes. In his recent biography of Robert Louis Stevenson, Mr. J. C. Furnas criticizes what he seems to consider a snobbish attitude on the part of Henry Adams and John LaFarge on their visit to Vailima, Stevenson's home in Samoa. I can't answer for Adams; he was an Adams, after all. With regard to Father a snobbish attitude does not seem to make sense. I would say rather that he disliked Stevenson's appearance simply because he disliked non-convention for non-convention's sake. He believed in old traditions; he reverenced the past in small things and great things, and had inherited from his parents a strong feeling of *noblesse oblige:* when you are out of the normal current of affairs and traveling around the Pacific Ocean, you should observe extra care to preserve your self-respect. You *might* neglect dressing for dinner at home in Newport—though I don't think he would—but still it would not be so important. But if you were in Tutuila or in Tahiti you would most undoubtedly dress for dinner, because otherwise it would be an insult to the hospitality of your hosts. The Samoans were an ancient and cultured race with great traditions of their own and coming from so many thousands of miles away to make one's home among them demanded an attitude of reverence and delicacy in their presence, with regard to what we felt as conventions in our life.

If there was a reason for being unconventional, such as the one recognized by the Chinese sage Chuang-Tzu, who played the guitar at his wife's death in order to be more in tune with the universe, Father could readily understand it. He himself saw no reason why he should not prowl out of the house clad in a purple kimono and straw sandals at dawn of a summer morning in order to observe the mist rising from the rocks upon the Newport seashore. It was only ten or fifteen minutes' walk from our old cottage down to Easton's Beach and the Cliff Walk, and since nobody was up at that hour and there was only one policeman on the Bellevue Avenue beat, and none to the east of it, why should Father not walk down

there and take a look at the sunrise in the way that would
seem to be most suitable for such contemplation? He had no
yearning to be eccentric or odd; he would have been just as
glad to make the trip in a tuxedo, if a tuxedo would have
helped contemplation. But the kimono put him in close contact with the landscape and thoughts behind the landscape
and the Creator who made it.

He simply wished to see the center of the world's mystery
and put himself in the best condition for seeing it, and sometimes he found it necessary to get as mad as hell. He also wondered whether, without a knowledge of geology, he could
paint the mountain ranges that he viewed as he sailed by the
islands of Tahiti. One never knew where Father's inquiries
would begin, or where they would cease; but they always
ended somewhere—they never went off into the void. There
was a thread, a reason which enriched either his mind or the
mind of those who talked to him. Even when he was most
exasperating, he continued to shed light.

Father did not make friends rapidly. In manner he was reserved and inquiring and critical in approaching people. It
was physically distressing to him to shake hands; disagreeable
for him to be introduced, and always somewhat of a shock to
make a new acquaintance. Yet he was singularly faithful to
his friends once he had made them, loyal to them to the very
end; in his whole life I never knew of an abandoned friendship. Friendship for him meant a continual intercourse of
word, thought, and interest.

In my childhood the most picturesque of all the *dramatis
personae* connected with my father was Mr. Okakura Kakuzo.
Mr. Okakura was a Japanese, a devout Buddhist, and a very
distinguished writer whose works have been translated into
English. One of his most delightful writings described his
pilgrimage to Tibet as a Japanese devotee. For us children
he was a subject of incessant interest. I vividly remember his
stay with us at Newport, how he insisted on wearing his

Japanese costume and sat on the stuffed parlor chair with his feet tucked under him, characteristic white Japanese stockings on his feet and straw sandals on the floor.

I ventured to ask Mr. Okakura, though I was only about eight years old at the time, his view of the white race. Mr. Okakura kindly explained that the white race had nothing to boast of; in fact, confidentially, it was rather deplorable. I asked him for particular reasons. First of all, he said, look at your homes where a multitude of pictures are hung on the wall without regard for sequence of time, place, or logic. They stay there indefinitely and contradict each other in every possible way. Compare your cluttered homes with the Japanese home, where each day of the year the owner unrolls a single *kakemono* and hangs it up on the wall for the family to contemplate. Mr. Okakura mentioned other aesthetic questions. For instance, he said, you consume milk, which is taken from the interior of a cow, as well as butter and cheese—a nauseating practice. As for your morals, look at your dances where men and partly disrobed ladies embrace intimately in public, whirl their bodies around and stamp to the sound of loud and strident music until all hours of the morning.

I didn't relay these disagreeable ideas to my parents or brothers because the talk was confidential and, after all, Mr. Okakura was our guest. I remember his distress once when he stayed with us in New York—I think it was in 1896—and went out for a walk dressed in his costume. He strolled from Fifth Avenue east on Tenth Street, and the further east he went the more unsympathetic he found the atmosphere, until he arrived at the block between Second and First Avenues. There he found the atmosphere not only unsympathetic, but hostile; various objects, he said, were thrown at him to emphasize the hostility. He had felt that walking toward the East things might have become more placid.

Mr. Okakura was indeed a great gentleman. He knew an enormous amount about tea, and the ceremony of drinking it. As a result, Father invested in a complicated lacquered tea outfit out of which we drank Japanese green tea with rather disastrous results, since it was extremely strong and seemed to have the effect of making everybody talk without being able to stop their conversation.

Among the other foreign visitors in my childhood, few were more interesting than the sculptor, Frédéric Auguste Bartholdi, designer of the Statue of Liberty, and his wife. The first plans for New York's famous Statue were worked out in 1876 by Monsieur Bartholdi in my father's studio in Newport. The Bartholdis were guests of my parents in Newport at the time, and a curious situation unexpectedly arose. My father—I don't know exactly how—discovered that Monsieur and Madame were not man and wife. Madame—née Bheux de Puysieux—had been a model, and Bartholdi was past forty at the time he met her. Though a prominent and prosperous artist, he was still in one respect immature and afraid: his mother was strongminded and imperious and he was certain she would not countenance a marriage with a girl who worked as a model. It was a problem, how to save the honor of the Bartholdis, not to mention the reputation of the LaFarge family itself. But Father and Mother, in their simple way, put the matter up to the pair and they agreed to get married. A priest could not be called in, since the Bartholdis were Protestants, nor did the pair belong to any religious affiliation known in Newport. It was decided, therefore, to invite the Rev. Dr. Ellery Channing, a Unitarian minister, to perform the marriage, which took place in the parlor, on the southern side of the house on Sunnyside Place. The bride was properly given in marriage by my father as her American "relative," and when the story reached France it was accepted even by Madame Bartholdi senior, who became firm friends with her daughter-in-law.

Of course, my acquaintance with the Bartholdis began after these events had taken place. To me the Bartholdis were exciting people not so much because of the Statue of Liberty as because they were the first French persons I had known out-

side of Franco-American relatives. I became a devoted intimate of young Madame Bartholdi through a familiar American product called popcorn. She had never seen popcorn and
was fascinated by it. In the winter evenings she and Monsieur
sat before the coal fire gleefully watching the delightful transformation of the grains into toothsome tidbits. Madame Bartholdi was so intrigued that after their return to Colmar, in
Alsace, she wrote and asked me to send to her a package of
popcorn with a "popper," a little wire device on a red stick
that you used in roasting the corn. Among my youthful bibliog-
raphy I treasured the letter in which she and Monsieur wrote
back saying they had received the popcorn, had unwrapped
the "popper," and had popped corn in their own fireplace.

The Statue of Liberty had been born in a financial sense
in the year of my own birth. In 1880 the Franco-American
Union had succeeded in raising funds for the Statue through
a lottery, and 300,000 tickets were sold at one franc each. The
people of France had met the challenge to their generosity,
and the Statue of Liberty was assured. On October 24, 1881,
the 100th anniversary of the Battle of Yorktown, the first rivet
was placed in the Statue of Liberty, "to be erected in New
York in remembrance of the ancient traditions of friendship
which unite the United States to France." By the next year,
as Bartholdi predicted, the Statue of Liberty loomed large
over the rooftops of Paris. On July 4, 1884, in the name of
the Franco-American Union it was formally presented to the
American Minister, Mr. Norton. It was then disassembled,
marked, prepared for shipment, and in May 1885 the Statue
of Liberty, carefully packed, left France bound for New York
harbor.

Many years later in New York I became acquainted with
Miss Emma Lazarus, who read me her wonderful lines inscribed on the base of the Statue. Miss Lazarus and the Bartholdis have long since passed away, but the Statue still stands.
It is curious to think that such a cosmic symbol took shape
in the brain of a man who enjoyed sitting by a fireside popping

corn with a skinny little child. Yet of such events is woven the tissue of this incredible world.

Considering that Father was at home so seldom in my early childhood that he hardly figured then in my life at all, and that even in later years we seldom saw him for more than five or six weeks annually, it may seem surprising that I, along with my brothers and sisters, conceived for him so deep an affection. That this was the case is attributable beyond measure to the tact and patience of my mother.

CHAPTER TWO

Mother and Father

⇒⇒ ⇐⇐

Father first came to Newport in the spring of 1859 to work in the Church Street studio of William Morris Hunt, earliest interpreter of the French school of painting in America. Hunt had two young Bostonians as students, William and Henry James, neither of whom developed into painters, though they were equally talented. Henry James in his *Notes of a Son and Brother* states that William Hunt had "no thoroughgoing élèves save John LaFarge and my brother."

At that time the center of attraction for the youth of Newport was a twenty-year-old young lady, Margaret Mason Perry. LaFarge had made her acquaintance through the James brothers who, from later accounts, seemed to have risked more than they thought at the time. Apparently the romance began when LaFarge and Margy Perry took a long walk out to the Spouting Rock on the Ocean Drive, a favorite promenade for Newporters in the early days.

Margaret's father was the late Dr. Christopher Grant Perry, one of the sons of Commodore Oliver Hazard Perry, and a nephew of Oliver's brother, Commodore Matthew Calbraith Perry, who achieved fame in 1853 by opening up Japan to the Western world. There is a curious relevancy in the latter, since John LaFarge had already possessed from boyhood a keen interest in things Oriental and Japanese. In childhood, he had edited with his brothers a little manuscript paper in French entitled *Le Chinois* and, as an undergraduate at St. John's College at Fordham, he had made the acquaintance

17

of Father William Monroe, S.J., who had been a naval officer and a missionary in Japan and had brought back a number of Japanese art objects.

Margaret Perry's mother, Mrs. C. Grant Perry, was Fanny Sergeant of Philadelphia, daughter of Thomas Sergeant, Chief Justice of the Supreme Court of Pennsylvania. Mrs. Perry, or Nonna as we always called her (pronounced Noh-na), was herself a great-granddaughter of Benjamin Franklin (Benjamin Franklin's daughter, Sally Franklin, married William Bache; their daughter Sally Bache married Judge Sergeant). Mrs. Grant Perry, like many of her family, bore a strong resemblance to her revolutionary ancestor, from whom she had inherited a tradition of kindliness and culture and a friendly manner with people in general. Though, as a devout Episcopalian, she disapproved in a general way of the Church of Rome, her attitude was tolerant compared to that of her mother-in-law, old Mrs. Commodore O. H. Perry, known to us as Grandma Perry, a vigorous and trenchant character.

Grandma Perry, so my mother informed me, and it was confirmed by other members of the family, had a fanatical hatred of everything Catholic. She firmly believed that the Church was the Scarlet Woman, and my mother remembered her teachings on that score, which were closely associated with the idea that the sun would turn blood red before the Last Judgment. Mother's earliest remembrance was of the sunset viewed from one of the upper windows of the old Perry mansion on Thames Street. Looking out over the harbor, she was alarmed by the red glow of the western sun as it sank over Goat Island; she really thought the end of the world was coming.

Another tradition about Grandma Perry took the edge off her fearsome side. As a little girl of five, she was taken to play on Easton's Beach, at the western end of which lies a rugged, rather flat-topped rock covered with barnacles and seaweed, over which I used to scramble as a small boy. Grandma Perry was marooned there by the rising sea and had to wait several hours until she could be rescued when the tide went down. It used to console me to think of her standing helpless in her little pantalets waiting for the tide to turn; it made up for the story of the Scarlet Woman and the blood-red sun.

Romance, in Mother's case, blossomed in a romantic Southern atmosphere, as a result of her friendship with Mrs. Mary Porter of Louisiana. The friendship itself was natural enough, since Newport in ante-bellum days was an annex of the deep South, a haunt of Southern summer residents. It was only after the war that the summer colony was drawn from literary Boston, and eventually from plutocratic New York. In the 1850's and earlier, wealthy plantation owners from South Carolina, Georgia, and Louisiana built palatial homes at Newport and beautified the town by their generosity. Already acquainted with the Perrys, Mrs. Porter invited Margy Perry to visit her historic plantation in the Evangeline country on the banks of the Bayou Tèche. Nonna gladly sent her daughter there for the two consecutive winters of 1858-59 and 1859-60.

From Father's point of view, lovely Margaret Perry's absenting herself from Newport was a serious matter. He considered the situation alarming because she seemed to be gathering more admirers in Louisiana than she had in Newport. This would never do. William James, whom Father referred to affectionately as "that donkey," circulated a report that she had already been proposed to by a person called Johnson and had turned him down. Henry James's apocalyptic-minded father announced that she was the only really attractive girl in Newport. Down on the plantation one of her ardent admirers was youthful Edward Douglass White, future Chief Justice of the United States, who in later years ventured to acknowledge to two members of my family that he had been desperately in love with Margy Perry. It was time to act. Being literary, LaFarge acted by writing, and started a series of letters, enclosing two or three neatly folded letters at a time in one envelope.

These he followed up by arranging for himself to be invited

to the plantation at the beginning of April 1860. He prepared
for his visit by sending a series of carefully thought-out written
proposals and arguments. These Margaret studied gravely and
concluded that they were unquestionably of the type which
her mother designated as "love letters"—letters conceived and
phrased in the proper style of 1860 Rhode Island and Louisiana amatory correspondence. The last of the series announced
his coming and was followed after his arrival by a series of
drawings of the plantation and Bayou in a little sketch-book
where with his painstaking pencil he managed in a tiny space
to convey the impression of vast space and mystery—a romantic background for fateful conversations.

There were several points to make clear to Margaret Perry
in these letters. The first, obviously, was that he loved her.
This he repeatedly expressed in the most appropriate fashion,
in language that could be properly scrutinized by her mother
in case the letters came into maternal hands:

I have spoken of you to my mother, who is ready to love you,
nay who loves you already . . . not, dear, (as I wished to tell you)
that I am in a hurry to marry—(to marry you is another thing, for
I thus own you) even with you, my dear, dear Margaret, it is to me
a sad step. I feel how serious it is, trust me, and its pleasures cannot conceal from me its dread chances. But with you, dearest dear,
a life, I believe, will pass happily: recollect though that you are
to love me *forever*—and *that*—even if my love for you were to die,
which indeed I cannot believe it will. Does that appear *too* hard
to you?

He was fascinated with Margaret's spiritual personality as
well as by her outward person. Of the latter indeed he says
nothing, doubtless lest her mother think that he was carried
away with some wayward and dangerous passion. Only in the
thirteenth and last letter of the series does he use the expression "passionately." Marriage for him is to be a union of
minds. She is to be, according to her own expression, "a spiritual wife." "We are," he says, "to be friends in conference, as
well as lovers." Thereby they can avoid "what you fear (and
I too), the loss of the lover in the husband or wife."

As an intellectual lover Father felt that he should communicate to his bride his mind as well as his love. In *Notes of a Son and Brother* Henry James describes the youthful mind of LaFarge, the "intellectual":

He revealed to us Browning, for instance; and this, oddly enough, long after *Men and Women* had begun (from our Paris time on, if I remember) to lie upon our parents' book-table. *They* had not divined in us as yet an aptitude for that author; whose appeal indeed John enforced to our eyes by the reproduction of the beautiful series of illustrative drawings, two or three of which he was never to surpass—any more than he was to complete his highly distinguished plan for the full set, not the least faded of his hundred dreams. Most of all he revealed to us Balzac; having so much to tell me of what was within that formidably-plated door, in which he all expertly and insidiously played the key, that to re-read even after long years the introductory pages of *Eugénie Grandet,* breathlessly seized and earnestly absorbed under his instruction, is to see my initiator's youthful face, so irregular but so refined, look out at me between the lines as through blurred prison bars.

Although "Harry," as his intimates called him, made no mention of the fact, this initiation into Balzac and explanation of Browning was not confined to the James brothers; Margy Perry too was a partner, sharing this "esoteric" information. It was part of the intellectual formation of Father's bride-to-be. In his letters of January 22 and 25, 1860, he expounds the theory which lay behind his recommendation of her reading Balzac, a theory which obviously did not motivate his initiation to the James boys:

Dear Margy, how I love you; I believe too that you love me, and much, sweet, perhaps more than I love you—and I need such an inequality: you must love me the most. Recollect the words of the *Imitation* "whose love hath bounds, loves not"—and do you recollect what I told you once returning from a walk? I think that of the *Spouting Rock,* that I wished to be very much loved. I will exact it all from you to the last drop, Margaret. The greatest love must be on your side and "J'aimerai qui m'aime." . . . I was glad that you liked *Eugénie Grandet* and I felt that you would like it, great work as it is. How well you felt, Dear Love, that I gave it

you with another intention than that you should see how love
often ends when it exists only on one side, and that you might see
that Eugénie loved to the last and as the old Royalists phrased it,
"quand même." Thanks for your promise of reading French—it
would do you good, Dear, even were it not bringing you nearer
to me.

He queries her as to whether she has read Ruskin's *Modern
Painters* and hints at a criticism of Ruskin which he was to
expound in magisterial form thirty-four years later in his
lectures before the Buffalo Art Museum, holding that Ruskin
erred by failing to see that the artist is essentially "not a rea-
soner but a seer." "When we meet in that case," he wrote her,
"I could tell you what I do not like in him and where I think
him very wrong—but there is nothing else in English. His
great success has depended upon his having said things *every
decent* painter knew in his heart, for the first time in such
great English but he is unfortunately more of a litterateur
than artist. It would be better the other way, for his truth.
Enough of literature—do not take this to heart, if you do not
read him now, we will read him some days of our *long life
together.*"

To her inquiries about Browning and the illustrations he
made for the poems, John LaFarge replied in detail and at
length in the same letter:

Let me tell you, Dear, that my ideas of *illustration* are not common ones. I would no more think myself bound to represent the
exact picture conveyed by the poet, than I would think of rivaling
him. The artist is at a disadvantage, he has lines and the other
has words. If the words were weak the illustrations might be superior—if not so the picture is complete. The same happens in any
literal description of a picture—no description can equal the picture itself. The best are *commentaries* or gloses [*sic*]. The artist
should illustrate by a poem of his own as the writer does, by music
of his own, as the musicians do. An example. The lines of Keats
upon Chapman's Homer. That, love, is the only way I believe—I
need not reason it. It seems simple enough, does it not? I use big
examples but the feeling remains the same. Much more could be

said, but that can be discussed later—and probably with others than yourself.

Apparently he was subject to a certain amount of teasing from William James.

I have just answered a letter of Willie James, who in it asked me how I had *borne* the absence of the Perrys. I could not resist telling him a little more than he asked, that is to say, that I had no reason to contradict all that I told him about you this autumn. So that when this summer he learns our engagement, his father may recollect what he said one day this autumn. They were all saying something in your praise—as I believe is more or less customary with regard to you—when Mr. J. [senior] interrupting himself said, "But Mr. L.F., I am sure, appreciates Miss Perry." I must say, it gave me *great pleasure,* for the *"old gentleman"* is a *pretty good judge* and *a frank one*. Don't blush, Dear, but I forget you are not given to that amiable weakness.

Much more than Balzac concerned the young lover in his approach to Margaret Perry. It was the question of religion. Wrote Henry James: "He was there, and there to say—intensely among us but somehow not with all *of* us; he being a Catholic, and apparently a 'real' one in spite of so many other omnisciences, making perhaps by itself the greatest difference. He had been through a Catholic college in Maryland, the name of which, though I am not assured of it now, exhaled a sort of educational elegance; but where and when he had so miraculously laid up his stores of reading and achieved his universal saturation was what we longest kept asking ourselves." (The college, of course, was Mount Saint Mary's College in Emmitsburg, Maryland, from which he was graduated in 1853. His first three years of college were at Fordham; his senior year at Mount Saint Mary's.)

Both mothers were concerned—Bonne Maman because her son would marry a Protestant; Nonna because her daughter would marry a Catholic, something that no Perry or Sergeant had ever done. Cautiously remarking that she is not to be too much disturbed about "temporal matters," Margaret observes:

"You know that my wealth is not as large as it is made out, though neither of us runs any chance of starvation." He says: "In this family I know you will soon become a *sister*. All are ready to see you and you are loved before you are known. How will it be on your side? Alas—that difference of religion should come at all between us as therein, Love, lie one or two of the questions we are to determine beforehand." Obviously there was the question of the religious education of their future children, as well as of her own integrity and peace of conscience. LaFarge remarked that he was "a skeptic"—skeptical of any religion except the Catholic faith. But since he was so skeptical as to admit nothing but the Catholic faith, he could not see how, from a skeptical point of view, the children could be educated in any religion but his own. Yet he would not ask anything of her that would do violence to integrity. He was sure that she could satisfy her conscience while agreeing with him. He writes to her on February 20, 1860:

You must know, Dear, that I shall not try to influence you unduly—and the expressions you have used in your last letters regarding the extent to which you would go to be nearer me—are as much as I require of you. I am sure that we are much nearer in our religious opinions than many would think, and as long as you can believe that (according to the Christian meaning) souls can be saved in Catholicity, you have granted enough for the present. I should be happier to see you a Catholic, you know, but only because I am a doubter, and I can only see *that Church or none*—but according to all Catholic meaning you cannot enter it without full faith. It is *not*, Love—and that is one of my many reasons for respecting it—a charitable and religious association to which one can belong as well as to half a dozen others—like most Protestant sects. I do not want to preach, though. I merely said this—my own dear Margaret—in answer to what you so sweetly said "that you would not be *half a Catholic*"; you must be *sincere* in your belief. There is no need of your not being so—nor does the Catholic idea allow of anything else. I am glad to know, Love, what you say about your mother with respect to her tolerance, and I am sure that hers would but increase if she knew any Catholic families. I say *knowing* not merely to be *acquainted* with them. But now accept my assurance, Dear, that what you tell me on this subject is all I expected—believing as I do that your next letter will bring acquiescence in what I proposed. If you have written otherwise when you receive this, do not, my dear Margaret, be troubled at all. We must find some way of settling it and we shall (DV). We can *reason,* I hope, like *friends,* AND *lovers.*

Along with these serious questions of love and eternal salvation ran a characteristically didactic vein. Engraved upon the ring he sent to her January 1, 1860, was the word "AVE." He explains the meaning of this in detail: "Soldiers cried *Ave Imperator,* and *Ave Maria* we Catholics use in blessing the Virgin Mother blessed among women. The word means more than our Northern tongues can give. All this (if thought out of place) will do for your philological education. Anything is a good excuse, Margaret, to talk to you a little longer." He also affectionately reminded her to head her sentences with capital letters.

My mother, according to her account, became a Catholic shortly after her wedding on October 15, 1860. Convinced of the truth of the Catholic Church before marriage, she did not wish to seem to have become a Catholic in order to have a Catholic ceremony. As she explained to me, her faith came naturally. It was the unfolding of a spiritual blossom that had already begun to grow. "I had no conflict," she would say. "What your father told me was simply what I had instinctively felt all my life. I was instinctively a Catholic. It was the completion of what I had already had in my heart." Father's gift of lucid explanation—for he was an unparalleled pedagogue—was supplemented by their acquaintance with Father Isaac Hecker (of the famous breakfast food family), the founder of the Paulist Fathers, who was a frequent guest at the LaFarge home. One of its treasured possessions is the pencil sketch, "Father Hecker Reading Goethe," which hangs on the wall of the old house in Newport.

I think one thing that helped my mother to assimilate the teachings of the Catholic Church was the fortunate circum-

stance that the preaching at old Trinity Church in Newport
had been of a high spiritual order. One of the former pastors
of Trinity, the devout though parsimonious Reverend Dr.
Alexander Mercer, wrote some thoughtful studies in the life
of Christ that could have been written by a Catholic author.
These, Mother told me, were among her favorite readings in
childhood. I think, too, the denunciations of Romanism by
Grandma Perry, her grandmother, had a reverse effect on her
youthful mind; they showed simply no connection with what
she saw in reality.

She had pondered a great deal over the situation of the
Catholics themselves. The first Catholics in Newport were a
minority. Vividly impressed on her imagination was a scene in
her youth when she had seen some of the Irish Catholics of
Newport stoned by rowdies. A small congregation of some
two hundred people worshiped at the little frame church on
Mount Vernon Street before the fine red stone Gothic church
of St. Mary, Star of the Sea was built. Mother told me of her
first Sundays at Mass. To attend the Catholic service she had
to pass by Trinity Church on Spring Street, pass by the graveyard where her ancestors from the founding of the Colony
were buried, pass by the pews where they and all her friends
and relatives had worshiped, and make her way to a back
street to which she came as a complete social stranger. Being
sensitive, a rather shy and retiring person, she found it by no
means easy, especially as everything she did was known, commented on, and speculated about in Newport.

Devoid of any intellectual Catholic contacts outside of
Father and the members of his family, and the occasional
visits of Father Hecker, my mother thirsted for more knowledge of her new-found faith. It was difficult actually to carry
out the promise to instruct her children in her new religion,
especially for the first arrivals. The situation improved when
the others came along, and in time she accumulated through
reading a fairly thorough and exact knowledge.

Among the works on my mother's bookshelf which she pondered over and invited me to read were those of St. Francis de Sales and of the Jesuit writers, Lallemant and Caussade. Lallemant's *Christian Doctrine* she absorbed with particular intensity, especially when she learned that Lallemant had been the spiritual teacher of the great Jesuit saints and martyrs, Isaac Jogues, Jean de Brébeuf, and their companions. One of Mother's favorite writers was Father Frederick Faber of the London Oratory, and she initiated me into his works in my childhood. A volume of Lallemant or Faber was usually propped up against her silver coffeepot on our breakfast table. Another of her writers was Coventry Patmore and still another, of course, was Newman, particularly his treatise on *The Present Position of Catholics,* which she used to read aloud to me. The most profound element in her religious life was her intimate devotion to the Blessed Virgin Mary, and she made on one or two occasions a mysterious reference to Our Lady in connection with my birth.

As time went on Father found himself increasingly absorbed in his work. It took him from home, and with his absence from home came a rift in the web of domesticity for which he had prepared so elaborately in his courtship correspondence. It finally dawned on Mother that she no longer completely possessed her John. The knowledge came to her quietly while she was staying at his mother's estate at Glen Cove, Long Island, after the birth of her second child, my oldest sister Emily. John LaFarge had left her to go to New York. "I knew then," she said in later years, "that your father no longer had the same complete affection for me. I knew there was no more sense in weeping. He was going to lead his own life, and I said to myself, this will be my life from henceforth; I must face it and do the best I can."

John LaFarge had given her all his love, but some of it he had afterwards withdrawn. He also had helped her to realize a divine faith which was far more precious to her than any earthly love. This faith he could never impair and it was completely her own, sealed by her own mind and conviction and her own unshakable will. In the sturdy ship of this faith she sailed the stormy seas of the threescore years that remained to her on earth.

Father proceeded to establish a lifelong pattern of living and moving half in and half out of his own household. The death in infancy of his third child, Raymond, deeply moved him. Although he seldom depicted his own children, he did portraits of Raymond both before and after the child's death. Raymond's life could have been saved by modern surgical methods but they were not understood at the time. The shock of this death brought John LaFarge to his senses for a time. For the next two years he made his summer home with his family in Newport on Paradise Avenue near his beloved Paradise Valley and the Sachuest Beach, passing the winters in various rented houses in the town.

In 1865 his fourth child was born and christened with his father's own name, John. His full name was John Louis Bancel LaFarge, after my great-grandmother's family, the Bancels de Confoulens. The child's aunts took to calling him Bancel instead of John, so very soon the John was completely dropped, and he remained Bancel LaFarge the rest of his life.

My sister Margaret was born during the Paradise Valley period. She, besides myself, is the only present survivor of all the children. Those two years after Raymond's death, says Margaret, were the two happiest years of our family life. They might have lasted had not Father's absorption in his work once more gained the upper hand. His stained-glass project claimed all his energies, and his illnesses (real or imaginary) sapped them. After attending a performance of *Disraeli* by Henry Irving, my mother remarked: "It was so nice to see Sir Henry Irving playing Disraeli with his diplomatic illnesses. They did remind me so much of your father."

The ardent lover and the genial partner of the Paradise Valley household contrast distressingly with the irritable and absentee parent of later years. Yet there was not one of his

children who did not love him, and they loved him to the
end with all his oddities and angularities. There was always
a deep sense that Father was genuine, that his peculiarities
were a kind of superstructure, and that beneath it all he did
love us. Sharp as was the contrast, it still did not necessarily
fix the stigma of insincerity upon his earlier ardent professions. With all his mental complexity, as I have said, there
was no great moral complexity in John LaFarge, not half as
much as one finds in supposedly simple, matter-of-fact people.
Father said to me one time that the people you should be particularly wary of are those who have blue eyes and look you
square in the face. They are, he said, the most deceitful. And
it was one of his theories that the plain, straightforward man—
though his thoughts might be simple—can have a twisted
heart.

I think no great probing is needed to see where his trouble
lay: In the youthful simplicity that underlay his sophisticated
and controlled exterior, Father had not realized the terrible
pull his own chosen profession would exert upon him, how it
would absorb his time, his mind, and energy, and lure him
into a total forgetfulness of life's ordinary obligations. His was
the philosophic detachment of a genius, but he was afflicted
also by the genius' fatal tendency to be lost in the world of
his own creativeness and thereby to lose contact with the ordinary humble things of life.

Nor did he forewarn himself sufficiently lest another spell
be cast upon him, that of the white magic of women. As St.
Patrick said, and Oliver St. John Gogarty after him, "Beware
of the magic of women and of the smiths and of the druids."
The druids in Father's case were the gods of his own professional genius. The smiths were presumably the patrons as well
as the employees whom he had to placate or sign contracts with
or pay, as the case might be. And the women were not the
coarse, seductive and sensual type, but women of intellect, of
high social standing, though some were honeyed flatterers.
They were captivated by a man who transcended the crassness

and crudeness of the social and business world around them.

On such matters a man's children cannot speak too apodic-tically. Possibly there was something graver in the case, but reports of such did not reach us. He did, however, it was plain to see, become used to being discreetly courted by a world of admirers. It was easy and natural to relax in that congenial atmosphere and to postpone the prosaic care of a home and family. To postpone, yes, but never wholly to neglect. We were still his, as he was always ours.

My mother was a tremendous walker. She and I took long walks together on the beaches and along the cliffs on the south shore of the Island. In later years we bicycled together. When I was about fourteen I remember walking with Mother along Easton's Beach. It was a dull, gray day and Mother had been a bit silent. Then she said: "There is something I think you ought to understand. You ought to know that your father does not properly look after us. He means well, but nevertheless I am at times forgotten, and there are times when I must turn to Almighty God for help." It was a simple thing simply stated, but it made a tremendous impression on me. I had a feeling of pride, a quiet satisfaction. I had vaguely sensed something of the sort, but Mother had never complained. From that time on I was to be a partner with her and share her problems, her anxieties and heartaches. I felt manly and protective.

In the old highboy desk in the dining room at Sunnyside Place, Newport, my mother would always lay a small statue of St. Joseph in a little drawer when Father became too for-getful. She would simply leave the statue there. St. Joseph never failed her and Mother, though she was anxious and dis-tressed, never became unnerved or upset. She knew that in the long run God would provide.

The fact that we did love my father in spite of his peculiari-ties is due in great measure to my mother, because she always taught us to love him. It is extraordinary, but true, that I never once heard her utter a bitter word. She was always insistent that all of us children must understand him, that he was not like other people and that he never would be like other people, that he was just himself and it would be very foolish of us to expect anything else. "Your dear father," she would say, "is perfectly unreasonable. He could not be more unreasonable and he causes us all a great deal of trouble, but we must take your father for exactly what he is."

There was an amusing side to this too, because knowing him as she did with such sharp intuition, she could see his likeness in his children and she would note in me any paternal traits. Every now and then she would say: "Well, you're acting just like your father," especially if I was a bit too particular about my person or inclined to be fastidious.

At home we all knew what to say and what to do when he returned, the times that he was to be left alone, places where he was not to be disturbed, objects that were not to be touched. And yet I don't think it worried us, because his visits were so extremely interesting. Father was always reading in his free time. He read incessantly, with great rapidity, and remembered everything he read. I discovered as a child that if I spoke to him when he was reading, he would always be genial. No matter how absorbed, he was ready to talk if he had a book in his hand. If he lacked a book, some mischief might be brewing. But the moment he held a volume, particularly a French book, holding it close to his myopic eyes, peering at it through his layers of spectacles, I knew that he was open to unlimited conversation. One would not dare to think of speaking to him when he was painting or writing.

I never could quite make out my father's religious practice. I might say that the whole thing was a question of *en principe*. He believed in going to church, he knew he ought to go to church. He would go to church if he could get organized and straightened out and somehow arrive there, and *then* his attendance was thoroughly simple, childlike, and reverent. He followed the Mass from his missal with utmost devotion. He talked to me about the two kinds of priests. One type of priest, he said, is superior in his conduct to the Mass. The Mass for such a man, he said, is functional. It is something he is using to express his own personality. He is a person *performing* an act or a liturgy. The other type, he said, lives for the Mass. The Mass is infinitely superior to him; he, only a servant of the Holy Eucharist, looks up to It and is humbled by It. And Father was extremely sensitive to the difference.

The question might be asked, how could a man so drift away from a wife who was completely suited to him, for she was indeed his very perfect wife who loved him, understood him, and spent herself to do his bidding. But as she herself remarked years later, perhaps the fault lay in her absence of self-assertion. Mother was not assertive by nature, but eventually through reflection and the strengthening of her inner spiritual life she formed her own brand of firmness of will and then exercised a strength which derived not from this world. In later years when things became particularly critical Mother did force herself, she said, to face up to Father and to meet him point-blank with a positive refusal.

"If," she said, "I had put down my foot firmly when he left Glen Cove after Emily's birth and said then that I would not tolerate a divided household, I believe that he would have capitulated." This was my own experience with him in later years. It was the old case of facing a domineering person with a flat and firm expression of will.

In later years there were three occasions on which she tested this out. The first came when, after remaining a couple of years in Newport, Father planned for her to stay near him while he was in New York. She had spent the summer visiting Bonne Maman at her Shrub Oak estate and Father proposed that she should remain there for the winter, make that her headquarters and keep the family there so as to be within easy reach of him while he was working in New York. My mother met this suggestion point-blank. "I refuse," she said, "to have my life spoiled by being imprisoned at Shrub Oak." And that was the end of the proposition. The second instance came when it was a question of my leaving for my studies for the priesthood, and the third was when she insisted upon going abroad to meet me during my vacation. In each of these three cases, Father capitulated. It was unfortunate that she did not make him capitulate the very first time.

With all his faults, there is one thing with which my father cannot be charged, and that is hypocrisy. He never tried to justify his neglect of his home or his family. His conscience remained clear as to principles. He knew his real responsibility, and he was always uneasy on this matter, and would therefore come back to his home unexpectedly and would be all the more concerned when he was away. In this respect he differed sharply from the current attitude that seeks by intellectual reasons to justify rebellion against the law of God. For that type of mind, he had no use. He displayed a certain amount of mild anti-clericalism and skepticism but, when it came to matters of principle, he never questioned the basis of human life and human conduct.

CHAPTER THREE

Newport and New York

-»» ««-

In the spring of 1879 my mother was visiting in New York. At that time she was already forty years old, her health was failing, she was in considerable straits financially, and our home life was a very complicated affair indeed. Father at this time was head-over-heels in an unfortunate suit with Louis Tiffany about his stained-glass methods, claiming that Tiffany had appropriated his ideas, which of course Father had not had the foresight to patent.

Dropping in at St. Francis Xavier's Church on Sixteenth Street, New York, my sadly troubled mother decided to ask the advice of her confessor who was, I believe, a young French-Canadian Jesuit, Father Alphonse Pelletier. She told him she had already had nine children, including one stillborn, and that her last child had died in infancy. Every natural reason seemed to militate against having any more. My mother told me many years later that she asked her confessor whether it would be wise, good, or prudent to have another child with the probability of its death or of adding to her burden. The priest simply told her, go ahead and try it again and trust in God. The result—a year later on February 13, 1880—was my emergence into the world.

My coming was unexpected in many ways. Mother had kept her pregnancy secret from Father, since she was afraid of his complete collapse because of his anxiety over the lawsuit. It was only after I had actually arrived that the fact was announced to him. What were his emotions I never knew. I was brought into daylight by a colored midwife in the southwest second-story room of the old house on Sunnyside Place in Newport, which is still the LaFarge home. According to legend, people would stop my mother as she wheeled me in a perambulator and express a word of sympathy when they saw her feeble baby, pale and apparently half-lifeless. It was assumed I would not live so there was not much bother about formalities at my baptism. As a matter of fact, I was baptized not in the church itself but in the convent rectory. Those present were my sister Emily as godmother, and Sister M. Borromeo, the Superior of the Sisters of Mercy. The priest significantly forgot to enter my baptism in the register, something I discovered at the time of my Ordination: the register contains only the name of John L. B. LaFarge (my brother Bancel) at a date fifteen years earlier.

My earliest recollection is watching flames flickering through the isinglass of a little iron stove in our nursery as I played with white threads from the spread of my crib. I began reading the large-print section of *St. Nicholas* magazine at the age of five.

They tell me I was a rather philosophical and observing little fellow for a boy of five. In 1885 when Mother took me on a trip to Jenkintown, Pennsylvania, to visit my grandmother Perry on the old Lober estate, she wrote to my older sister Frances:

I fully meant to keep my promise of writing to you yesterday, but was so tired and spent so much time with Nonna, I could not manage it very well. . . . This place is lovely and John is perfectly happy here and enjoys every moment. To begin at the beginning—as soon as we got into the cab John said, "I like driving," and soon after he said, "I like traveling when you don't have to walk." When we arrived as far as St. Joseph's Church he said, "We wouldn't have got as far as this if we had walked!" Before that he said, "Are you a traveler?" I said, yes, that he was one, too, which seemed to please him very much.

I followed this up by asking Mother, apropos of nothing: "Who was your father?"

Very shortly after that I began my first schooling in a private day school conducted by Mrs. Walter N. Hill, whose sons, Perry and Walter, and daughter Catherine became my staunch friends during my boyhood and early youth. The two Hill boys were my own age and took the place really of brothers. Mrs. Hill, a pious woman, respected my Catholic faith and was amused whenever we were supposed to learn a verse or two from the Bible and, rather militantly I fear, I quoted the Douay version, having been carefully prompted by my mother. Most of the boys and girls at the school were children of Navy officers. The Mahans, Belknaps, the Breeses, were all my childhood playmates.

At home discipline was put in force largely by my oldest sister Emily who had two means of repression, the gentler of which was to lock me in a large closet until my tantrum was over. At this dramatic moment "a small bird" would appear with a chocolate cigarette, and on agreeing to be good, I was allowed to come out of the closet and consume it under Emily's watchful eye. The second, more dreaded punishment, was to be almost suffocated on the bed with a pillow. Either of these ways served as a sufficient deterrent. With my mother, mild as she was, orders meant orders, though she didn't know until later years what Emily's methods had been.

The principal treasure of interest to young boys in our Newport home was my brother Bancel's splendid collection of birds' eggs. They were carefully ticketed and bedded in cotton wool in the numerous shallow drawers of a handsome hardwood cabinet which Bancel guarded with a little brass padlock and key. It was always a big treat when my older brother allowed me to approach his wondrous cabinet. On top of it he had installed a collection of curios picked up in the course of his wanderings. Among these was a bullet labeled: "Found on the field of Waterloo."

This bullet started wheels revolving in my mind. What was there in this bullet that made it different from any other bullet exactly the same size, weight, and chemical constitution?

What made it, in other words, a bullet from the field of Waterloo? And suppose it had not been from the field of Waterloo? Would there in that case be anything science could possibly find in this bullet that would make it different from the real Waterloo bullet? What was the significance then of this "coming-from-Waterloo" business? I had to wait until my grown-up courses in philosophy before I could venture an answer.

Mother decided not to send me to our parish school, so I attended the red-brick Coddington Public School on Mill Street after my primary years with Mrs. Hill were over, and later graduated from Rogers High School, also a public school. Teaching in the Newport public schools was of a high order. The teachers were strict, of the good old New England variety, showing full consideration for my religious beliefs.

The background of my boyhood was the sea, the open sea of the cliffs and beaches, the closed sea of the harbor and Narragansett Bay. At night when I lay in bed a roar from Easton's Beach to the east of us meant approaching stormy weather. The beach was only ten or fifteen minutes walk from our house and frequently on a winter's evening my brothers and I would stroll down to the western end of the beach to watch the vast heaving waves under the moonlight. When a storm had passed and all was quiet I would listen for the distant bell buoy far out to sea off Brenton's Reef—named for Jahleel Brenton, an ancestor of ours—at the entrance of the harbor. That distant tinkle always signified a welcome change in the weather and the promise of a splendid day on the morrow. The goal of many walks and later bicycle excursions was Paradise Rocks, Bishop Berkeley's Seat under the Hanging Rock, and the curious miniature world of mountain, valley, and forest that extended for a mile or so back from Sachuest Beach.

From my older brothers I learned great reverence for seamanship, in which they excelled. I saw little of my brother Grant. He was away from home most of the time during my boyhood, and his rare visits did not suffice to impress his personality clearly on my mind, though I was fascinated by his repeating-watch that played chimes when you pushed a button. Bancel was my mentor in the world of boats and crafts and all outdoors. Under his guidance I acquired a fair knowledge of sailing, and with that a passion for the harbor, particularly the ship chandlery offices on Long Wharf, and Swinburne's cavernous marine tackle shop on Thames Street along the harbor.

At school we memorized Longfellow's pathetic poem, "The Skeleton in Armor," and I was impressed by the thought that Norsemen had settled here centuries before the earliest English colonists. The Old Stone Mill (or the Old Stone Tower, as it is now called), a circular affair of neatly fitted slate slabs standing in eight pillars, was only five minutes' walk from our home. Dr. Ellery Channing, founder of the Unitarians, and the portly figure of Uncle Matthew Calbraith Perry, "Conqueror of Japan," were familiar statues in Touro Park. The Old Mill was supposed to have been built by my mother's ancestor, Rhode Island's first governor, the seventeenth-century Benedict Arnold (not the eighteenth-century traitor). But there still lurked the possibility that the Norsemen might have had something to do with all this, a theory still stoutly defended. I was curious about the Norse and all the more so when at the age of ten I examined in our library at home a collection of books in Danish, Swedish, and Icelandic that my father had gathered on his tour of Europe before his marriage. I saw no reason why I shouldn't learn to read these books. Mrs. George Bliss, the wife of the librarian of Redwood Library, knew Danish and was so taken with my interest that she undertook to teach me.

The most glorious day in my Norse period was the arrival of a Viking ship in Newport Harbor in 1893. I spotted it from the window of the Coddington school that looked out over the harbor. As soon as school was out, I rushed down to the Mill Street wharf, untied a skiff and paddled out to meet the sailors, try a few Danish words on them (courtesy of Mrs. Bliss), and learn of their experiences. Another red-letter day was the arrival in town of a native of Iceland, Mrs. Sigridur Magnusson, the wife of a professor at Cambridge, England. I went swimming with her at Easton's Beach, where she taught me a few words of the spoken language. I was intrigued by the fact that she looked more like a rather plump elderly Irish woman, and learned from her that the Icelanders possessed considerable Irish blood and that the island off the main harbor at Reykjavik was called West Men's Island.

At the same time I had been struggling with French. My French teacher, Mrs. Francis, was a good Belgian lady who by some quirk of fate had married a stuffy Newport non-practicing physician. Mrs. Francis gave lessons in the school, but I also took lessons from her in the four-story frame house on Gibbs Avenue. In winter she occupied the second floor but in the heat of summer moved to her summer residence, which was oddly enough on the third floor! When this poor soul died, I failed to attend her funeral. Mother reproached me for this neglect, asking why, as her old friend and favorite pupil, I did not give her that last sign of affection and respect. My mother's reproof profoundly affected me. It revealed a nasty stock of egotism and selfishness which up to that time I had only dimly suspected in myself. It proved that I could be just as mean by *not* doing certain things as I could by doing others.

The Redwood Library I have mentioned was close to Touro Park. That venerable institution consisted of a reading room, library, and museum of local antiquities. Visitors still view in the center of the main room the replica of "The Dying Gladiator." Recent attempts to remove the statue have been unsuccessful, I'm told, and the present librarian informs me that he will probably continue to die there indefinitely. Before the present rear wing of the library was built, there was a large back porch on the east end which nobody ever visited. I discovered this magical hiding place myself and spent long

summer afternoons there sitting on the floor of the porch
poring over sea stories and biographies. One day in August
when I was about thirteen, I finished devouring Boswell's *Life
of Johnson* and a feeling of desolation came over me as I
turned the last page. I debated with myself for some time
what I should read next, and listened to the katydids in the
horse-chestnut trees for advice. Then the bright idea occurred
to me, why not read the two fat volumes through again? It
was a wise choice and I shall never regret it.

At home we observed the happy practice, so little in vogue
now, of reading aloud. Father read frequently to us on his
family visits, and my uncle, Professor Thomas Sergeant Perry,
Professor of English at Harvard University, was also a delightful reader. A fine Russian scholar, he introduced us to
Turgenev, and I knew by heart the dialogue between the
Jungfrau and the Finsteraarhorn. One day he pulled out of
his pocket some rather battered newspaper clippings which
he said were taken from a local newspaper in Bombay. They
were written by an obscure British journalist, a man called
Rudyard Kipling, and were entitled *Soldiers Three*. For hours
Uncle Tom would read to our delighted ears the adventures
of Ortheris and Mulvaney. He had also dug up the Omar
Khayyam verses by Edward Fitzgerald. Since I had considerable trouble with my eyes, I loved to be read to.

In the long evenings under the oil student-lamp made of
brass which periodically glug-glugged, my mother would read
aloud most of Dickens, Trollope, and Jane Austen, as well
as the guide books of Augustus J. C. Hare, *Walks in Rome,
Walks in Florence*, etc. Reading of Hare was the signal
for me to consume my nightly glass of hot Horlick's Malted
Milk. Mother's memory was so clear and her imagination so
vivid that the characters in these books became part of our
daily life. Later when we visited Great Britain and the Continent much of this reading came to life again and we relived
the scenes of *Barchester Towers* or *Pride and Prejudice*, and

walked again with Augustus Hare, recalling the austerely sober flavor of Horlick's Malted.

The signal to end the reading came, a signal not always obeyed, when the curfew rang from the Pelham Street Church at nine o'clock. Newport life was regulated by bells. At 7 A.M. the church bells of the town rang for people to rise and start work. At twelve the lunch bell sounded. At one it signaled to resume work, and at nine came the curfew. On stormy days when there was only one session in the school a very welcome special bell was rung. Around 1890 St. Mary's Church, the first Catholic church in the town, inaugurated the Angelus bell at 6 A.M. and 6 P.M. This raised the number of bell-ringings per diem to six. On still evenings we could hear the town clock in the Rhode Island State House strike the hours. My earliest ambition was to be the town clockwinder when grown up, and at diverse times I climbed into the State House tower to see how it worked.

I was proud of the fact that Rhode Island was the only state in the Union that boasted two capitals. Every year in May the Legislature sailed from Providence to Newport by steamer, a two-hour trip down Narragansett Bay. The newly inaugurated Governor was driven through Newport in an open barouche in the midst of a grand parade. The day of his inauguration was for some strange reason called Election Day. It was celebrated like the Fourth of July with fireworks and firecrackers, and everybody drank pink lemonade. This officially opened the one-month Newport session where affairs relating to Newport County were transacted. Everybody seemed to have such a pleasant time. It was a comfortable world to grow up in! A world divided into many segments and layers of people and our family in one way or another shared in all of it.

Close in our neighborhood dwelt representatives of Boston's intellectual mid-century colony. The bulky frame cottage next door, built by Stanford White, was inhabited successively by the Tiltons and by Miss Katharine Prescott Wormeley, who

had translated nearly forty works of Balzac and other famous
French authors, and also—wonder of wonders—included a harp
in the furnishings of her elaborate music room. Also in hailing
distance lived Miss Sarah C. Woolsey, the biographer of Fanny
Burney, Mme. d'Arblay, and Jane Austen, and more famous,
under the name "Susan Coolidge," as the prolific writer of
such juveniles as the *What Katy Did* series. Miss Woolsey possessed no harp, but she was a giantess, close to seven feet in
stature, and was marvelously hospitable to small boys. An object of my occasional pilgrimage out on the Island was the
awesome Julia Ward Howe, who wrote "The Battle Hymn
of the Republic."

The older set of colonists was largely eclipsed by the
mauve-decade splurge of New York palace-builders in the gay
'90s, so superbly satirized by Edith Wharton. I knew Mrs.
Wharton as a boy, and though I never saw her again in later
life, the remembrance of that personality is extraordinarily
clear: I still see her slight, alert figure reclining upon her
wicker chaise longue, in a corner of the verandah at the house
at the end of the Cliff Walk, quietly interrogating me over a
teacup upon my religious beliefs, as if she were looking for
something desperately needed, but only vaguely knowing
her own needs.

From our quiet back street we heard across the fields the
ping of tennis balls every August when the star players contended in the annual tournament at the Newport Casino. I
felt the usual small boy's once-in-a-lifetime thrill when my
brother Oliver brought the famous Ollie Campbell (who today knows of Ollie Campbell?) home to tea. I even succeeded
in photographing Ollie Campbell's foot as it projected in the
seat ahead of me at the tournament. The Havemeyers' tally-ho
coach; Mrs. Stuyvesant Fish's incredible parties; the fantastic
building exploits of the Goelets, the Van Alens, and the Van-
derbilts—all were part of the big show that surrounded me
every summer. But I preferred for the most part the long

afternoons of reading in my hiding place on the back porch of the Redwood Library.

Greater and lesser lights on Bellevue Avenue and the Ocean Drive were more the social concern of my older brothers and sisters. My own summer friends were for the most part from a different group. I preferred the nautical-minded folk who occupied the old houses on Washington Street and "The Point," as it was called, fronting on the outer harbor north of Long Wharf and to the east end of the Naval War College, which was the chief architectural exploit of canny, old white-bearded cousin George Mason. From Philadelphia every summer came the Quaker families, the Hallowells and the Smiths: white-haired, ruddy, robust Hester Morton Smith, her sister Anna, her brother Bill, close friend of my brother Bancel. Bill was drowned on a Sunday morning trying to save a crippled friend when their boat had capsized off Brenton's Reef in a sudden squall. The event was particularly poignant because Bancel was to be one of the party, but at the last moment he figured in his sober way that he did not want to miss Mass. I haunted the marine workshop of Bill Smith's younger brother, Ed. The Smiths, strict disciplinarians, were my nautical advisers. They helped me rig up my own first craft, a Swampscott dory. I was long pursued by their reproaches when I returned to the wharf late one August evening, after allowing myself to be caught in a tide rip off Rose Island.

Closer to my age were the Fairchilds from Boston, a redheaded family of whom the third boy Nelson—Neil as we called him—was closest to my own age. Off their wharf I first learned to swim by the simple process of falling overboard when nobody was around and deciding the best thing to do was to strike out. It was from their slowly drifting cat-boat that I overcame my timidity and plunged into the brilliant, clear, green salt depths five or six miles offshore on lazy summer afternoons. I must have cadged a lot off the ever-hospitable Fairchilds, but it seemed quite natural and nobody ob-

jected. They were wonderfully decent and understanding people with a grand home life, and it seemed to me that, like the
ocean itself, they were God's gift to help steer me through the
difficult years of adolescence.

Outside of the firm alliance with the Hills and some of the
neighbors on Church Street, I had few friends among the old
Newport townsfolk. The Hills were proud possessors of a hand
printing press, and at the age of ten or so I undertook to edit
a monthly magazine entitled *The Sunlight,* which we sold for
two cents a copy to our friends and relatives. Along with *The
Sunlight* type font came a set of miscellaneous woodcuts with
no relevance to one another or to anything else. The only way
to utilize the cuts was to build a story about them. I was com-
missioned to undertake this, and solved the problem by antici-
pating Buck Rogers and contributing a story of a "Trip to
Mars" in monthly installments. Since no one could dispute
what might be found on Mars, one was always able to insert
one of the woodcuts. The copy was prepared on a typewriter
that my aunt Emily LaFarge, Mrs. Jack Lawrence, had presented me at Christmas. There were no keys, properly speaking. You turned a little handle to a particular point with your
right hand and pressed down on a bar with your left. However,
I was immensely satisfied with its performance and felt I had
derived from it a certain literary inspiration.

The extraordinary thing was that we continued to produce
The Sunlight for so long a period, some ten or twelve issues,
until all the woodcuts and possibilities of the planet Mars
were exhausted. We featured also local news, information
about Rhode Island history, school items, political prophecies,
etc. In short, it was a miniature magazine, a page of which
my sister came upon a few years ago in our old Newport home.

A Yankee small boy's curiosity about mechanical devices
made me haunt the power plants, waterworks, dynamos, en-
gine rooms of the town and vicinity. One day I came upon a
little book that told how to install electric bells. Immediately
I began to install them in our house and those of the neigh-

bors. Good Mrs. Dyer, who boarded the Anglican minister at the Church of St. John the Divine on Washington Street, close to my nautical haunts, asked me if I would install an electric bell in her house because the minister, a High Church clergyman who was called Father Buckey, wished something of the sort. I gladly consented and attached an electric bell to Father Buckey's desk for his convenience. He was absent at the time and I took the occasion to leave on his desk a copy of a pamphlet on Anglican Orders, which I had carefully studied from cover to cover. Two or three weeks after that Father Buckey said good-by to his congregation and went to Baltimore for an interview with Cardinal Gibbons and later was received into the Church. He eventually became a Catholic priest and spent his last years as Monsignor Buckey, the pastor of St. Matthew's Church in Washington, D. C. Whether this had any connection with my proselytizing, I do not know, but the event left me with a sense of awe and wonderment.

My interest in mechanical devices led me to a disconcerting discovery. It seems my zeal for things mechanical was in inverse ratio to my skill in mechanical achievement. In all that I undertook with my hands there was a fatal absence of manual facility. I found I was another example of a curious division that runs through every generation of the LaFarge family; some of us start with our brains, and some with our hands. My nephew Tom LaFarge, one of Bancel's sons, explained to me once how he and his brother Ed started first to use their hands and then let their brains carry out what their hands had instinctively started. But his older brother Bancel, he said, starts with his head and after he has worked it out allows his hands to take over. I did not even have young Bancel's skill. What I thought out could not be transmitted to my hands. I could not wield pencils or pens or brushes or anything that required the use of my fingers.

I have agonized remembrances of a few winter evenings when I took "writing lessons" from a sad-looking young man called Sisson down at his house on Spring Street, where I had to use a curious double-jointed pen and sit at an acute diagonal to the table. The capital "D" was my nemesis. I could never achieve the elaborate Spencerian-system flourishes, and my awkwardness was increased by inward rebellion. It was like being obliged to dance when you could not even walk properly, so that I succeeded in producing only a shaky tangle of scrawls. Poor Sisson gave up in despair. "I guess you ain't made to write!" he declared, and to my great relief Mother sadly dropped the lessons. I was somewhat consoled when I learned that my erudite uncle, Professor T. S. Perry, suffered from over-flexible fingers, although the deformity did not affect his handwriting.

Beautiful, clear, distinctive, fluent handwriting was the characteristic of all my brothers and sisters and my uncles and aunts. The Sisson experiment made my writing infinitely worse; from becoming poor it became practically illegible. My English instructor at Harvard, the late Charles T. Copeland, affectionately known as Copey, summed it up in a word when he said: "LaFarge, your handwriting is Gothic and that's all there is to it."

This handicap of poor co-ordination troubled me in everything that required physical exertion, and was accompanied with a natural muscular debility. I had equally poor luck when it came to any drawing or painting. I was quite hopeless. In public school when I was aged thirteen, I was excused by the drawing teacher, Miss French, because, she said, lessons were absolutely wasted on me. I finally put the matter up to my father and asked him if there were any sense in my trying to do anything in that line, and he frankly said, "No, you have absolutely no talent for drawing or painting. Just forget all about it." It was a great relief to my mind. Yet curiously enough I did succeed—to my own puzzlement and everybody else's—in winning a city-wide drawing contest by using a simplified charcoal smudge that my brother Grant obligingly taught me.

The further you are from England, said Lewis Carroll's Carpenter, the nearer you are to France. And so I found, as a compensation, that I was the only boy in the family who was musical. My sister Emily, though she had not cultivated it, had much of my musical sense, which we inherited from my mother. In my childhood I loved to hear Mother playing old Swedish folk songs. When she observed how much I enjoyed listening, she said I might take piano lessons from Miss Annie Kelly, a young lady who lived on the further side of Touro Park. I was so eager to begin that I struggled to attend my first lesson through drifts of snow on the day of the worst blizzard that, to my knowledge, Newport had ever known. When we spent two winters in New York, 1895 to 1897, I took piano lessons from an excellent teacher, an English Jew named Victor Benham, who at once set me studying for perfection on a relatively easy piece—Chopin's *Nocturne* in E Flat Major. During my four years at Harvard I studied both piano and organ with the highly competent Walter Spalding.

At Harvard, too, I pursued harmony and counterpoint as well. I never developed any talent for composition and I don't think I ever would have made very much of an impression anyhow. I had picked up enough to read off a score of a quartet or symphony and hear it in the mind just as if the instruments were playing. This to me was a great satisfaction and joy. What trials I inflicted on the rest of the family by my fairly diligent practice I shall not know until the next world. My sister Frances toward the end of her life recalled reproachfully "the everlasting tinkle" of Bach and Mozart. Frances, incidentally, betrayed in later years her own modest but real share of artistic gifts through her exquisite botanical paintings of plants and flowers.

I was very much disturbed by the fact that I seemed to be considered a prodigy. It was all the more humiliating because as a prodigy there were so many things which everybody else can do that I would like to have done and done well. But somehow or other they seemed to slip past me. The only comfort was that the boys and girls my own age never taunted

me with the prodigy business, simply took me for granted for
better or worse. My uncle, Dr. William Pepper, Provost of
the University of Pennsylvania, who in summer lived a few
blocks away from us on Greenough Place, was particularly
interested in my intellectual capacities. Uncle Willie's personality reminded me of what I had read of Prince Albert, the
consort of Queen Victoria. He was optimistic about human
progress and had a burning desire to improve himself and
everybody else in his vicinity, including his own three sons, the
youngest of whom, Perry Pepper, he addressed in French at
the top of his lungs. He studied Spanish at the breakfast table
and was on the watch to see that everybody used their time
profitably. When I was twelve years old he presented me with
a copy of Newman's *The Idea of a University,* figuring that
since I was a Catholic I should, of course, be able to understand Newman, and as a university official no subject was
closer to his heart. Out of respect for Uncle Willie I dipped
into *The Idea of a University* but found I could neither float
nor swim. However, it probably started in my mind a sort of
perspective of Newman whose work I explored more deeply
in later years.

Of my relatives on my mother's side Franklin Pepper, Dr.
Pepper's second son, was closest to me, hardly a year older, a
straightforward, manly, serious lad. Though we had little in
common, fundamentally he was one of my earliest playmates
and I felt very keenly when he bravely lost his life during the
First World War. In my youth I saw little of my relatives on
the LaFarge side.

Beneath this varied and seemingly full world of friendships
and interests, I felt a certain sense of loneliness. I had hardly
any Catholic friends; certainly none who in any way remotely
shared my own tastes and interests. The Sorzanos, a delightful
Spanish Cuban family, were for some years our closest neighbors, and one of the boys, Leonardo, became a lifelong friend.
He graduated from Georgetown in 1900 and I was present with
him at the Georgetown Jubilee in 1950. Curiously enough it

was Leonardo Sorzano, always a loyal son of Georgetown, who dissuaded me from my original plan of choosing Georgetown for a college. From pure freakishness, as he afterward told me, he invented some stories about life at Georgetown, complaining particularly about the quality of the food. This touched a very sensitive point, for at the time I was laboring with a sort of recurrent nausea and immediately Georgetown became associated in my mind with certain physical sensations. The food at Georgetown certainly could not have been worse than what I endured later during my four years at Harvard.

As my twelfth year approached, I experienced the growth of an all-dominating purpose in my life. That was to become a Catholic priest. I did not feel that there was anything in me that made me particularly suited to the priesthood. The priest must be a man of the people, all things to all men, and personally I was somewhat reserved and fastidious. The priest's work was arduous and demanded a robust constitution, and I was struggling periodically with ill health. The priest was to be the soul of unselfishness, and I was naturally egotistic and self-centered. I did not feel that I was the material of which priests were made, but the conviction grew in me that somehow or other it was something that God wanted of me. That conviction, I feel, was the work of God's grace.

The idea of the priesthood began to take shape in my mind as the result of two gifts. One of these was a Latin Missal from Father Philip Cronan, the assistant at our home parish of St. Mary, Star of the Sea in Newport. Shortly after that someone presented me with Cardinal Manning's beautiful book *The Eternal Priesthood*. I am not sure whether the latter was from Father Cronan or Father William I. Simmons, pastor of the Church of the Blessed Sacrament in Providence, who was an intimate friend of my father and of my two oldest brothers. My brother Grant was architect of Father Simmons' church, and all three had helped to decorate it. Father Simmons was a former member of Father Hecker's Paulist Congregation.

My attraction to the priesthood was not primarily to the duties or mode of life or a priest's position in society or any of his other attributes. I was attracted to the essence of the priesthood, to the priestly function itself, that of the Mass, and particularly its closeness to Our Lord Jesus Christ himself, for Whose personality I felt an intense attraction and for Whose friendship I increasingly longed. I was, as it were, not attracted liturgically, because I did not serve Mass until shortly before I went away to study for the priesthood. Nor was I particularly familiar with the local clergy. I knew little about their lives and habits and ideas.

At an early date, I think when I was only seven years old, my mother had consecrated me to the Blessed Virgin at the altar of St. Mary's Church. I remember that I always wore blue suits in my childhood as a token of that consecration. It made a profound impression on me, so that I felt that I belonged to her in some special way, that she would guard me, watch over me night and day, and that I owed to her an extraordinary fidelity of thought and action. Then too, an early impression was made on my mind by the immense stained-glass window in St. Mary's Church, which I gazed at Sunday after Sunday. This window represented the fifteen mysteries of the Rosary, the various symbols of the Church and of the Passion. I never wearied in trying to figure it all out, though in my childhood I had some bizarre ideas as to what the various items meant. The central figure represented Our Lady's Assumption, and it annoyed me no end that she was depicted in so ugly a fashion. In later years a new central figure was inserted, but the window itself could never be changed substantially, because Miss Emily Harper from Baltimore, who had contributed the main part of the funds with which the church was built in 1860, stipulated that the window should always remain.

I was deeply impressed by my First Communion, which I made in Philadelphia at the age of ten. (Seven is the average age for children of today.) I was staying for a month with my grandmother, Mrs. Grant Perry, and her daughter and son-in-law, Dr. and Mrs. William Pepper. This was my first city experience and I thoroughly disapproved. I resented the idea that houses should be built in blocks with no grounds or garden around them. It was all so confining. I felt intolerable homesickness as I watched the old horse-cars tinkling their way wearily along Spruce Street. With chin in hands I looked out of my grandmother's window through the little "gossip's mirror," the better to see the passers-by. My mother took this occasion to arrange for my First Communion which I made at the Arch Street Convent of the Religious of the Sacred Heart, after being instructed by Mother Biegan, R.S.C.J. I resolved then that the little white ribbon which I wore on that occasion should remain white as far as possible in my own soul. The Holy Eucharist on that occasion became the one great central overwhelming fact of my existence. At that time it could never be forgotten.

I do not recall any personal influence that encouraged me in my idea of the priesthood. Nobody had suggested it. I had no relatives in Orders or in religion except one remote cousin, Mother Binsse, a religious of the Sacred Heart, whom I had never seen. The priests I had known were excellent men but they did not appeal to my imagination. Our pastor, Dr. Philip Grace, was definitely of the old Irish school, a grand soul with his top hat and his long coat and his elaborate hour-long sermons, in which he quoted Greek, Latin, and Hebrew. He was paralyzed in one arm as a result of a partial stroke, and had just the one gesture of lifting up his left hand by his right. We stood in the utmost awe of Dr. Grace. His eyes moved in contrary directions, and I was sure he always kept one eye fixed on me. Mother reassured me by explaining that he only saw out of the other eye and the gaze was not like that of the Ancient Mariner's.

The local clergy were kind and holy men, Fathers J. Tully and James Looby, Father Cronan, and Father James Coyle, pastor of neighboring St. Joseph's Church. The Passionist

Fathers preached a mission at St. Mary's in my childhood and I was impressed by the saintly bearing and the eloquent sermons of Father Alphonsus, C.P., the leader of the band. But my home atmosphere was uncongenial to the idea of my being a priest. The family were just not interested, and while my mother rather approved of the idea she never pushed it in any way. Newport society certainly was utterly uncongenial to the idea of my becoming a Catholic priest, and it was as remote as the North Pole from the thoughts of any of my youthful companions.

There were plenty of other attractions. My father rather hoped I might become a professor, as he called it, and so confided to his friend, Henry Adams. The Navy was attractive and I often fondly imagined myself as commander of one of the procession of vessels that passed through Newport harbor. There were other careers to dream about, and since I was a bookish type of boy there was always room for something in the field of scholarship or libraries, if more strenuous careers proved impracticable.

Moreover, I had the severest idea of the priest's life. I conceived it as entirely devoid of any natural pleasures. I just couldn't see his human side at all. Consequently when I saw my first film, a shot of seminary students at Catholic University, they impressed my then priggish mind as singularly unkempt. What, I asked myself, would my parents and the neighbors say if I were to join that group? I am convinced this point would have been cleared up for me if, in spite of its shortcomings, I had attended the parochial school. I thought of the priest's life as one of social exile, cut off from even the innocent pleasures of society, isolated from its cultural life, working instead among the poor in the heart of the big city and dramatically at the beck and call of every beggar. It was only some years later during my college days that I thought of the possibility of being a priest and professor at the same time. I was profoundly awed by the dignity of the priesthood, the priest's association with the Eucharistic Lord, and his apostolic functions.

Reading of spiritual books did much to build up in my mind a doctrinal foundation. Someone presented me with a volume entitled euphemistically *A Pocket Bible,* a large, fat, ugly volume of the Douay version printed on flimsy paper in fine print, with unduly large margins, badly bound in shabby cloth. I used to wonder what pocket it could possibly fit, yet I treasured it and almost slept with the Bible under my pillow at night. I did in fact sleep with another book under my pillow, *The Young People's Encyclopedia,* which I had nearly learned by heart. I read the Bible through conscientiously three times from cover to cover, reading much that I could not possibly understand. The heroes and heroines of the Old and the New Testament formed an inspiring picture in my mind and when I was troubled I took refuge in the Book of Wisdom or the Psalms. I was proud of the fact that the Catholic Bible contained so much more than the Protestant Bible and astonished my public school teachers by reciting the complete list of Catholic books: First Kings, Second Kings, Third Kings, Fourth Kings, etc., to the delight of my fellow pupils.

Mother had purchased a complete set of the works of Father Faber, which I read by the hour. I would retire to my room at night, light the little student lamp and read far into the early morning. The man's own personality attracted me. My grandmother Nonna's patience with her continual headaches made me sympathize with Faber and admire his seeming cheerfulness under the same affliction. I learned from his books the grandeur and sweep of Catholic dogma. Three impressions were particularly lasting: a vivid picture of the immensity, grandeur, and beauty of the transcendent God, the story of the Creator; the intense humanness of the God-Man, the mystery of the Incarnation, especially in the mysteries of Bethlehem; and third, Faber's shrewd psychological analysis of the worldly mind, of which I saw plenty around me.

Certain moments stand out in my childhood and boyhood as peculiarly related to the emergence and growth of my sense of a priestly vocation. Father Cronan repeated simple advice in the confessional month after month—to have a pure intention in all that I did. The words meant little to me at the time. I had only a vague idea of a pure intention, but as time went on the words began to mean something. I began to see that a pure intention was identical with complete sincerity in dealing with God and neighbor and, having understood this, I felt a sense of direction. Another moment that meant much to me was the Hour of Adoration spent on the First Friday of each month before the Blessed Sacrament. The Hour of Adoration was established in St. Joseph's Church, then in the old wooden building on Newport's Mall, which was converted later into a motion picture theater after the erection of the handsome new church farther north on Broadway. I know that I was astonished to find how the Lord Himself helped one meditate on those occasions. I would start the hour with nothing particular to offer Our Lord, and yet help always came and I became conscious that it was a two-way street, that most of the work would be done by the good Lord Himself if I would only show my willingness. The hour which I'll always remember came on a hot First Friday afternoon in August. I had been sailing all day, was sunburned, overheated, and dog-tired. It took quite an effort to drag myself into the church and spend the hour on my knees, yet on that occasion I felt the Divine Presence most vividly, as if the hand of the Saviour were taking hold of mine and helping me over the rough paths of prayer.

My boyhood studies were complicated by an interruption that I experienced in high school. At the beginning of my second year at Rogers High in Newport I developed what afterward turned out to be acute appendicitis. I was out the remainder of that second year, much of the time merely resting in bed, too weak even to do much reading. I developed an intense antipathy toward various kinds of food and lost weight and was generally miserable. Finally, my mother made the important decision I have mentioned earlier and moved to New York for two years.

During those two years I became acquainted with one of the city's great linguists, J. Dyneley Prince, Professor of Semitic languages at Columbia University. Through Professor Prince I came to know a group of elderly Gaelic-speaking Irishmen who met every week or so over beer and cheese somewhere around Second Avenue and Thirty-fourth Street and cultivated the mysteries of the Gaelic language. I was initiated into their group, picked up quite a little Gaelic, and was elected as secretary.

Father was infinitely amused at this and wrote to Henry Adams about it. Henry had written to Father that he was sending him a Polynesian boy, son of one of the dignitaries whose acquaintance they had made traveling in Tahiti. Mr. Adams begged Father to look after this fourteen-year-old boy during his New York stay. Father replied that he would be very glad to marshal the younger element of his household to entertain the youngster. He said he figured that I was the only one who could do anything much about it, though I would probably not be interested in the young savage except possibly from a purely linguistic point of view, since I had recently become an authority in the field of Gaelic. The Polynesian lad never turned up and personally I have no recollection of his name ever having been mentioned. If he had arrived he probably would have added something to my linguistic repertoire.

During those two years in New York I made the acquaintance of two profoundly intellectual priests, each of whom greatly helped me to formulate my hopes and plans. Shortly after my arrival in New York, as a fifteen-year-old lad, I called upon Father John Prendergast, S.J., who was the first Jesuit with whom I ever conversed. He produced at first sight a copy of Leaf's Homer and made me read him the English while he explained to me some of the majesty of the Greek. With his deep-set eyes, shock of black hair, and great cape slung around his gaunt form, Father Prendergast imaged the Old Testament prophets to whom he was passionately devoted. Hearing that my grandmother Mrs. Grant Perry (Nonna) was interested like himself in the conversion of the Jews, he started a correspondence with her on the topic that lasted until his death a year or so after.

Another important contact of those two years was with the learned and saintly Dr. Herman J. Heuser, Professor of Scripture at Overbrook Seminary, near Philadelphia. I became acquainted with him through W. R. Claxton, my sister Emily's husband, and whenever I visited my sister I would bicycle over to Overbrook and pow-wow with him in his book-lined study. Here was a source of limitless information on a hundred and one questions that had piled up in my youthful mind. Patiently he answered them for a while, and then he suddenly turned to me and said: "Look out, young fellow. You are merely cultivating your intellect and neglecting your heart. What you need is less brains and more heart."

This simple advice impressed me profoundly. I began to see there was danger in mere braininess and that disaster lay ahead if I were overbalanced in that direction. At the same time, the magnificent Vesper services every Sunday afternoon in the Church of St. Paul the Apostle, and High Mass at St. Francis Xavier's on Sunday mornings, seemed to open another window on my spiritual world and aroused in me a deep feeling for the sacral majesty of the Church's worship.

From the musical angle my chief treat were the Philharmonic concerts in Carnegie Hall. (In those days there was a dead spot in Carnegie Hall close to the stage in the second or third gallery, which I believe was afterwards removed.) The first opera I ever heard was Von Flotow's *Martha* of which I best remember the interpolated "The Last Rose of Summer." I attended the performance with my sisters and other members of the family in the box belonging to Mrs. Winthrop Chanler, an old friend of the family. In the middle of the opera the semi-comedy turned to tragedy when the *buffo* suddenly died right in the midst of a dance scene, surrounded by a bevy of maidens. The opera, however, kept bravely on and the heroine's voice trembled as she sang for the last time "The Last Rose of Summer." My own emotions, already overcome by all this, were still more confused when I discovered toward the middle of the opera that I was wearing russet shoes with a tuxedo and black tie. Altogether my first opera night was an unforgettable experience.

Another experience of this period was my first black bowler hat. It blew off my head at the corner of Tenth Street and Fifth Avenue and I madly pursued it all the way down the Avenue, under the arch to the middle of Washington Square. Those two years were the first and only time in my entire life that I was able to live day after day in close proximity to the mystic sanctum of Father's studio at 51 West Tenth Street, learning to know its personnel and glimpsing periodically something of its complicated workings, especially in the fascinating stage-by-stage production of stained glass. During this period I suffered a second attack of appendicitis, and on recovering went through an operation in the spring of 1897. As a reward for behaving myself during the recovery period, I was taken home from Dr. Brewer's private hospital in an electric hansom, the greatest thrill in transportation.

That same summer I passed my college entrance examination. I had so much to make up that my parents short-circuited the process by engaging a tutor, Dr. Wilfrid Lay, a Columbia graduate student in psychology who coached me very well indeed, as Dean Briggs's letter was to testify. The Georgetown plan had been dropped, Columbia was almost my choice, but fair Harvard prevailed.

CHAPTER FOUR
Harvard College

⋙⋘

While Harvard was eventually my college, I took preliminary exams for Columbia University in the spring of 1897. I was about to take the finals in September when I decided, after considerable deliberation, that I preferred Harvard, though none of my three brothers were Harvard men. Grant had left home for the West after his high school, and Bancel's medical studies at the University of Pennsylvania were cut off after one year by the loss of one of his eyes through infection. Oliver preferred Columbia, having taken his college courses at the Columbia School of Mines. Grant and Bancel, however, were strongly favorable to Harvard, and so was my father, as well as Grant's friend, Theodore Roosevelt. But how was I to change plans on such extremely short notice?

I discussed my problem with my Newport friend, W. Kirkpatrick Brice, who immediately wrote to the Dean of Harvard College, L. B. R. Briggs. It was "desperately short notice," as Dean Briggs later wrote Kirk Brice, but the outcome was indicated in the following excerpt from Dean Briggs's letter, which Brice was kind enough to give me:

I knew that [LaFarge] would have time to finish his Columbia examinations, if he came out very badly in ours. . . . I scarcely dreamed of his passing enough examinations to warrant our admitting him as a regular student. Certainly he more than justifies your account of him; and if you can send us some other fellows who will come up on the second day of the examinations and get in, even with a little help from old preliminary certificates, we

58

shall gladly consider them. I regard the kindness as on your side rather than on mine.

I greatly needed some practical counseling as to studies, and it came from an unexpected source. My brother Grant was taken very ill in 1897 at his summer residence in Saunderstown, Rhode Island. Theodore Roosevelt, then Police Commissioner of New York, dropped in one day to see him. Out of their common interest in Western hunting and wild life conservation, an enthusiastic friendship had sprung up. They took many exploring trips together in the Rocky Mountain territory, and Laura Roosevelt, T.R.'s wife, was a particularly dear friend of Grant's wife, Florence Lockwood.

On this occasion, when I happened to be visiting Grant, Mr. Roosevelt warned me not to raise my voice, as words carried easily from the parlor of the little frame cottage. He was intensely concerned about Grant's condition, which happily turned out to be needless alarm, though Grant had been in bad shape for several months. His talk then turned to my own problems, and he asked me what my future plans were. He already knew of my tastes, and urged me very strongly to carry right through the entire four years of college with Greek and Latin. Mr. Roosevelt's counsel was the only concrete advice I received before entering college, as I found my relation with Professor W. M. Morgan, the adviser assigned to me at entrance, to be quite perfunctory. In later years I never regretted that I followed T.R.'s suggestions.

I journeyed to Cambridge completely alone and with few acquaintances among the undergraduates except Nelson (Neil) Fairchild, Jack Hallowell, and some others who were summer vacation companions on the Newport "Point."

I could not live at college as if in a seminary. But I did impose upon myself a fairly strict regime that I hoped would best fit me for seminary life of which, incidentally, I had only the vaguest notion. The backbone of this regime was my weekly visit (and confession) to Father Thomas I. Gasson, S.J., an Englishman by birth, Rector of old Boston College on

Harrison Avenue. I had learned of him from my solitary Jesuit friend, Father John Prendergast of New York.

As to friendships, my brother Oliver, handsome, jovial, and blessed throughout his generous life with hosts of friends, young and old, offered me advice when I was leaving for Harvard. "Believe me," he said, "don't choose your friends by their exterior. You will find the pleasantest fellows are often the most disappointing. Choose your friends carefully." A simple prescription, yet it worked, and I can honestly say that I do not recall a single friend at Harvard of whom I was not more or less proud in later years.

First days at Cambridge were dismal enough. Slatternly Mrs. Bradt's boarding house on Oxford Street was neither collegiate nor homelike. My neighbor was a sallow, bespectacled farm boy from upstate New York. Food was bad, and evenings were dreary. However, I soon found my bearings as I became interested in my work. But I must admit that I was disappointed in the way the classics were taught, especially in the junior and senior years. The tradition of the German university hung heavily over Harvard in the days of President Eliot and the professors adhered rigidly to grammar and points of erudition. When I longed to fathom the spirit of Aristophanes or Aeschylus it was disappointing to spend hours of study on the structure of the Greek stage. When I came to my senior year, the first class in fourth-year Greek was for me full of anticipation. Professor W. W. Goodwin, author of *Greek Moods and Tenses,* adjusted his twelve-inch feet (the poor man was sensitive on this subject) behind the little green curtain that hung in front of his desk. We were starting, he said, the Nicomachean Ethics of Aristotle. I knew nothing about Aristotle, but was anxious to know what he would have to say. I thought that Goodwin, as the foremost Greek scholar of Harvard and one of the foremost Greek scholars of the world, would have much to share with his students. "Aristotle," said Professor Goodwin, stroking his patriarchal white beard, "was a philosopher. I shall say nothing about his philosophy. If you wish to inform yourself on that subject you can visit the library and look up Zeller's *History of Greek Philosophy*. My exposition of the ethics will be confined to the topic of Aristotle's use of moods and tenses." In later years, however, when I was teaching the Greek classics to students of my own, I experienced the satisfaction of treating Aristotle as genuine literature, in spite of Goodwin's introduction.

It was a year before I eventually recognized President Eliot, though I saw him almost every day crossing the campus. His appearance was forbidding and still more ominous was his observation to students that he was not concerned with their welfare or progress in the university. It was the university's function, he thought, merely to hand out the information; it was that of the student to absorb it. Though the elective system provided no guidance, it did provide some opportunity for those like myself who had a more or less definite idea of what they wanted to do. My mind was not fully made up to the priesthood, but I felt that the logical course for me at Harvard would be one that would tend in that direction. As a result of my conferences with Rev. Dr. Heuser I felt that some day I might teach Scripture, and anyhow, a priest, I reasoned, ought to know something of Scripture in the original languages. So for three years, sophomore, junior and senior, I studied the Semitic languages, Hebrew, Syriac, and Aramaic, with youthful but white-haired and white-bearded Professor Lyon, and the venerable Professor Toy.

Later on I realized I had cheated myself to some extent by not following the crowd who filled the halls for the lectures of Barrett Wendell and Lyman Kittredge. The English department was one place in the university where you could find good teaching, as contrasted with mere academic lecturing in the German style. Luckily for my needs, freshman English was obligatory, and "Copey" Copeland submitted me to his rigors. I knew that he took a dim view of an essay I wrote on the psychology of emptiness of thought, since the theme paper was empty of thought. However, "Copey's" famous readings made up for everything you might otherwise suffer at his hands. It came to me with a strange start, the very day I began to write these lines, to read in the newspaper that Charles T. Copeland had just passed away at the age of ninety-two. I don't know of any American English teacher in our time who inspired and helped young writers more; I know he encouraged me to try some writing, and as a result I was elected to the editorial board of the Harvard monthly.

My most fruitful ventures were almost all extracurricular. Professor Dickinson Sergeant Miller, a distant relative of Mother, and not connected with the university, used to gather some of us in his room of an evening and read with us the English romantic poets, particularly Wordsworth whom we plowed through from beginning to end. Dickinson's subtle, perceptive, and curiously detached mind kept his little circle of after-hour students everlastingly on the alert. I greatly treasure the experiences of those rewarding evenings.

Professor George Santayana also held his Wednesday evenings and read poetry to a small circle of students, but with characteristic good taste did not read his own work. I attended two or three of those gatherings but quickly decided they were not for me. Santayana's personality was somehow antipathetic. From what I heard of his conversations with other students, I had reason to surmise he was as hostile to the Catholic faith, and indeed Christian thought, as any dyed-in-the-wool bigot or utilitarian. I was particularly irritated by his appearing in public as the exponent of the good, the true, and the beautiful in classical and Christian culture. I knew personally two Harvard men whose religious faith he had badly shaken, if not completely destroyed—one a man somewhat older than myself, a Catholic, and the other a classmate, a devout Anglican.

Santayana apparently found me an interesting and unique specimen, and would single me out for his penetrating glance. He soon sensed that I was on my guard against him, and began to query me on my faith in an insinuating fashion. I finally replied rather bluntly that I very much resented the tone of his inquiry. And that was my last appearance at his Wednesday evenings.

Although Santayana in his youthful days attended services at the Jesuit Church of the Immaculate Conception in Boston (where I used to visit Father Gasson) and, for a time, was captivated by some of its great preachers. it is more than doubtful whether at any time he could really have been called a Catholic. Certainly, contrary to general opinion, he was not brought up as one, and actually was exposed to very little Catholic influence in his youth. He could not be judged by the same standards as one who had once enjoyed the faith and then deliberately abandoned it. He was apparently one of those complex characters in whom contradictory tendencies contended. Nevertheless, the unfavorable impression he left on me in my youth was not just my own. Others today confirm it who recall his earlier Harvard influence. In later years at Harvard his attitude toward those who held positive religious beliefs appears to have grown less aggressive.*

The happy discovery that music was an elective led me to enroll in the courses of harmony and counterpoint with the desultory Professor J. K. Payne and the scholarly Walter Spalding. I soon learned that it is one thing to understand the theory of music or read orchestral scores and another to compose. The latter gift you either have or haven't, and I was a have-not. Since my friend Emma Forbes Cary of Cambridge was as good a judge of music as I knew, I played for her my latest composition, a piano prelude or something of the sort. She listened placidly and at the close remarked graciously: "It is *very* impressive." That settled it for me. However, I derived from the course immense love and appreciation for good music.

More fruitful were my private lessons in piano and organ with Walter Spalding, and it was grand fun practicing the

* For a thoughtful and sensitive Spanish appreciation of Santayana see J. Iriarte in *Razón y Fé* (Madrid), July-August 1953.

organ in Appleton Chapel. Spalding was a virile, gentlemanly fellow, a pleasure to work with. He gave me good advice, and told me bluntly that I was introspective.

Of all my courses at Harvard the most completely satisfying was French medieval history, given in my senior year to about thirty of us by Professor Charles Gross. Professor Gross jarred with his high-pitched voice and unpleasant lecturing manner, but he was an ideal teacher. He prescribed ample supplementary reading and treated the great epochs, particularly the disputes between Pope Boniface VIII and Philip the Fair, with thoroughness and objectivity. At last I felt I could grasp something really substantial. Another course, Professor Ashley's on medieval agricultural economics, was also stimulating. While the topic was too technical to be of much practical use, it did serve to make the European scene intensely interesting and provided me with a background that was of great use in later years when I was trying to solve some of the social problems of a rural community.

Since no religion was taught at Harvard, except Protestant theology in the Harvard Divinity School, several of us, including Robert L. Hoguet of the class of '99, and several of my own class—Joe O'Gorman, Nelson Vanderhoof, Walter Desmond, and others—arranged with my friend Father Gasson, the Rector of Boston College, to give us some talks of an apologetic nature on Catholic teaching, under the auspices of the practically defunct Harvard Catholic Club. Rev. Dr. Matthew Flaherty of Brighton Seminary also showed an interest in our project.

These lectures were a feeble substitute for the religious atmosphere of a Catholic college, but they were highly rewarding because of the apparent utter lack of interest in the spiritual welfare of students at Harvard. That is not to say that we Catholics suffered from any formal opposition. Certain professors were reported as being anti-Catholic, but you could avoid their courses. The indifference of the place weighed

heavily on us. In the smug 1890s young people were not
troubled by thoughts as to where the world was going. Religious matters were rarely discussed; it was simply considered
not good form.

Then, too, conditions under which a Roman Catholic of
my background practiced his faith were not particularly
cheering. No contrast was sharper than that between St. Paul's
Catholic church on Auburn Street in Cambridge and Trinity
Episcopal church in Boston's Copley Square. The latter was
a magnificent monument to the architectural genius of Rich-
ardson and the decorative brilliance of my father's painting
and glass. In the former I had many lonely and disturbing
hours. St. Paul's was a plain wooden structure, homely outside and devoid within of any attractive features. On an alternate Sunday we heard the rather depressing discourses of
the famous Father William Orr concerning the state of his
own health or the sins of his parishioners, including those
of the well-known campus character, ancient John the Orange
Man with his diminutive donkey cart. Father Orr frequently
denounced the vices of Harvard youth in general. I was more
fortunate when I listened to the assistant, Father J. J. Ryan.
His talks were of the homespun variety, but I discovered that
some sentence in each of them somehow helpfully applied to
me.

I resented St. Paul's for the false picture of the Catholic
Church it gave to the Harvard community, of Catholic worship, of the dignity of the priesthood. I deplored this situation
so much that three years after my graduation, while home
during the summer vacation from Innsbruck, I pilgrimaged from Newport, Rhode Island, to Old Orchard Beach,
Maine, where Bishop William O'Connell of Portland (the
future Cardinal O'Connell) was summering, and asked him
point-blank if he wouldn't do something to provide spiritual
help for the Harvard students if and when the Pope made him
Archbishop of Boston. "For that's what they say will happen to

you, Your Lordship," I remarked with some interior quaking.

To my surprise, His Lordship listened attentively and made no deprecatory remarks. He said if by the grace of the good Lord such an event were to happen, he would take proper measures and see that the Harvard Catholic students were looked after spiritually. Then he put me at ease by inviting me in swimming. While ducking the salt waves, I looked to see if he wore the episcopal ring in the ocean, and discovered that he did not. He then requested his Chancellor to take me to the hotel, where I was provided with a fine Maine shore dinner—all of which proves that there was a certain advantage in being young and ecclesiastically guileless.

I resented St. Paul's and yet in a way gloried in it. It struck me as being the Church's blunt way of telling the world, and especially the Harvard world: "Here the Faith of Christ and the Sacraments of Christ depend on no earthly dignity or outward appeal to the imagination." St. Paul's appeared to Harvard and Brattle Street pretty much, I imagine, as the worship of the early Christians looked to the cultivated Greeks and Romans. Some of the violent remarks made about the early Christians by pagan emperors were quite similar to what was said by fashionable Bostonians and Cantabrigians about St. Paul's. In its essence the worship on Auburn Street was the identical worship of the catacombs, and the Host lifted up by its priests was the same Body of the Lord for Whom the martyrs had shed their blood.

Though Trinity Church was a complete contrast, it was the Rector of Trinity, the Rev. E. Winchester Donald, who first told me that I would one day be a Jesuit. (The E in his name, I deviously discovered, stood for Eliphaz.) Dr. Donald indeed probed with his mind a bit further into Catholic matters than he was able to propel himself with his will. He had been deeply impressed by the courtesy and keen reasoning of the reply published in 1900 by Father Timothy Brosnahan, S.J., former president of Boston College, to Harvard President

Charles W. Eliot's wholly unprovoked attack in the *Atlantic Monthly* for October 1899 on the Jesuits and Jesuit education. As Dr. Donald himself remarked: "Father Brosnahan, throughout this dispute, made no pretense of being a gentleman, but showed himself a thorough one. Dr. Eliot made all pretense to be a gentleman but failed evidently to be one at all." To Father Brosnahan the Rector eventually unburdened his heart, stating frankly that were it not for his family and his position he would have joined the Catholic Church.

The name of Phillips Brooks, Dr. Donald's famous and eloquent predecessor, was enshrined in the newly inaugurated Phillips Brooks House in the Harvard Yard. Along with other religious bodies of the university the Catholics were assigned a room in Brooks House. In my sophomore year I was given two hundred dollars to spend on furnishing the Catholic room with suitable reading matter. I bought a supply of books from Kenedy and Benziger but after I'd put them on the shelves I noticed that nobody ever used them. It was discouraging.

I had considerably more success my senior year when I was entrusted by the student volunteer association with organizing the annual old clothing collection for student charity. It was the first—and for a long time the last—time that I ever organized anything. Somehow or other we gathered several dozen barrels of good clothing, which we shipped to Mrs. Booker T. Washington, wife of the president of Tuskegee Institute. I was happy when Mrs. Washington replied to my letter with a gracious note of thanks. At the annual meeting I had to make my report, but had never before spoken in public. When I opened my mouth, no sound seemed to come out, but from afar off, away across the hall, my own voice made intelligible and connected phrases, so that I was able to go on.

Not daunted by the obvious lack of interest in the books I'd selected for the Catholic room at Brooks House, I succeeded in prevailing on the authorities to invite Dr. Herman Heuser of Overbrook, my learned friend, to speak in Appleton Chapel, where he made a quite remarkably solemn impression with his German chin whiskers, gold spectacles, and professorial manner. But I was disheartened when the Rev. Dr. Aiken, of the Catholic University in Washington, delivered a dry and factual lecture on Emerson at the Fogg Art Museum. It was as if a Bostonian lectured in Richmond, Virginia, on the glories of the Confederacy.

At different times in my life the question has been put to me how I, a priest and a Jesuit, member of an Order whose major work in this country is in the field of Catholic education, felt about studying in a secular institution. Later on, when I actually taught in a Jesuit college, I had a chance to compare notes on the two types of education and form some impressions. I believed, and still do, that a Catholic youth is apt to suffer a definite loss in not attending a Catholic college. I have heard Catholics, even churchmen, expand on the apostolic opportunity for a Catholic boy in a non-Catholic institution to influence his—usually pagan—milieu. I do not deny such a possibility, but I think it could be argued in the case of foreign schools to a much greater extent than in this country. I do not recollect that I myself had much influence on my fellow students or the faculty. Some individuals, like Santayana or William James, might have been mildly curious as to what a Catholic would say or do under certain circumstances and there were always a few to whom one could speak directly and put a straight question about the Faith. On the other hand, I was aware of lives which were spiritually wrecked by poor moral example or ignorance or by the mere weight of indifference and the spirit of social conformism.

The disadvantages of a secular college do not excuse a Catholic college from living up to its own very high vocation, which is to interpret the total Christ to a living world. Otherwise it fails of its established purpose. Having experienced a non-Catholic education, and having witnessed the great improvement in Catholic college teaching in later years, I appreciate the resources and realizations of à Catholic school.

In a Catholic college, even a very ordinary one, I might

have learned many fundamental things about my religion which I had laboriously to make up in later years. And I would have been spared isolation from those whose outlook resembled my own. This isolation, in spite of the many agreeable features of my life at Harvard, was much the hardest to bear. It made me greatly cherish men who in any way held similar spiritual ideals. Outstanding in that number was Paul Rooney, a graduate student from Saint Louis who later became a Franciscan friar: a physically frail, but spiritually and mentally robust soul, who was consumed even as a college student by a truly Franciscan love of the poor.

Cambridge in the '90s was unique: a city of over seventy thousand people with no railroad station, no hotel, and no restaurant. The Harvard Union eating arrangements had not yet been established, so students were dependent either on Memorial Hall, which was architecturally magnificent but gustatorially deficient, or on the so-called boarding houses, which were expensive and almost equally unappetizing. The average Harvard student managed somehow, however, but with my rebellious interior I was hard put to work out a system of survival. I cooked my breakfast in my room, picked up an egg sandwich at odd moments at the Hasty Pudding Club, and eked out the standard fare by an occasional meal with some of the more hospitable folk of Cambridge or Boston. An unfailing resource was the exceptional soup dispensed by my cousin Miss Agnes Irwin, Dean of Radcliffe College. Miss Irwin explained to me gravely that it was considered excellent manners to ask for a *second* plate of soup, since that implied the soup was so good that nothing else could equal it; being young and hungry, I agreed. Every Sunday afternoon I could count at precisely six o'clock upon a superb and beautifully served dinner at the town home of the brilliant Napoleonic historian, the kindly, sturdy, and hunchbacked John C. Ropes. Anyone on Mr. Ropes's list of undergraduate guests could share that Sunday dinner, but only the six who arrived first.

Mr. Ropes, in his fatherly way, explained to me that what I needed for the good of my soul was to forget my rather select companionship, summer in a plain country hotel, and learn to know the common crowd. I saw the logic of his idea but somehow never got around to it. For the four years of my college life I still found it impossible to shake off a constant feeling of utter physical weakness. I tried the gymnasium, tried rowing on the Charles River, and skating on Spy Pond—most sublime of all physical thrills on a moonlit January night— taking long bicycle rides, exercising any way I could, but always the same helpless feeling returned, and I found myself again on the flat of my back.

One bright spot in a spiritually bleak world was the friendly Brattle Street home of Miss Emma Forbes Cary, the patient listener to my piano playing. She was the sister of Mrs. Louis Agassiz of Agassiz Museum fame. Miss Cary herself was one of the most remarkable women I have ever met. She was a convert to the Faith, but with an entirely different type of experience from that of my mother. She had suffered, she said, a violent conversion, a struggle, "as if cut to pieces," almost a death struggle against an intense repugnance and brought to a conclusion only by long, scrupulous argumentation. Miss Cary was a brilliant pianist and somewhat of a poetess, and a staunch friend of the students, who had more or less the run of her house. For some thirty years she had served on the Massachusetts Prison Commission, the first woman ever to occupy such a post, and she had been entrusted with some of the most delicate and difficult youth problems the Commission had had to meet. Her capacious bulk was irradiated by tremendous humor, good nature, and general jollity. A curious contrast was her companion, the supremely spinsterish Miss Lisa Felton, daughter of one of Harvard's former presidents.

Of William James, then teaching psychology, I had little experience outside of two or three perfunctory visits to his home, and his brother Henry James was only a name I had heard at home. I was therefore mystified one afternoon in my junior year when, after a knock on the door, a rough-looking, burly individual stamped into my room in Hilton Hall. He plumped himself down on the sofa, looking very much like a piano-mover come to see about his job.

"My name," he said, "is James. Robertson James. I am the younger brother of William and Henry."

I had heard of Robertson as a sort of black sheep of the James family, though he and his brother Wilky as young men had fought in the Civil War and William and Henry had not. We struck up acquaintance and under his somewhat dilapidated exterior I found Robertson James vivacious, entertaining, and rather curious about religion. He spoke with affection of my father and my mother and revived, as Henry did in later years, old memories.

My musical interests, outside of the lessons I took with Walter Spalding, centered chiefly around the concerts of the Kneisel quartet in Sanders Theater in Cambridge, and of course the Boston Symphony. One of my happiest memories is the trio of piano, violin, and cello, to which I contributed the piano part, at the home of my uncle, T. S. Perry, at 312 Marlboro Street. His oldest daughter Margaret played the violin, punching me in the back with her bow for better tempo, and his second daughter, Edith, the cello. The third daughter, Alice, later Mrs. Joseph C. Grew, was a pianist in her own right.

Since Aunt Lilla Perry was a Cabot, the Cabots drifted into the picture, and every now and then we played along with Handasyd Cabot, their cousin, who occupied the awesome position of a cellist in the Boston Symphony Orchestra, though for how long I do not know. From a musical standpoint Handasyd was a curious phenomenon. With his brilliant technique, he performed stunts with the cello, but could not keep perfect time. Something in the Cabots refused to swing along rhythmically.

In addition to the music, Aunt Lilla's translations from Plato and the Greek lyric poets came in handy at examination

time, and I admired her proficiency. She became involved,
not to her benefit, with Mrs. Piper and Spiritualism, and
brought her complacent husband and the girls somewhat under
its baneful influence. In later years the results were tragic. To
me it was curiously pathetic to see such intelligent and cultivated people, so wise, charming, and thoughtful, guided by
these curious psychics who directed even their smallest actions.
They could not even pack a trunk or order a meal without
consulting Mrs. Piper's "control," the mysterious Dr. Phinuit.
This kind of religious idiocy seemed like God's rebuke to a
certain social pride and self-complacency.

One of my last talks with Uncle Tom Perry was just at the
outbreak of the First World War. He presented the curious
spectacle of a brilliant, noble-hearted man who lacked a philosophy with which to meet something tragic and tremendous.
His sister Frances, my Aunt Fannie—Mrs. William Pepper of
Philadelphia—an Anglican, was deeply religious, though definitely conventional in her outlook on life. But Uncle Tom
wandered in a fog, as it were, of decency and good will. The
evil in the world, he said, made his blood boil. He clenched
his fist and gesticulated, but then there was nothing more to
do except let his blood boil a little more.

With Aunt Lilla we always wondered what would happen
next. She dyed her hair bright green when she meant to dye
it black. She stored a hundred bottles of fermented milk or
Kumyss in our cellar at Newport and forgot to fasten the corks
securely, so that it all exploded during the night and was
found spread around the property. She fainted at every emotion, and was in a constant dither as to what the spirits might
say next. Yet she had a good heart, was kind and devoted to
her family and children, and she certainly added to the pic-
turesqueness of Boston and Newport life.

A big event in my junior year at college was my brother Bancel's engagement to my Boston acquaintance, Mabel Hooper,
one of Mr. Edward Hooper's five daughters. I owed more to

my brother Bancel than I have at any time in my life been able quite to express. Bancel himself had not had the benefit of a college education. He had started a year of medical study at the University of Pennsylvania at the instance of our Uncle Willie Pepper. Then his eye became infected and for a year, at the age of twenty, he sat in a dark room under continual watch lest the other eye should be lost too. Happily the other eye was saved but he dropped all further idea of medical study. Walking in my father's footsteps, he took up painting and became a competent mural painter. Bancel was by nature a thorough sportsman, and an extraordinarily accurate observer of nature. Skilled boatman, fisherman, and shot, he delightfully combined sportsmanship with his art. He would spend a day at the seashore or on the marshes with a gun in his hand and a paint box strapped to his back. When the birds did not flush, he would set up his easel and start to take notes or to paint. He was a silent soul. As a child he never spoke until he was five years old, and did not say very much even after. His loss of an eye cut him off from much reading. On the other hand, with his orderly mind and his keen memory he possessed a fine business sense and put order into my father's chaotic affairs. In earlier years my father valued his work immensely, but in later times considerable friction developed. But it was largely Bancel's foresight and continual watching over my own needs that enabled me to go to college and enjoy the advantages which had been denied him.

I was not sorry Bancel was marrying a Hooper. Periodic visits to the Hooper household were a soothing affair. The five slender blonde girls, with their subdued voices and measured language, would be seated in low chairs in their mansion parlor on Mount Vernon Street. You also sank into one of those chintz-covered chairs, and the conversation was just stimulating enough, avoiding violent controversy. From the parlor window you looked out on the famous Shaw Memorial. This great relief sculpture of marching troops recalled earlier and heroic days when Boston's patriots were ready to lay down their lives for the freedom of slaves whose ordinary human rights they later so conveniently forgot in the "great betrayal" of the late '70s. My father's association with Edward Hooper and his brother-in-law, "Uncle" Henry Adams, was so long and intimate that I never felt as if the girls were anything but my older sisters. Their conversation with me was sisterly, too. At any rate, their home was a refuge if the going got too hard in Cambridge.

Though he was a Unitarian by profession, Edward Hooper entertained a deep devotion to the Blessed Virgin. It was a much simpler and less sophisticated affair than the metaphysical and somewhat enigmatic glorification of the Blessed Virgin familiar to us in the writings of Henry Adams. Every night, before they went to bed, Mr. Hooper gathered his five daughters around him and said a prayer to Our Lady. His oldest daughter Ellen married a Catholic, the late John Briggs Potter. Mabel, the third daughter, who married my brother Bancel, later came into the Catholic Church and brought up in the Catholic faith her four sons, Bancel, Jr., Henry, Edward, and Tom. The last-named died at sea in December of 1942, while returning home, as commander of a small Coast Guard cutter, from months of patrol duty in the icy Arctic.

Entering college in 1897, I had the distinction of being a member of the first graduating class of the twentieth century. By general agreement of its members, the class of 1901 was a vast improvement over the expiring nineteenth century's last gasp in the class of 1900. We also felt we were setting a standard which the class of '02 might admire but never attain. The genius of the class was the poet Robert Frost, and some lesser celebrities clustered around his melodious name. In general, however, the class of '01 prided itself through the years on being the class of the *homme moyen,* standing on its widely distributed merits, not on the borrowed radiance of a few celebrities.

Harvard class membership in the President Eliot days did

not necessarily mean sociability. In fact, it was quite normal not even to converse with a fellow classman unless you had been introduced to him. Clarence Saunders, an incredibly reticent millionaire from Cleveland, and I ate our tasteless meals together for a good while at a boarding house on Auburn Street without speaking. I was determined not to be the first to break the ice. It was a couple of months before Saunders unbent sufficiently to comment on the pudding. Only when the class anniversaries began to roll around in later life did class membership first become a matter of consciousness, then of conscience, next of pride, and finally of a very real and noble pleasure. We are inordinately proud, for example, that Jim Lawrence, elected class president in 1897, still presides at this writing over his not too depleted flock.

My own first consciousness of the Harvard class of '01 as an entity with a very human heart was in 1921. Members of the class that year astonished and moved me more than I could say by collecting a substantial sum to aid in building my church of St. Nicholas in St. Mary's County near Patuxent, Maryland. Instigator of this plan was the former class treasurer, John White Hallowell, my former summer companion in Newport. Jack Hallowell died six years later and with him passed my closest bond with the class, until those bonds were resumed in very recent years. The two members of my class with whom I have kept up the most continuous correspondence are Joseph A. O'Gorman, mentioned earlier, and Erich Stern. Erich, a stocky young lad from Milwaukee, was somewhat of my own serious type of mind and many a talk we had on subjects of common interest. He had a spiritual philosophy of his own which struck me at the time as being wise and which has worn well through the years.

The ceremonial closing of my college years was a solemn affair, for unrelaxed graduates of 1901 did not ask to have their degrees casually sent to them by mail. I was sorely tempted to continue what had become a fairly pleasant life in Cambridge, but I had already cast the die in my own mind for actually taking up studies for the priesthood. Father Gasson had suggested that I should pursue my studies at the University of Innsbruck in Austria, where he himself had taken his theological training a few years previously as a Jesuit scholastic. This greatly appealed to me, for from what I could learn the theological faculty of Innsbruck was composed of outstanding men. Moreover, the idea of studying abroad, particularly of studying in a university of the German type, and in the Alps, had its special attraction. The decision meant no small sacrifice on Father's part, and once more the same persons came to my assistance as had presided at my entrance into college—my brother Bancel and Theodore Roosevelt.

Bancel faced the financial problem bravely and during my course at Innsbruck, as in my years at Harvard, arranged, sometimes in the face of serious obstacles, for my material needs. Father had not been averse to my notion of studying for the priesthood, but when it came to the showdown I could see that he entertained other plans, so that he hesitated somewhat, as did my oldest brother Grant. The hesitation, however, was broken down chiefly by Mr. Roosevelt. As he had advised on my entrance to college, he now spoke up to Father and Grant on my behalf. The boy, "T.R." insisted, has a vocation. God has sent him certain lights and certain graces, and it would be folly not to let him follow them. He was an eloquent advocate and his counsel won the day.

I intended to study for the Diocese of Providence, but I went entirely on my own, without any obligation to the Bishop of Providence, the Most Rev. Matthew Harkins. When I said good-by to my mother in Newport in July 1901 it was the only time in my life that I had ever seen her weep, and yet in this as in so many other matters she was my staunchest supporter.

For some reason or other, which neither she nor I could ever explain, she begged me on that occasion: "Don't let them make you a Jesuit."

I replied: "Mother, dear, nothing can ever make me a Jesuit."

In later years we were somewhat mystified over this. The idea of becoming a Jesuit had not remotely occurred to me, in spite of Dr. Donald's prophecy, and did not occur to me until more than three years later.

Father surprised me by his interest in every detail of my proposed trip, and arranged for me to meet some of his old New York friends—W. C. Brownell, the literary critic, the art experts Bernard Roelker and A. F. Jaccaci, and others, at the Century Club. As I was about to say good-by he drew me into a corner of the Graham Library, on the Century's third floor, where we would be undisturbed, saying that he wished to give me a special bit of advice.

"Old man," he said, "you are going to Europe. You will visit London, Paris, Vienna and many other places. You are still young, you are still a man, and you will come across a certain type of woman," using more precise language. "You are not thinking of anything wrong, but you will be away from home. I hope you will never get into any trouble of this sort, but if you do, remember I am here to help you, and don't hesitate to send me a cable. I'll come to your aid."

I was a bit taken aback by Father's frankness, for I did not expect to be involved in that particular kind of complication. Yet his concern deeply touched me. Fortunately for myself and for his peace of soul, I did not get into trouble with the ladies; though his own anxiety for my welfare must have been on his mind and may well have been the reason for an amusing incident which I recount in Chapter Six. I saw enough, however, during my four years abroad to know that Father's apprehensions were not fashioned out of cobwebs; Father knew the world, and he knew youth.

PARS VERNA

⟫ ⟪

Spring is the time of decision: what and when to plant; what weeds to uproot and fallow ground to be cleared; what fields to cultivate with Heaven's gracious gifts and with what tools. Spring, too, is the time of sprouting and unfolding: God unrolls the sequence of His great plan, the Mysterium Dei—Lent—Passiontide—Resurrection—Ascension—Sending *of the* Holy Spirit—*for the whole world, and for each soul in particular. The Spring volume is a story of sharp penance, anxious uncertainties, and new-found joy.*

CHAPTER FIVE

Innsbruck, Alpine Sanctuary

—》》 《《—

I sailed for Europe on the S.S. *Grosser Kurfürst* in July 1901 in the company of two of my classmates, Henry Varnum Poor of New York and Benjamin Blake of Boston. The trip was delightfully calm, and the three of us bunked in a big cabin on the top deck, next to the Captain's.

At our first landfall, England's southern extremity, the Lizard, I spotted through the spyglass an old stone house with an odd little stone barn, and gazed at it long and thoughtfully—my first sight of the Old World. My regret at not being allowed ashore increased at the sight of Cowes, preparing for the yacht races, and again when passing in the bright sunshine the Isle of Wight, which reminded me of home.

Bremerhaven was a complete disappointment to me. Henry Poor remarked that the young fellows there looked as if they had taken a flying leap through a clothing shop and a few articles had somehow stuck to them. Bremen itself was better, though I was disappointed, in a way, that things looked pretty much as I had imagined.

At Amsterdam, however, with its endlessly variegated houses and its magnificent Rijksmuzeum, my spirits lifted. At Rotterdam I felt as if time had vanished when I saw Rembrandt's *Presentation of Our Lord,* with its intense lights and its ghostly figures. I was struck by the way the people seemed to enjoy the great works of art. I was both helped and wearied by my endlessly sedulous companion, Henry Poor, who

81

tramped mercilessly through the galleries, Baedeker ever in hand.

In Rotterdam I decided I should go to confession. I found a Jesuit church and made a venture in French.

"For your penance," the confessor said, "you may recite the litany of Our Lady."

When I returned to the pew to say my penance I realized that I did not know the litany of Our Lady by heart, and that I had no English or French prayerbook. Seeing a pious young lady praying in the corner of the church, I asked her if she spoke French. She said she did.

"Would you lend me your prayerbook?" I said.

"But my prayerbook is in Dutch. Do you know Dutch?"

I gave a vague answer and opened her prayerbook at the litany of Our Lady. My Dutch knowledge was fragmentary, but I conjectured that the Blessed Virgin would understand and accept my effort.

I bade good-by to Blake and Poor at Munich and thence traveled by stagecoach to Innsbruck. Stopping there long enough to get my bearings, I kept on via the Austrian Südbahn and Brenner Pass by slow train to Brixen (later Bressanone) in the South Tyrol, in those days still in Austrian hands.

There I was the guest of Baron and Baroness Schönberg-Roth-Schönberg, at their summer home, Schloss (Castle) Pallaus, on the outskirts of the town. Baron Schönberg was a papal chamberlain, who passed his winters in Rome. His wife was an American lady, born Elizabeth Ward, daughter of Mr. Thomas Ward of Boston. Her nephew, George Cabot Ward, was a law student at Harvard in my day and had spoken to me of his Aunt Bessie on various occasions. The Schönbergs made up for their childlessness by their hospitality. Among their close associates in Rome were Cardinal Rampolla, Secretary of State under Pope Leo XIII; Cardinal Merry del Val, who held the same office under Pius X; Dr. William O'Connell, Rector of the North American College, later Cardinal and Archbishop of Boston; Holland's Cardinal Van Rossum, and many others.

A Saxon convert to Catholicism in his youth, Baron Schönberg was disinherited by his father and "adopted," as he said, by Pope Pius IX. The Pope gave him a place at the Vatican Court where he functioned for the rest of his life. He was Roman to the core and was enormously annoyed at people who complained of irreverence in Roman churches.

"Speak about irreverence," he said on one occasion, "my first Sunday in the United States was in a Catholic church in Boston, and the pastor talked about nothing but raffling a silver tea-set. Nobody in Rome ever talks from the altar about silver tea-sets."

The Baron offered me some practical advice about board and lodging in Innsbruck, and was anxious that I should make the acquaintance of Father Hamilton Macdonald, an English convert priest and Navy chaplain, who would soon be visiting in those parts. Father Macdonald was a Scotsman, an old Etonian. From what the Baron said, I gathered that he would be helpful to me in trying to make up my mind as to whether to settle definitely upon Innsbruck or Rome for my theology. The Baron's own views inclined in both directions. He was as Roman-minded as any non-Roman could be; yet he immensely respected Innsbruck for its fine tradition, its outstanding faculty and Regent; and he was an old personal friend of Innsbruck's Rector, Father Johann Nepomuk Mayr, S.J.

I returned to Innsbruck for a couple of weeks and established myself in living quarters. Theological students at that time were not obliged to live in the Canisianum (or Theologisches Convict or Convictus, as it was also called), the residence, with its rules and "way of life," run by the Jesuits. Classes were held at the University of Innsbruck, a state institution. As a free-lance I preferred to live for a time outside the Convictus and learn something of German student life.

My room on the second floor at No. 3 Adamgasse was separated from the street by a cold, green, rushing mountain stream that ran right through the town. There was a coffee or chicory factory in the building, and the water wheel which operated the machinery turned night and day. (When I revisited Innsbruck for the first time, in 1951, almost fifty years later, I strolled from the hotel along the Adamgasse, and discovered the old water wheel. During World War II the stream bed had filled with rubble, and the wheel was inoperative, but the sight of it brought back to me the faint, all-pervasive smell of chicory and the perpetual rumble of the ancient machinery which made me believe in my dreams that I was voyaging back in a paddle-wheel steamer to the United States.)

For I soon became appallingly homesick in that room, and felt as if I had been dropped to the bottom of a well. My homesickness led me to desperate measures: I rented a grand piano, a Blüthner, for less than I had paid at Harvard for an upright Ivers and Pond, and somehow got it into the apartment, to the amazement of the landlady, Frau Feichtmeier, a sad-faced little woman who was English by birth and had married an Austrian.

When I visited Brixen again, the Baron took me for a long walk over the fields and into the town to see the Prince Bishop of Brixen, the venerable and half-blind Most Rev. Dr. Simon Aichner, an authority on Canon Law. I found his person and manners pleasantly simple, but his strongly Tyrolese German somewhat hard to understand. He was anxious I should go to Rome, saying: "The Holy Ghost tells me you should go to Rome." But since the Holy Spirit, speaking through the Prince Bishop, had not specified a time limit, I saw no reason why that should affect my plans for the current year. The Bishop was deeply disturbed by the militant movement, called the *Los von Rom-Bewegung*, which was attempting to organize an active anti-Catholic political party in Austria and Germany. It had made itself felt even in the Tyrol which, like all predominantly Catholic countries, never lacked its quota of anti-clericals.

On September 23 I received a telegram informing me that I would find Father Macdonald at Gerstein. When we met, he advised me to stay in Innsbruck, and gave me many arguments in favor of it as opposed to Rome. An old friend of his, another English convert priest, the Rev. Adrian Knottsford-Fortescue—widely known in later years as an authority on the Roman relics—was an Innsbruck man, and had told Macdonald much about its advantages. I took long walks with Father Macdonald through the woods on subsequent visits to the Schönbergs, and gathered from him bits of simple, homely wisdom, such as advice on certain details of personal appearance and bearing. I profited greatly from the example of his high, apostolic ideal.

Back at Innsbruck in October I began my lectures in Philosophy under Father Joseph Lercher, with Schiffini's dry Latin textbook, followed by the first classes in Scripture with Father Leopold Fonck. All this was after I had filled out various forms, checking them first with the redoubtable Father Matthias Flunk, dean of the Jesuit theological faculty, and then with the still more redoubtable registrar, the Herr Quaestor of the Königlich-Kaiserlich University, dreaded by students for his tart remarks and grouchy disposition.

The calm and dignity of the Innsbruck theological faculty and seminary contrasted with the uproar in the rest of the University that I ran into occasionally as an extern student. The German-speaking students, by far the majority, protested against lectures given in Italian by the Austrian-Italian professors in the School of Law, and insulted the Italian Professor Menestrina. The Italians held a counter-protest meeting at Berg Isel, a resort on the south side of the city, and I rode home with a crowd of them in the streetcar.

That evening they demonstrated in front of the Statthalterei, the Government House of the Tyrol. The next morning the Germans stamped and blew their trumpets. The Italians demonstrated again before the Statthalterei, but this time

seven of them were arrested and put in jail. The next day the
University Senate told Menestrina not to lecture any more.
The Germans had not been arrested because they had demonstrated *inside* the University, where the police could not enter.
Walking past the University, I saw a little placard on the door
saying that "the honored students are politely informed that
the University is closed for the rest of the semester."

That stopped the Germans, but the Italians still raged. They
appealed to the Italian deputies in the (Vienna) Reichstag,
and one of these, Malfatti, brought up a bill in the House
asking for an Italian University in Trent or Trieste, the two
Italian cities. A few days later in a letter to the University
Senate the Minister of Public Instruction replied saying, "New
faculties are not created overnight."

In these demonstrations, I noted, the German Catholics took
no part, and they made the Rector very uncomfortable by
sending a delegation to protest against the closing of the University, explaining that they were 400 in number, and "with
the theological students, 600." The student affair was my first
sampling of the German-Italian dissensions that continued to
plague the Austrian Reich during the successive years: the
fruit of a hopeless conflict between pagan German nationalism
and an extreme, often highly anti-clerical Italian nationalism:
a foretaste of Hitler and Mussolini.

My first experience of an Austrian public political discussion proved to me, as I wrote to my mother, the need of "a
strong will and a calm mind" to seek the truth. Posters advertised that Herr Engel (pastor of one of the churches in Hall,
the neighboring town) would speak on behalf of the Christian
Social Party, and opponents were invited to give utterance
to their sentiments.

The enormous hall with frescoed walls and a great, high
timber roof was lighted only by candles, one on each table.
It was crowded mostly with peasants and workingmen. The
pastor, a tall, thin man with a hatchet face and a cracked voice,
spoke eloquently for about an hour, talking of the *Los von*

Rom movement in Austria, which was united with the German nationalist movement, and the attempt to destroy the Austrian Empire and build up an all-German non-religious Socialist state. Father Engel spoke clearly and intelligently about Luther, showed the noble estimation Luther himself had of the peasants and the workingmen, talked of freedom and charity and then described the St. Vincent de Paul Society, Bishop Von Ketteler, the thousands of Catholic charitable institutions over the world, and especially in Austria, Archbishop Ireland, and many other things, bringing forth figures and statistics. His words were followed by great applause and a rest of five or six minutes.

Several persons then spoke: a young Lutheran missionary, a Catholic, a professed atheist, and a Socialist leader, who was baited by the audience to express opposition to the Jews. Father Engel closed the meeting, still talking with ease and good form. At the end the Socialists went out shouting *"Los von Rom."* But the Catholics kept their tempers and drowned them out with a hymn.

My experience of this meeting was a foreshadowing of the tragic contradictions that were to mark life in the eastern European world in the decades to come: the nobility, vitality, and strength of the genuine Christian Democratic movement and its strong hold on the common people; yet the impasse it reached whenever it allowed itself to drift, as was the case with Luëger in Vienna, into the facile paths of anti-Semitism.

I attended the solemn ceremony of immatriculation in the Innsbruck University, the *Imperialis et Regalis Universitas Oenipontana,* and wrote to my mother: "The Rector came in and made a stupid, hesitating little speech, then called the names with considerable difficulty, for there were Germans, Poles, Czechs, Italians, Slovenians, Croats, and Hungarians. He even choked at my name, mumbling something about 'Chawn LaJartch,' after which it was my turn to give the so-called 'solemn handshake' (*feierlichen Handschlag*) to the Uni-

versity Secretary." I discovered later that the trouble with
my name came from my American, or English, script. My
letter F looked in German like a J, and henceforth I amended
that item in my straggling handwriting. A French name attached to an American was a cause of perplexity for German
eyes and ears.

A few days before Christmas, Count Schaffgotsch made me
feel humble by visiting my apartment in person to return the
ceremonial call I had paid upon him in compliance with
Baron Schönberg's request. The old gentleman was most simple and genial, and regaled me with stories of Father Tuzer,
one of the former theology professors, who used to take a
generous pinch of snuff every time he had to make an impressive pronouncement. Snuff was still in order among some of
the old-timers, and I was a bit uncertain as to whether it belonged simply to the *ancien régime,* or was in some way connected with the Society of Jesus. The doubt was not cleared
up until I finally landed at St. Andrew-on-Hudson at Poughkeepsie, New York, after my return to America and saw no
snuff.

The American colony, self-styled "American Exiles," celebrated Thanksgiving in as traditional a style as possible, and
usually managed to secure a turkey. For my first Thanksgiving
abroad, I was deputed to make a fifteen-minute speech on
President Theodore Roosevelt. (I had learned the news of
President McKinley's assassination when a newsboy cried
"Extra!" late at night along the Adamgasse. All he had to sell
was a little slip of paper with the bare announcement of
"McKinley Murdered!" upon it.) Since I was still highly diffi-
dent about speech-making, my only reliance was on a collection of jokes for the occasion. The banquet was held, *de more,*
at Frau Gerlach's ever-hospitable inn at Schwatz, an hour's
ride by tram from Innsbruck.

I ate my meals at a table furnished by Frau Evers and her
daughter, for theological students only, in the more modern-
ized residential section of the town. "All the Paters recom-

mend it," I wrote, "and I believe she is their protégée, having two theological sons of her own." The food was excellent, considering the price: 56 kronen or $12.04 a month—about $3.00 a week. Once a week good Frau Evers provided for us what in liturgical language might be called a "commemoration of the preceding," a little basket affair with dozens of tiny compartments in which bits of vegetable, meat, pickle, etc., were neatly chopped up into a sort of *hors d'œuvre.*

Four of us ate at Frau Evers': Heinrich Chardon, a Rhinelander from Trier; Adolph Traurich from Kreuznach, and a solemn and habitually perplexed blond Swiss youth, Baron Victor von Ernst. Our conversation consisted largely in getting Von Ernst straightened out with his studies, and in heated arguments between the two Germans and myself. It was the best possible school for the German language. In the case of Heinrich Chardon it was also the foundation of a precious and life-long friendship.

For the good of my soul, I joined the student sodality. Father Oberkamp, S.J., whom I had met at the Schönbergs', had organized a number of Catholic university students as a unit of the Blessed Virgin's Sodality or Marianische Kongregation. These were men studying in the other university faculties: law, medicine, and philosophy, as well as the theological students who, like myself, during those first months, were residing not in the seminary but in the town. Father Oberkamp considered himself a bit of a radical, going so far as to tell the students he had no objection to their staying up as late as 11 P.M. three times a week. Anyhow, they liked him, and I was glad to accept his invitation to join the group.

Forthwith I was appointed organist for the weekly sodality meetings, and played the German sodality hymns on the little harmonium when we met every week in the blue-frescoed Princes' Chapel of the great Jesuit University church. I was always proud to have had this first and only experience as a member of the Sodality, functioning as it did in the very chapel constructed for its use centuries before. When I revisited the

old place in the spring of 1951 I made my way at once to explore the Princes' Chapel. It had been badly bombed out during the war and I had heard that it was all gone, but to my
delight I found it completely restored, the same old chapel
with a window looking into the sanctuary of the church, and
even a harmonium like the one I had played fifty years ago.
It seems strange now that I had to cross the ocean and become
an Austrian university student in order to join a traditional
Catholic organization such as one ought normally to find in
every American parish. But then that was precisely a commentary on what was lacking at Harvard, as well as in many
Catholic parishes of the period.

Though in my three months of town life I did not have the
opportunity to become a full-fledged member of one of the
famous Couleur-Corps, or *Verbindungen* (university student
fraternities), with their visored and specially hued cap, swag-
gering costume, and other paraphernalia, I did sit in on some
of the Kommerses or festive occasions of the yellow-capped
"Austria" (Catholic Austrian membership), where the chairman shouted *"Silentium!"* as we rattled Salamander with giant
beer-mugs on the mighty oaken table, and the new arrival
from across the sea was called upon to make a speech, the more
nonsensical the better. Since I was not ready for a German discourse, I saved the occasion by reciting, to hilarious applause,
the names of the way-stations on the Old Colony Railroad
between Boston and Tiverton, Rhode Island.

As the days grew shorter and my loneliness increased, I
took long walks in the dusk through the nooks and byways
of half-medieval Innsbruck, wearing an old worn raincoat. I
reached the nadir of depression when on a rainy night a
youngster hailed me with the expression: *"Bettelstudent!"*—a
hobo student.

The acute, practically physical feeling of homesickness was
relieved, however, in a curiously unexpected way. From
friends at home I carried an introduction to an English lady,
Miss Mary Howitt, daughter of the poet and poetess William

and Mary Howitt, known chiefly through their ditty, "Will you walk into my parlor, said the Spider to the Fly?" Miss Howitt invited me to walk into her parlor in the villa section of the town, where she resided with her companion, the Baroness Frankenstein. But my experience was pleasanter than that of the fly. She offered me a good cup of hot British tea, with British muffins to boot, talked of common friends, and made me feel as if I had escaped from the grim Alpine surroundings. It was absurdly trifling, yet it broke the spell, and I began to feel more like a normal human being. I have often thought of that experience in dealing with young people who come from abroad to this country.

Christmas I spent in Munich in a plain little hotel drearily called "The Three Ravens," *Hotel Drei Raben,* and while there frequented the museums and the Court Theatre, and attended my first Midnight Mass.

After my return from Munich I had had enough solitude, and decided to follow the example of the other students from the United States, as well as of my three German friends, who were entering the seminary. I entered with them at the close of the year and made my first spiritual retreat, which was given by Father Hugo Hurter, S.J., famous professor of Dogmatic Theology. Father Hurter was an incredibly vivacious and original personality. The retreat was ideal, a vivid, direct, and complete revelation to me first of my own interior, a perspective, as it were, of what the inner life really could mean; and secondly, it was an introduction to the living Christ of the Gospel, to His teaching, His personality, His Passion and Resurrection, in a way that I had never even dreamt of before. I came out of retreat a new man filled with enthusiasm, with peace of soul and a resolution to carry on.

Once within the seminary walls, I found myself, in every sense of the word. The Canisianum was a plain, fairly modern four-story building, attached at one end to a couple of old private residences, awkwardly separated from one another by a private family which could not be displaced. I lodged in the ancient four-story Pfeffersberghaus, which must have been a stately burgher residence in its day. The further side of the seminary led to the Jesuit residence built four centuries previous by the great apostle of northern Italy and southern Germany and Poland, St. Peter Canisius.

The university buildings were once the Jesuit college of Innsbruck, but now belonged to the Austrian Government. From the upper stories of the university building a passageway led into a tribune looking over the sanctuary of the University church. There on Sundays we attended a late High Mass. The church itself was in charge of the Jesuits, but the building was the property of the Austrian Government. The Government also paid the choir that sang at the High Mass, and had complete control over it.

Outside of the bedrooms there was no heat whatsoever in any part of the buildings. Corridors, dining hall, capacious lecture rooms where the professor climbed up in a lofty pulpit and the listeners sat on the hardest of wooden benches, were completely devoid of heat. In the chapel the holy water froze solid in the bronze fonts, and an acolyte serving Mass had to beware lest he freeze his fingers on the heavy eighteenth-century silver cruet trays. In the evening we lined up in the courtyard to fill our jugs for drinking and washing. During the first two years there was no plumbing, and nature's needs were cared for in fairly medieval fashion.

In class I swathed myself in cloak and galoshes as for an old-fashioned sleigh-ride. Twice a day, at 4 A.M. and 4 P.M., the old apple-faced Diener, or house servant, chucked oak and pine logs into the fire chamber of the immense brick stove that heated the bedrooms. Thick walls and double windows kept the rooms warm by day and night. The food was plain, but well-cooked in Austrian style, with plenty of Wiener Schnitzels, Kugelupfen, Kaiserschmarrn (or omelet pancakes with prune sauce, popularly referred to as Stiefelwichs or bootblacking), and a viertel of red wine or seidel of Tyrolese beer,

with other delicacies. After a day's duty in the open a glass
(not a cup) of highly recommended Rhum mit Thee made
existence bearable. I groaned a bit over some of the primitive
features of the life, but began to thrive and enjoyed during
those four years a health I had never known before.

When the wind blew from the south the wretched sirocco,
a dry wind with low air pressure wrangled everybody's nerves
and sent some of the more sensitive souls to bed. But when
the wind was from the north, all was different. Then the
mighty Frau Hitt and her stony companions of the Nordkette
mountains shielded us from the icy northern blasts so that
when winter in one sense was at its worst it was at its pleasantest, with clear icy air and sparkling sunlight.

Those were the days before the elaborate ski craze and
funicular railroads. We tramped endlessly; in winter there
was informal skiing, and in summer, spring, and autumn no
end of mountain climbing. Somehow or other I did my own
share of tramping, more than ever before or since. On regular
class days the names of one's walking companions were posted
or *"gesteckt"* on the sign-board by the door, always of different
nationality; a Swiss, for instance, with a couple of Americans,
and a North German and a Bavarian with a Pole.

German was the universally prescribed language, for most
of the foreign bishops had sent their students there to learn
German, and each seminarian once during his four years had
to preach a German sermon in the dining hall to the tune
of rattling plates and clattering knives and forks. I knew only
one exception ever permitted, Count Bylicki, a whiskered
Pole, who absolutely could not enunciate any German.

On holidays you could choose your companions *ad lib,* and
the "American Exiles," the American group of some thirty of
us, found their own haunts, gravitating often to the ever-
hospitable inn at Schwatz, an hour's trip to the east. Innsbruck
itself made up for its bleak location by a wonderful wealth of
glorious excursions in every direction. A half-hour ride on the

train and an hour's walk brought you into perfect mountain valleys.

You could travel in those days from New York to Innsbruck, and from Innsbruck to any place in Britain or on the Continent, with no passport. All you needed was an item of identification. I carried merely my photograph as a matriculated university student, marked with the registrar's stamp. You changed foreign money without exchange regulations and the customs regulations were of the utmost simplicity. A few elderly women at the French border picked over your luggage a bit. Otherwise you were carefree.

In Italy you traveled comfortably for two or two and a half lire daily—about fifty cents—for board and lodging, and for a gulden—also about fifty cents—one could get along very nicely all over the Tyrol with three meals a day and a bit of wine thrown in.

Once the great hurdle of departure from home had been passed, and after the grim days of initiation and loneliness in the Alpine town and the shock of entering an entirely new life were over, I felt as if I were liberated and had emerged from a shadow into glorious sunlight and inspiring companionship.

CHAPTER SIX

Cor Unum et Anima Una

>» «<

Some months after my arrival at Innsbruck I received a letter in the familiar handwriting of my father written from his Tenth Street studio. It covered two or three pages and its contents might be summarized as follows:

My dear, beloved Son—Some time has now elapsed since you crossed the ocean, and my heart is ever anxious at the thought of all that might have befallen you. I follow you night and day with my thoughts and prayers. You are a long way from home and from the care and safeguards with which your parents have surrounded you. You are in a strange land among strange people, and for a young man of your age there are very many temptations to wickedness. It is so easy to forget virtue and to learn vice. How unfortunate it would be if you were to lose the benefits of a promising career. For this reason, therefore, I feel it my obligation to warn you against these dangers and to urge you when the voice of temptation besets you to seek the guidance of wise and prudent men and to listen to the counsels of wisdom. Hoping that your health is not impaired and that you can properly dispose your life, I am, your devoted parent, John LaFarge.

I was utterly mystified by this communication. It was as unlike my father's style as I could conceive; nevertheless, the handwriting seemed unmistakable, until on closer examination I became suspicious, though I could not yet solve the mystery. A year or two later I learned from Father that the letter was written by a Japanese studio helper, a somber individual who mixed Father's paints and did odd jobs on the frescoes. He used to wear a long coat, a black tuxedo, resembling in fact the traditional undertaker. This good youth felt that it was his duty to his master to be solicitous about the son, and he considered it a delicate compliment to Father to imitate his handwriting, even though unable to imitate his style. Father's regular Japanese servant, Awoki, explained to me that imitating handwriting was not considered such an invasion of privacy as it would be in this country. For the Japanese the sacred object was rather one's personal seal.

If any such dangers as the letter envisaged had previously existed, they were considerably lessened in my new surroundings. No one could be long at Innsbruck without catching the spirit of the house and of its director, Father Michael Hofmann, the Regens (Regent) or Rex, as he was familiarly called. Life, as I said, was plain enough. Our chapel contained no seats but only kneeling benches. If you were weary of kneeling you could stand.

As far as the course of study was concerned, you could walk out, hire a room in a nearby boarding-house, and quietly continue your class attendance as an extern student. Under present papal regulations, this would interfere with your standing as a seminarian but it was possible in those days. While you were in the house, however, you were expected to live up to its traditions and regulations, called *consuetudines*, "customs."

The Regent explained these in detail and related everything to one great central idea: our entire life whether as individuals or as a community should be modeled after the example of our great High Priest, Jesus Christ. We were to be men not only "after His Heart"—that is, according to all the prescriptions of a priestly ideal—but were, as far as humanly possible, to make His Heart our home and to share His attitude toward the whole world. The *anima una* was not only the spirit of the house or Convictus, but it was the spirit of world-unity in Christ to the labor for which we were to devote our lives.

The Innsbruck program drew dynamism from a positive compelling idea that was tremendously helped by the very surroundings in which we lived. Veneration of the Heart of

Jesus was the great devotion of the Tyrolese people, and *Herz-Jesu fest,* the second Sunday after Corpus Christi, was the Tyrol's national feast. Its stirring hymn to the Sacred Heart was the Tyrolese national anthem, and so greatly did it appeal to me that after my Ordination I brought the music of the hymn back here and had English words set to it. No person was better fitted to interpret this idea and spirit than Father Hofmann, himself a Tyrolese peasant who had learned as a child his Canisius, as the catechism was called, in a mountain village of the Tyrol.

The motto *"Cor Unum et Anima Una"* expressed the spirit of the house itself, the spirit of the early Christians, "who were of one heart and one mind." In Rome the many nationalities among the theological students observe their international spirit in the lecture room or on state occasions, but at Innsbruck we all lived together in harmony and friendly rivalry. Each of the nationalities received its own mail and its own papers. Each sang its own songs and contributed to the variety of the place; but still we were all one family, drawn from some forty different peoples and from at least ten different religious Orders who shared the common life, keeping a quota of their own religious observances and wearing their own religious habits. Our community life, however, was entirely distinct from that of the Jesuit students, though they attended the same lectures.

The Austro-Hungarian Empire accounted for some twelve of the different national groups. The most intense national feeling possibly was among the Czechs, whose antagonism to Hapsburg Vienna could have been so greatly alleviated by a little more tact and kindly interest on the part of old Franz Joseph I. Some more tact too might have been exerted by foreign visitors, such as my somewhat unrealistic uncle, Professor T. S. Perry. Uncle Tom was invited to lecture in Prague on some phase of English literature. He took the occasion to explain to the Czechs how concerned he was about differences arising between them and their Imperial Government.

These differences, he thought, could be solved if they would give up the Czech language, which the majority of people find difficult anyway, and would all speak German. To his disappointment his hearers did not seem enthusiastic.

Among the Germans I was surprised to find how strong was their consciousness of their particular land or section of Germany, how little feeling there was for Germany as a whole. This was, of course, before World War I. If you asked a German his nationality he would say, I am a Bavarian, a Württemberger, a Pfalzer, or a Saxon, as the case might be. But if he said, *"Ich bin ein Deutscher,"* you knew that he was a Prussian.

Among religious orders, the Conventual Franciscans (with the black habit) were closest to the American colony, as the American Province of the Order was generously represented at Innsbruck. The American colony itself did an educational job on the pious Father Regent. As he himself confessed in later years, he was quite suspicious of the Americans when he first took up this work. They seemed to him uncouth; he shared the general European idea that they were wild and unruly. His suspicions were confirmed when he found one of his American students studying St. Thomas while reposing his feet on his desk. But, as he later explained, his views soon changed. He found that when he entrusted anything to an American to be done, it was done. The Americans proved to be men of high spiritual ideals, firm character, and a spirit of simple, humble devotion that he later referred to as a model for the rest of the community. As the years went on his love for the Americans deepened. He joined in our annual Thanksgiving banquet at Schwatz, where we treated him for the first time to ice cream and strawberries. We explained that the title the American colony had adopted, "American Exiles," was not an expression of mourning but was merely a bit of quaint overseas humor.

Many years later I had the joy of welcoming Father Hofmann to New York on the first stage of a trip he made around the country. Bishop McLaughlin of Paterson and I treated him to a steamer ride up the Hudson River, and he was divided between his admiration for the superb scenery, which he said completely surpassed the Rhine, and his mystification that the colored people on the steamer actually spoke English.

After the First World War, the "American Exiles" and the American alumni put their hands to the plow in full earnest and raised the funds with which a new Canisianum was built, not at the old site but in a more modern part of the city. In 1951 I had the great satisfaction of visiting this handsome building for the first time.

It was a new experience for an ex-Harvard student to remain in such close personal touch with the professors, to be able to knock on their doors and confer with them day by day about one's work, for there was always access to their rooms. Tradition prevented both students and professors from asking and answering questions in class: it was considered to be against academic dignity. But other times we were free to approach them; and on their part they made every effort to aid us with our work both in class and out of it. Classes were conducted in Latin, with the exception of Church history, but the Latin was not such a formidable obstacle as an outsider would be apt to think. Among the professorial lights were the Jesuit Fathers Hugo Hurter; Jerome Noldin, author of three famous volumes on moral theology; Joseph Kern and Joseph Mueller for dogma; Leopold Fonck for New Testament exegesis; and Emil Michael in Church history.

I enjoyed the scope, the vigor and the clarity of the Innsbruck teaching, which was as good as one could expect under the rather rigid restrictions of a German state university, but there was one serious handicap. The theological faculty schedule allowed no place for a thorough grounding in scholastic philosophy, such as is traditional in Catholic seminaries. For the first year a makeshift was provided, solemnly called *propaedeutica*. Unfortunately it was taught in uninspiring fashion. This hit me hard precisely because I had learned no scholastic philosophy at Harvard and had thereby missed the key to the more speculative part of doctrinal teaching.

The spiritual training at the Canisianum did not favor practices, however edifying at the time, which the students would not continue in later years. From the very beginning we were taught to understand and carry out certain fundamental relationships with God our Lord that we would be able to preserve all through our lives as priests. Chief among these was the daily meditation. At Innsbruck you were supposed to make a half-hour meditation in the morning before Mass, alone in your room. Nobody watched or kept tab on you. If you neglected it, nobody was the wiser. But in point of fact the majority of the students adopted permanently the practice of meditation. The evening before, we assembled in the auditorium where "points of meditation," in the traditional fashion, were outlined to us for fifteen minutes. The daily practice, too, of the examination of conscience—a short period, again in private—was one of the fundamentals.

I lay stress on these because I have often heard priests and bishops who were educated there remark that they owed most of all to Innsbruck the practice of meditation. One meditated on the life of Christ, on the Gospel, on the fundamentals of the Faith, on the liturgy of the Church and other matters that would be of aid.

From the liturgical standpoint, the high spot of the year at the university was the solemn Matins service and Midnight Mass chanted by the seminarians at Christmas. The low point was the High Mass on Sunday, which we were obliged to attend and which was sung by the Government-paid university choir. Their chattering became so offensive that on one occasion an athletic American seminarian from the prairie country hurled his prayerbook at the prima donna's head. It had the desired effect.

Depressing in old Austria-Hungary were the remnants of the system of paternal religious interference, or Josephinism, exemplified by the Emperor Joseph II at the end of the eighteenth century. The town itself presented odd contrasts of great piety and of anti-religion. Members of Catholic student organizations, such as the Austrian and Swiss red caps, attended the university. On the other hand, the green-capped Pan-Germans, the predecessors of the Nazis, were blasphemously offensive. At night we often heard their loud-mouthed brawling in the streets.

Those were the days when the Catholic Center Party was in its glory and the famous triumph of Windthorst over Bismarck and his Kulturkampf was part of the great legend of German Catholicism. We did not foresee then the woes the Center Party would suffer in later years. The rise of German nationalism was troubling, even in those days, and the extreme unhealthiness of the Pan-German movement was plain, more plain in Austria probably than in Germany itself, for the Pan-Germans sought to carry on their propaganda especially in Catholic regions. In the little inns one found matchboxes with Pan-German inscriptions on them appealing to the friends of Germany, that is Prussian and Protestant Germany, to "stand fast against the enemy in a strange land," the enemy, of course, being Rome penetrating from the South:

> *Den Brüdern im bedrängten Land,*
> *Ein treues Herz, hilfreiche Hand.**

The supreme liturgical solemnity at Innsbruck was the magnificent annual Corpus Christi procession, but it was marred by the very fact that the Government was supposed to contribute to its splendor. Government officials were forced to attend, and the professors of the university were obliged to march, not always to their liking, in the procession.

The Mayor of the town was said to be a "Liberal," as was the Quaestor, the red-bearded, gaunt official from whom we obtained our certificates at the beginning of the course. He

---

* For brethren in a hard-pressed land,
A loyal heart, a generous hand.

was famed, as I said, for his short answers and his general dislike of seminarians. I happened to learn that he was interested in sea shells, so in the fall of 1904, after I had been home to the United States, I brought back a collection of sea shells from off Easton's Beach in Newport and presented them to him. From that day we became staunch friends.

The beadle or *bidellus* of the theological students was Count Clement von Galen from Muenster, who won great prominence during the Hitler regime when he preached Sunday after Sunday in his cathedral against the Fuehrer's policies. Von Galen was created a Cardinal by Pope Pius XII at the same consistory in which Cardinal Spellman and Cardinal Glennon of St. Louis received their red hats. He shared, however, the fate of Cardinal Glennon and died soon after his return to his native land. Even as a student he was a prominent figure. Like Saul, with his tall, powerful figure he stood head and shoulders above the rest of the crowd, and was respected for his straightforward and democratic personality.

I had become acquainted to some extent with the great German Catholic social movement which had been inaugurated around 1848 by Wilhelm von Ketteler, Bishop of Mainz. It was a curious coincidence, incidentally, that old Dominie Thayer, Presbyterian clergyman from Newport, whose funeral I attended during my first year at the Rogers High School, visited Europe in Ketteler's time and in his famous diary, published some years ago by the Newport Historical Society, expressed a desire and a hope that Protestantism and Popery, as he expressed it, should heal Europe's social disorders by appealing to the content of their respective teachings. I read much about the wonderful life-work of Von Ketteler and through reading at table and conversation with the professors and some students, learned the progress the social movement made in Switzerland and in France, culminating in the great encyclical, "On the Condition of the Workingman," or *Rerum Novarum,* of Leo XIII in 1891.

One of my most interesting companions at the seminary was Edward M. O'Rourke. He spoke no English and, on my first meeting with him, I spoke French. I asked him his nationality, and he made the surprising reply: *"Je suis irlandais."* I learned that he was born in Russia of parents whose Irish forebears had left Erin some three centuries before.

Later on, after his ordination, he became rector of the Catholic seminary in what was then St. Petersburg, and complained to me that the seminarians had only ninety workdays in the year, what with all the Russian Orthodox holidays, the Catholic holidays, and the holidays of the Imperial family. After the Revolution he became Bishop of Riga, still later was exiled and way-stationed in Poland, and finally landed in Rome, where he died in the convent of the Fathers of Mercy. We traveled considerably together and kept up correspondence, as far as war conditions would allow, until near his very death. From O'Rourke and from two other Poles—Korzonkiewicz, later a canon in Cracow, and Matzura—I learned a certain amount of Polish.

In the summer of 1902 my mother and sister Margaret joined me in the Tyrol and together we visited the South Tyrol and the Schönbergs, the Gröden Valley, and later on Bavaria.

At my Easter vacation the following year I met them in Rome and had the privilege of seeing Pope Leo XIII in a general audience in his very last months. I recall him as a frail, waxen figure, like a being already out of this world.

The Schönbergs insisted that I should call on Cardinal Rampolla, the Secretary of State. I had no reason for doing so and I disliked visiting distinguished people when I had nothing to propose. However, he received me most graciously. While I waited for the audience his secretary, Monsignor della Chiesa, stepped out and recited the Angelus. At its close he recited the following prayer to the Guardian Angel, which I had not known before and have since always recited three times each day:

Angele Dei, qui custos es mei,
Me tibi commissum pietate superna,
*Custodi, protege, rege, guberna.**

Della Chiesa later became a Cardinal, and ultimately Pope Benedict XV, so I can include him in the catalogue, five in all, of the Popes whom I have at least seen with my own eyes. I also had an interview with Spanish-born, English-bred Cardinal Merry del Val who was in favor of my continuing my studies at Innsbruck, not of changing to Rome.

Pope Leo XIII died on July 26 of the same year. Immediately after his death there appeared at the Innsbruck seminary Cardinal Puzyna, Archbishop of Cracow, who was on his way to the conclave in Rome to elect the new Pope. Visiting us on his return trip he told us, not without a certain exultation, how he had pronounced the veto against the name of Cardinal Rampolla who seemed to be gaining the majority in the election. This he did in the name of the Emperor Franz Joseph of Austria. It was the last time that such a veto was or ever could be exercised, since Pius X, Joseph Sarto of Venice, who may or may not have owed his election to that circumstance, abolished the privilege.

This insolent bit of political interference was just another instance of certain miserable results that can flow in our times from the union of Church and State. It is difficult to know which is more disastrous in the long run, the meddling of ecclesiastics in the affairs of the country beyond their actual competence, or the meddling of the State in Church affairs, which is very apt to be the result of the former. A vicious circle is set up with disastrous consequences for all.

Baron Schönberg later read to me passages from his diary concerning the election of Pius X. "I was much impressed by the dignified part which Cardinal Rampolla took in every-

---

* Angel of God, my guardian dear,
    To whom His love commends me here;
  Ever this day (night) be at my side,
    To light and guard, to rule and guide.

thing. He did not *propose* Cardinal Sarto (who was elected) but did urge the others to vote for him. The Archbishops of Prague and Vienna refused to have anything to do with [the Austrian veto]." Cardinal Rampolla said to the Baron, as the latter visited him after the election, *"Vous voyez que Dieu n'a pas besoin des hommes pour l'Eglise"* (You see that God does need men for the Church).

Pius X, the new Pope, was a lovable person, much more fatherly than Leo XIII; like a very good, holy bishop, the Baron said. He told me that the Pope was so generous that, as Cardinal Sarto of Venice, he had pawned all his possessions. When the time came for him to appear on the balcony of St. Peter's, at the proclamation, he could muster nothing but a cheap tin cross instead of the silver bishop's cross, which he had pawned. Some were troubled about this circumstance, but he was not at all disturbed. "No one will notice," he said. "It looks quite like the real thing."

CHAPTER SEVEN

"Cand. S.J." and Ordination

━━»» ««━━

Innsbruck, unlike many other clerical seminaries, made no special provision for its students' vacations. It ran no summer villa or even a summer school. The idea of Father Hofmann and of the Canisianum in general was that vacation gave foreign students a wonderful chance to see Europe, and allowed those who came from nearby places to return to their homelands and give account to their own bishops. Classes closed late, somewhere around the 31st of July, and began in the first days of October. The town in summer was intolerably hot, with a peculiar kind of dry, burning heat, and few cared to remain there.

Longing for a sight of western Europe, I joined my mother and sister in Paris in the summer of 1903, and together we toured the northern cathedrals and the valley of the Loire. My mother was an ideal traveling companion, thoroughly posted on geography through her perusal of Baedeker and Augustus J. C. Hare, as well as the hints that my father always provided for her. Her wiry person was not easily wearied, and her retentive memory made the recollection of her trips months later almost as interesting as the traveling itself.

Brittany was a "must" on my trip. As a youthful linguist I was curious about the Breton language, akin to the Gaelic, and was interested in discovering that our French cousins, the Barre de Nanteuils, lived near Morlaix in the picturesque province of Finistère.

Our visit to Morlaix revealed to me the warmth and cohesiveness of French family life. Auguste de la Barre de Nanteuil was my father's first cousin. His father, Pierre de la Barre de Nanteuil, had explored the United States in his youth and had married Adèle Binsse de Saint-Victor, sister of my grandmother LaFarge. Great-uncle Pierre and great-aunt Adèle had stayed with my grandfather at his home in LaFargeville, New York, near Watertown, and Auguste was born there, returning in due time with his father to France. He married Caroline LeFlô, daughter of General LeFlô of Napoleonic fame. They made their home in Château Nec'hoat, just outside of Morlaix. They insisted that they were my uncle and aunt, *"à la mode de Bretagne,"* and we always referred to them as Uncle Auguste and Aunt Caroline.

Father wrote in December 1891 to Henry Adams—planning a European trip—suggesting that he should visit our cousin Auguste. He would discover, said Father:

A French family where English is spoken, a Catholic legitimist, and so forth. Both he and his wife speak English. Naturally I prefer the wife. Her father, General LeFlô, was exiled in the early part of the Empire and was afterwards Embassador [*sic*] to Russia, where she was with him, as he was a widower. . . . De Nanteuil himself is a very nice fellow, has never done anything but take a "legitimist" interest in matters; of course he has written. He is less *arriéré* than many about him: he is to me very French. . . .You might meet some of the neighbours—*bien pensant*—and shock the little abbé who has charge of the children, as I did.

I never heard that Adams visited the Nanteuils, though I think that, if he had, some of his reserve might have melted under their general simplicity. If Father had shocked anybody during his stay there, all traces had vanished. His visits were remembered as part of the family tradition. The old Château Nec'hoat parlor and library were full of his drawings and paintings, as well as portraits of various members of the family both in France and in the United States.

Uncle Auguste was a good Royalist who wrote various pamphlets on political questions and believed that the clergy

should be generously endowed by the State, but he was a
moderate by nature, as well as a faithful Ultramontane: a
Catholic first, and with all his patriotic fervor a Frenchman
afterward. Hallowed was the memory of his brother Alfred
who had lost his life fighting as a Papal Zouave for the Pope in
1867 in the tragic battle of Castelfidardo in the Papal States.
I don't recollect that Uncle Auguste was overburdened with
theories on society, but as a former pupil of the French sociolo-
gist de Bonald, and admirer of Frédéric le Play, he was nonetheless concerned with the social problems of the time. He
was a friend of Albert de Mun and I learned from him of the
personality of some of the conservative pioneers in the French
social movement, such as de Mun, Léon Harmel, and de la
Tour du Pin.

In France at that time the fanatically anti-clerical Government made it difficult for any Catholic to refrain from bitterness. At Morlaix I witnessed the cruelty and undemocratic
action of Emile Combes, recently elected Prime Minister, in
demanding the expulsion of the religious congregations. The
Sisters of the Holy Ghost, whose mother house was in Brittany
and who also had a house in Morlaix, were given notice of
their dissolution. These humble workers for the sick poor
had the choice of either returning to the world or seeking
exile. Like countless other Religious, they preferred exile, and
sought asylum in England, which gave them a home denied
them by supposedly Catholic France. The day of their departure they came to lunch at Nec'hoat. We offered them what
cheer we could and the entire household accompanied them
to the railroad station where Uncle Auguste with tears in his
eyes waved to them to the very end.

The great struggle for the Congregations was brought home
to us somewhat more closely because Deputy Henri de Gail-
hard-Bancel was a relative of our family on the side of my
great-grandmother Bancel. For fourteen years, 1901-1914, Gail-
hard-Bancel led a heroic battle in the Chamber of Deputies

on the school and religious order front. He helped fight the battle of the expelled Carthusians, and gave courage to the four Jesuit Provincials of France when they took the decisive step that meant their expulsion.

At Morlaix the members of the family closest to my own age were Yvonne, daughter of Aunt Caroline and Uncle Auguste, who later married Baron Joseph du Halgouët, formerly an official of the French Embassy in London, and Alfred her brother, who died gallantly at Dixmude in World War I. Yvonne spoke English, was active and adventurous and an antidote to any provincial stuffiness which might oppress Nec'hoat. In fact the neighbors were scandalized because Mademoiselle la Vicomtesse rode horseback around the country unaccompanied by a groom. A note of pathos crept into my visit when I was driven one afternoon to visit a household of five lonely, well-born spinsters in the neighborhood. Aunt Caroline informed me that they were growing a bit *triste* because time was passing and so far few young men had come their way. Numerically they resembled the five Hooper girls whom I had known in Boston, but in no other manner. Alas, their countenances fell at the sight of my soutane and Roman collar. The best I could offer was a few kind words of greeting.

The desire to explore the Breton countryside led us to the modest inland summer resort of Huelgoat, in those days unknown to foreign tourists. I struck up an acquaintance with the curé and picked up a few phrases of the Breton language. In good French family style all of us, old and young, went for a long promenade in the woods one lovely afternoon. All was going serenely until I stepped plump into a bees' nest. With bees swarming inside my clothes, I let out a yell, tore off my cassock in the face of the horrified relatives, and raced for the local apothecary. I explained to his bewildered ears that I had been attacked by *abeilles*—that is, bees—and not by *abbé's* as he first thought I said. He came to my rescue with a lotion that really worked, though for a day or two I felt sickish as a result of the stings.

Leaving France we went by steamer from St. Malo to South-hampton, and thence by train to Rye in Sussex, where we spent a couple of weeks with Henry James. We lodged at the Mermaid Inn, where my mother said her room reminded her "somewhat of Noah's Ark." The inn was one of those pictures-que affairs, but unfortunately, the food was not quite equal to the artistic surroundings. This deficiency was helped by various meals at Lamb House, Henry James's stately, square brick residence in the vicinity, where much more considera-tion was paid to foreign tastes and appetites.

Mr. James had meticulously prepared for our coming and had written in his unmistakable syntax to my sister concerning the Mermaid: "Neither the establishment, nor the place, nor the privilege is candidly 'good enough.' With relatives and companions *passe encore*—though, as I originally wrote you, even then expectation should be pitched low."

The four of us took long walks about the countryside, an intensely interesting experience for my mother, since it was her first visit to England. She felt, she said, as if she had stepped into one of the novels of Jane Austen or Anthony Trollope, most of which she almost knew by heart.

In his *Notes of a Son and Brother,* Henry James recalled the long walks which he took in Newport in the early 1860s. There were "three or four of us," he wrote, "who walked in those days, or I should say, if pushed, the single pair in par-ticular of whom I was one and the other Thomas Sargeant [*sic*] Perry, superexcellent," for T.S.P. and H.J. were insep-arable. James had much to say of a third member of the "three or four," my father, John LaFarge, "intensely among us, but somehow not withal of us," who was obstinate in maintaining his "serenity." Of the fourth in the party, T. S. Perry's sister, Margy (Margaret Mason Perry, my mother), there is no word, though her personality played no small part in the life of the youthful James. But it was in her company that after some forty years these walks were now resumed, not along Newport's shores and cliffs, but over the meadows of Sussex.

Our walks were followed by a decorous meal at Lamb House. Mr. James twitted me for having picked up some Germanic expressions as a result of my life in Austria, such as saying *please* when I meant *yes*. At Lamb House we could study him at work in his Georgian garden pavilion, the Temple of the Muses, as he called it, where he paced up and down a strip of carpet and dictated his discursive novels, made more discursive by dictation.

I did not undertake to enter much into the conversation of my mother and Henry James about the past, since it was more or less private and belonged to a period that pertained little to my present career. Henry James, in truth, was the sole living friend who, knowing my father, could sympathetically comprehend the many factors that had helped to create the contrast between the LaFarge of the Bayou Tèche and the LaFarge of the Tenth Street studio building and the Century Club.

Years after our visit to Rye my mother mentioned casually, in matter-of-fact manner, that she was the only woman with whom Henry James was ever deeply in love. In view of his concern for Minny Temple, who seems reflected in certain heroines of his novels, there might appear to be no basis for such a remark. Nevertheless, Mother's habitual caution and reserve in speaking of herself gave it a certain weight. Current with us children was the notion that the *Portrait of a Lady* was in some fashion inspired by my mother; but if so, it was no close likeness, and she herself thought otherwise. She did believe, however, that her ghost flitted through some of the other stories.

However much Henry James may have puzzled the rest of the world, for us he was a warm-hearted, thoroughly human and fatherly companion. He was gravely interested in my career, and I imagined that he was conscious of a certain meaning in it for himself. As in the case of my father, the personality of the man himself seemed simpler than the artist's or scholar's work with its necessary shadings and nuances. James certainly was deeply conscious of his indebtedness to Father, a relation that is strongly emphasized by the latest and most competent biographer of Henry James, Leon Edel, who calls my father "the original inspirer, the first to prod Henry to a constructive writing effort." Speaking of Father's early portrait of Henry James, which suggested a stained-glass window and which the subject himself considered the exhibition of "a rare color sense," Mr. Edel remarks:

LaFarge was indeed to become a master of this medium. . . . His interest in stained glass and cathedrals was to set his friend Henry Adams upon the exploration of Mont St. Michel and Chartres. Thus John LaFarge, who lived so large and full a creative life himself, fed the lives of two other creative personalities— the young Henry James and, in later life, Henry Adams. . . . For Henry James he opened "more windows than he closed." The windows he closed were those of the practice of art. He let Henry daub but encouraged him and pushed him to write. He taught him that the "arts were after all essentially one." He gave Henry the sense of a young man who feels secure, who knows what he wants to do "a settled sovereign self." And as Henry talked with him, he felt surer of himself, he too could become sovereign.*

After our departure his solicitude followed us to London where he dined with us in our rooms in Brompton Square. He wrote to me on September 28, 1903, as follows:

My dear John:
I rejoiced to hear from you, all the more that your news seems to be of the best. I am particularly glad that your Mother's London quarters soothe and satisfy her from the first. You have all clearly the gift of falling on your feet. If the world were more felicitously arranged, I should now be in London too, to give you the benefit of my long experience of it—an idea that makes me wistful as I think of the hundred places to which I might personally conduct you—the innumerable opportunities for "talking about" that the great city gives. Your Mother and Margaret seem

* *Henry James: the Untried Years* (Lippincott, 1953), pp. 163-164.

slightly pathetic to me, left to struggle alone with the mighty
monster—yet I reflect that their solitude is probably already tem-
pered by your friendly contacts and encounters, and that a few of
these things, in London, have a trick of becoming many before one
knows it.

Little limited Rye has, since you left, kept up its simple habits
of breaking out into grassy walks and making small uplifted pictures and flushing with pink sunsets—all it knows how to do. My
motor ride, with my young cousin, over to Burwash and the
[Rudyard] Kiplings, proved a thing of great beauty every way, and
I quite groaned with regret all the while that you were not there
to see and to admire. Kipling is settled in an extraordinarily beautiful old house, of Charles I's time, in a wonderful Happy Valley
which he himself mainly owns, and the impression is well worth
a long pilgrimage. I was quite proud of the beauty of the land for
our 20-mile drive, as I was able to show it to my companion in
the splendour of last Friday morning.

For the rest, our history has been—books and Bigelows. Eleven
cases of the former have at last descended on me from town, after
long relegation there, and the latter have very gallantly been helping me these two days to sift and dust and arrange them—no light
task, which has left us all with rather aching backs and languid
legs. But it's been amusing and interesting to every one but Max,
who has thought us great idiots and been ashamed of us for pursuits so alien to his own tastes and so incompatible with a proper
amount of attention to himself. He lies near me now as I write,
wriggling and squealing quietly in his dreams and reminding me
that as it is more than 1:00 A.M., I ought to be doing likewise. So
I bid you all goodnight, or good morning, while I listen in intense
stillness of the Rye small hours to the scratching of my pen, the
ticking of my old clock and (I am sorry to say) to the heavy patter
of the rain in the garden.

Give my very best to your companions, and believe in the great
pleasure our reunion here has brought after so long years to yours,
my dear John,

Affectionately,
HENRY JAMES

Concerning Edith Wharton he wrote to my sister in January 1904 that he found her "with a slightly cold but quite individual grace." And again, though he greatly liked her, he
found her "a little dry," and added: "But she is too pampered

and provided and facilitated for one to be able really to judge
of the woman herself, or for *her* even, I think, to be able to
get really *at* things."

Henry James carried out his idea of visiting the United
States and my brother Oliver arranged for him to make a trip
to the West Coast, which he found pretty confusing. He seemed
to be unable to take it all in. The last we heard of him was
after the outbreak of the First World War. He wrote to my
mother on August 21, 1914 (he had sent to her a copy of his
book *Notes of a Son and Brother*):

That I have made the unspeakable Past live again a little for
you is delightful to me, and I am touched by the terms in which
you tell me so—indeed by the very fact of hearing from you at all.
There are passages and pages in the book which Tom and you
are the sole persons living who will have understood, and to be
linked with you still in that way, after all the years—well, is something that I feel as a blessing. . . .

I wrote you under the black cloud of portentous events on this
side of the world, horrible, unspeakable, iniquitous things—I mean
horrors of war criminally, infamously precipitated. What point of
danger the situation may have reached this soft mid-summer Sunday night we shan't know till the morning; but the air is full of
the wars, and rumors, and I brace myself with the fear of the
newspaper. These are monstrous miseries for *us* of our generation
and age, to live on into; but we wouldn't not have lived—and yet
this is what we get by it. I try to think it will be *interesting*—but
have only got so far as to feel it's sickening. However, I wanted to
write you only tender and happy things—and send my faithful old
love to Margaret. And I am yours and hers all constantly and un-
forgettingly.

The summer of 1904 I decided to spend my vacation at home,
feeling that I could make better plans for the future if I knew
something of how things looked after three years' absence.
Accordingly, after the Innsbruck examinations were finished
in July, I set sail on the S.S. *Finland* of the Red Star Line.

Arriving in New York, I regretted having returned and
began to think of all that I could have seen or done if I had

stayed in Europe. However, it proved profitable in another manner. I made my way to Newport where my father was at home by himself. My mother and sisters were out on the West Coast and, for the first time in my life, I found myself alone with him, and he in a relaxed and genial mood.

I recall now his mildly malicious joy in narrating a dream about Heaven. Arriving, finally, at eternal beatitude, he set about to explore the new surroundings. On the very outer edge of the parapets of Heaven he discovered the distinguished banker, Jay Gould, from whom, to my knowledge, he had never received a commission for any work. In his polite manner, Father congratulated Mr. Gould on being saved, like himself. "That's all very well, Mr. LaFarge," mournfully replied Gould, "but there is not much to crow about. I only squeezed in here because I once gave a donation to a church. But now that I am rescued, all St. Peter will let me do is to sit here for eternity with my feet dangling and looking off into space."

Concerning me, Father wrote as follows to Henry Adams: "John returned from Europe in due ecclesiastical form. I have him here now in Newport, where he has turned out to be quite charming and human, and will probably be improved by the acquaintance of the laity. He is really very charming, though I say so, and I shall miss him again when he goes." This does not sound like a very enthusiastic remark from a father about his son, but in his case it meant much; though it was nearly fifty years later in looking over his old correspondence that I discovered he had thus unburdened himself in my regard. He was more ironical as to my proficiency in Greek, which he remarked had grown as rusty in the short time since I had left college as was his after most of a lifetime.

Father worked busily, as was his custom, during the day, dictating, painting, and generally ordering everybody around. But delightful were the long August evenings, when he would balance his cigar in the fingers of his left hand and gesticulate mildly with his right and tell of his experiences in the South Seas.

In all his talk about the Islands and their people he sounded always the note of profound respect for them as human beings and children of our Common Father. To my knowledge, Father was the first white man outside of the missionaries to visit those islands and write about and paint them sympathetically. The Islanders were not natives for him; they were personalities for whom he felt a kinship, an affection and a genuine love. When he was adopted into the royal family of Tahiti, he did not consider it as just some kind of quaint ceremony, but felt it as a profound honor. He had a particular regard for the famous Christian Chief Mata'afa and loved to tell the story of how Mata'afa was warned not to cross the beach because the German guns would be firing on him; but the old man expected to attend Benediction at the Catholic chapel at a certain time, and since he was going to honor the Lord of the Universe, he refused to be intimidated by any shots aimed at him.

Our conversations that summer ranged over many subjects. What I had picked up at Innsbruck of the scholastic theory of knowledge seemed to fit in closely with Father's concept of the artistic perception of truth—that the mind correctly perceived truth, but perceived it according to the mind's own mode and intelligible activity. Indeed, as Algernon Cecil observes: "The Schoolmen were artists in thought. . . . They saw a primrose as it was in deed and in truth; and the eye of their mind pierced to the significance of pure form."* With all his sensitiveness to every phase of the subjective, Father staunchly defended objectivity of truth both in the moral and in the physically perceptible order. And he lucidly distinguished between the accuracy with which all artists, from the cave men to Rembrandt and Velasquez, have always *felt* the visible world, and the inaccuracy with which they have represented it.

* *A House in Bryanston Square* (Harcourt, Brace, 1953), p. 169.

Father's dislike of humbug made him annoyed with the type of person who is easily scandalized because someone was having difficulty with the Church authorities, or because of the supposed worldliness of prelates. The Church, he insisted, employs, according to the Holy Spirit's own wisdom, men who are knowledgeable in a worldly fashion and can deal with the world on its own terms. She does not expect her spiritual life always to be much enriched by her more conspicuous servants, of high or low degree. Often, their chief role is as ambassadors to the world, and they are chosen for their kinship to it. The spiritual life of the Church, as he expressed it, is carried on "by anchorites in cells and lonely missionaries on far islands in the sea and by humble, devout people everywhere." (For my own part I have observed that some of the most genuinely unworldly souls are prominent persons charged with much responsibility. They carry a hidden load in great patience under continued criticism.)

There was quite a rumpus at the time about the Nun of Kenmare, an Irish lady who had left the Church because she felt she was being persecuted by the bishops. Father remarked in her regard: "The lady had the support of the Pope. What more must she have? All she had to do was to go on with her work and be persecuted. The bishops in Ireland are in a very difficult position. They must mediate between the Church and the heretical great people." He had little sympathy for the modernists, but remarked rather maliciously that possibly in Rome they were somewhat kinder to Lord Acton than they would be to Dr. Döllinger since Acton was a distinguished English nobleman and Döllinger was a crusty German.

I visited a number of the clergy during my stay at home and spent a while with Father Simmons, at the Church of the Blessed Sacrament in Providence, Rhode Island, of which my brother Grant was the architect. My visits to the rectories left in me a strange and uneasy sense that they did not fit into my concept of my own future priestly life. I felt that as a priest I might better live under a rule bound more strictly to poverty and to obedience than was the case with the diocesan priests. It was only a vague feeling of disquiet, but it laid the foundation for thoughts that were to mature some months later.

In the early autumn of 1904, it was not easy to quit the fireside in Newport, with its conversations and comfort and peace, and start across the ocean to the distant crags and glaciers of the Alps. The return journey, however, proved unexpectedly agreeable. I took a slow steamer, two weeks from New York to Genoa, with only seventeen passengers on board and complete calm the entire distance. One of the passengers was Eugene Kelly, brother of Tom Kelly, who had married my cousin Emérance de Sallier du Pin in Watertown, New York. We stopped at Gibraltar on the way over where I merely glimpsed Spain in the distance, and thence to Genoa.

From Genoa I made my way to the north and arrived late at night in Brixen absolutely penniless. Somehow I had miscalculated my resources and I threw myself on the mercy of Herr Hans Heiss, the proprietor of the Hotel Zum Elephanten. Mr. Heiss received me pleasantly enough as I arrived at midnight, and told me that all grades of rooms were occupied, save the sacrosanct archducal suite. Opening the locked door and the windows and pulling back the covers on the sumptuous four-poster bed, he told me to forget all my troubles financial and physical and get a good night's rest. Certainly I never felt more like an Emperor than after that endless journey. Mr. Heiss's account was settled later.

I continued to ponder the impressions of my home visit until the annual retreat in January 1905. Then the solution to my problem appeared before me with such startling plainness that I was quite taken aback.

In the course of the eight-day retreat, a meditation is frequently assigned for the fourth day in which the retreatant considers the visit of the Christ Child to the Temple. St. Ignatius lays before him two courses of life, that of the commandments, as he calls it, corresponding to the Saviour's obedient domestic

life at Nazareth, and that of the counsels in which the retreatant considers the possibility that he, like the adult Jesus, may
be called to leave even his own father and mother and conse-
crate himself entirely to the service of God.

I returned to my room in the old Pfeffersberg house, knelt
down and made the meditation, as I had made all the previous
ones, and had made that particular meditation several times
before. But now it seemed plain to me that there was only
one course, and that was to become a Religious.

It was not that I lacked appreciation for the sanctity of the
diocesan priesthood and all its abundant opportunities for
good. I simply saw with extraordinary distinctness that my
personal concept of a priest's life was of one bound by poverty
and obedience, in addition to the priestly chastity, which is
common to all the priests of the Latin Rite. The idea of being
a priest and of not sharing the poverty of the great High Priest
seemed to me intolerable. I could not reconcile myself to the
idea of owning property, having anything of my own when
He Himself was without a place to lay His head. It is true
the diocesan priest is bound by obedience to his bishop, but
I felt that I had need of more: of penetrating the great mysteries of the obedience of Jesus Christ, of assimilating myself
in some way to that inner holocaust, that sacrifice of perpetual
adoration and love by which He fulfilled the will of His Father on earth.

These thoughts followed me for a couple of days during the
retreat, and then on the sixth, the day of Election as it is
called, I placed a sheet of paper on the standing desk in my
room, divided it by a line in the middle, and wrote on one
side *"pro"* and on the other *"con."* For *"pro"* I concocted
eight reasons similar to those I have mentioned; for *"con"* I
only discovered one. (I do not remember now what it was.)
Then I walked up and down the carpetless floors of that room
for an hour trying to explore what I was perfectly positive
must somehow be present, some more reasons to put on the
"con" side; but the *"con"* never came.

I talked the matter over with the Retreat Master, Father Fonck, and he said quite simply: "You have a vocation to the Jesuits." I told this story many years afterward to a couple of Dominican friends who raised their arms simultaneously to Heaven and in mock horror exclaimed: "It was just there that you went wrong. You were lost to the Dominicans, and what the Dominicans would have made of you." Well, I guess I was. At any rate, I had no further doubts, and for the rest of that year it was only a question in my mind of what further steps I would take.

When Easter came around I again availed myself of the opportunity to visit Rome and set off in company with Tom McLaughlin, who was then ordained, for Rome via Venice and Assisi, one of the most fateful journeys of my life. (Many years after that event my nephew, Tom LaFarge, traveled the valleys and hillsides of central Italy in a donkey cart laden with maps and sketchbooks, and caught the spirit of the Umbrian landscapes and the blossoming fruit trees of the countryside, which he expressed in his radiant chapel of St. Francis of Assisi in St. Matthew's Cathedral in Washington, D. C.)

McLaughlin and myself, cassock-clad, explored the Assisi hillside on a glorious April morning. An old peasant accompanied us part of the way trying to drive a reluctant sheep before him. The old man jabbed a stick right and left and expressed no small annoyance to the two young *preti* at his failure to keep the sheep on the path. It was then that I realized how theology itself might occasionally offer some quite unexpected helps.

A couple of months previous, in the treatise on "Grace" at Innsbruck, Father Kern had read to us the words of St. Augustine that the Church recalls on Wednesday in Pentecost Week. The mind, says Augustine, is drawn by love. The soul, too, has its pleasures as has the body. Men are drawn to Christ; they are forced to follow Him. But they are moved toward Him by delight: "delight in the truth; delight in blessedness; delight in justice; delight in eternal life." "Show me a lover," says Augustine, "and he knows what I am talking about." Thus, he says, the Father draws men to His Son, to faith in Him, the Son of the Living God. "Show a green bough to a sheep, and you draw it after you. If you show goodies to a child, you will draw him." And so, says Augustine, if all men are drawn by their earthly pleasures, why should men not be drawn by that which is the supreme delight of the soul, the beauty, the goodness, the truth of Christ, "whom the Father hath revealed?"

"Show a bough to a sheep." I broke off a leafy apple bough and told the old man to try holding it before the sheep's nose, instead of prodding him from the rear. "San Agostino!" said McLaughlin. The old man grinned at the funny foreigners, but waved the bough in front of the sheep. It followed him far down the hillside and both vanished into the leafy distance.

"For what," says St. Augustine, "does the soul crave more than for the truth?" *"Quid enim fortius desiderat anima, quam veritatem?"* That was what I wanted and I had set out for Rome to find the ultimate truth in my own life. I had decided what God was drawing me toward, and was satisfied in my own mind that Rome was to confirm it.

My most wonderful experience on that Easter trip was receiving Holy Communion from the hands of Pope Pius X. The Innsbruck seminarians enjoyed the rare privilege of attending the Pope's private Mass on Holy Thursday morning. No others, I was told, except the members of his own immediate Vatican household, were privileged to attend the Mass. After Mass, we knelt in a semi-circle in the antechamber to the chapel. The Holy Father blessed each one of us in silence. When he came to me—I was about in the middle of the semi-circle—he stopped and gazed straight at me with his gray-blue eyes, it seemed to me for ages, before giving his blessing and passing on. During those seconds I could look directly into his face, which was fresh and fair, rapidly passing from pallor to a ruddy glow. Why he looked at me so steadily I do not know, but I had a feeling that his grave glance penetrated into my very soul.

For our breakfast we were treated by the Monsignori to a quaint black-fast repast of mixed chocolate and coffee, macaroons and sherbet in gilded cups. This was the same year in which Pius X issued his famous decree on frequent Communion, opening the gates of the Holy Sacrament liberally to all the Faithful, restoring thereby the practice of the early Church.

In Rome McLaughlin and I had the good fortune to lodge with a hospitable Italian family named Rossi De Gasperis, a form slightly different from that of the former Prime Minister of Italy. Our stay with them revealed to me a real Italian home, just as I had already learned to know a French household, and in later years would savor the charm of a Spanish home when visiting my old friends, the Sorzanos, in Havana.

I lost little time in making contact with the Jesuits. At that time the Jesuit General and his staff resided in the German college, whose students were familiar to all tourists in Rome by their brilliant red cassocks. I was directed to apply at the office of the English Assistancy, for the separate American Assistancy or national grouping of American Jesuit Provinces had not yet then been set up. The Jesuit Assistant helps in communication and transaction of business between the General and the various provinces in a certain country or district or region. The United States then was part of the English Assistancy.

I paused a long time at the door, on which was the sign *Assistentia Angliae*. I even held my hand up in the air and reflected that all I needed to perform was to bring it down on the door and my fate would be sealed forever.

Finally I knocked and the door was opened by Father Chandlery of the Assistancy, a homely, gracious soul known particularly for his guidebook for English-speaking visitors in Rome. He arranged that my companions and I should have an audience with the Father General, Father Martín, a Spaniard; and we were presented to Father Martín in due course, who proved friendly and sociable. Father Chandlery had informed Father Martín of my wish to be received as a candidate for the Jesuits, also that I was close to the date of my ordination to the priesthood. When I met Father Martín in private audience I assured him that it would be entirely a matter of his preference whether I should be ordained a priest before entering the Society or afterward. If it was His Paternity's decision that I should not be ordained before entering and should make the usual years of preparation in the Society before finally advancing to ordination, it was wholly agreeable to me.

Nevertheless I did hope that I could have the privilege of being ordained first, since my family was coming over, quite a bit of preparation had been made for my first Mass in July of that year, and, moreover, I was concerned about my father. Father had been so much won over to my priestly vocation and showed himself so sympathetic on my recent visit and so interested in the prospect of my ordination, that I felt if it were postponed he would become discouraged and possibly alienated. Father Martín took the whole idea sympathetically and gave me the very welcome answer that, as far as he was concerned, he left it entirely with the Father Rector of the Jesuit college in Innsbruck.

Accordingly, on my return to Innsbruck I presented the case to Father Rector, the famous and rather redoubtable John Nepomuk Mayr. Father Mayr decided for my ordination provided I could get the requisite permission from my Bishop. Most of the seminarians never came in contact with Father Mayr, as all our dealings were with our own director, the Regent, Father Hofmann. He was close to his eighties, with much of the bearing of an old nobleman, though it was carefully explained to me in good Austrian style that he was not a nobleman but was one of the *very* high bourgeoisie of Vienna. Father Mayr had me put through the usual questions

asked of candidates for the Society of Jesus, and I was duly
registered as a prospective Jesuit—*Cand. S.J.*

The only one of my Innsbruck companions who had predicted my future vocation was a fussy little Hungarian nobleman who sat next to me during my first year in the philosophy
classroom. He once shrugged his shoulders in irritated fashion
when I raised some question at the close of class and said, "You
will be a Jesuit. I always know them." Up to that time no
one had made that prediction except the Rev. E. Winchester
Donald in Boston, and nobody made it again until I finally
reached the decision myself.

I then had to take up matters with my own Ordinary, Bishop
Matthew Harkins of Providence. A candidate for the priesthood in the Catholic Church must produce in advance some
guarantee of support after ordination, in order that he may
not be a burden on the Church's charity. Such an assurance,
or title as it is called, may be provided by a Church benefice,
if he has a claim to it, or by the fact that he engages himself
explicitly to the future service of his bishop. If he is a member
of a religious community, the community, of course, guarantees to care for him on the "title of poverty." At that time,
however, the pledge, or mission oath as it was called, to the
service of an American bishop contained also a pledge not to
join a religious order. This pledge I could not utter in conscience. The only course left was for the bishop to permit me
to be ordained on the so-called title of patrimony, which
meant that you would live on your own fortune, or at least
your family could easily provide for you. Though ordinations
under the title of patrimony have been frequent enough in
later years, I could find only two cases before my time where
they had been permitted to an American priest. Writing to
the bishop I explained to him respectfully that I expected
anyhow, whether I was ordained or not ordained, to enter
the Society of Jesus in the near future.

I anxiously awaited the reply and even began the three days' retreat for the subdeacon's orders without having heard from him. On the third day of the retreat the longed-for cable arrived: "Title of patrimony is conceded." I had received minor orders in the December previous, and now I could look forward to my ordination to the priesthood on July 26, 1905, in the University church at Innsbruck along with others of my classmates.

The magnificent ceremony, always the most moving ceremony in the Catholic Church outside of the consecration of a bishop himself, was performed by the Most Reverend Joseph Altenwaisl, Prince-Bishop of Brixen, whose diocese at that time included North Tyrol and Innsbruck. The candidate for ordination dons a set of priestly vestments at one period during the ceremony and an interesting touch of color was provided for some of us by brilliant blue vestments that dated from the eighteenth century.

At my first Mass my mother, my sister Margaret, my cousin Mr. Henry Bancel Binsse, the Baron and Baroness Schönberg, and several others were present. I consecrated the Body and Blood of the Good Lord and held Him in my trembling hands for the first time in the lovely little Princes' chapel, *die Fürstenkapelle,* in the tower of the University church. Father Rector Mayr, of his own accord, offered to be my assistant at the Mass. He was so old and feeble that I was in acute fear every moment lest he tumble over, and two or three times had to stretch my arm out to support him. However, all went happily and I was infinitely glad that, after so many vicissitudes, the great goal had at last been reached.

My brother Bancel was unable to attend my first Mass. In a long and deeply affectionate letter from Villiers-sur-Morin, dated August 9, 1905, he expressed his regrets as well as his congratulations:

. . . You are my brother so that the great step which you have taken means much to me, inasmuch as it sets an example and awakens in me a desire to perfect my own efforts in giving to my fellows the best I am. . . .

Your life so far has been marked with great success while mine has been about a failure, but fortunately I am not discouraged and one reason is that I have you as an example. It is a great comfort to me to know that I have you to turn to for advice and help at times. . . .

You are young and have reached your foothold sooner than you expected and now with the confidence you must have gained with the determined struggle you have made you can more clearly see your road before you. . . .

You have all my love and sympathy; I have nothing else to give you except my friendship which, of course, you have always had. . . .

It was hard for me to decide not to go to your first Mass and I can't get over feeling my regret and absolute chagrin at not being there, but I had so much to consider that I think in fact I know for my work at least it has been much better that I stayed here and threw myself into it rather than have another serious interruption.

Tho' I got a tremendous lot from Italy, it upset me entirely and only now I am beginning to get into the frame of mind so that I can apply myself once more to my painting. . . .

(Bancel, incidentally, did not mention in this letter what I believe was the deciding reason for his remaining at Villiers-sur-Morin: the poor condition of his wife's health, which caused some anxiety to him and to her sisters.)

I was under no obligation to apply for the Society immediately and could have spent two more years working for a doctorate in theology, a *rigorosum,* as it was called, as did quite a number of my classmates. Tom McLaughlin was halfway on the road to his doctorate. I believed, however, that when God calls you it is safer to walk fast, and so I applied for entrance into the New York-Maryland Province of the Society of Jesus at Poughkeepsie, New York, in autumn of the same year.

During the four months that elapsed between my ordination in July and my entrance on November 12, the eve of the Feast of St. Stanislaus, I was, so to speak, an ecclesiastical free-lance, with no other obligation than to say my daily Office and observe the proper decorum of a priest. This decorum was aided by the fact that at that time I was unusually thin. It blessed me with a very ascetic appearance and secured for me that respect which seems to be the privilege of thin ecclesiastics.

I celebrated my first Solemn Mass at the village of Steinach, on the Brenner Pass south of Innsbruck, where I remained for a while with my mother and friends. Present at this event was Father John J. McGlinchey, later Monsignor McGlinchey of the Archdiocese of Boston. I had met McGlinchey in Rome on a visit to the North American College and we have often recalled the event.

Particularly precious was the experience of living as a guest of the Pastor of Steinach, one of those scholarly, saintly peasant priests who surprise you in the most unexpected places in Europe. I performed there my first Baptism for the daughter of the Mayor of Steinach, and entered her name proudly in the parish register. At the neighboring village of St. Jodok, where I also sang a High Mass, I was amused—since there was no use getting scandalized—at the good old custom of singing only one-half the Creed. The choir sang vigorously up to the *sepultus est* and then stopped there, apparently unable to proceed further. But the choir's delinquencies were balanced by the beautiful ceremony of the blessing of the fields on Rogation days, when the Blessed Sacrament was carried far and wide over the countryside, a custom which has been inaugurated in some of the country parishes here in the United States.

My last days in Europe were spent in London, as the guest of Father Hamilton Macdonald. He was at that time chaplain of the Religious of the Sacred Heart at Hammersmith, where he also taught catechism to the children and chuckled over the little girl who asked him gravely: "Did God make Hammersmith?"

At the urging of the Schönbergs, and of Father Macdonald as well, I called on Lady Herbert of Lea in London. The door was opened by an affable young Irishman quite different from

the traditional solemn-faced butler. Lady Herbert, girded
with a denim apron and busy dusting her furniture, was extremely hospitable, and told me that she was, so to speak, a
poor rich woman owing to her various charities and demands
on her time.

At Lady Herbert's home I met the Baron von Hügel, center
of so many dramatic incidents of the current modernist movement, whose writings Macdonald and I had already discussed.
He was a man of limitless kindness, of mystical personal piety
and vast erudition. My four years of contact with German
scholars who had managed to combine clear thinking and
sharp reasoning with patient research made the profundity
of his Teutonic thought less awe-inspiring to me than it
seemed to be to many of his British and French admirers.

It was a beautiful trait, I thought, for him to seek so deli-
cately to understand and sympathize with the minds of those
who differed from him doctrinally. Indeed without this, intercourse between Catholic and non-Catholic is impossible. Catholic truth can gain acceptance only by persuasion, not by
bludgeoning. Respect for the inviolability of another man's
conscience is a prime requisite for all religious dialogue.
Nevertheless, I could not quite see why Von Hügel needed to
be so extremely apologetic about his own faith. His mind, so
broad toward dissenters, seemed narrow in judging his fellow
Catholics, and he was quite hoodwinked by that insatiable
egoist, the arch-modernist Père Alfred Loisy. There were narrow-minded men at Rome, as there were narrow-minded men
at Innsbruck, such as the elderly Jesuit who informed our
class that America was essentially a wicked country since it
was ruled by an atheistic government. Nevertheless, I could
not see the picture in the perspective that seemed to haunt
Von Hügel and his associates. Cardinal Merry del Val and
the entourage of Pius X may have been lacking in some finer
degrees of sympathy, but nevertheless they were not narrow-
minded people. They were deeply concerned about the problems of the Church in the field of modern thought and were
honest in trying to meet them.

The modernist movement, which was then in its heyday, seemed to me to have switched Catholic thought, especially Catholic Scriptural research, into a blind alley, from which the drastic action of Pius X in his encyclical *Pascendi* would later rescue it. Father George Tyrrell's writings, so attractive in their outward form, had proved an ashen deception. At the time of his leaving the Society of Jesus, my mother told me that the very first time she read one of his volumes she had said to herself instinctively: "This man will one day leave the Church." To me the chief offense of the modernists was the perversion of language, their cheapening of the very substance of words themselves, which are the most delicate and sacrosanct of man's instruments in the search for truth. If a man refused to believe that Jesus Christ rose from the dead, you at least knew where he stood and could argue with him. But what could you do with a man who said he believed in the Resurrection, but understood by it nothing more than a subjective consciousness that he was somehow or other more at harmony with the rest of the world? However, it is only fair to recall that the modernists adventurously tackled the solution of difficult and urgent questions which later theologians did face, and faced with far greater success.

On my way to London from Innsbruck I had made a detour to Lourdes. No pilgrimage was scheduled at the time and the pilgrims were few. It was an ineffable privilege to offer Mass in the shrine, and I was deeply touched when a bishop undertook to serve the Mass for myself, a very young neophyte. Writing of Lourdes in later years for the *American* magazine, I summed up the question of the miraculous cures in a sentence that the motion picture, *Song of Bernadette,* featured (without credit to the author): "For those who believe in God no explanation is needed; for those who do not believe in God no explanation is possible." On the way to Lourdes I stopped off at Bordeaux and proudly inscribed my name in the guestbook of the cathedral as *"Cand. S.J.,"* to the puzzlement of the verger in charge.

I said good-by to London and to Macdonald with a heavy

heart, for I guessed I should never see him again. Until shortly before his death he continued to write to me about his fine work for the sailors and seamen.

Arriving in New York I presented myself at once to the Rev. Thomas J. Gannon, S.J., Provincial of the Maryland-New York Province, then residing at St. Francis Xavier Church on Sixteenth Street. He arranged that I should enter the novitiate on the eve of the Feast of St. Stanislaus, which falls on November 13. When the appointed day came so many odds and ends turned up that, in my absentminded way, I arrived almost too late for the very last train on the New York Central for Poughkeepsie at 9 P.M. To my horror the gate was already closed and the conductor was shouting "All aboard." I feared that if I missed that train I would be in a dreadful state about entering the Society, and yelled to the conductor, much to his bewilderment: "For heaven's sake open the gate and let me through! I am *leaving the world* on this train and *must* make it!" I made it.

When the cab from the Poughkeepsie station finally deposited me at the novitiate, where happily they were awaiting me, the Brother took my meager baggage and brought me to my room. There, to my consolation, I found that I could sleep in pajamas just as I had always done. Somehow or other I had formed an idea that in the Society one wore a long white nightgown and used a red pocket handkerchief, such as I had seen produced by professors at Innsbruck. Aversion to nightgowns and red cotton handkerchiefs were my two greatest immediate repugnances on entering the Religious state.

After a good night's rest I found myself the next morning quite at home. After Mass the Novice Master, Father George A. Pettit, S.J., came to greet me, and to my confusion I found that he was the gentleman whom I had greeted the night before as a Brother. The Brother who had accompanied him I had taken for the Novice Master and addressed him as such. We had a good laugh, and my days at Poughkeepsie started off in a cheerful atmosphere. It was curious that after the rigors of Innsbruck, to which I had become acclimated, it took me some time to get used to the relative comfort of an American institution. Like many a European I somewhat longed for the sharp contrast between the cold corridors and the cozy, even if stuffy, cell where one lived and prayed and studied.

When I wrote from Innsbruck to my father that I intended to become a Jesuit, he was at first a bit disturbed. I don't know just what he had in mind for my future, but on further consideration he became completely converted to the idea. He still retained an affectionate regard for the Jesuits, under whom he had studied as a boy for three years at St. John's college, at Fordham, and had picked up through the years considerable knowledge about the Society. He liked their spirit. He liked particularly the idea that I was choosing, as he thought, the best, and would not admit of any compromise in my ideals. And his peculiar notion that I was somehow or other professorially inclined was more accommodated than if I had become simply a parish priest.

Two days after my ordination he wrote from Newport to Henry Adams: "Of course my wife and Margaret are abroad and with John at Innsbruck. I send you a clipping from the newspaper which will give you the news regarding him, which is so serious to me." When I arrived in New York I found that my father did indeed take it seriously but cheerfully. Parting from him was friendly and a good augury for future relations. Father's mind paused and picked many a flower on its devious route, but he respected those who walked straight according to their convictions.

On the advice of Father Pettit, I kept up correspondence with both my parents after entrance into the Society. Somebody, I do not now recall who, apparently told Father that his son would not be able to write to him after becoming a Jesuit, so he sent me a much disturbed letter from Paris, to which I immediately replied that such an idea was nonsense, and that I could not understand how anyone could have created such an impression. Father was so relieved that he did not even bother to read the rest of my letter, and immediately wrote as follows (letter undated) in a characteristic bit of whimsy:

I read a few words which settled that absurd business, invented by some busybody, regarding correspondence between us. Still, there are idiotic things done by important people of your Order, notably, that wild raid of Fr. Sherman, I believe on horseback, passing through the country which his father ravaged and desolated. I wonder how his superiors in the Church could have allowed this, if discipline continued during vacation time. It was so absolutely wild, so far away from a clergyman's life and so certain to make a tremendous row and stir up all the worst feelings of human nature. Never, I know, will you do such a thing and therefore I do not hesitate to quote him.

The reference was to Father Tom Sherman (Thomas Ewing Sherman, S.J.), son of General Sherman of Civil War repute. Father Sherman, a generous soul, had become more or less deranged about the time this letter was written. He had told everybody of his plan for making a pilgrimage through Georgia along the line of his father's devastating "march," but I do not think he ever succeeded in carrying it out. As for myself, I found it sufficient to confine my raids, at a later period, to the woods and streams of southern Maryland.

At Christmas time I wrote to Father my regrets that I could not be on hand to give him my Christmas greetings in person, but had to depend upon sending them by my "not very skillful hand on paper," and I added:

Some wise man once said that you could tell a person's character by the way he sharpens a pencil; many say that you can judge by the handwriting. If this be true, I fear that according to either criterion I have no character at all. So I must try to struggle on through life without one. At present I do not feel the loss. Perhaps it is so much baggage the less.

Let me add, incidentally, that my handwriting from 1901 to 1906 was definitely the best I have ever enjoyed, before or since.

CHAPTER EIGHT
The Manner Is Ordinary

~»» «««~

Of life in the Society of Jesus its founder, St. Ignatius Loyola, remarks (Rule 4): "For good reasons, having always in view God's greater service, the manner of living as to external things is ordinary, and has no regular penances or corporal austerities obligatory on all." This means that the novice coming from a seminary for priests, as I did, finds a regime which in general resembles that of his seminary. The Jesuit wears no prescribed and traditional habit. He does not recite the Divine Office in choir, and penitential practices are voluntary. This absence of certain typical monastic customs, however, is partly made up for by longer periods of prescribed mental prayer and examination of conscience and certain specific community devotions. The difference lies in the manner in which all life is carried out, as expressed in the Institute (rules of the Order). The spirit is one of complete simplicity, and a poverty which makes up for the lack of austerity by its absolute dependence, even in the smallest details, upon explicit permissions and conformity to common life.

St. Ignatius was anxious that the "genuine progeny of the Society" should be distinguished by "true and perfect Obedience and abnegation of will and judgment," even though they may easily suffer themselves "to be surpassed by other religious orders in fasting, watching and other austerities in food and clothing, which each according to its institute and rule holily adopts." The novice learns to lay great stress on mutual helpfulness, humility, and charity. This is no easy matter when

133

so many different temperaments live day in and day out in the closest possible association.

Externals of the different Orders greatly differ, and members are very conscious of these differences. But if the founders themselves were to reappear and talk over their work, they might be more at harmony than some of their commentators, although they differ greatly in their manner of approach to a common problem. In every case the road to be followed is the royal road of the Cross, a sacrifice to God of man's pride and sensuality, of the disordered inclinations which are a consequence of Original Sin. Through the rules of the respective Order, a building up of "the new man in Christ" is to be achieved.

What the Ignatian rule lacks in outward austerity is amply supplied by the strictness and thoroughness with which the Ignatian ideal is to be fulfilled in every detail under all possible circumstances, independently of environment, place, age, or condition of body or mind. In fact Rule 51 prescribes how one should behave in the very act of death.* Nothing is more demanding than the "ordinary manner of life." The words of the canonized Jesuit scholastic, John Berchmans, are often quoted: "The common life is my greatest penance." This is true in whichever sense you take it: the *common* life—that is, with other members of the community in common living—or the *ordinary* life as lived according to the spirit of Ignatius. In both senses it adds up to as great an offering to God of one's pride and egotism and sensuality as can be devised.

The noviceship is no automatic process. The Master of Novices leads but he cannot drive, and the Order itself may lead its subjects but it cannot force them to obey. It is up to them to choose not only to follow their vocation, but to use their own initiative in every detail. Despite all the care with which

---

* "As in the whole of life, so also and much more in death, everyone of the Society must make it his effort and care that God our Lord be glorified and served in him, and that those around be edified at least by the example of his patience and fortitude, joined to a lively faith and hope and love. . . ."

the Order sifts its candidates there is no infallible process. In
the last analysis it rests on man's complete honesty and sincerity with himself and God. The aim of the Jesuit life as
explained by its founder is to clothe the man in the "vesture
of Christ," His vesture of humility and as a means to humility,
humiliations themselves. But it is the individual's decision
whether he wishes to put that vesture on or to seek to escape
it. If he wishes honestly to learn the humility of Jesus Christ
he must take the means to that end, and there is no means
toward learning humility except through accepting the humiliating experiences that everyday life provides. The novice, too,
must learn many a matter-of-fact lesson in everyday virtues.
It was the special contention of the late Father Timothy Brosnahan, S.J., one of the most lucid minds I have known and
critic of President Eliot, that one should strive to be, by God's
grace, first a thorough man if one wants to be a saint; that one
must, for instance, practice the requirements of ordinary justice before one aspires to the demands of charity.

On entering the Society an "angel"—in the shape of an older
novice—is provided to guide the newcomer and show him
where to black his boots, how to make his bed, and dozens of
other practical details. To my good fortune, my "angel" was
a fellow-novice priest like myself, Father Daniel J. M. Callahan, formerly a professor at Seton Hall College in Newark.
Father Callahan was an old Roman student and we made many
comparisons of Roman and Innsbruck usage. The two of us,
except for a few details proper to a priest, lived the life quite
in common with the other novices. His companionship saved
me from any sense of solitude. Father Callahan was blessed
with a keen sense of detail, an exact fidelity to minute prescriptions, yet he was saved by a robust, practical sense; all of which
was a vigorous help for me in trying to adjust myself to the
ideals of a religious order.

During noviceship the candidate of a religious community
learns to know life by practical experience; at the same time,
the community learns to know the candidate and forms a

judgment of his fitness for the Order. The most important
time of the two years is that given to the Spiritual Exercises
of St. Ignatius, which in their completeness last for a month.
At St. Andrew the Long Retreat, as it is called, is given in
the month of October, and our retreat closed on October 30,
the feast of St. Alphonsus Rodriguez, just prior to the Vigil
of All Saints. The retreatant lives through, as it were, the experiences of the founder of the Order, Ignatius Loyola, in the
cave of Manresa. There Ignatius saw revealed to his mind
and will the plan of the future spiritual campaign that determined the rest of his life, and embodied his experiences in a
scheme of prayer, meditation, and self-examination entitled
the "Spiritual Exercises."

There was little enough to converse about when visitors arrived, for the world of a novitiate and the outside world are
quite distinct. One caller, however, in the course of my first
year, was a young Episcopal clergyman, Rev. John Diman of
Newport, Rhode Island, founder of St. George's School in
Newport. Mr. Diman was a friend of my mother. Like her he
was a native Rhode Islander, and like a number of other young
men, he was accustomed to visit her for counsel and encouragement. Shortly before his ordination to the Episcopal ministry,
John Diman had mentioned to my mother the fact that he
was uncertain just what he really wanted to do as a minister.
He did not relish pastoral work, so Mother suggested to him
that he start a school. He liked the idea, acquired the use of
the old Cliff Hotel, a rambling wooden structure overlooking
the sea on the Cliff Walk, and later on obtained the beautiful
property overlooking Sachuest Beach, which is the site of the
present St. George's School.

I don't know exactly why he came to St. Andrew to see me,
except that we had always been sympathetic and he was interested in the Catholic Church and had made many inquiries
about it. Some years later, Mr. Diman became a Catholic, sac-
rificed his position as Headmaster of St. George's, and joined

the tiny congregation of English Benedictines at Portsmouth
that had been founded by Dom Leonard Sargent. Under Dom
Leonard's guidance he established the Portsmouth Priory
School, which became one of the best-known Catholic prepara-
tory schools in the United States. When the Portsmouth Priory
School was built, quite a number of the contractors who had
provided their services—plumbing, construction, etc.—for St.
George's kindly offered to work for him at Portsmouth at half
price.

Shortly before his death in 1950 I had a long talk with Father Diman at the Priory. He told me at the time something
he had mentioned to me on several previous occasions—that
his visit to St. Andrew had made a profound impression on
him and was a turning point in his conversion to the Catholic
faith. I asked what particularly impressed him about it, and
he said it was the fact that he saw me so completely happy
there. He realized that St.-Andrew-on-Hudson had something
to give that he had been seeking all his life.

Between St. Andrew and Poughkeepsie lies the Hudson River
State mental hospital, an immense property two miles across.
There I had my first experiences of the ministry. I preached
my first sermon in the Catholic chapel of the hospital on St.
Patrick's Day and was immensely encouraged when, in the
midst of my discourse, a patient stood up and yelled: "Grand
work, old boy, let's have more of it!" I sensed then my possibilities as a preacher.

Occasionally I was sent to West Point where I said Mass and
preached to the cadets in the little Catholic chapel which my
brother Grant had built some years before; the cadets took
my talks more quietly.

The chaplain of the State Hospital for the Insane, Father
John W. Casey, had himself entered the Society as a priest
six years before Father Callahan and myself. He was a man of
great energy and constructive power and played quite a part
in my later years. The two fine Catholic chapels at the State

Hospital were Father Casey's achievement. He firmly believed in the therapeutic power of religious faith. To this point of view he converted the Hospital Superintendent, Dr. Pilgrim. Many a patient had found his or her way back to sanity—to light out of darkness, to use a patient's own expression— through visits to the chapel. Father Casey showed unlimited charity and understanding for the mentally afflicted, and the contact with them was less repelling than what I had expected.

Brief as was my experience at the Poughkeepsie State Hospital, it greatly helped my exercise in later years of the priestly office in the confessional. I began then to see what grew much more evident in later years, that the confessional can greatly aid persons who are suffering from certain types of mental disorder, but that it cannot do everything.

The confessor does learn not infrequently that many a supposed mental affliction is due simply to disturbed and guilty conscience. Such persons need contrition, honest confession, and sacramental absolution more than they need professional psychiatric treatment. The current and frequently frustrated dependence on the psychiatrist to heal all inner anxieties is one of the many penalties modern man must pay for the decay of his religious faith and practice.

On the other hand, the confessor cannot be expected to take the place of the psychiatrist and heal genuinely sick cases that demand skilled professional treatment. The spheres of the confessor and of the mind-doctor are distinct; and Pope Pius XII, in his recent address to the Fifth International Congress of Psychotherapy and Clinical Psychology meeting in Rome (April 13, 1953), emphasized the great and blessed work of a psychiatrist who works according to the highest standards of his profession. He did not ban psychoanalysis, as long as it is practiced within limits and respects the religious and moral conscience. The confessor's primary work is to absolve from the personal guilt that has been subjected to his sacramental judgment, and to aid people by personal counsel to avoid evil and practice virtue in the future. Where he meets with genuine mental cases, he fulfills a great work of mercy by advising them to consult a morally reputable and professionally competent psychiatrist.

Through the years since I had left Harvard, I had corresponded with my old Harvard friend, Paul Rooney, Father Francis Solano in the Franciscan Order. Toward the end of my first year at St. Andrew, I was grieved to learn from Rev. Father Anselm, O.F.M., his Provincial, of Father Francis's death from tuberculosis. He had died aged 29 after a brief missionary career among the Pima Indians at the San Juan Bautista Mission in Arizona. After a stay at Phoenix, he was sent to the Old Mission at Santa Barbara, California, in the vain hope that he might recover his health. "In this charming spot," he wrote, "with the quiet Pacific rolling before and the wooded mountains of Santa Iñez towering behind, I am to remain until able to resume active work."

But the work was never resumed, although his extraordinary cheerfulness and alertness of mind never left him even up to the moment of his death. On the morning of May 24, 1906, Ascension Thursday, just as the deacon had chanted the Gospel of the Ascension and extinguished the Paschal candle, Father Francis Solano died at the exact instant he had predicted, having carefully marked the portions of the Gospels which he wished to have read to him during the last moments of his life. He was buried in the Franciscan Cemetery at Santa Barbara. His short life, made long by its variety and intensity, had been consumed for his ideals of duty and God-given charity.

In the second year of my noviceship I reviewed my classical studies in the other section of St. Andrew-on-Hudson entitled the Juniorate where the young Jesuits pursue their humanist or classical studies after their two-year noviceship has been completed. An exception was made for my case and that of Father Callahan, since we had entered as priests. Young Mr.

John J. O'Rourke, S.J., professor of Greek, was an Oxford degree holder and had brought into the juniorate a flavor of Oxford culture and a passion for the classics. The sight again of Homer and Aeschylus recalled those glowing words of my father: "Anything made, anything even influenced by that little race of artists, the Greeks, brings back our mind to its first legitimate, ever-continuing admiration; with them the floating Goddess of Chance took off her sandals and remained."*

In the summer of 1907 I was sent to Canisius College in Buffalo to teach "humanities" in the freshman year, according to the Jesuit plan of studies. In this plan, the teaching was not departmentalized. One taught English, Greek, and Latin to the freshmen as a co-ordinated whole. To me it was an entirely new and difficult experience. Canisius College was still part of the old Buffalo German Jesuit mission under the German Province. Shortly after, in the fall of the same year, the mission was dissolved and the houses divided among the two Jesuit provinces of Maryland-New York and Saint Louis. The time of transition was difficult. The German Fathers suffered from a sense of frustration and disappointment. They had been buoyed up by a great hope for a new Germany in the new world. In fact, Father Bonvin, Swiss by birth but a fervent German nationalist, confided to me that the saddest event in American history was the refusal by the Wisconsin legislature to sanction the use of German as the official governmental language of the state of Wisconsin.

The Fathers strongly differed as to the teaching and use of German in the school. Some of the older ones, particularly those in parish work, believed there should be no compromise, that the German language must be taught in school, must be the vehicle of instruction and of preaching. English was discouraged because, as they held, once you learned English you absorbed strange American ideas and departed from true orthodoxy. On the other hand, the younger group, among whom were several rather older men, were quite as well convinced

---

* *Considerations on Painting,* p. 187.

in the other direction. The dispute continued with increasing
bitterness until the dissolution of the mission. I was placed
more or less in the middle. With my knowledge of German
acquired from Innsbruck, my familiarity with German customs, I felt at home with the German Fathers, and it was odd
once more to hear reading at table in German, including some
of the books and magazines that I had listened to for four
years at Innsbruck.

Teaching was a bewildering task, since I had never had any
experience teaching anything except a very fragmentary course
in English and German during the juniorate, and by some
accident the college at that time lacked the clearly defined plan
of studies and daily schedule customary in Jesuit institutions;
so that the curriculum was in a fluid condition. However, the
standard of scholarship was high, with a fine, old tradition of
rigid study. The teacher was perfectly free to exact from the
boys a degree of homework that would be unheard of today.

The second semester brought relief. I was transferred to
Loyola College in Baltimore, exchanging positions with young
Father Miles O'Mailia. My soul began to thaw out in the more
congenial atmosphere of Baltimore. I could hardly believe
my ears when, at my first entry into the classroom, the boys
one by one walked up to me and said, "Good morning,
Father!"

I taught there only one semester, much to my regret, as I
would have loved to continue teaching the Humanities once
I began to grasp something of the procedure. It was enormously interesting to note contrasts between the Jesuit plan
and that of the Harvard classical system. In the Jesuit idea
the three branches, vernacular—which in our case was English,
Latin, and Greek, were grouped around a central concept, the
specific literary genus of "poetry." Poetry was understood not
in the limited sense of verse but in the wider sense of creative
and imaginative production, *poesis* in the Greek sense or in
the sense of Horace's great didactic work, the *Ars Poetica*
which was prescribed for freshman Latin. The students' atten-

tion was concentrated not so much on studying the language as studying the production itself, for which language was the vehicle. Such teaching, of course, might seem superficial from the point of view of classical erudition; it could become dilettante, or a mere instrument of the professor's whims. Nevertheless, it offered vast possibilities at the hands of a teacher who entered thoroughly into the spirit of the idea and was imaginative and somewhat creative besides. It was interesting working with a small roomful of boys who learned to know one another and know the teacher as well, with whom one established a real companionship.

The Society looks upon teaching in the colleges as an interlude for her young aspirants in their scholastic studies. As a priest I was not obliged to review my studies. But Father Callahan and myself decided we would avail ourselves of the opportunity and would review our philosophy and theology. Accordingly, we left for Woodstock in July 1908, arriving there, curiously enough, in a small snowstorm, by no means common in Maryland that time of the year.

This was the golden opportunity which I had missed in Innsbruck of really acquiring some grip on the fundamentals of scholastic philosophy. Those two years at Woodstock were for me the time of the greatest natural intellectual satisfaction that I have ever experienced. Once I grasped a bit of the essence of Thomism, it was intensely interesting for me to review some of the modern philosophical theories that I had glimpsed during my Harvard and Innsbruck years and see where the divergencies arose, as well as occasional correspondences.

In scholastic circles of recent years there has been considerable revolt against the use of the strict syllogistic method and a demand in many cases for its abandonment in favor of a more discursive type of demonstration. Certainly, the strict scholastic method can be exaggerated and it would be absurd to confine philosophical discussion to that single pattern. Nevertheless, I have never shared the extreme distaste for it. One of the most stimulating exercises for the human mind is to combine both methods, that of rigid syllogistic demonstration along with a free commentary and informal exposition.

During these two years I was particularly absorbed by the scholastic doctrine on Being, that wide scope of thought that includes the infinite and the finite under one analogous concept. Though at first it seemed to be the driest possible formula of words, the concept of the analogous nature of Being grew in my mind with astonishing luminosity. I began to realize that the notion of Being itself was the opposite of static; it was dynamic and creative.

During my second year the Rector of the scholasticate, Father Anthony J. Maas, who was a great Scripture scholar, asked me if I would work on a translation of a German article for the *Catholic Encyclopedia,* that magnificent work of scholarship issued under the presidency of the late Father John J. Wynne, S.J. I toiled pretty hard at that at a time when I was not feeling any too well, for I still had to struggle with some of my interior organism. I labored particularly on the exhaustive and exhausting article on the Hierarchy, which presented bewildering problems in terminology, involving words for which we have no equivalent in English. Father Maas was anxious to satisfy my eagerness for work and it was a welcome task, but it did not pay well in the long run and I had already accumulated a burden of fatigue when I took my final M.A. examinations at the close of the two years of philosophy.

In July the scholastics from Woodstock, both the philosophers and the theologians, pilgrimaged in a steamer to St. Inigoes in St. Mary's County down at the juncture of the St. Mary's River and the Potomac, for three weeks of holiday known as "Villa." There we camped out in a four-story frame building enjoying a sun-scorched outdoor life, which was

splendid for the vigorous but trying on the less robust. The
second year of my villa plus the heat and the examinations
left me pretty well weakened.

On my return I learned of my father's grave illness in New
York. Superiors gave me permission to visit New York and
see him in the hospital, which naturally raised the question of
his returning to the Sacraments. In good French style he had
no desire to talk about that particular matter and it was
not easy to bring it up. However, he referred repeatedly to
his affection for his early teachers whether at Fordham or
at Mount St. Mary's, and he was not averse to speaking on
the question of religion. He had written to me at Woodstock, asking for some suggestions for a spiritual guide.

One memorable day I put the matter to him directly, saying that the time had come to settle the question. I quoted
the words of the *Dies Irae: "Quaerens me, sedisti lassus,"*
"Seeking me, thou hast sat weary." These words moved him
deeply: he said that he could not forget them. We agreed
that he should see one of the four priests whom I had suggested, Father Henry C. Semple, of the Southern Jesuit Province, who was then visiting in New York and was himself a
Mount St. Mary's man.

Father had already completed his work on the four lunettes
in the Statehouse at Saint Paul, Minnesota, which represented
the four law-givers—Moses, Socrates, Mohammed, and Emperor Justinian. He had enjoyed, he wrote to Adams, doing
Socrates' portrait, since Socrates was a sculptor, and much of
his talk, as told by Plato, was "studio-talk," only better than
what you get now-a-days. We passed hours discussing the
philosophies of the four law-givers and I did a certain amount
of research for his very last major achievement, the four
murals for the Baltimore Court House.

After I returned to Woodstock he wrote to me on July 3,
1910, from the Albemarle Hotel in New York, as follows:

Dear John,

I was much pleased with Father Semple, so much so that I wished I could see more of him and he promised to do his best that way. The matter which troubled me he handled in (a) very satisfactory way and moreover talked charmingly anyhow. I'll say more in his praise some day.

Thanks indeed

Yours affy,
JLF

When Father was able to move he left for Newport where, unfortunately, his mental condition was not so good. He became restless and irresponsible, and caused us, particularly my mother, an intense anxiety. He finally agreed to go to the Butler Hospital in Providence for a complete rest. He entered in July 1910 and remained there until he passed away quite suddenly on November 14 of the same year.

Father Maas, the Woodstock Rector, woke me out of a sound sleep to inform me of Father's death, so that I could catch the early morning train for Baltimore and thence to New York and the funeral. The sudden awakening was a terrific shock to me. I had already suffered an intense nervous shock when I was awakened the first night of St. Inigoes' "Villa," by the cries of one of my brethren suffering from a nightmare. I was deeply distressed that I had not been able to be with Father at the end. However, I was comforted later on when I learned that he was kindly cared for in his last days by the Catholic chaplain of the Hospital. Shortly before his death he had sent to Henry Adams a final message—"all manner of good-bys"—through the hands of his old friend Mrs. Cadwalader Jones.

Death had not taken Father unawares; indeed he had long pondered over it and learned, as it were, to live with death in prospect. At the close of an earlier letter (undated) he wrote me:

One thing delights me that I came across, as it answers certain feelings. Justin (the Martyr) writes to uphold the value of the

Cumaean Sibyl and tells how he saw "himself" the suspended
bronze urn in which her ashes were and [makes?] the usual appeal
from such fact. Then comes in a very different gentleman, Petro-
nius "Arbiter," to whom I referred at once. He tells how the little
boys and girls went into the Temple at Cumae on hot days, let us
say, for coolness and some fun, I suppose. And they called up the
Sibyl, and asked her what she wished for in her urn. And she said
"Death."—Nothing is new. But this is fine, I think. She might well
be tired. But so with others.

Three years earlier he had written me:

I saw something of the thing myself, as I was supposed to have
the same trouble last summer, and I had to prepare for death in
a very short number of hours. It is a curious experience, and I
think out of all proportion with our habits. Only it seems a little
severe that one should have to go through that several times over.
Even the philosophy which must come, as you say, from Mr.
Thomas Ward's house along the street, is not sufficient to make me
dwell on the occasion with pleasure. This letter is merely in answer to yours. I have been thinking of writing to you on more
serious subjects than death.

Father was buried from the Church of St. Francis Xavier
with a Solemn High Mass, and laid to rest in the LaFarge
vault in Greenwood Cemetery, Brooklyn.

Shortly after his death the New York *Herald* for December
4, 1910, published a long and generous tribute that he characteristically paid to a fellow-artist and former neighbor in
the Tenth Street studio building: Winslow Homer. He had
completed it while "resting" in the hospital. Father's intense
labors, continued to the very finish, exemplified in his own
life one of his favorite mottoes: *le génie est une longue patience*. Always he returned to the idea, as he himself expressed
it: "The consciousness of having powers above the common
require all the more, as proof of having attained, that we
should have care of small things; that we should cook the
meals and sweep the house." *

At the marked revival of interest in his work at the Metro-

* *Considerations on Painting*, p. 249.

politan Museum of Art exhibit in New York in the Spring of
1936—a revival to be credited in great measure to the tireless
devotion of his critic and artistic biographer, the late Mr.
Royal Cortissoz—I recalled Father's theme, expressed formerly
to his own pupils in that same museum. He told them they
could look upon the world through the same windows
through which each great artist had looked upon it, and
added: "The very fact that it has all been done is enough
to assure you that it can be done again, done as never before."
He was convinced that the most genuine merit of all that he
crowded into his busy seventy-five years was the inspiration
for others to do the same, but do it far better, and with still
loftier and purer intent.

At Woodstock after my return I tried to get what refreshment I could by long walks, rest, and so on, but with no success. Finally, the Rector called me to his office and in his own
homely way he put the matter up to me:
    "You have the choice, Father LaFarge, of being a live jack-
ass or a dead lion. Personally," he said, "I think it is better to
be a live jackass."
    This meant, in less metaphorical language, that the time
had come to give up the idea of pursuing a strictly intellectual
speculative career. The Rector judged, as did Father Provincial, that I would recover my strength better if I were in
some active work which would not be too much of a strain.
So I said good-by to my classmates at Woodstock. For the
time being I was assigned to St. Thomas' Manor, St. Ignatius
Church, in Charles County, Maryland.
    Wearing an old pair of work trousers and a cassock, I packed
up my few belongings along with a few books and manuscripts
I was allowed to take with me and the House delivery wagon
carried them to the railroad station at the foot of the hill.
A little good-by party gathered in my room and, as the time
for the farewells approached, I suddenly realized to my dis-
may that my only pair of respectable trousers was packed up

with the rest of my clothes. Time was running out. There was
a frantic rush down the hill, unpacking of the trunk, and a
still more frantic rush up the hill, and vesting myself with
proper garb I caught the train for Relay, Maryland, and from
Bowie took the local line down to St. Thomas' Manor. I was
at St. Thomas' for only a short time, just enough to get a
bit of rest, and then was sent to Old St. Joseph's Church at
Willing's Alley in Philadelphia where I acted as assistant in
the parish, with that most delightful man as Superior, Father
Daniel O'Kane.

After three weeks of peaceful work at Willing's Alley, news
came that I was needed by Father John W. Casey as assistant
in the hospitals and penal institutions on Blackwells Island
in New York harbor, now known as Welfare Island. In this
capacity I experienced eight of the most tremendous months
in my life, for they opened up to me a vast vision of the
tragic as well as the human side of life. I had had a glimpse
of this in Poughkeepsie State Hospital, but Blackwells Island
was the real thing.

In those days the workers on the Island were almost completely
isolated. The approach by the Queensborough Bridge had not
yet been made, and the only way to reach the Island was by
a little ferry boat from the foot of East Seventy-second Street
in Manhattan. I don't mind acknowledging that my first feelings were pretty much of terror.

Blackwells Island had a bad name; to be sent to the Island
was only short of being sent to Sing Sing. Patients in the
charity and hospital divisions of the Island hated to acknowledge that they were sent there as patients, since the very name
suggested a stigma. At the south end of the Island were the
State Penitentiary and the New York City Hospital. With
these I had nothing to do. Father Richard Ryan, S.J., cared
for these as the Catholic chaplain.

Shortly before I arrived on the Island, Father Ryan, a frail
elderly man, had rescued a fellow from drowning in the river

by jumping overboard and bringing him to shore. He was cited for a hero's medal before the Board of a famous foundation. After quite an examination, they asked Father Ryan what he was thinking about when he jumped overboard. "I saw a man in the water," he said, "and thought I had better pull him out." They then decided that he should have been conscious of the fact that he was performing an heroic act. Unfortunately, the idea of heroism had never occurred to Father Ryan, so the medal was not bestowed.

Father Casey was in charge of three institutions: the City Home, in the center of the Island, with 3,300 inmates, of which 2,800 were reputed to be Catholics; the Work House with over 900, mostly on drunken and disorderly sentences from six months down; and the Metropolitan toward the north with 1,500 patients, of which 500 were largely chronic or neurological, and 1,000 were tubercular. Father Casey resided at the extreme northern end of the Island in the orderlies' quarters, with a room facing out on the East River.

I was installed in the Work House itself where the chaplain was provided with a large study and an adjoining small bedroom. There was no chapel in the Work House, though on Sunday Mass was celebrated there in the hall upstairs, Catholics first and then an Anglican service. I enjoyed, however, the privilege of keeping the Blessed Sacrament in a little closet off the study.

I arrived at the Work House late in the evening, tired, confused and, as I say, somewhat terrified, and lay down with considerable apprehension for my first night inside the walls of a prison. An electric bulb shone in through the transom on my bed. I had just dozed off in a fitful slumber around midnight when there came a loud knocking on the door. I was told to hurry at once to the hospital tier, that one of the prisoners was out of his mind and dying at the same time. It was my first experience of visiting the cell blocks. With my anxious dread of night awakening, it was quite a rude initiation.

My work was divided among the different institutions. Father Casey had systematically examined prisoners of the Catholic faith as they came in. If they reported themselves as Catholics, which the majority did, I interviewed them briefly.

It was interesting to learn the various ways in which people can become officially D.D., or drunk and disorderly. In fact all of these prisoners, both men and women, were quite innocent. They had arrived from the other side of the East River by a mere accident. As one old fellow put it, "Just three tablespoonfuls, Father, with a half glass of hot water to prevent the bad effects of a quinine pill, and then I find myself here." Indeed, some of them cultivated special devotions, such as one pious lad from Brooklyn who felt he had a vocation to be a Jesuit lay brother and had even applied to our Provincial, Father Hanselman. On later inquiry I found he had a particular devotion to the poor and had been seen praying in the vicinity of the poor box in our St. Ignatius Church in Brooklyn. He accompanied his devout practices with a gum-tipped wire which he occasionally dipped into the poor box. I considered his vocation too special for us to handle, and suggested that he might adopt a more secular mode of living. Yet with all their faults and ruses, a bit of kindness was never wasted on men and women who found themselves adrift in the impersonal toils of a city institution.

In all the institutions, but particularly in the Metropolitan, there was plenty of work instructing converts. Then there were the hospital wards to be visited. The best thing was to go the rounds of all the wards where there were bed-ridden sick people at least once a day, preferably between eight and nine in the evening, to take a look so as not to be called out too frequently at night. On Sunday I said Mass in the Work House hall, where my acolyte was a composed and competent twelve-year-old altar boy called Johnny Hartigan, son of the Superintendent of the City Home: Monsignor Hartigan he is today. Mass was also celebrated in the City Home's barn-like old "chapel." The evening before, confessions of the old people ran from 400 to 600 in number. I celebrated two Masses and I preached at both, but the congregation was practically the same for the two. The old folks figured that if they came to the first Mass they might as well attend the second, so preaching was rather uninspiring.

The climax came about the middle of my stay there when Father Casey was ill for a protracted period and I was left alone with all three institutions to look after. In those days we did not receive the extra help from the Jesuit houses which was inaugurated a few years after I left. The old tuberculosis wards were, perhaps, the most depressing of all the spots in that grim, shabby, and overcrowded world. Ward H and Ward Q in the old TB building were notorious. If you entered Ward H or Ward Q you were proverbially stepping into your grave.

Gloomy and depressing as the institutions were, another side to the life began to dawn. A hospital, after all, is not just a building housing patients; it is also a family with a life of its own and a spirit of fellowship. With Tammany in supreme control of Blackwells Island, the administration was not ideal. Yet a friendly spirit prevailed among the officials, the nurses, doctors, wardens of the Work House, matrons, and everybody else. One had the distinct feeling of living in a great and rather jovial family. The nurses were a wonderful group, and Father Casey had organized a flourishing nurses' sodality for which we held special services in the little wooden chapel which then served the Metropolitan. After I left, Father Casey built the Met's present splendid Catholic chapel. Chief Warden of the prison was James Fox, a great friend of Father Casey, a warm-hearted, enlightened man who introduced a simple form of shop work for the prisoners and did as much to rehabilitate them as possible. Even the women prisoners with their bedraggled careers revealed to me much that was hopefully human beneath a forlorn exterior.

During my eight months on the Island I administered the

Sacrament of Extreme Unction some three thousand times.
I had heard and read much of the power of this sacrament,
about which Father Kern, S.J., had lectured so eloquently
at Innsbruck. Now I had the chance of witnessing this power,
and it was dramatically evident before my eyes. So many times
that I could not count them, I would see a change come over
the patients the moment they had received the holy oils.
These people were simple; they were derelicts and all earthly
comfort and hope had left them; they were thrown on the
Creator, and the Creator made good His word. He was a hundred per cent "there," in a vigorous, dramatic manner that
often took my breath away.

On one occasion I was called to a woman—she was an East
European German afflicted with some neurological trouble,
out of her mind, raving and tied by the usual bandages to the
bed. For hours and days no means had been discovered of
calming her. She glared at me; something seemed to repel
her from me. Yet the moment I merely touched the edge of
her eyelid with the holy oils she relaxed, fell back quietly on
the bed, took a deep breath and from that time on until her
death was peaceful, tranquil, and rational.

Other contacts cast a far-reaching light into the realm of
the spiritual, such as the helpless kids in the children's wards,
who took their crosses as nonchalantly as they would an extra
lesson at school; or old John Lennon, with only 32 cents to
his name, who had lain four years in a bed on the top floor
of the West TB pavilion, and had only one worry in the
world: "Why does God seem to treat people so unequally?
The rich folk in Fifth Avenue have only hell to look forward
to; yet He's given me, a sinner, His grace and with it the
hope of heaven."

Innsbruck and Woodstock were schools of knowledge, but
Blackwells Island was a school of life and death.

GLEN COVE, NEW YORK, 1861-62. *Standing, left to right:* Mrs. John LaFarge (Margaret Mason Perry); Mrs. Louis LaFarge (Johanna Stack); Louis LaFarge; Thomas Sergeant Perry. *Seated:* John LaFarge senior and (foreground) Aimée LaFarge, his younger sister.

My mother (1918) and father (1907). The picture of my mother was taken on the porch of our house at Sunnyside Place in Newport.

The author in childhood and at age 15.

As a young priest in the summer of 1905, and in the garden at Newport in the autumn of 1905, with my brother, Oliver H. P. LaFarge, and my mother.

Parish meeting at St. James, St. Mary's City, Maryland, in the summer of 1919. Mr. Joseph Gurskey is in the top row, extreme left and Mr. James H. Carroll, extreme right.

The first pupils of St. Alphonsus School, St. James Parish. Mrs. Jennie Beale is at extreme left and Mr. Clem Beale at rear.

A weekly forum meeting at the Catholic Interracial Center, Vesey Street, New York City.

The Editorial Board of *America* at Campion House, New York City, October, 1948. *Left to right:* Fathers Conway, Hartnett, Gibbons, LaFarge (editor-in-chief), Masse, Keenan, Duff, Gardiner.

CATHOLIC INTERRACIAL FORUM—Panel group in tribute to St. Francis Hospital, Charleston, West Virginia, in 1951. *Standing*: Richard S. Zeissler, American Jewish Committee. *Seated, left to right*: Dr. John E. Moseley, prominent Harlem physician; Rev. John LaFarge, S.J., Chaplain, Catholic Interracial Council; Rev. Marshall Scott, Presbyterian Institute of Industrial Relations.

Annual retreat of the Catholic Laymen's Union at Glenmont, New York, in July, 1953. An open-air round table with the author.

PARS AESTIVA

꒰꒰ ꒱꒱

Summer days are the longest: days crowded with struggle, days that work up swiftly to the year's climax and start the year's decline. On June 24, close to the sun's turning-point, John the Baptist reminds us that Christ will increase as our own sun lessens; Peter and Paul (June 29) bid us look forward and outward over the races and peoples of mankind; Ignatius, Alphonsus, and Dominic (July 31, August 2 and 4) invite us to a campaign of truth and love, and Mary in her supreme hour (August 15) bids the humblest and weakest take courage. Summer days pass quickest. The Breviary reader, still fancying that much of Summer remains, is surprised to find that it is over. September, the beginning of the Autumn season, is already at hand.

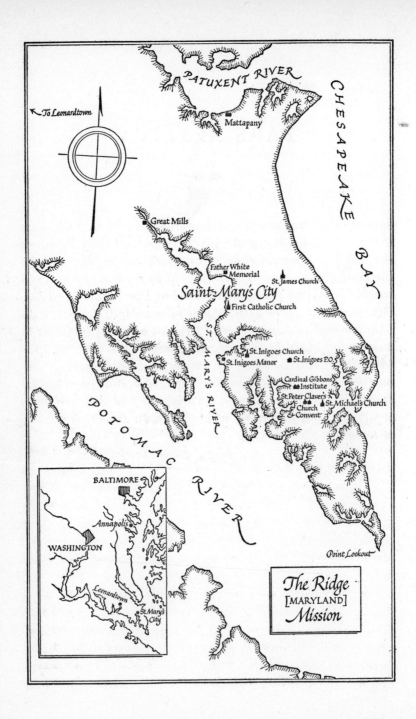

To Leonardtown

PATUXENT RIVER

CHESAPEAKE BAY

Mattapany

Great Mills

Father White Memorial

St. James Church

Saint Mary's City

First Catholic Church

ST. MARY'S RIVER

St. Inigoes Church

St. Inigoes Manor

St. Inigoes P.O.

Cardinal Gibbons Institute

St. Peter Claver's Church & Convent

St. Michael's Church

POTOMAC RIVER

Point Lookout

BALTIMORE

Annapolis

WASHINGTON

Leonardtown

St. Mary's City

The Ridge
[MARYLAND]
Mission

CHAPTER NINE

Leonardtown Arcadia

⇉⇇

On the afternoon of September 13, 1911, Father Michael Hogan, a fellow Jesuit, and I went by train from New York to Washington, thence across the city in the trolley to board the steamer at the old Seventh Street wharves. The steamer ran three times a week to the various wharves along the shores of the Potomac River and Chesapeake Bay. Leaving Washington at four it passed Mount Vernon, Indian Head, Maryland, and then switched over to various spots on the Virginia shore, arriving finally at the Leonardtown Wharf in St. Mary's County about three-thirty or four in the morning. The boat continued its weaving way between Maryland and Virginia. Turning around Point Lookout at the mouth of the Potomac River and proceeding up the Chesapeake it arrived the following morning in Baltimore, a journey of forty-eight hours in all. Trips on the old Chesapeake line, though tedious if you were in a hurry—which you never could be in that part of the world—were agreeable enough. Accommodations were spacious and comfortable; you were well fed with a fried oyster or crab dinner according to the season, and tolerable weather made the time pass all the more pleasantly.

I was assigned as assistant pastor to the Church of St. Aloysius in Leonardtown, while Father Hogan was assigned to one of the many Jesuit missions that depended on the Leonardtown church. His mission comprised two churches, the Sacred Heart and the Church of the Holy Angels in St. Mary's County. All St. Mary's County had been in charge of the Jesuits since the first white man landed there in 1634. Charles County, too, had been entirely in charge of the Jesuits, but about forty or fifty years previous, some of it had been taken over by the Archdiocese of Baltimore. The Jesuits had some twenty-two Jesuit missions or parishes in Charles and St. Mary's Counties. These were run from three centers: St. Thomas' Manor, near Bel Alton in Charles County; and Leonardtown and St. Inigoes in St. Mary's County.

Six Jesuit Fathers were stationed at St. Aloysius Church, Leonardtown: the pastor (also Superior of the Community), the Very Rev. Laurence J. Kelly, S.J., a native of Philadelphia; Father Hogan who was in charge of the two churches already mentioned; Father Joseph Schmidt who attended the missions of Morganza and Mechanicsville; Father Timothy O'Leary who was pastor of St. John's Church at Hollywood, one of the oldest of the Maryland settlements; Father William Stanton of Newtown and Medley's Neck; and myself.

The missions covered an enormous territory when you considered the slow and difficult transportation of those days. With one exception, the roads from Leonardtown to Mechanicsville were mere dirt roads, impassable in winter and anything but easy in summer, so that much travel in olden days was by water. The missionary often spent several days on the road, and slept in the homes of parishioners who traditionally offered him the best of their hospitality. Many of the better old manor or plantation residences kept a special "priest's room." Some, like the Bushwood residence near Sacred Heart Church, were provided with an altar. Mass was celebrated periodically.

The southern Maryland missions were traditionally known as the Counties. Apart from the boat which made that slow trip three times a week, weather permitting, there was no other way to reach St. Mary's County except a tedious and complicated land trip by jerkwater railroad plus horse and buggy. The Counties were in somewhat bad report because they were rural instead of urban, and few of our Eastern clergy had any rural background or were sympathetic to country life.

The people who lived in this isolated region were of a different national or racial origin from our traditional Catholic parishes. Irish and Germans among them were so rare as to be practically non-existent. The white people who made up three-fifths of the population were descendants of the old English Catholics who emigrated with Lord Baltimore in the *Ark* and the *Dove* and others who came from England in later years but at one period or another had become converted to the Catholic faith. They had no sense of any past European background. In fact, the absence of historical sense among the Maryland Catholics, except with a few educated persons, was disturbing. St. Mary's County was just "home," where they grew up, where their ancestors had lived, and their mental perspective reached no further back. Their piety was traditional; they were steadfast, family-minded, highly devotional with a strong moral sense, a strict observance of the proprieties of life and of decency in their language and conduct. On the other hand, they lacked the vigor and aggressiveness of a typical Northern Catholic parish.

The people were independent and frank in expressing their opinion of "our priest," as they called him. Yet they habitually bewailed the former pastor, as a matter of etiquette. When Father Hogan succeeded Father Kelly as pastor of Sacred Heart Church he was immediately peppered with lamentations as to why his superior had taken "our dear Father Kelly away." What can we ever do without him, they wailed, quoting his sayings, his actions, his views on everything. "You would think," said Father Hogan, a somewhat irascible Irishman with strong ideas of priestly authority and dignity, "that I had murdered Father Kelly."

Northerners who were assigned to work in the Counties were sometimes disconcerted at finding that part of their charges would be Negroes. Until I went to St. Mary's County the only Negroes with whom I had come in contact in a priestly way were in the municipal hospitals of Blackwells Island in New York.

Father Kelly, the pastor of Leonardtown, was young, energetic, broad and apostolic in his outlook, patient and human, with a good sense of humor and an incredible sense for detail. He was indeed a model pastor, and I was fortunate to have learned pastoral work under so competent a guide. Father Kelly was painstaking about the instruction of the children, and personally supervised their spiritual condition.

My four years in Leonardtown as assistant pastor of St. Aloysius Church were a grateful change from the strain of the Metropolitan Hospital, the Work House, and the City Home. True, the life had certain hardships, chief of which was the sense of separation from intellectual companionship. Yet it was a full life in its way, occupied by the daily Mass and Sunday Mass with its sermon, instruction of converts, baptism of children, care of the sick in all kinds of unique circumstances, marriages, sacramentals and devotions of various kinds, many of which were traditional in our Jesuit parishes. Visits to the homes, work with the young, catechism at home and outside, promotion of recreational life, filled the time. Along with this I was always conscious that in some way or other it was the land of the Most Holy Sacrament. For three hundred years the Saviour had dwelt in or traveled these forests, farms, fields, and bays in His Eucharistic presence. Back in August 1768 the people of St. Ignatius Church at St. Thomas' Manor had formed a "Guard of Honor" for daily twelve-hour adoration of the Blessed Sacrament and the list of adorers still remains, names still familiar—Birch, Bowling, Digges, Edelen, Jenkins, Neale, Pilkington, Yates, etc. It was the land of Mary and the land of Jesus, a land of peace, a territory untouched by war except for a slight passing event during the War of 1812.

I studied the geography and maps, and the character of the population, their social strata, their traditions, and in this way learned to know human beings in their many aspects, in contrast to the hospital and prison, where I saw only fragments of human life—infinitely precious fragments but detached from the main current. I could observe an entire social process, thus gaining very practical knowledge. Once more I could apply to myself the advice that good Father Heuser had given me in my boyhood, that my heart and not my head must find its due place. It meant that I renounced some congenial intellectual pursuits, but the book of life compensated.

My assignment was to cultivate the outer regions of the extensive parish, a radius of about six or eight miles from the church, divided by various water courses and swamps which made the routes long and circuitous. Several hundred parishioners were scattered over all this parochially rather uncharted area, many of whom had not been visited by the priest for years, children who had never made their First Communion, people who had been baptized but never entered in the baptismal register for some reason or other, and even adults who had never come in contact with the Church. The aristocratic sacristan of the church, stately, meticulous Miss Jane Margaret Fenwick—popularly known as Miss Madge—helped me locate and catalogue the absentees.

I established eight catechetical centers for both white and colored in various outlying parts of the parish and trained a group of catechists. Each of these eight centers I visited weekly and armed myself with all the visual aids and apparatus that were available at that time.

Life with Father Kelly was not monotonous. On the doggiest of dog days, August 3, 1914, after the outbreak of the First World War, the bells of St. Aloysius Church in Leonardtown and other Catholic churches in St. Mary's County were rung to celebrate an event that no Catholic church has ever, to my knowledge, celebrated before or since. In the battle against the demon Rum the dry Catholics and the Methodists had won a substantial victory over the wet Catholics and the equally wet Episcopalians. Local option had triumphed in the "land of the fiddle and the flask." The continual battle pro and con distressed me. Visiting clergymen from Baltimore, Washington, and points beyond delighted in poking fun at us and expressing their amazement at what was going on. This did not, however, disturb Father Kelly, however much it may have pained him interiorly. He was no Manichean; though he abstained himself, he saw no reason why somebody else should not take a drink. He simply wanted to stop the undue consumption of liquor and abuses in selling it, and to that end did not hesitate to use the services of Wayne B. Wheeler and his famous Anti-Saloon League—which one of our local dry orators persisted in calling the Anti-Loonsa League.

The feud enlarged as time went on. The campaign met with spirited opposition from the local judiciary, and more issues entered its orbit. However, God's grace prevailed and the opposing Judge was reconciled. He and Father Kelly shook hands, made up, and were friends from then on. Later the ill-starred Eighteenth Amendment put its curse upon the Maryland countryside. Like certain types of unskilled, amateur anti-communism, Prohibition achieved the precise opposite of its professed aims.

Southern Maryland was occasionally referred to as an Arcadia by its Jesuit visitors, and the people themselves agreed. Talking one day with an old farmer on the Jesuit Manor property at Newtown, I asked Mr. Abell what he thought of the world in general. The world in general, said Mr. Abell, consists of three kinds of people: first, us folks (that is, the people of St. Mary's and Charles Counties, Maryland); second, furriners (people from Maryland's Eastern Shore, Baltimore, California, China or Sweden and other outlying parts); and the third kind of people, said Mr. Abell, were those damned Virginians. Virginians, be it explained, were extremely annoying because they crossed the Potomac River and interfered with the Maryland oyster fisheries.

Placid as was the faith of the Marylanders, there were plenty of examples of heroic sanctity. Catholic parish saints are not much known to the general world, but explore and you will find them. Miss Rose Nuttall, a slender lass who looked as if she had been born and bred in the Scotch highlands, lived on the other side of Bretton Bay from Leonardtown in a tiny cabin with an invalid fisherman father and her helpless mother; did everything, cooking and attending to all their needs. Yet every morning Rose would row two miles across the bay in her little skiff, tie it to the mooring post at the wharf and walk up hill two miles more to the church for Mass and Communion. In addition to this, Rose took upon herself the poor of the parish. It was her job, she felt, if anybody was in want, to provide for them anything that was needed. She gave particular care to an invalid brother Gregory. Even though he lived in the town she still managed to find time to look after him.

Uncle Cass Adams, as he was called, a venerable Negro, lived in the adjoining parish of St. John's at Hollywood, one of the original southern Maryland parishes which dated from the earliest days of the Colony. Father Timothy O'Leary, S.J., had built a little chapel chiefly for the Negroes at a place called California, which is four miles from Hollywood. Between the two places ran a narrow clay road dug out of the soil. Every Sunday morning Uncle Cass walked the four miles from his home in California to St. John's Church in Hollywood for early Mass and Communion, home again for his breakfast, which he cooked himself, then trudged once more to St. John's for the late Mass and after the late Mass returned the second time, sixteen miles in all for his rheumatic limbs. When I asked Cass Adams why he did this, why he did not consider one Mass enough, his answer was simple: "You can never have enough of the good Lord." In addition to this he cared for a little mission church and engaged in other charitable activities as well. One could catalogue no end of people like this: men and women who walked miles to church or traveled in boats or with balky horses; children who trudged alone through

the woods and over the fields in order to attend catechism or
to serve Mass.

People loved preaching, especially in the outer missions.
In many cases they complained if the priest cut his talk too
short. If they had made such efforts to get to Mass, they felt
entitled to something reasonably substantial. At St. Aloysius
Church I gauged the length of my sermon by looking at the
gallery. A young farmer called Stumpy Nelson rested his lanky
limbs there next to the organ loft. Stumpy was pious enough
and would consider me intently for eighteen or at the most
twenty minutes. At the expiration of that time he invariably
turned and gazed out the window. This was a signal to pero-
rate.

The Faith had survived in this place under circumstances
somewhat similar to those which the Irish had experienced
in the old country. The southern Marylanders had suffered
a hundred and forty years of penal laws, persecutions not violent or bloody, but nonetheless humiliating and harassing.
They were educationally handicapped; they were obliged to
pay taxes for the support of churches and minister other than
their own; they were debarred from civic office and were in
continual danger of annoyances of every description. They
lived under a perpetual social stigma, something that most
people feel more keenly than open persecution.

Like the Irish, too, they lacked the assistance to the Faith
of much that appeals to the senses and the imagination. No
beautiful churches or cathedrals adorned their territory. The
best were plain brick edifices erected toward the end of the
eighteenth century by Father Charles Sewall and Father James
Walton and their successors. Adornment was scant: a few simple statues and rather crude decorations. Usually the altar
linen, vestments, and other appurtenances were beautifully
cared for, since the people, both white and colored, took great
pride in keeping church and sacristy immaculately clean. Altar
societies were an old tradition of the mission, and the priest,
if he paid the slightest attention to his people, had no need

to suffer from shabby or soiled altar linens or injured vest-ments. The only appeal to the ear was the country choir and a few simple old sodality hymns sung at the various devotional meetings and the usual series of rather plain devotions, the rosary, occasional novenas, and once in a while a rousing mis-sion and a sermon. But no great pilgrimages, magnificent or-gans, or beautiful stained glass supplied those aids which helped to keep the Faith alive in the towns and countryside of Europe.

In the case of the Negroes the miracle of the preservation of the Faith was still more striking, for in a subdued and sober type of Catholic Christianity theirs was a still more subdued position. Yet they wore their proprietorship proudly and sel-dom complained that they did not share some of the religious advantages of their white brethren. The Negro choirs were of recent date and in general the Negroes had been content to sit in silence while the white choir did its best in the organ loft. At a Negro sodality meeting they sang the familiar hymns, but the spirituals were unknown. Evelyn Waugh's observa-tions about the Negroes of southern Maryland in his *Life* magazine account of U.S. Catholicism were blunt and some-what exaggerated, but nevertheless the tribute was justified.

Arcadian was the hospitality shown to the priest, traditional among the English Catholics and carried on by their success-ors. It was expected that the priest should feel free to stay at any house he wished where there was room to accommodate him, and he would be provided with clean linen, with quiet and what comfort could be afforded, and, of course, abun-dantly fed. Feeding the clergyman is an honored Anglo-Saxon tradition. It was said of the late Judge Freeman in the Seventh District of St. Mary's County that whenever a priest entered the Judge's front gate a chicken died in the back yard. If you stopped to talk to any of the inhabitants whether they were working in the fields or on the road or in the garden, they would request you to "light (alight) and go by." "Go by," meaning to stop. Families of the parish divided the task of providing a priest's breakfast and lunch, a combined meal after the late Mass on Sunday. This was called "eating the priest." The first time that I said a late Mass in one of our missions a sweet-looking little old lady dressed in black introduced herself as Mrs. Pettit with the startling remark: "Father, I am the lady who eats the priest during the month of August"; whereupon she produced a large hamper full of sandwiches, chicken, cold vegetables, salad, jellies, toast, and everything one could desire. The priest's horse was cared for and a little fodder was usually bestowed in the back of the buggy. Once a year a cart was driven around the parish, to which everybody contributed. Conveyances could be borrowed *ad libitum* since it was understood that when the priest wanted to go anywhere it was to move by the quickest and easiest way possible.

In times of trouble, provision was made for cases of dependent persons and for accidents which in more modern communities are taken care of by public agencies. True, there was and still is a poorhouse with its accompanying farm. This county poorhouse was known as the "Porus" house, which, incidentally, was not an ignorant mispronunciation of the word "poor" but derives from an old English pronunciation of poor with its accompanying genitive case. Very few people were sent to the "Porus" house. They were taken care of one way or another. Old folks lived with their children, pretty contented and happy as a rule. The mentally handicapped were also given special care.

For several months one winter in Leonardtown a curious whistle was heard at intervals. It sounded like a hoot owl. The whistle was blown by Jody Clements, a youth of low IQ. Jody had good will and came of a well-known local family, so it was decided to make him the town watchman with instructions to blow the whistle every half-hour. He stayed on the job until it was decided a town watchman was not needed since everybody knew pretty much what was going on anyhow. Despite his handicaps, Jody did not wish his condition to be exaggerated. On one occasion when he had been pretty sharply pushed, he remarked: "Perhaps I have no brains, but at least I've got an ounce of sense."

Maryland boasted an old tradition of sociability and conviviality. Church festivals and dances were part of religious life. These provided for the support of the Church and the priest, and on the other hand brought the people together socially. The Maryland Jesuits carried on the old English tradition of encouraging social life and dances for the young. The same tradition was brought into Kentucky by the early Dominican Fathers, which conflicted with the more austere ideas of the French missionary pioneers. This brought the priest close to his people, made him feel a sense of companionship and also enabled him to study them, and keep check on the sheep and the goats. On the other hand it meant being involved in what Father Kelly referred to as a thousand trifles. Innumerable were details about festival supplies, schedules of prices, and so on. In general it was for the best.

A picturesque feature of entertainment were the tournaments, where knights decorated with appropriate insignia rode their charges from opposing directions, spearing rings with the lance and carrying off the honors for their respective parishes—the Knight of St. John, Knight of the Sacred Heart, or Knight of Medley's Neck. Each one pledged loyalty to his queen and if he was the winner she was crowned the Queen of Love and Beauty. Election candidates, according to tradition, made campaign speeches at these tournaments, featuring a flowery Southern oration, with compliments to the fair ladies, God bless them, and much bombast about the glories and the beauties of southern Maryland, combined with a down-to-earth political appeal. The chargers were usually plain farm nags, though occasionally more highly bred horseflesh was enlisted.

When the Bishops of Canada issued their famous injunction against dances and entertainments of like nature under church auspices we were somewhat bewildered, since their example was supposed to be followed by the clergy in this country. We appealed, therefore, to the auxiliary Bishop of Baltimore, Most Rev. Owen B. Corrigan, who knew the country well since he had been down there many times on his Confirmation visits. Bishop Corrigan's directions were prompt and precise. Certainly, he said, dances were a matter for very careful attention by the Church and abuses should not be tolerated. It was the duty of the clergy first to see that these dances should be promoted if possible once every week, and secondly, a priest should always be present on the dance floor from the beginning to the end, the end to be at midnight. So that settled the question. And in general the idea of the Maryland pastorate was that the priest should be with the people first, last and always.

The people expected the priest to know their homes and take an interest in all their affairs. This in turn was a compliment, one might say, to one's life of celibacy. For a priest's celibacy is a true fatherhood, as that of the woman dedicated to life in a religous community is a genuine motherhood. The priest is emphatically not just a pious bachelor. He is wedded to the Saviour's work in this world, and celibacy is the obvious, congenial expression of the priest's relation to God and man. As a practical ideal, celibacy cannot be separated from a priest's inner life of prayer and self-denial, and it presupposes the vigorous cultivation of a manly, well-rounded character.*

One Christmas Eve I said Midnight Mass at St. Mary's Academy in Leonardtown. It was a still, frosty night. After the

* "To be reared in a Catholic country where celibacy in the service of God is regarded as a high vocation is a preparation for the life of celibacy; to be reared believing in a Protestant definition of human behavior that regards sex as regrettable but inevitable . . . is a very poor preparation for celibacy. To those so reared, celibacy is neither a privileged nor a tolerable state. . . .

"The Catholic position that both celibacy and marriage are holy states, that the body is not inherently evil, but that man must fight against himself to use that body wisely and well, permits a different sort of celibate adulthood." Margaret Mead, "Sex and Censorship in Contemporary Society." *New World Writing, Third Mentor Selection* (The New American Library, 1953), p. 9.

celebration of the Mass at the Academy where the girls had sung their carols I drove over the silent roads to the old chapel of St. Francis Xavier at Newtown Manor about six miles from Leonardtown. A gentle snow was falling and the carriage lamplight mildly illuminated the flakes. It would seem faint by our modern standards of automobile lights, but in those days it looked quite charming. Everything was absolutely peaceful. I crept into the big square bed at the old brick Manor House at Newtown, in the historic "Priest's room" where Jesuit missionaries for two centuries had slept before me, and celebrated the other two Masses the following morning. It had seemed to me, as I drove along that road, that there was a synthesis of pleasant pastoral life. There was plenty to do, it was quiet but active, and yet I felt in my heart that I must not yield to that state of mind, since a very different picture lay behind it all. There was much to be done and it would be fatal to taste a lotus leaf.

The physical handicap of transportation could not be left out of consideration. Only after the coming of the auto and good roads did we appreciate the amount of time and energy formerly used up in merely getting around the country by such means as were available by land or water.

It is hard to say whether the buggy was worse in summer or winter. In winter the only protection was a pre-heated brick or a charcoal stove at your feet. For rain you could attach a rubber curtain. Sophisticated buggy riders purchased various attachments from Sears, Roebuck and Montgomery Ward, such as a small electric battery and lamp and isinglass side curtains. In summer the dust, the green flies, horseflies, and mosquitoes descended upon man and beast alike. A standard article of clerical clothing was the long linen duster, time-honored in the Maryland Jesuit Province. With the Jesuit clergy the end of the horse and buggy era marked the passing of the linen duster. At country funerals the words, "Remember, man, that thou art dust and unto dust thou shalt return," applied in the present tense. A long line of fifteen or twenty buggies preceding the pastor filled the air with a yellow cloud and you choked as best you could. In summertime horses were soon exhausted under the relentless sun. Switching their tails and tangling them over the dashboard, they heaved their sweating sides and gasped as they plodded along the dusty road.

Yet the buggy had its compensations. You could pick up people along the road and you were not in danger of hitchhikers as you are with the auto. I picked up 106-year-old Aunt Pigeon one day, known more formally as Mrs. Mary Jones. Aunt Pigeon made her way every morning on foot from her little cottage to the church of St. Peter Claver at Ridge, a distance of about three quarters of a mile. She said that in her girlhood she had traveled on foot a good eight miles from Mr. Dominic Smith's plantation, near the southern extremity of the county, to old St. Ignatius Church. She and the other little colored girls—and it was during the slave days—went barefoot, carrying their linen dresses wrapped up in a bundle. When they approached the church they hid in the woods, put on shoes and stockings and little white dresses and attended Mass, and then reversed the process as they went home. I asked Aunt Pigeon how it was that she kept such wonderful vitality and cheerfulness at the ripe age of 106. She was the life of the place in a hundred different ways. "My prescription," she said, "is very simple. Just love God and dance. I have danced all my life." Aunt Pigeon told me she got her name because in her childhood she danced the Pigeon Wing. "Even now," she said, "when I am all alone, I hop around a bit for myself."

The long drives offered a chance to meditate, to think out sermons, plan lessons for instructing adults and children, or if you were of a literary mind you could think out an article. During those journeyings I began to ponder about the possible application of the social doctrine of the Church, of which I had heard so much during my Innsbruck years, to the problems of the world in which I was then living. I wondered whether some of the hardest nuts of a social kind might not be cracked if we really took earnestly the Church's social teaching and applied it to the human relations that I saw around me. Although things went along fairly calmly under a patriarchal form of life, those relations would become a source of discord and bitterness as soon as the place was opened up to the outside world. The young Negroes of the County whose fathers and mothers had been content to do odd jobs for present or former landlords, to help out on the tobacco farm or to do some work around the fishing boats, would feel very differently when they were obliged to seek occupations in the city and would run up against the stiff walls of racial discrimination. I wondered, too—the question haunted me—whether the Church might not speak definitely about the rural economy, whether a message could be obtained from the Church itself to enable the people to feel more pride in their land and more interest in keeping the integrity of their Catholic homes. These thoughts were pretty vague, yet they began to take some shape in my mind.

There was a certain compensation in the very leisureliness of the buggy. Of a summer night, if it was not too torrid and the moon was full, you rolled along the road under the richly fragrant locust trees while the dashboard light sent a feeble gleam ahead; or later in the season you passed the tobacco fields with their aromatic fragrance. The horse took care of himself. He knew his way back if you were on the homeward stretch, and even if you were leaving home, as a rule he had a pretty good idea where you were heading. In fact, it was sometimes a bit embarrassing, because old horses became so acquainted with the habits of their masters that you could guess where your predecessor spent his time. They liked to turn in at certain gates. Father Clem Lancaster, who had been twenty-one years in the County, left me his sorrel horse Morgan who was twenty-five years old. Despite his advanced age Morgan was still surprisingly active. It had been stone-deaf Father Lancaster's habit to stop and speak—a one-sided discourse—if he met anyone traveling in the opposite direction. Morgan would come to a dead stop when we met anyone, ex-

pecting a little conversation to be started up. It was a good
suggestion and I found myself falling into the same habit.
After all, if you stopped the passer-by always thought that you
really did want to talk to him, so I found myself in a little
while stopping and conversing with half the countryside. It
was one of those ways in which you can learn something from
a horse. When I first started to drive my Ford, it took time
to realize that the Ford had no memory, that holding the
wheel was not the same thing as holding the reins. You could
not depend on an auto to take you home or to avoid a false
turn or keep out of the ditch.

The most spectacular event in which the horse featured was
the Holy Thursday cavalcade instituted in Holy Week of 1912
by Father William Stanton, pastor of the mission churches of
Medley's Neck and Newtown. Father Stanton had been a val-
iant preacher on the Jesuits' New York-Maryland Province
mission band, and he loved doing big things in a big way.
Stocky of stature and with a full beard, astride a horse he
looked like General U. S. Grant. This resemblance annoyed
one of Father Stanton's chief parishioners, a vigorous farmer,
who admired Father Stanton's organizing power and zeal and
thoroughly enjoyed his magnificent sermons, but resented, as
he said, being bossed by anybody out of Boston, Massachusetts.
When in a mellower mood, however, he would ring up either
Father Stanton or myself on the party-line telephone and confide to us the two dominant themes of his emotion: he considered Cardinal Gibbons the greatest man that ever lived, or
else he would say plaintively, "I had a good mother, yes, I had
a *good* mother." That was usually the sign for a little more
personal admonition to be administered the following Sunday
by Father Stanton, who would recall to his parishioner what
his mother would doubtless have expected of him under present circumstances.

The cavalcade was organized in honor of the Saviour in the
Most Blessed Sacrament on Holy Thursday. It was a solemn
visit to the church and the Repository. The first participants

were the boys of Leonard Hall, the Xaverian Brothers grammar and high school nearby at Leonardtown. They were marshaled by Brother Gregory, C.F.X., and led by Father Stanton on his steed. Four banner bearers were decorated with blue and white sashes. The boys—all mounted—formed a hollow square before the church and were there addressed by the pastor Father Kelly, by Father Stanton, and myself. They then dismounted, entered the church and recited prayers before the Blessed Sacrament. In the following years of 1913, 1914, and 1915 the cavalcade grew, when young men and boys from the outlying parishes along with their parents were invited to participate.

Close to the spirit of the Holy Thursday cavalcade was that of the Corpus Christi Procession, which occurred for the first time as a public procession on June 16, 1912. Anyone visiting the town of Leonardtown on that occasion would have thought he was in some village of Bavaria or northern Italy. Protestant neighbors were kindly and reverent and care was taken not to give offense. It lacked the grandeur of the Corpus Christi procession at Innsbruck but also the bad impression afforded in Innsbruck by recalcitrant state officials. The procession started on the grounds of St. Mary's Academy and continued down the main street of the village to the front of St. Aloysius Church. All three altars were set up in the open air where the usual Benediction services were held. The altar boys, whom I had trained myself in the liturgical chant, furnished the music. White and colored, old and young took part in this solemn tribute to Our Saviour.

I wrote to Baroness Schönberg early in 1912, asking her if she could obtain a signed photo of Pope Pius X, with a blessing for the choir. In response to the petition which I composed for her, on July 6 of the same year a splendid photo arrived, with a five-line Latin message in the Holy Father's handwriting: "Cordially congratulating Our beloved children and begging for them from the Lord those rewards that are stored up for all who sing the divine praises, as a token of Our gratitude and good will we lovingly impart the Apostolic Benediction."

The Baroness wrote that she had been singularly fortunate in securing the message, when others were no longer able to obtain his signature. He sent his blessing, she said, not only to the boys and myself

but to the parish priest, and clergy, and *all the people*—to the whole parish most especially also. He sat at his writing table between the crucifix and statue of the Curé d'Ars, a wonderful picture of strength, and purpose, and humility. When I asked his prayers for someone afflicted with many trials and discouraged, he looked at the crucifix and said: "No day passes that trials, and very heavy ones, do not come to me. Tell this to ——. But one must never lose courage, never lose cheerfulness; always bow in humility to the Master's will. He wills it, and it is good."

I tell you privately, what you may know, as it has been in the papers:—but the Holy Father disclaims all merit, and does not wish the things mentioned in any way, through his prayers several miracles have been performed. Who knows but he will be canonized some day? A saint he is now.

The photograph was sent to Baltimore to be framed. It is now hung in the sanctuary of St. Aloysius Church.

The musical studies of my youth served me in good stead in my parish work, especially with the children. With the help of a cultivated and enthusiastic young couple who had recently settled in our neighborhood, Mr. and Mrs. Ralph Cullinan—he Irish, she Mexican—I managed to get organized the St. Aloysius Choral Club, a dramatic and musical society. Unexpected talent turned up among the young folk, and we gave some fairly creditable performances. My efforts at training a sanctuary choir at St. Aloysius Church inspired me to explore the theory of plain chant, the "ritual melody of the Church," as my friend Dr. Becket Gibbs so appropriately terms it. Opinions differ as to how far the chant can be made acceptable to a modern congregation, used to a different type of music. Within definite bounds, and through experience, I formed a rather optimistic idea on this point. But apart from such disputes, I could not reconcile myself to the fact that American Catholics, living in a country where traditional culture has a more or less Protestant flavor, should be indifferent to the vast *cultural* treasure of the Church's liturgical music; some of it echoing the folk-songs of ancient Ireland or the still more ancient melodies of the Jewish synagogue; much of it composed by saints and masters like Pope Gregory I; known by heart to Catholics of other nationalities; laden with historical associations; some of it borrowed by Christians of other denominations or appropriated by great musicians, such as Richard Wagner, who used it for his *leitmotifs*. The treasure is easily available and not over-mysterious; yet even to university-bred Catholics, it is practically a sealed book, many hardly knowing of its existence.

It seemed odd that it should take a convert to the Catholic faith, like Mrs. Justine Ward, to do spadework in arousing Catholic interest and appreciation of the chant, especially in the schools. She had explained to me in detail her "Justine Ward Method" for teaching the chant and teaching the fundamentals of vocal music at the same time, and I did some experimenting with her ideas. I found they worked, and some of her learning proved unexpectedly helpful.

On a visit to Washington in the winter of 1913, the idea occurred to me to call upon Father's old companion, Henry Adams. He was then living on H Street, in the historic John Hay residence. Miss Aileen Tone, his gifted secretary, and a friend of Mrs. Ward, had done considerable research for him in the field of medieval studies, when he was in Paris. Mr. Adams had received from France a consignment of medieval liturgical volumes, and counted on Aileen to find some explanation of the plain-chant notation which they contained. Aileen, at my visit, asked me if I could help, so I spent an hour with her at Mr. Adams's piano, explaining to her the basic ideas of the chant and its notation, as I had derived it from Dom Mocquereau, the great Solesmes Benedictine authority, through Mrs. Ward: the twofold movable clef (F or C) on the four-line staff; the equal note-length and the free rhythm; the varieties of accent and phrasing, etc.—enough to enable her to sing some of the melodies in turn to "Uncle Henry," as he was known to the "honorary nieces" like Miss Tone who assisted him in his work. For Aileen it was the introduction to a subject of lifelong interest.

Mr. Adams, who had already suffered a stroke, welcomed me warmly and, as Aileen observed later in retrospect, with a notable sense of liberation. We sat by the open fire in the big living room while he talked long and affectionately about Father, whose presence he greatly missed, even though—as I heard many years later—some slight estrangement had grown up between them not long before Father's death. On different occasions he had shown much interest in my life and work as a priest. A couple of months or so after my ordination in 1905, he had written from Paris to his niece, Mrs. Bancel LaFarge (Mabel Hooper):

Perhaps John will kindly stick me into his Mass. I need it more than you. I've not the least objection to being prayed for. For that matter I have no objection to being taken to all the churches there are. Why not? Any one of them is good enough for a sinner like me. I'm afraid the objection would come from the Church. In all my life I've never met a Church willing to touch me. After all, I have to belong to a State, under the same conditions, and have to pay my taxes and admire the Senators. My rule is to conform. It is the only path of freedom. . . .*

He indicated to me he was inwardly troubled, and was searching for a religious faith, yet it was not easy to press the matter further. One thing none could venture with Henry Adams, not even his nearest and dearest: that was to put to him any questions. I might have learned more if at the time I had known better the intimate, spiritual side of his nature that he partly disclosed to Mabel. I was hopeful that I could

* *Letters to a Niece,* by Mabel LaFarge (Houghton Mifflin, 1920), p. 113.

pay another visit and enjoy further conversation, but traveling from Leonardtown to Washington was not easy, and I did not see him again.

In his last months he deeply missed the company of Monsignor Sigourney Fay, secretary to Cardinal Gibbons, who was then visiting Rome. He had conversations with Monsignor Fay, and in the summertime at Beverly Farms would insist upon driving his priest-friend personally to the church every morning, though he would not enter while the Monsignor said Mass, and spent the time walking on the beach. On one occasion, a feast of the Blessed Virgin, he upbraided the Monsignor for casually remarking that he would put off reciting his daily breviary office until they had returned from their afternoon drive. "Our Blessed Lady," said Adams, "will not tolerate that sort of thing. Today is her feast and she wants her office said in time. Please go up to your room and finish it, and then we can take our drive." As Father Fay left to fulfill this imperative command, Adams added, in a grave manner: "She is my *only* hope."

It seems evident that Henry Adams's religious convictions were more definite than his somewhat elusive exterior gave the world to believe. If there is doubt on the matter—and some-one can always make a case for skepticism—certainly the benefit of the doubt would seem to rest with one who could write the passionate "Prayer to the Virgin of Chartres," which was found after his death in a little wallet of special papers. "These verses," said Mabel, "were apparently written just after the *Chartres* book and while he was contemplating the *Education*, and were shown by him to only one friend, a 'sister in the twelfth century.' One can understand that he did not care to publish them during his lifetime for he did not wish to lift the veil. In this 'Prayer' Henry Adams makes an act of faith in the Son's divinity."*

---

* *Letters to a Niece*, pp. 26-27.

The "sister," of course, was the late Mrs. Winthrop Chanler, herself a lover of the plain chant, as indeed of all things fair and holy.

Aileen Tone, however, had learned of these verses * during his lifetime, as did Mrs. Ward Thoron (Mabel's sister, Louley Hooper), to whom he sent the only other copy. Remarking that he considered himself really more of an artist and poet than anything else, he had asked Aileen to remove the packet of manuscripts containing them from a drawer in the huge desk in the Washington home. After warning her that he would probably break down from emotion and be unable to continue, he started to read the verses, but soon was too overcome to continue. "Take them up to your room," he told her, "and finish them for yourself."

When Adams's faith sought personal outlet, however, it encountered a wall of self-centered secretiveness: the painful fruit of a lifetime's disillusionment and inward revolt—against the age, against American jingoism, against the political scene in Washington, against his own personal limitations. In his riper years when under normal circumstances some sort of stoical philosophy might have enabled him to break from his shell, "Uncle Henry" was utterly crushed and driven in upon himself by the tragic death of his wife.

Not unlike Simone Weil, child of a later generation, Adams seems to have rationalized, as it were, his own inner hesitation—or refusal. He spoke of himself as a Catholic. To a friend who asked him what particular "church" he meant when he talked of "the Church," Adams scornfully replied that the question was pointless, since there could be and was but one Church.

Singularly enough, the intimates who surrounded Henry Adams in his latest years were mostly persons who themselves

* The verses contain the prophetic "Prayer to the Dynamo," in which the atom gives godlike power to its master, the American people (for whom Adams speaks), only to slay us: "Seize, then, the Atom! rack his joints! / Tear out of him his secret spring!"

early or late, in one way or another, had passed through the
lowly portal that confronts everybody who begs of the Church
the gift of eternal life: John LaFarge, Daisy Chanler, Justine
Ward, Mabel LaFarge, Sigourney Fay, Aileen Tone. . . .

Adams closed his life peacefully, in his sleep, keeping his
secret to himself. I have never been interested in wishful spec-
ulation on matters that remain a closed book. The perfection
of life's end is measured not by the absence of suffering, but by
the sincere sorrow and humble hope with which we go to meet
our Creator. "Uncle Henry" may have found his way before
the end into the Catholic faith, if not by explicit profession,
at least implicitly by a true spirit of penance and genuine desire. I was content to leave it that way, and after my return
to Leonardtown to say Mass for his soul.

As I continued in my work of catechizing and home visiting,
I became more and more aware of three outstanding problems
which lay concealed under the peaceable exterior of the St.
Mary's County community. The first was the deplorable condition of the schooling; the second was the condition of the
local Negroes; and the third was the rural life problem.

The public schools, with very rare exceptions, were mere
one-room schools, inadequate for the white children and a
mere farce, in many cases, for the colored. Some of the colored
schools ran only four months of the year, weather permitting,
and the teachers in some instances were themselves not educated beyond the fourth or fifth grade. The public-school teachers were, many of them, noble and devoted people. They
tackled a tough task, managing anything from four to seven
or eight grades in one room, and did surprisingly well under
the circumstances, but the circumstances were impossible. The
few youths of the patrician class, so to speak, could obtain an
education outside by attending Mount St. Mary's in Emmitsburg, Georgetown University, or other Jesuit schools. The
girls, again of the "better" classes, attended St. Mary's Academy in Leonardtown. Strangely enough, after 300 years there

were no Catholic parish schools. It is true that sometime in the
'70s Father Pye Neale, I believe it was, had attempted a school
with a lay teacher in the neighborhood of Great Mills, but it
only lasted a short time, though the blackboards and desks still
remained in my time. At Leonardtown itself, Saint Mary's
Academy for girls, and Leonard Hall School for boys fulfilled
some of the functions of a parish school. But they charged
tuition and many children could not attend them.

In view of my budding concern about the rural life question, my interest was aroused in the work of the Xaverian
Brothers who conducted Leonard Hall Academy one mile to
the north of our Rectory in Leonardtown. They had obtained
a fine piece of property there and had begun work the year
before Father Kelly arrived on the scene. His predecessor, Father Edward X. Fink, S.J., had urged the Xaverian Brothers
to start an Agricultural School, since he, too, was conscious
of the rural life problem. It also was a finishing school for
the youth of the parish.

As the school chaplain, I said Mass there every morning,
and gave a weekly talk to the boys. I found the work there
so interesting that on one occasion, after giving my afternoon
conference, around three o'clock, I forgot that I had come
with a horse (who was tied to a tree outside in the usual manner) and walked home, ate supper and eventually went to
bed. Just as I was drifting off to sleep (it was a pleasant summer
evening), I recalled that the poor animal was still standing
tied to the tree. I rose, walked the mile to the school, found
him angrily champing the bit and pawing the ground with
his feet, and brought him home to his oats and hay.

As for the Negroes, I obtained a better perspective of their
condition and their needs—which I shall speak of later—after
I had been transferred to the southern section of St. Mary's
County. This transfer resulted from the opening of a new field
of work, that of ministering to the recently arrived Slav colonists * at St. Mary's City.

* See Appendix I.

I first learned about the colonists in 1914, and immediately
my curiosity was aroused. Father Emerick informed Father
Kelly that these people were in great distress. Many of them
could not speak English, and there were many Catholics among
them. As I had already acquired some facility in speaking
Polish, I concluded that the Slav language could not be difficult to master. Accordingly, I got in touch with Father Emerick
and some of his parishioners who were acquainted with the
Slav colony, and paid a visit to them.

My first contact with the Slavs was from the James H. Carroll home on St. Inigoes Creek. The Carrolls arranged for one
of the leaders of the Slav colony, Mr. John Balta, to meet me
with horse and buggy. Mr. Balta drove me through the colony
and introduced me to all the members on the different farms.
Father Emerick had already set up a small structure, a future
chapel, to be used for catechism instruction at a place about
two miles toward Chesapeake Bay from St. Mary's City. St.
Mary's City was the first capital of the old Maryland Colony,
when it contained, it was said, sixty houses. In the year 1702
the capital was removed to Annapolis. The place had disappeared, even as a village. All that remained was a Protestant
church, a few large farms in the neighborhood, and a non-
sectarian girls' boarding school, St. Mary's Female Seminary.

Though the newcomers impressed the old-timers by the dili-
gence with which they used their large prayer books, and by
other signs of devotion, they were looked upon with some suspicion as foreigners out of another world. As people got to
know the Slavs, feelings became more friendly. Storekeepers
commented that Slavs paid their bills at once, in cash, and
fulfilled all their business agreements.

Father Emerick and I arranged a Mass at the little chapel,
which he had baptized St. James Chapel, after Father James
Brent Matthews, who was superior of the St. Inigoes Mission.
The Slavs were welcomed and responded generously. I
preached a Slav sermon as best I could, heard confessions, and
gave them Holy Communion. Most of them were agreeable

to deal with. The women seemed to be somewhat more refined
and intellectual than the men. Throughout my experience
with the Slav people, I was always impressed by the fine bearing of their womenfolk.

From the religious point of view, the colonists presented a
puzzling spectacle. Certain families, indifferent at first, became
active and practicing Catholics later on. The Czech families,
five in number, were fanatical Hussites, who brought their
antagonisms from the old country. They were also influenced
by propaganda (see Appendix I) that impaired the faith and
practice of at least six of the Slovak families, and turned them
into hostile and often pugnacious enemies of the Church. I
welcomed the opportunity to bring some spiritual aid to this
group of colonists, for whom their own National Slavonic Society had made no spiritual provision.

CHAPTER TEN

Glory Lit the Midnight Air

⇶ ⇷

On September 2, 1915, I was transferred to the other mission center of St. Mary's County, located on St. Inigoes Manor. The residence of the mission was on Priests' Point, at the mouth of St. Inigoes Creek, where it joins the St. Mary's River. The Jesuits had moved to St. Inigoes in 1702, when the Catholic colony came to an end and St. Mary's City was removed to Annapolis. The original manor house, built in 1730, a large structure in traditional colonial style with a spacious central hallway and then two smaller wings, had burned in the year 1878 and only the wing remained. With the burning of the manor house many valuable records perished. The remaining structure consisted of a few rooms and a chapel of later date. We took our meals in the housekeeper's frame house nearby. Some grand old pecan trees planted by an early missionary shaded the lawn with its magnificent cluster of box bushes. At the gate of the residence stood a handsome fig tree, prolific in luscious fruit.

At St. Inigoes were only two others in the community, Father James Brent Matthews, the Superior, who had charge of the missions of St. George and St. Nicholas, and Father Abraham J. Emerick, a veteran ex-missionary in Jamaica, B.W.I., who cared for the missions of nearby St. Ignatius and St. Michael's at Ridge and St. George's Island. I was entrusted with the new plan for the Slavs and other parishioners at St. James's, as well as helping out in the various other missions as might be needed.

181

It was three miles by a dusty road from St. Inigoes Villa to the Post Office at St. Inigoes, where our only telephone connection was. One mile on the way to St. Inigoes Post Office was St. Ignatius Church, built by Father James Walton in 1790. It was then in fair condition, and had been restored and improved at various times. (Later on the church was abandoned for practical purposes. Recently, through the zeal of Lieutenant Commander Chaplain Cunningham of the Potomac Air Base, voluntary labor of officers and men, and the cooperation of the local clergy, the chapel has been restored as an historic monument.) In old colonial style, the Negroes occupied pews in a gallery extending almost to the altar on both sides. The ground floor box pews of the church extended on both sides of the altar. The altar itself was raised by several steps, and standing there one had a curious sensation of hovering between heaven and earth. The pews in the gallery and the pews beneath were an equal distance from the preacher, which helped to emphasize gestures.

We celebrated Mass at St. Ignatius on the second and fourth Sundays of the month. In the afternoon I would board a sailboat at the wharf of the manor residence, sail two or three miles across the broad expanse of the St. Mary's River over to St. George's Island, a low-lying, sandy, wooded tract of land between the river and the Potomac, and say Mass on Monday morning for the people of the Island. On the fifth Sunday of the month I visited the Holy Face Church at Great Mills. This oddly shaped old wooden structure owed much to the benefaction of Mrs. Maria Cecil, a parishioner who had great devotion to the sacred countenance of Jesus as depicted traditionally on Veronica's Veil. The old church no longer exists, and its place has been taken by a handsome modern structure on the nearby hill, with rectory and parish school.

The Negro parishioners were mostly descendants of former slaves from the old manor or were from the neighborhood. Most of the colored people followed a three-fold economy.

They would work one-third of the year as farm hands, another third as fishermen or oystermen on the nearby St. Mary's River and tributaries, and the other third they would give to tending their own patch of farm land around their homes. Near St. Ignatius was a small settlement, partly Negro, called Beachville, with tidy little homes and gardens. Among the Negroes of the parish were a number of outstanding personalities. An inspired missionary whom I have mentioned earlier, Father Pye Neale, S.J., himself a member of one of the old historic Maryland families, had helped in the '70s to develop among them a sense of cohesion and solidarity, by founding for them a well-organized beneficial society, parent of other such societies among the Negroes of southern Maryland.

From the earliest period mentioned down to the time when I first came in contact with their descendants, the Negroes had been considered by the Jesuit missionaries as entitled to the same degree of spiritual ministration as the whites. Their homes were visited individually, their children carefully cate-chized, their sick taken care of, both physically and spiritually, and the sacrament of marriage was scrupulously promoted and safeguarded. As far back as 1749 Father George Hunter dur-ing his annual retreat noted that "Charity to Negroes is due from all, particularly their masters." Father Hunter also estab-lished some sort of a school for Negro children where they would be taught some simple vocational skills.*

The older Negroes, like old folk everywhere, liked to talk of bygone days, even the days of slavery before the Civil War. They referred to the slave days usually as the "bad times," spoke with great affection of benevolent masters, and recalled unkind, even vicious masters, who inflicted long and painful hours of work and harsh treatment. Another set of reminis-cences turned around the disagreement that occurred with the origin of St. Peter Claver parish and led to the establish-ment of a separate church for the Negroes. Father Tynan, S.J.,

* See Appendix II.

the pastor of St. Michael's, was so concerned at this event that he closed St. Michael's Church for several weeks and hung crepe on the church door.

The old people spoke with great bitterness of a tragic event which occurred in 1838. Some of the slaves from the manor property were sold to slave merchants who carried them to Louisiana and Georgia. This was one of those unfortunate instances where fundamentally well-meaning people blunder into an act objectively of real cruelty. Such blunders are largely due to officialdom and negligence in considering all the contingencies and human factors. In 1833 the Maryland Mission of the English Province became a separate Province with Father McSherry, S.J., as its Provincial. One of his first concerns was this matter of the ownership of slaves. The matter was represented to the Father General in Rome and in 1836 Father General decreed that they should be sold, laying down certain humane conditions to be strictly observed.

The execution of the sale was entrusted to Father Thomas Mulledy, then head of the Maryland Province, an excellent priest and a distinguished educator, who seems nonetheless to have been singularly short-sighted in the way he went about it. An agreement was made in 1838 with two apparently honorable individuals from Louisiana, Dr. Batey and Governor Johnson. The Negroes were sold to these gentlemen and transferred to Georgia and Louisiana. Plans, however, worked out badly. The Negroes from Maryland were deprived of ordinary ministrations, and were without priest or church. As a consequence the majority of the descendants of the Maryland ex-slaves drifted away from the Catholic faith and were brought up as Methodists or Baptists.

Of the original manor slaves only two families remained, one in Charles County, the Suetons, and in St. Mary's the descendants of Aunt Louisa Mason and her husband Bob. This matriarch, the mother of eighteen children, was buried at St. Ignatius Church in 1910, the most elaborate funeral, it was said, that had ever been celebrated at that church, and it was my first experience of a funeral in southern Maryland. Aunt Louisa would never admit emancipation. She held that in her own right she was always attached both to the Jesuit property and to the Society of Jesus itself. Moreover, she was attached not to the manor property as such but to the Glebe farm, which was the farm reserved for the use of the mission-aries themselves, as distinguished from the other farms which were at the service of the Jesuit Province. She referred to her-self always as a "Glebe slave." As a person affiliated with the Order she insisted that each year when the Father Provincial came she should be included in his annual visitation of the residence and be permitted to render to him her spiritual account for the past year.

Of her numerous family none were more respected than two wonderful old ladies, Mrs. Charity Lee and Mrs. Josie Barnes. Mrs. Barnes's husband, Daniel Oliver Barnes, died in 1931 at the age of seventy. For a time he had conducted a parochial school for the colored children. It had only run for two or three years, to my recollection. But his teaching had nevertheless made an impression. Charity Lee's husband, Ham Lee, was not living in my day. He had been, said his wife, "a fiddler and an oysterman, a musician and a farmer on the land."

The following items I recall from conversations with the two old ladies as well as with centenarian "Aunt Pigeon" (Mrs. Mary Jones), Columbus Butler, and a few other old-timers. I noted some of them at the time and my successor, Father Horace B. McKenna, S.J., checked on others in later years, when he also talked to the Negroes of winter evenings.

Aunt Louisa Mason's mother was a pure African. Her father wanted such a person as a wife. Her mother was an orphan child and was treated so badly that a man called Henry Mahoney pitied her and married her. Harry Mahoney, he must have been an Irishman once upon a time. Nobody knows where the Mahoneys came from. One of Aunt Louisa's uncles, Robert Mahoney, said he wouldn't serve nobody. His master, who was a very nice man, said he had done enough work and so he could go. In order to get freedom, you worked yourself out of slavery. And so Robert Mahoney who was a working person did jobs as a carpenter, and he bought himself the freedom of his wife and his youngest daughter. Robert's youngest child, who was smarter than he was, went North to Philadelphia.

Robert returned before Henry Mahoney's death to see him. He then heard another daughter was coming from Philadelphia on a visit. Then he got frightened because it was possible that if he didn't do something about it the Paddyrollers would catch her. The Paddyrollers (patrols): they were men who used to ride around on horseback and keep the slaves from running away, or bring them back if they escaped. And so he had to think out a plan. He put a cover over his head so he couldn't see his daughter. Robert was always very truthful, so he gave the girl enough money to go back North, and then he told the searchers when they came around that he hadn't seen her. "Where is your daughter?" said the Paddyroller. "I haven't seen her," said Robert. And true it was, he hadn't seen her. And they weren't smart enough to know that he was telling the truth.

Some of Aunt Louisa's ancestors were called Joyce, and they were from away back and they came from England. And Father Zwinge,* he said the tradition was that they came over in Lord Baltimore's time, and that Lord Baltimore gave the Joyces to old Father Thomas Copley who came right after Father Andrew White. The priests used to come and talk with Aunt Josie's mother, who had "an elegant memory" so it must have been the truth. Grandpa Harry Mahoney was a saving man and so he saved the house, which we still have today.

* The Rev. Joseph Zwinge, S.J., the treasurer of the Jesuit Province who had charge of the farms.

Daniel Barnes, like Ham Lee, too was an oysterman when he was young and a farmer at fifty cents a day. He built his mother's house, and then he built him his own house, because his wife Josie made him rent a place belonging to Prophet Medley, a Methodist, and she wouldn't go into her mother's house. Josie and Charity helped the husbands to grub up and make a garden. They had food all through the winter, cabbage, potatoes, two or three hogs up to April. They had a barrel of meal and a barrel of flour and had very little money. Now people say it's too hot to work one day. Then another day people say it's too cold to work. People today are always fussy and never contented. They are always worrying. People in old days didn't do so much worrying. Well, maybe the work made us rheumatic, and perhaps it gave Josie strength to survive to be seventy-eight years old. People can't make out in the city unless they have a steady job, because they have everything to buy. So now they have to go on relief. Some of this was in the Depression days but Josie says that relief is bad, except for the old and helpless. Relief makes people less independent. People had only little in the old days, and they wanted little. And some say that they were better off. But we cannot go back to the old days; we must take care of ourselves.

Before the [Civil] War the common schools were very good. Children were tougher. Late after the War there were colored schools, a good many schools, and they all had men teachers. Houses in the old times were better. Colored people had log houses and mud floors. They were plain and they were small, but they were solidly built and they didn't shake with the wind. The Negro children had no shoes. When you were grown up you got one pair at Christmastime. When these shoes wore out folks went barefooted until Christmas came again. Clothing was all one piece and it was wool. No one then bought stockings or suspenders.

There were not many Jesuit Fathers around then. People did not have so many priests to care for them as they have today. Father Pacciarini came once a month. He was large and stout. Father Vigilante was tall and thin. All the Fathers were pleasant. Much land has grown up since the [Civil] War. One-third more land was worked in those days than is worked today. Now the trouble is you can't get labor. Before the War there was more labor and there was more money. The white children all had shoes and plenty of clothing. Well, every generation is weaker and wiser. They drank as much then as they do now, but they didn't drink in the stores and on the roads. They always had it at home. Just because it was there they didn't bother about it so much and didn't drink so much in public.

The old folk then did more practice of the Faith. The young folks in those days wanted to go to church. Said Charity Lee, people wouldn't stay in church to hear Father Vigilante preach. He was a good old soul but they couldn't understand him. Some priests preached long; some of them less. The life of people as regards goodness and kindness was just about what it is today. They did not, it is true, practice frequent daily or weekly Communion. But, said Charity Lee, they need Holy Communion nowadays as a protection against wickedness. In fact, we need all the grace that the good Lord can give us.

Some priests were harder and some were gentler than others. Father Carberry was gentle. Father Thomas Lilly and Father David Walker were harder. Folks in those days knew the catechism. They had catechism Saturday afternoons in St. Inigoes Church. Uncle Bob Mason used to learn his daughter Josephine, up the road. White and colored were all in the same Sunday school. So it was at St. Michael's in Father Tynan's time, though they were not in the same classes. The whites sat on one side, and colored on the other. Father Gubitosi* was kind and he taught Josephine Barnes her ABC's.

Before the War white people were wealthy. The Dominic Smiths' Negroes and the Campbells' Negroes had plenty to

* Later in the Denver, Colorado, Jesuit mission.

eat and clothes. So they made a little money. They could have a little land and grow things on the side, vegetables and poultry, and sell them to people. And they could do extra jobs and they could go fishing, and they had little enterprises of their own. The colored people in Jarboesville had horses and were free. The Paddyrollers, who were whites, beat the Negroes to death. This was before the War.

The Negroes never forgave Father Mulledy for selling them into exile in Louisiana and Georgia. Father General had said to get rid of slavery, but he told them to do it as easy as possible. They weren't to do anything harsh or wicked. Father Carberry was terribly unhappy over it. He prayed and he prayed and he pleaded with the Fathers and begged that such a dreadful thing might not happen. He told the folks that he was praying, and asked them to pray with him. But they outvoted him; they went over his head and Father Carberry's heart was broken. When the time came for the wicked men to take the Negroes away, Father Carberry warned some of them about it and so a few of them escaped, went into the woods and there they lived in starvation and thirst for days so they could escape the slave traders who were after their bodies and lives. People wept and cried when the ship came that took them away. Once they were gone the people who had stayed came out of the woods and Father Carberry welcomed them; he was so happy that at least some had escaped. He was a good and holy man. Why were there not more like Father Carberry?

Father Tynan started the Sodality of the Blessed Virgin for white people at St. Michael's. The white people didn't take hold of the Sodality. It was something new, and they didn't like anything new. So Father Tynan started one for the colored at St. Michael's about 1902. St. Peter Claver's Hall was built for entertainment and it was built also to be used by the Sodality. It had been built for two or three years before the colored people had left St. Michael's and used it as a parish church.

The trouble at St. Michael's was at Christmas about 1905. Mrs. B. said she couldn't play the organ after any colored person had used it; so Father Tynan told her to play at the Christmas Mass and she refused even that. So the colored people played at the late Mass Christmas day and then some young white men praised their singing, especially Agnes Biscoe's singing of the hymn: "Glory Lit the Midnight Air." Then they all disputed in church at the door and Father Tynan told the colored to go to St. Peter's. He told all of them to go, but some colored still went to St. Michael's for a while, and occasionally they would drop in to Mass on the way to work, would go there for the First Friday when the priest was not at St. Peter's. Mass was every other Sunday at St. Peter's and they would stay home on the odd Sunday. On every Sunday they had Sodality meeting except in winter. Father Tynan kept the crepe on the door for a month and it worried Mrs. Herbert, the St. Michael's sacristan.

(Another witness to the past was Mrs. Mary Swann Welch, aged ninety, whom Father McKenna interviewed on July 29, 1934, in Charles County, near Bel Alton, Maryland.) At the time of the War, said Mrs. Welch, she was ten years old. There were so many soldiers; they were always on the road. They were good-mannered men. She used to help in looking for Mrs. Surratt, the boarding-house keeper who had harbored Abraham Lincoln's assassin, Wilkes Booth. Before the War, as was said by Mrs. Barnes and Mrs. Lee, there was more money. People got along better; they had more money and more things. They made better crops. People did not have to work so hard. Nobody was stuck up over the others. Now if you ain't got plenty of money you ain't got nothing. They had the same crops in those days as they have today: corn, tobacco, and wheat. "Everybody" owned at least one or two slaves. Her father had six slaves. Some had a hundred. Some on every farm.

This last item reminds me of a fact often forgotten, that quite a number of the free colored people themselves kept slaves.

The buying and the purchasing of slaves became so completely a matter of commercial economy that nothing about it seemed incongruous. Similarly, no one thought it incongruous when the Carmelite nuns at Port Tobacco in 1790 brought a few slaves into the convent farm as their dowry.

On Decoration Day each year the Negroes visited the old cemetery adjacent to St. Ignatius Church on St. Inigoes Manor and adorned the graves of those who had died in the wars. On this occasion Father Brent Matthews would deliver a stirring speech urging them, as was his wont when he could talk informally outside the church, to make themselves economically independent. As expressed in their own words he was "a great advocate of horses, getting property and getting deed for it. He spoke thus more than any of the others." A practical farmer himself, he believed that they should get away from the hand-to-mouth, garden-patch existence which dated from slave days. After his address the Negro parishioners would file down a winding path behind St. Ignatius Church to the little harbor of Church Cove with its tangled honeysuckle, its boxwood and laurel bushes and tiny sandy beach. There they threw flowers into the water for those who had died for their country and were buried at sea.

The plain fact was that the interests, spiritual or temporal, of the Negro in that region could never be handled in any rational and Christian manner save by men of imagination, energy, and a certain imperviousness to the terrific claims of timidity and human respect. No easy formula existed in the past; none exists today, and in all probability there will be none in the future. No matter how tactful and apologetic the pastor might be, he was told that he was moving the Negro "out of his place" the moment he treated him as a human being. He came in conflict at once with an age-old tradition by which Negroes were not to be considered as persons in their own right but only as persons subject to another's right, as servants.

What added to the complication were the feelings of discontent and resentment that plagued the white population as well. As countrymen they were neglected by the city; as white Catholics of English-speaking descent they were in a small minority amid the vast Protestant population in the United States and for that reason they stood at a certain disadvantage in the face of a well-entrenched Protestant minority in the section, old land-holding families with a high social status. And the Negro Catholics were at a certain disadvantage as a tiny island of Catholicism, as it were, in the great sea of Negro Protestants in the United States.

The tragedy is not so much that any great mistakes were made. The Fathers were conscientious men, kindly men, men of pure and devoted lives. Some of them were honestly bewildered by the rural and Southern atmosphere, coming from Northern and often scholastic environments; others more knowledgeable of the South were over-comfortable in the companionship, spiritual rather than physical, of the white majority. No, the tragic element is rather that positive, bold, and constructive steps were not taken at a much earlier date when simpler means would have accomplished such a vast amount of good. This was particularly true in the field of education. Imposing as were the Jesuit educational achievements elsewhere, they were, practically speaking, of no aid at all in the educational problem that faced the Maryland missionary. As far as education was concerned, he worked in a vacuum. The work was to be accomplished not by striking a few heroic poses, not by the bull in the ecclesiastical china-shop. It could only be the fruit of patient and determined and planned effort.

Let me add that there were always men and women among the white population of the parish who showed themselves singularly free of a narrow and prejudiced attitude toward the colored people. Some of these were educated persons who benefited by outside contacts; but some were just honest Catholics who knew their faith and practiced it integrally in one of its most difficult and sensitive areas. Social disapproval is hard to endure under any circumstances, but it is well-nigh intolerable in an old Southern community of English descent.

Only when one has lived in such a community does one realize what stings and barbs can sink into a sensitive soul from a few choice sneering remarks. As I have met and known these persons who resisted prejudice over the years—and some of them, thank God, today—I certainly respect them. The bitter and prejudiced people are a minority, small, but noisy and aggressive. The trouble was and still is in such communities that this minority so easily takes the lead and sways a large number of people who are fundamentally well disposed but are simply unable to face any strong form of marked disapproval. The person—clergyman or layman—who yields and is obsequious to the noisy demagogue may suffer inwardly but avoids outward trouble. It is the old story of the rise of all political passions and ideologies.

I was once asked by a prominent Catholic missionary who had devoted his life to work among the colored, "Why is it that we missionaries know so little about the Negroes? I and my companions," he said, "have worked for a lifetime among the Negroes but their minds still remain to us a closed book. Have you had the same experience?"

I told him emphatically not. Individuals among Negroes as among whites or any group of people were reticent or deceitful, but I never found particular difficulty in ascertaining their point of view. I hinted that possibly his difficulty arose because they sensed that he had a very definite theory as to where the Negro should be, what his "place" was and that he should not be moved out of that place. Naturally in talking to a man who believed that the Negro should always be "kept in a certain place," they would be secretive.

The question of separation or segregation did not arise in southern Maryland at that time. The attitude of the Negroes was rather one of pride in whatever institutions they had. They referred with enthusiasm to the schools and churches that had been established for them in Washington, Baltimore, and Philadelphia. They spoke with pride of their own church, their own nuns, acolytes, church organizations and of their own priests, whenever the latter visited them. But Negroes in southern Maryland, and throughout the nation, came deeply to resent any attitude on the part of white co-religionists which would seize upon the establishment of "special works" for the Negro as an excuse for excluding them from places of worship attended by the whites, or would assign to them an unequal status in such places of worship if admitted.

Lasting without shadow of change was the record of that great flame of faith that for three centuries had glorified the lives of Maryland's black folk. Nevertheless, patriarchal conditions were vanishing. Without adequate schools, the Faith would perish, and the folk themselves would be defrauded of their legitimate development.

CHAPTER ELEVEN

The Ridge Schools

⤜⤚

In the fall of 1916 I started celebrating Mass at St. James's on alternate Sundays. In this way the people of the vicinity, whether Slavs or native whites or Negroes, could practice their religion. The meeting place had been inaugurated by Father Emerick merely as a catechetical center and entertainment hall. It was his belief, as an old Jamaica missionary, that you should always start by ringing a bell, sounding the Angelus, and letting the evil spirits know they were no longer wanted around the premises. Accordingly, his first procedure had been to purchase a bell and erect a tower for it outside the church. The windows of the plain box-like structure had originally belonged to the old church of St. Ignatius on the Manor. Later on I was able to house the bell in a proper tower erected over a vestibule in the front of the church. Through the kindness of Mother Katharine Drexel, Foundress and Superior of the Sisters of the Blessed Sacrament for Indians and Negroes, I was able to build a commodious sacristy back of the church with a priest's room over it. There I would sleep when I had any particular work to do at the church.

From the Manor residence a narrow red clay road led through a dense and lonely forest. The Slavs got together and helped us to clear the land. A couple of stumping bees with a windlass laboriously extracted the tree roots. A new barn sheltered the horse and buggy and a corn crib over it was well stocked with corn provided by the parishioners, while a nice black snake dwelt in the corn crib for the purpose of discouraging rats and other marauders.

We had as yet no water, so I engaged the services of old Rufus Hughes, otherwise known as Froggy, an elderly long-bearded Negro who went barefoot and was supposed to be infallible in discovering water. He was supposed to use a divining rod, but actually he would trace where two lines of vegetation crossed and at the juncture he would place a well. He found such a juncture in front of the church and, sure enough, we hauled up abundant, cold, and delicious water, although muddy in appearance. If you closed your eyes, you were satisfied with the drink.

Collections were small at St. James's, hardly a dollar or so, but grew as time went on. This was supplemented by a dollar-a-month envelope contributed by the families of the parish, instead of the traditional pew-rent. Small as were the cash offerings, service and personal care were generous. The house-keeping of my quarters over the sacristy was managed by a colored neighbor, Mrs. Rosie Hawkins, who still resides in the neighborhood. Mrs. Ida Cullison, a white lady with a numer-ous family of boys and girls, was at hand for all emergencies. Particularly helpful was the unfailing hospitality of a culti-vated Baltimore family. The summer home—some three miles distant—of Mrs. Carroll B. Blick and her gifted daughters was a sort of oasis in the desert. The entire family sought from me instruction in the Catholic faith, and I received them into the Church, along with their English governess, Miss Lawrence.

Miss Nanny Hebb, a young lady who had been teaching at the now defunct one-room district school in the vicinity, opened a school for the white children, with Miss Clementine Clarke (now a Sister of Mercy in Baltimore, Sister M. Carmel) as her assistant. On weekdays, a large canvas curtain was let down in front of the altar and the church building was used for a school. We started off happily with about sixty children.

On the following January 2, 1917, I opened the Negro

school, for which I had obtained five and a half acres of property from a firm on the Maryland Eastern Shore. It was a rainy
day and the teacher, Mrs. Jenny Beale, had but one pupil.
Anyone else would have been discouraged or depressed under
those circumstances, but not so Mrs. Beale. With unfailing
instinct she knew that once the school was started it could not
help but grow. She was placid, imperturbable in her manner,
with a gentle voice and a fine sense of humor. She had attended
the convent school of the colored Sisters, the Oblates of Providence, on East Chase Street in Baltimore, and had never lost
her love of culture and her boundless belief in the capacities
of the colored children. The more ragged and disreputable
their outward shape, the more she was convinced that you
could train them. She taught them good manners, how to take
care of themselves and become really fine representatives of
their race. Once while walking through the forest I heard a
small boy shouting among the scrub pines: "Where's you
gwine?" And another small boy answered immediately: "Doan'
say gwine. Say go-ing": a typical sign of Miss Jenny's work.

As yet I had not made my third probation, or tertianship,
which comes in the Society after Ordination to the priesthood
and the completion of theological studies. For those who enter
as priests, as I did in 1905, the tertianship is usually made
about ten years after entrance.

So I began my tertianship on the first of September in 1917
at St.-Andrew-on-Hudson, Poughkeepsie, New York. Instructor of tertians was the gifted preacher Father John H.
O'Rourke. The tertianship is called *schola affectus,* the school
of the heart. One reviews the early lessons of the novitiate
in the light of experience and the responsibilities of the future.
The Long Retreat is made for another thirty days and the
Institute of the Society is studied and explained. A number
of other features characterize the year. In general it is a time
for laying a second spiritual foundation for one's life work.
The tertianship is a profound provision of the founder of the

Society of Jesus and has been adopted in one form or another
by other religious communities both of men and of women.
St. Alphonsus Liguori, founder of the Congregation of Re-
demptorist Fathers, prescribed a similar period of rejuvena-
tion.

Memorable for me in that year was walking across the frozen
Hudson at 25° below zero and preaching at the funeral of the
saintly Mother F. X. Cabrini, later canonized. She was interred
temporarily at the mother house of her order at West Park,
New York, where in 1906, during my noviceship, I had
preached my first retreat.

The tertianship, apart from its purely spiritual character,
gave me a chance to set my whole work in a new perspective.
Though my physical condition had not improved, superiors
seemed to wish me to keep on with my work in St. Mary's.
When I returned permanently to my old post in June 1918,
I found that the residence had been changed from Priest's
Point to the Church of St. Michael at Ridge, some six miles
distant. Ridge received its name from the fact that the village
overlooked the two sides of the fifty-mile-long ridge which
runs the entire length of the southern Maryland peninsula.

Father Emerick had kindly taken over the direction of the
two St. James schools during my absence. There was no problem with regard to the colored school, as Mrs. Beale was a
permanent and eminently satisfactory institution, but the
teachers at the white school were leaving, Miss Clarke to enter
religion and Miss Hebb to take up other plans. Moreover,
we faced a severe problem of financial support. The Negro
school did not present so much difficulty owing to the help
which was provided by the Sisters of the Blessed Sacrament
for Indians and Negroes, as well as by the Board of Colored
Missions through Father Kramer in New York. But nothing
was established for the white school, and I began then a long
and arduous struggle for funds which was carried on the
remainder of my time at Ridge, until the Sisters of St. Joseph
finally came and lifted much of the burden off my shoulders.

Moreover, the schools had multiplied. September 20, 1918, we opened a white school at St. Michael's conducted by the Missionary Servants of the Blessed Trinity, a group of four ladies who were not as yet strictly members of a religious community but were devoted to missionary life. They started in utmost poverty. Then at St. Peter's we started a school for the colored children under a lay teacher, Miss Sadie Biscoe, a rough-hewn character of great integrity, devotion and energy. Soon her school, too, was filled with eager aspirants.

The years 1918 to 1922 were years of struggle, in many respects the hardest years of my life, certainly those in which I felt most helpless and abandoned by everything human. I also struggled with a refractory digestion, not aided by various dietary ventures. I felt deep revulsion at having to seek out-side aid for my work. I could appeal to plenty of friends and relatives in Washington, in Philadelphia, and New York, and they were suprisingly considerate and generous once they understood what I was doing. But it was extremely disagree-able to me to pass the hat and talk money to people when I really wanted to do something for their own souls. I shared on a small scale the experience of countless missionaries, foreign and home, when they try to obtain support for their works.

I began the appeal in Washington with meetings at the homes of old family friends like Mrs. Russell Sturgis and Miss Sarah R. Lee and Miss Wilcox. Then in New York I followed the same plan with such people as Mrs. Schuyler N. Warren, my cousin; Miss Agnes Keyes, Miss Mary M. Kearney, and Mr. and Mrs. John G. Agar. To all of these and hundreds of others living and dead, I wish I could express my gratitude adequately. I do express that gratitude as a priest at the altar.

The necessity for obtaining funds forced me to come out of my shell, however, to think over problems with a wider per-spective, and to study the unusual history of the place where I was working. This bore fruit in a lecture that I held at the Catholic Club in New York City on January 16, 1922, under the auspices of the United States Catholic Historical Association. Apparently very few, if any, of our Catholic laity knew anything about St. Mary's City and the origins of Maryland.

I spent five years looking for Sisters to take up the school work at Ridge, and interviewed some sixteen or seventeen Superiors of different religious communities. Some even traveled down there to visit me. The Missionary Servants of the Blessed Trinity who, as I said, were not actually a religious order, were the soul of zeal and charity, but their work was more social service than educational. After their departure in June 1919, I fell into a trap. I can chuckle over it now, but then it was no laughing matter.

The services of a group of Third Order or Tertiary Carmelites had been recommended to us, and I was able to house them in the convent newly erected in the summer of 1919. The question of the convent had been a great dilemma: I could not obtain Sisters as I had no convent, and nobody was interested in building a convent with no Sisters to use it. I finally resorted in the spring of 1919 to the two mightiest patrons whose feasts were near—St. Patrick (March 17) and St. Joseph (March 19). I prayed to both of them diligently. St. Patrick's Day arrived and nothing happened, but the following day, March 18, I received a check for $5,000 from my old friend, Miss Agnes F. Keyes. To this day I never knew whom to thank, St. Patrick or St. Joseph. On closer acquaintance, the Tertiaries turned out to be refugees, one might say, from different communities. The Mother who had organized the group was an eccentric. They had little knowledge of teaching, they seemed to have no idea of the religious life, and they were involved in perpetual struggle with the Mother. Things got so bad that I reproached the Mother Superior for her peculiar conduct and that of her group. She did not take it very well and remarked with some acerbity: "I would like you to understand that I may have a good many faults but I am strong as h—— on humility." Well, she may have been strong on humility but she needed ordinary common sense and some knowledge of her job. My impression was that the good lady had simply gathered a group of malcontents around her, clothed them in picturesque costumes, and set out on an adventure. They took charge in the fall of 1919, but by November the situation was so difficult and their lack of authority was so complete, that Father Emerick and I were obliged to do all the teaching for the boys in both white schools. Meanwhile I had to carry on my begging. The white school at St. James's itself became uninhabitable because of water in the cellar, and had to be abandoned. Classes were held in my little bedroom over the sacristy. Meanwhile rumors developed about the nuns. Finally on April 26, 1920, I said good-by to the Mother Superior and her companions.

The lowest point had been reached when I entered the schoolroom at St. Michael's and saw written on the board in large letters: "Can the blind lead the blind?" A storm of criticism descended upon us from all sides. Financial matters continued to plague us and I was obliged to see if I could pick up a few pennies around the big cities. One bright spot remained: Mrs. Beale continued quietly with her little colored school, placid and competent as ever. It would have been more sensible for me to have transferred Mrs. Beale to one of the white schools and I believe that, after the first shock, they would have been grateful to have her teach. When the Tertiaries left in April 1920 the School of Social Service of the National Catholic Welfare Conference in Washington, D. C., nobly came to my aid. Two members of the faculty, Miss Cook and Miss Boland, came down and held the fort until the white school closed at the end of the term.

In May of that year, Mother Josephine O'Connor, an English-born Superior in this country of the Sisters of St. Joseph of Chambéry, France, came to consider the possibility of working at Ridge. She sized up our difficulty and decided to come to our rescue at the end of two years. How then to bridge the gap before she could send her Sisters? That was accomplished, in a quite original fashion, through the aid of Dr. Caroline R. Martin, a talented farm girl who had worked her way through college and acquired a medical degree and a good local practice. Later Dr. Martin became a leading authority on records in the New York hospital system, improving the hospital records of Manhattan and Brooklyn; some of her ideas were taken up by the British government. Dr. Martin was sympathetic to the problems of youth. She was a vigorous personality, who knew the people of the County well. From local families she invited several girls to form a little temporary teaching community. The girls led a quasi-religious life, with meditation and Mass in the morning, preparing their lessons for the following day each evening and keeping silence after night prayers. So Dr. Martin, with her girls, staffed my two white schools from September 1920 to June 1922.

In August 1922 the Sisters of St. Joseph, sent by Mother Josephine O'Connor, arrived from their mother house in Hartford to take up school work at Ridge. I had first become acquainted with them through my associate on Blackwells Island, the Rev. John W. Casey, S.J., whose sister and brother had welcomed the first band of St. Joseph Sisters to this country.

For the St. Joseph sisters pioneering at Ridge was particularly difficult.* Nothing could be less like busy, noisy Hartford, Connecticut, than this remote countryside where they heard no sound at night save the chirping of crickets and the occasional yell of a screech-owl. A good quota of physical annoyances confronted them—troubles with heating, water supply, etc. Until we consolidated it with the white school at Ridge a couple of them traveled daily by Ford and lumbering horse-bus through the mud or snow to the school (St. David's) at St. James. But theirs was love at first sight for the country children, who lost no time in reciprocating. I had prophesied to the Sisters that they would obtain candidates for their community from the new mission, and the prophecy was gener-

---

* The story of Mother Josephine O'Connor and the Sisters of St. Joseph, along with many details of their beginnings at Ridge, is told by Katherine Burton in *Mightily and Sweetly* (St. Anthony Guild Press, Paterson, New Jersey, 1948).

ously fulfilled. Today twenty-five girls from the Ridge schools have joined the Sisters of St. Joseph, besides several girls and boys who have joined other religious communities. Two priests of the Archdiocese of Baltimore, Father John B. Peacock and Linus E. Robinson, started the first schooling of their lives in the Ridge schools.

In the fall of 1924, the colored Oblate Sisters of Providence came to take over St. Peter Claver school, which had been consolidated with the other colored school. Their community had been founded in 1829 in Baltimore by the Sulpician, Father Hector Joubert. Conditions at Ridge were difficult for the Oblate Sisters too. Their own convent, about a mile from that of the St. Joseph Sisters, was under construction, thanks to a generous grant from the then Archbishop of Baltimore, the Most Rev. Michael J. Curley. In the meantime the only place to lodge them was in a couple of small rooms, heated by tin stoves, at the rear of the church. The rest of the church, a flimsy frame structure, was unheated save during services, and it was a bitterly cold winter.

Immediately the colored Sisters won the respect and affection of the entire community. They brought new life into the Negro community of Ridge and the vicinity. They set an example of gracious manners, and showed wonderful devotion to the people, their homes, and their children.

Through the generosity of my friends the Misses Austin, I was able to obtain funds so that my successors could build a high school for boys and girls at Ridge, and a grade school at Great Mills, some twelve miles distant, also in charge of the Sisters of St. Joseph. All of these institutions have flourished far beyond any of my expectations, and take care of many hundreds of children who today travel to them by bus from all nooks and corners of a spacious countryside.

I was occasionally asked why I was so persistent in trying to start the Ridge schools in view of all the difficulties connected with them. My answer is simple. It is because the Church is not complete without its schools. That has been the traditional attitude of the missionaries of the Church. I was assigned to work for the community and for the development of the Faith among its people, and I felt that this could not be accomplished without schools, especially if one considered the very nature of our Faith. The Faith for us is a deposit, entrusted by the Eternal Son of God to human hands at the foundation of His Church, to be passed on intact until the end of time, yet forever growing in meaning with the development of the human race. The gift of Faith must be perfected through study and the hearing of the Word. I had seen personally the effect of mere custom Catholicism in the Old World, how the Faith had decayed under routine and the devastating influence of a state-controlled Church. I wanted to see our Catholics intelligently believing and able to stand on their own feet.

I wanted to see them well-rounded citizens, prepared spiritually for life and its problems. With the opening up of this isolated section there would be a fierce battle to preserve the homes from disintegration; divorce, family absenteeism, juvenile delinquency, all these would attack the home and could only be met by an integral spiritual preparation based on the firm foundation of the Faith. And only through a Catholic school would sacramental life and particularly Eucharistic worship become integrated into the lives of the children.

This conviction eased the tedium of trying to raise money for the schools. Sometimes I asked myself if I had not gone too fast and too far. Perhaps I did. I would doubtless not have embarked upon all these projects if I had foreseen all the difficulties. Happily I did not foresee them. And they did keep me from devoting part of my time and strength to a more remote mission parish, that of St. Nicholas, one which dated from the foundation of the Maryland Colony.

From St. Inigoes Manor you reached St. Nicholas through the long lane of the Three Notch Road, the oldest road in Maryland, only in very recent years developed into a state road.

In my time it was only a path, one might say, through the woods. The priest lived over the sacristy of the old eighteenth-century frame church. A curious little door about five and a half feet in height marked the entrance to the priest's apartment. I asked Henry Chapman, the colored sexton, how it happened that the opening was so diminutive. The door, said Henry, was built by Father Gubitosi, a former pastor, "and he was a low priest."

During the four or five years I had charge of St. Nicholas I labored to complete the church begun by Father Matthews, but still only a shell of concrete blocks. At Mass one morning while I was reading the Gospel a black snake fell on my head, and set the ladies of the congregation scrambling up on the pews. The snake's intentions were harmless, but he symbolized the condition of the building; snakes do not drop on one's head in completed churches.

On wintry Saturday nights, after supper at the sexton's cottage, the glowing coal stove and the oil lamp were my companions in the priest's quarters. To while away the time, I tried my hand at reading Russian, and worked through Dostoyevsky's *Crime and Punishment* with the aid of a dictionary. With a little practice I found the story absorbing enough to keep me up to late hours of the night, and thoroughly suited to the ghostlike, graveyard surroundings. Outside, the whippoorwills entertained me with their extraordinary power of repetition. One morning I counted one old fellow to see how long he would persist; he repeated "whippoorwill" 375 times in succession, sounding a little groggy toward the end.

At St. Nicholas the story got out, which I made no serious attempt to combat, that I ran a still where I made bootleg whisky. This was, of course, during Prohibition days. The fact that I did not drink was taken as possible confirmation, because people who are not seen to drink are supposed to be drinking considerably in secret. I used to meet an old Holiness preacher occasionally on the Three Notch Road, the Rev. Mr. Gatton, who told me that in his church there were no sinners. "All sinners," he said, "I expelled from the church." When I asked what sins he referred to, he listed card-playing, drinking, smoking, dancing. Since such sinners were in perfectly good standing in St. Nicholas Parish, I was unable to measure up to his standard.

Circumstantial evidence pointed to the existence of the still. An eyewitness was Peter Biscoe, a colored Methodist undertaker, who did not reside in the neighborhood. Mr. Biscoe was conducting a Negro funeral and in need of a plank for the burial. He appealed to Henry Chapman, who kept everything carefully locked. Unlocking the church tower basement, he told Mr. Biscoe he could get the plank. Peter entered the bottom chamber of the tower and observed there a number of interesting objects. One was a large bin of corn which I kept for the horse (Henry insisted on locking the corn up, and doled it out only when strictly needed). He viewed also a copper kettle which my cousin Mrs. Schuyler Warren had sent me—a baptismal font, discarded from a country church in Tuxedo, which I never found practicable. A large supply of tubing was connected with a gasoline stove with which I had tried unsuccessfully to heat the church. In addition to this an abundance of soft drink bottles were left from a recent church festival. All this Mr. Biscoe took in with a jaundiced eye, saying nothing at the time, but drawing mental conclusions. Possession of a still was, of course, a misdemeanor under Prohibition, but the local observance of the laws was quite lenient. If anyone of prominence happened to be in jail for violating them, he was allowed to return home over the week end, since County officials held that it was not civilized for a man to absent himself too long from his family. During the week the people of Leonardtown would visit the jail with delicacies and give little serenades on the lawn outside. In the case of my supposed "still," no further developments occurred.

Happily I was able to complete the church, largely through the generosity of Mr. George C. Jenkins of Baltimore, a saintly

Catholic citizen who was devoted to the place, and then through the help of two wonderful spinster ladies in New York, Miss Kate and Miss Julia Austin, relatives of Mr. Warren Austin, former U.S. Ambassador to the United Nations.

The St. Nicholas congregation was three-quarters colored, one-quarter white, and all services were held in common. I was impressed by the two races' common interest in the community, especially in the preservation of the life of the family. The countryside was going to be transformed, forces for good and evil from the rest of the country would soon invade it. If the home forces for good were divided, whether in the church or in the civil community, it would bring only weakness at home. It seemed to me some basis could be found on which all groups would work together in the community for defending the best traditions of the past. Everyone in the community, the white people and Negroes alike, had a common stake in the future and at some point they could no longer act separately but would need to recognize their new type of interdependence.

The traditional interdependence was that of the Negro working for the white man and the white man seeking a colored man to do a job. Now the Negroes were becoming economically less dependent, each his own man, as they would say, and the whites on the other hand were freeing themselves from human help through the aid of farm and household machinery. What would be the effect of such a change? Would the two races drift completely apart, or would they realize that they were still bound by a common interest, one that might not be so rigidly economic as in the past, more cultural and civic and spiritual, yet none the less genuine? At any rate, somehow they would be *obliged* to discover a common working basis, if they were both to survive. The Cardinal Gibbons Institute, secondary school for Negroes which I helped to establish at Ridge, was an attempt to reach such a common basis.

CHAPTER TWELVE

The Cardinal Gibbons Institute

⇛ ⇚

At the beginning the Cardinal Gibbons Institute seemed like manna from Heaven, whether one considers its first form or later development. The whole project began one Sunday afternoon in November 1916, when the three of us, Father Matthews, Father Emerick, and myself, who were then still living at the Manor House at Priest's Point, piled into Father Matthews' rickety Ford and made our way to St. Peter Claver's Hall, a few miles distant, which was the gathering place for the Negroes of the vicinity. A bill had been passed by the legislature providing for industrial schools in the different counties of Maryland. Meetings had been held with the colored people about the County for this purpose.

In the opinion of many the industrial school was held out to the colored people as a political bait by certain white politicians. After the plans for the state school had been proposed the three of us gave our opinion, and showed the impracticality of many features in the plans. We stated that we had long been considering the need and possibility of a colored industrial school for boys of eleven or twelve years and that such a school under Catholic auspices could obtain the patronage of His Eminence Cardinal Gibbons and help from other sources, and could obtain the services of teachers who would be far more competent than those we knew would be obtained under the other plan. Our plan, we explained, would be perfectly fair to Protestants as well as to Catholics and the institution would be entitled to state aid. These remarks were

208

met with considerable enthusiasm on the part of the audience, and some Protestants spoke endorsing our plan. We invited the proponents of the state school to join with us in our work, and since we were determined to put it through anyhow we suggested it would be better if they would work with us.

Plans were then formulated among the various clergy of the County for an industrial school for colored boys which should be a counterpart, more or less, of the St. Mary's Industrial School conducted for white boys in Baltimore by the Xaverian Brothers or Brothers of St. Francis Xavier. It was conceived definitely as a reform school. The Brothers were approached on the matter. On December 7, 1916, they agreed to take up the work. The following May the Provincial of the Brothers, Brother Isidore, C.F.X., and Brother Gerard, C.F.X., visited Ridge. A conference was then held concerning the purchase of property and the upshot was that a very fine estate of some seventy or eighty acres was purchased directly opposite St. Peter Claver's Church, extending from the high plane of the ridge down to the salt-water front of Smith's Creek which empties into the Potomac. The Brothers, however, who were so enthusiastic about the work at the beginning, found obstacles in their way. They soon sent word that they would not be able to carry out the plan of an industrial school. Nevertheless, we had the property incorporated under the name of the St. Peter Claver Institute, with the aid of one of the white parishioners of St. Michael's, Mr. Lawrence P. Williams. We had been enabled to purchase it through a generous gift of Cardinal Gibbons, who sent us a check of $8,000. It was decided then that any new institution we started there would be named after him and called the Cardinal Gibbons Institute.

With the death of Cardinal Gibbons and the coming of the Most Rev. Michael J. Curley, Archbishop of Baltimore, the opportunity for some revival of the plan for the Institute arose. I myself made some exploration along that line with the National Catholic Welfare Conference authorities in Washington. They had been extremely helpful to me with regard to the schools, and in the spring of 1921 they had assisted me with teachers and furniture. I talked matters over with the Rev. Raymond A. McGowan, Assistant Director of the Social Action Department, NCWC, Miss Margaret Lynch and Miss Agnes Regan, and others who were interested in my parish school work, and they suggested I should discuss the matter with Arthur C. Monahan, of the NCWC Education division, who had had considerable experience of Negro education in the South. Mr. Monahan was deeply interested in the project and recommended a quite different line of approach. He suggested that we drop the idea of a reform school and instead organize a school for the better type of Negro youth, those who were promising and fairly talented and for whom a school would open the doors of opportunity. Mr. Monahan visited the location and was favorably impressed by its physical possibilities.

He stressed several points in particular. First, the school should be co-educational, for both boys and girls. This from his experience had been found to be the most practical method, and it is interesting to note that when Mother Katharine Drexel established her Xavier University in New Orleans in 1932, she also hit on the idea of a co-educational school. Boys and girls alike would be educated with the same ideals, they would get to know each other under favorable circumstances, and the resulting unions would produce a new and more enlightened generation.

Secondly, Mr. Monahan proposed the idea of a Negro principal, someone who would himself be identified with the school and take a deep pride in it as an accomplishment of his own race; and thirdly, he urged us to seek very widespread popular support for the school through a far-reaching type of organization. Moreover, he suggested that the school should not be narrowly agricultural but should venture on a wider vocational character in accordance with some of the very successful methods pursued in the South.

Accordingly, on October 25, 1921, an organization meeting for the Cardinal Gibbons Institute was held at the NCWC

in Washington. Fathers Matthews, John W. Casey, and myself
attended, and Archbishop Curley presided. The following year
on February 6 Archbishop Curley approved the general plan
of the school, and on April 25 we held our first board meeting
in Washington. The Board was mixed in every sense of the
word: it included white and colored, Catholics and Protestants,
men and women, local southern Marylanders, Baltimoreans
and Washingtonians, and people from other parts of the country. The chairman of the Board was the Archbishop himself,
and the vice-chairman was Admiral William S. Benson, who
threw himself into the work with the greatest enthusiasm. As
a retired U.S. Navy flag officer he desired to devote himself
especially to this work for the rest of his life. The Board met
again on June 23, and July 11 visited its proposed location.
On July 15 Mr. Monahan made a more careful inspection of
the place.

Plans continued to be made through the next winter, and
the following spring, on June 27, 1923, the Board made a very
important decision, which was that the school should be religious in character. Though it would be open to non-Catholics
and would enlist their co-operation, still it would be definitely
under Catholic auspices and known as a Catholic school. An
executive committee was formed and Mr. Victor H. Daniel,
who had taught at Tuskegee Institute and also at the Borden-
town Manual Training School for Negroes in New Jersey, was
selected as principal, and his wife as assistant principal.

On September 3 the Knights of Columbus' National Board
of Directors sent us a check for $35,000. This princely gift was
obtained at the instance of a white citizen of Baltimore, Mr.
William S. Aumen, State Deputy for the Maryland Knights
of Columbus, an enthusiastic friend of the school and a member of its Board and Executive Committee. The sum was appropriated by their Supreme Board of Directors for the erection of the main building of the school. Later on two very fine
brick wings were added to this same building through the

generosity of the late Mr. James Byrne of New York, father-in-law of Walter Lippmann.

On October 14 of the same year a local Cardinal Gibbons auxiliary was organized in Leonardtown and others soon sprang up among the Negroes and some whites in different parts of the country. The Federated Colored Catholics, an inter-state Negro organization, took an active part and soon affairs for the Cardinal Gibbons Institute became a recognized part of Negro life. It gave the Negroes an immediate object to work for. There was tremendous interest in the whole idea of a project which was national in scope, the first national project undertaken by Catholics on behalf of the Negro.

The Institute building was dedicated on October 26, 1924. Father McGowan of the NCWC preached the sermon, and two Masses were celebrated, both by Negro priests, the late Father Unkles of the Josephite Fathers, and the late Father John of the Society of African Missions. On May 25 of the following year the trustees met in Washington, and Archbishop Curley presented Mr. Daniel with $1,000 to fit up the house which had been erected as the principal's residence. It was decided then to build a boys' dormitory, and an appeal was made to the Catholics of Pittsburgh. On October 18 of that year the handsome, one-story, brick and stucco dormitory was dedicated and named Boyle Hall: it was the gift of the Pittsburgh Catholics, money having been raised under the leadership of Mr. Houlihan, County Commissioner of Pittsburgh.

In the meantime Mr. Daniel had been holding conferences with the farmers in the vicinity and impressed them with the possibility of developing a program of better farming under the guidance of the Institute and in collaboration with it. Though some of the more conservative met these overtures with suspicion, the majority were heartily in accord. It soon developed that the Institute's plan of providing better homes for the people of the neighborhood, i.e., encouraging them to self-help in improvement of their homes, was a thoroughly practical idea. Mr. Daniel's simple gospel was readily accepted.

He would propose that one of these wretched one-crop farmer houses could be made a decent place for living. The usual technique was followed: panes of glass put in the dilapidated windows, fences repaired, proper toilet arrangements (outdoor of course) created according to simple and practical government specifications, and corresponding indoor improvements for the women's housekeeping. Farmers' conferences and fairs, agricultural exhibits followed in due course. The Institute became, as it was desired to be, a center of community life and of renewed hope that somehow or other the backwardness and apathy of the place could be overcome.

A memorable meeting was held at St. Peter Claver's Hall at which Mr. Michael Williams, editor of *Commonweal,* was the principal speaker. Mr. Daniel in introducing him remarked that the title of the *Commonweal* was particularly suitable for this occasion; people, he said, wail in the city and wail in the country, but if we all wail in common we shall see a ray of hope, so he liked the idea of the "commonwail." This intrigued Mr. Williams no end.

For our support we were obliged, like all such institutions, to look in great measure to outside aid. Though we obtained some funds from the General Education Board and some other organizations, we were largely dependent on the contributions of charitable individuals: many of them persons who had helped me with the other schools. My brother O. H. P. LaFarge headed the Executive Committee formed for this purpose, which was composed of persons of both races and included non-Catholic members.

From the outset, however, the Executive Committee faced a disheartening obstacle of general public indifference to anything connected with the South or with the Negro, coupled by special incomprehension for such a novel type of school. The Executive Committee functioned in New York, remote from the school's locus, and was in a somewhat awkward position as auxiliary to a project headed by the Archbishop of Baltimore.

It was difficult to keep our best friends and even our committee members posted on what we were trying to do, although I took them on various visits to the place. After the resignation of Mr. Monahan as secretary, the Board engaged in September 1931 the services of Mr. George K. Hunton, a friend of my cousin Schuyler Warren and a member of the New York Bar. Mr. Hunton was entrusted with the vexatious task of trying to work out plans for raising money and at the same time of being a liaison between the Committee and the Institute.

The financial problem might have been managed had it not been for the worst years of the Depression, 1930-1933. This affected all the members of the Committee, not only their actual fortunes but in most of them their morale as well. After the trial of several makeshift plans, the Institute was closed on December 31, 1933. Under the supervision of the local pastor, the Reverend Horace B. McKenna, S.J., it continued as a center for various activities of the local Negro community. Later, in 1936, it was reopened by Father McKenna as a secondary-level day school for the colored children of the vicinity, and in this reincarnation did and still continues to do excellent work. At present the classes are taught by the same Sisters who conduct the local Negro grade school, the Oblate Sisters of Providence, from Baltimore.

The Institute wished its young men and women to stand upon their own feet and take their place in society strictly according to their own qualifications. The lesson was impressed upon them that they were to seek no special favors because they were Negroes, but were to meet in competition with everybody else. The principles of respect for personal dignity and rights and the stress upon personal responsibility, as a necessary condition for complete integration in the larger American community, were akin to those that my nephew, Oliver La-Farge, has so skillfully elaborated in his lifelong work with the American Indians.

The school from the outset did an outstanding job in the community by co-operating with government and state agencies for the benefit of local farmers, white and colored, and by promoting adult education. Through its extension program it served as a center for community activities, exhibits, contests, etc. This feature of its work weathered all other vicissitudes. Even when the Institute was closed for several years the extension work continued.

The school was hampered by a revival of the original demand for a 100 per cent agricultural education. It was powerless, however, to afford under its limited budget the necessary professionally competent training. Furthermore, it was very doubtful if such an exclusively agricultural school as had originally been planned would have been worth the tremendous expense it would have entailed. Several years after the closing of the Institute in 1933, during the Second World War, the whole complexion of the neighborhood was changed by the establishment of the immense Patuxent Naval Air Base with the attractive jobs it offered the community. It is very doubtful if a straight agricultural school would have made its mark unless it had been conducted by some extraordinary personality— a Liberty Hyde Bailey, a Gabriel Davidson, a Father John Rawe, or some other agricultural genius—and even such a person would have been in dire need without proper support from capital investment.

Though the school was closed it opened a door to a new vision of the capacities of Negro youth both in their own minds and that of the public at large, along with a legitimate pride in their race and its great achievements. It aroused a large intelligent sector of the local people to a new concept of the dignity and opportunities of agriculture and the possibilities of the rural community. It worked as a powerful instrument with which to awaken the dormant consciences of the Catholic public who were forgetful of the abnormal situation of the Negro in the Catholic Church. It showed them that this situation impaired the Church's apostolate for souls in this country and abroad: not to speak of the dangerous inconsistency with the professions of our democracy itself.

Finally, the extraordinary amount of hard work and close thinking that had gone into the problem of keeping the Institute alive were turned into channels that were undoubtedly not picturesque and not as immediately and physically tangible as a school, but in the long run would open the doors of opportunity not only to the colored boys and girls in southern Maryland but advance the whole situation of the Negro and other racial groups in the United States. From this point of view the Institute was emphatically not a failure but was, as I see it, a predestined seed ground for the development of the Catholic interracial movement in the United States. Furthermore, the publicity about the Institute over the years aroused the interest of many Catholic leaders in the plight of Negroes and led them to inquire what could be done to promote more opportunities for the Negro in American life.

CHAPTER THIRTEEN
The Ark *and the* Dove

->>> <<<-

St. Mary's City, part of my parish of St. James, is now within easy access of Washington, D. C. The road runs straight south through Brandywine, Waldorf, Hughesville, and Leonardtown or Great Mills. Shortly before reaching St. Mary's City a road through the woods to the right leads to the Father White memorial.

In 1634 Father Andrew White, S.J., and two companions came to Maryland on the *Ark* and *Dove* with Lord Baltimore and his brother, Leonard Calvert. The first landing took place at Blackistone Island on the Potomac River near Leonardtown, but they remained there only a short time, since the island was not particularly habitable, and came down the river again nearer to its mouth, turned in at the St. Mary's River and landed at what is now Chancellor's Point.

The monument to Father White looks across a small bay in the river toward Chancellor's Point: a picturesque view. The brick structure is in the form of a segment of a circle, shaped like an altar with a fine piece of lettering in the center. On either side a few dark-colored bricks are inserted, taken from the original Catholic chapel at St. Mary's City. The property for the monument—several acres in extent, was the generous donation of one of my charter pupils at the St. James School, Mrs. Warren Dunbar (Susette Ridgell) and her husband. It slopes down to a little beach on the bay itself.

The architect of the memorial was my nephew, Christopher LaFarge, who had done work in his father's field of architecture before he made writing his principal vocation. Christopher's design is an attractive job, characteristically well-balanced and refined; he devoted great care to the lettering, which is marked out by gold leaf. The monument was erected in 1933 under the auspices of the Pilgrims of St. Mary's, and was used for a public ceremony for the first time in May of the tercentenary year 1934. Holy Mass was celebrated on that occasion by the Rev. Richard B. Washington, a collateral descendant of George Washington. I knelt in the audience with two or three of the local Protestant clergymen beside me, and explained to them the rites of the Mass.

I was often asked why so much of the land of St. Mary's County and southern Maryland was in the hands of Protestants and not in the hands of Catholics. The basic reason is that the Protestants were in the ascendancy in Catholic Maryland for 140 years of the Penal days. The old Catholic land-owning families seemed unable to retain their land, so that the Catholics, as a rule, were tenants rather than big land-owners. It is not correct to present the story of the foundation of Maryland as something exclusively Catholic, for Protestants also arrived on the *Ark* and *Dove*. They took part in the founding of the Colony and some of them—in fact, all of those who were among the original settlers—distinguished themselves by their friendly and entirely loyal conduct to a Catholic Lord Proprietary. They are not to be judged by the fanatical and sectarian actions of the Puritans, who came afterward; nor by the Royalist bigots who upset the former proprietary government when the Crown Governor was installed. Nevertheless, the full truth both as to facts and the meaning of the facts is seldom presented.

As early as 1916 I began to foresee the tercentennial of Maryland in 1934. I was astonished to find that among the Catholics nobody seemed to take any interest in the matter, either locally or in the adjacent cities of Washington or Baltimore. It was a reproach to Catholics that they had done so little in preserving the records of the past. Only in relatively recent times did we wake up to the historical treasures of the Church in this country in the colonial epoch and the early nineteenth century. The great historian Dr. Peter Guilday, Mr. Thomas F. Meehan of the U.S. Catholic Historical Society, Dr. Zwierlein of Rochester, Dr. John Tracy Ellis of the Catholic University of America, John Gilmary Shea, and others finally aroused a real Catholic historical sense which now is taken for granted. Some thirty or forty years ago there was comparatively little interest among Catholics in the early history of the American church. I saw boxes of old letters and diaries which today would be priceless, thrown on junk heaps because they were simply "old eighteenth-century stuff." I was not a professional historian, but I hoped that by making a little noise some attention would be paid to the treasures which we were on the point of losing, and again to some of the great issues which were being ignored. This seemed to me to be especially our duty as Jesuits, since we had been identified with the Colony from its beginning.

The Jesuits took up residence in Maryland on equal terms with the laity. Says Father Thomas Hughes in his *History of the Jesuits of North America:* "It was the first instance in the Catholic Church that the clergy had been assigned a place in a presumably Catholic community, at least a community that respected religion, and had no provision at all made for their temporal support." They provided for themselves and shifted as well as they could. The idea, incidentally, that the clergy could provide for themselves persisted down into later times. An eminent old Protestant worthy in Leonardtown, Judge Joe Key, gravely informed me on one occasion that the Jesuits "lived on the fat of the land." There was an idea even in clerical circles in Washington and Baltimore that the clergy lived in magnificence on large estates in their County missions.

On one occasion Archbishop Curley sent down to the Counties an official visitor to conduct the regular canonical visitation of the parishes. I was deputed to carry the Monsignor to the different churches in my Ford car over the muddy roads. Rain had been threatening and it was pouring as we started on our trip and it continued to pour throughout. The Mon-

signor apparently had expected to find rather palatial conditions in the Counties. Finally we were stuck good and fair in
the clay of the Three Notch Road.

"What shall we do?" he asked.

I said, "Nothing to do, Monsignor, but pray to St. Ignatius
and hope that he may extricate us."

While we were praying diligently, a local farmer, Mr. Bud
Carroll, came along with his team of mules and wagon. I explained the situation to him and he drove back to the farm,
returned with a block and tackle and hauled us out of the
mud. After his return to Washington, so I was informed, the
visitor reported a somewhat different picture of the conditions
under which the Jesuit missionaries lived in southern Maryland. He had learned, incidentally, how isolated the place was
in those pre-state-road days.

Local Catholic interest in early Maryland history was stirred
by a controversy originating with a letter published in 1922
in the *St. Mary's Beacon*. The Leonardtown council of the
Knights of Columbus had protested against the action of the
Maryland Society of the Colonial Dames of America in dedi-
cating on October 25, 1922, a memorial to Lionel Copley, the
first Royal Governor of Maryland. "The said Lionel Copley,"
they wrote in the *Beacon,* "was a narrow-minded bigot whose
outstanding accomplishment during his regime (1692) was the
repeal of the Toleration Act of 1649, once the proudest boast
of Maryland, and the enactment of an obnoxious and oppres-
sive law whereby the Anglican Church became the established
church of the Province and all taxables were assessed by the
poll for its maintenance and support."

The Rev. Dr. C. W. Whitmore, the Episcopal Rector at St.
Mary's City, replied in defense of Governor Copley, and the
Beacon's editor, the late Aloysius F. King, wrote in rebuttal.
This started one of the periodical discussions about the real
nature of the Religious Toleration Act of 1649, properly en-
titled "An Act Concerning Religion."

References to Governor Lionel Copley, criticized by the

Catholics, were countered with mention of Father Thomas Copley, S.J., who has been represented by Protestant historians as an enemy of Lord Baltimore.

The matter might have slept had not a Protestant historian called Johnson written a monograph on the subject in which he made out that Baltimore underwent a religious persecution from men who did not understand his ideas. With equal vigor Father Thomas Hughes, S.J., who did not like Lord Baltimore, defended the startling notion that Baltimore was quite un-Catholic in his policy, and compared his policies to the social-istic regime that led to the suppression of the churches in France. I undertook, as a kind of essay in historical ingenuity, to try to disentangle the controversy. I wrote a couple of arti-cles in *Thought* magazine about it, and studied the legal argu-ments which Johnson had raised. Later on Father Gilbert Gar-raghan, S.J., writing also in *Thought,* did, as trained historian, a better job.

The question of lay interference in Church affairs—a ques-tion which was to come up at various times in later years and which I had seen operate in my own time—was thus raised at the outset of the Colony. The layman has his status and his rights in the Church, but it is quite another thing to dictate and determine conditions under which the Church should pursue its own perfectly normal activities. Was Lord Baltimore a predecessor of the Emperor Joseph II of Austria and a suc-cessor of King John of Runnymede, or was he a fine Catholic gentleman annoyed and hounded by busybody ecclesiastics? These are questions for historians and for the reader who trou-bles to examine the records and make up his own mind. The affair looked to me like a very natural dispute between a high-minded, courageous, but woefully anxious promoter and men of equal mettle and caliber who toiled in hardship at an enor-mously distant spot.

The tercentennial of Maryland was due on the Feast of the Annunciation, March 25, 1934. Eleven years and one month before this event, we organized the Pilgrims of St. Mary's. The purpose of the organization was twofold. First, it was to create interest in Maryland's historical past and prepare the minds of the public for the tercentennial, and particularly the minds of the Catholic public for the part that the Church played therein. However, a policy of scrupulous fairness and friendly co-operation with our non-Catholic friends was to be observed throughout. The organization was also to serve as a sort of mission auxiliary. It would help to support the teachers of St. David's School, at St. James Church, which had been built by Mrs. David K. McCarthy in memory of her beloved husband.

The first chapter was the Washington branch of the Pilgrims. Later on a Baltimore chapter was founded with a numerous membership, its moving spirit the late Mrs. F. P. Scrivener, who with her husband was a diligent student of Maryland history. Branches were also established at Upper Marlboro and at Leonardtown in St. Mary's County itself. An incorporated group was established in 1926 with headquarters in Washington, a seal and letterhead, constitutions and by-laws. President of the corporation was the late William Franklin Sands, a former professor of Georgetown University, a Marylander by birth, and a man keenly interested in the history of his native state. In the years following the tercentennial the Washington chapter and eventually the chapters of Baltimore and Leonardtown lapsed; however, the Upper Marlboro chapter still continues. With regard to the tercentennial, the Pilgrims certainly achieved their purpose. They aroused great interest among Catholics and swung the sentiment toward solicitude and care for Maryland's Catholic past.

The Father White monument was actually a substitute proposal. The original idea was simply for a marker, noting the actual site of the first Catholic church in Maryland, built a couple of years after the colonists had landed. I considered it distressing that nothing had ever been done to mark the site of this first church. As far as any permanent foundation is concerned, it was the first Catholic church in the thirteen original colonies of the United States.

In company with Victor H. Daniel, principal of the Cardinal Gibbons Institute, and other neighbors, I had verified the site of the original chapel in a field adjacent to what was then the principal road between St. Mary's City and Ridge, 150 feet from the roadway. The spot was easily identifiable. Sufficient bricks of the original foundation remained in the ground to establish the location. The chapel was about thirty feet long and ten or fifteen feet wide. The bricks were baked by Richard Cox, whose name is recorded in the early archives; they were dirt-colored and longer and heavier than the ordinary brick.

The owners of the property had shown themselves averse to any project to mark the presence of the chapel. They explained that they needed the field for agricultural purposes; it was good soil and any kind of a monument would interfere with the plowing. I was all the more surprised therefore when Mr. James Bennett, son-in-law of the late Mrs. Brome, appeared one day at St. Michael's Rectory and said that they were considering offering the location itself to the Catholics and would entertain the idea of having some sort of a monument or marker erected. I replied that all we wanted was something extremely simple, just a mere marker. No, he said, they wanted something dignified that would have a certain artistic value. If I would make a proposal he would take it up with the family and they would consider it. Accordingly, I discussed the matter with Christopher LaFarge, who drafted a plan for a small symbolic altar and a brick canopy overhead with colonial or Georgian flavor. This, however, seemed to displease the owners, who believed it was too elaborate and became alarmed over the possibility that many people would come, leave beer bottles on the lawn, trample neighboring crops, and invade their privacy. I was puzzled by these objections in view of their offer. Anyhow, the whole project, after a long correspondence, was finally dropped. The spot remains unmarked.

If the plan is ever adopted of making St. Mary's City another Williamsburg, undoubtedly the Catholic chapel will be incorporated therein. Visitors to the place will find that the old

State House has been restored. This fortunately could be done because the exact specifications for the building both inside and outside are given in the Maryland archives. Several of my carpenter parishioners worked on it and took pleasure in showing me the details when I visited the place after its completion.

On April 27, 1925, at 11 A.M., I received a telegram from my sister Margaret telling of my mother's illness. I reached Newport the next morning at ten o'clock. I found my mother greatly changed from when I had last seen her. She spoke with much difficulty and at first was in great pain. My sister, Mrs. Frances Childs, and my brothers Oliver and Bancel were already at her bedside. Grant had just been there and would return. The morning of April 30 I brought her Holy Communion; she was then conscious and very alert. On Friday, May 1, she begged again to receive Holy Communion. "Do not postpone it," she said, "it would be unsafe."

"Shall I bring it now?" I asked.

"Yes," she replied, "bring it now."

On two occasions she joked with my sister Margaret about the number of people (a day nurse, night nurse, and members of the family) who were waiting on her. "Why not call in the neighbors?" she remarked. "And you might find a job for Zu Zu (the dog)." At her last conversation with Grant, just before I had arrived, she discussed French politics, in which she always took a lively interest. She asked his views on Edouard Herriot and Joseph Caillaux. She didn't like Caillaux and remarked, "He's like Sam Honeyman [an old Newport lawyer]—always worms his way back again!"

On Friday, May 1, her last full day on earth, she told us that in the night the Blessed Mother had helped her to obtain relief from pain. She failed so rapidly that day that there seemed little chance she would survive the night. At 6:15 A.M. Saturday morning Oliver and I were sent for. After I had recited the rosary, the Litanies, and other prayers, I left at 9:30 to say Mass for her, returning immediately to the house. Grant arrived from Saunderstown shortly before her death. At 2 P.M. death was imminent. Toward the end she appeared to see something which gave her great joy. Her face shone with a strange radiance, and she was on the point of speaking. At 2:35 she passed away, very gradually, breathing more and more faintly until one final gasp. It was the tranquil passing of a soul united with God.

That night all of us, brothers and sisters—saving my sister Emily, no longer living—met together for the first time in many years and told one another stories of Emily's odd adventures and mishaps in her lively youth. Perhaps it was just the natural reaction to days of tension and sorrow that made us so strangely lighthearted, but I felt it was more than that. It was as Mother had wished. "Death," Mother used to say, "is just a natural thing, like birth, and growth, and old age. When it comes, it will be familiar and welcome. The real grief is sin: that is death's sting."

The following evening a number of the priest visitors joined with me in the parlor to recite the Office of the Dead. On May 4, after the funeral Mass at St. Mary's, we buried her in St. Columba's cemetery, a few miles outside of Newport. For her gravestone she had chosen a translation of the words of the Psalm which the priest recites at the foot of the altar at the beginning of Mass: *"Send forth Thy light and Thy truth: they have led me and brought me unto Thy holy mount and into Thy tabernacles."* In these words, she said, were summed up her life's pilgrimage and her constant prayer that the light and truth which had guided her personally might reach the hearts and minds of the whole world.

The very day of my mother's departure I received a telephone message from our Reverend Father Provincial in New York, my former pastor Father Laurence J. Kelly, saying that I was to stop on the way back and see Father Wilfrid Parsons, editor of *America*. I have wondered whether it was my mother who somehow suggested the idea to the good Lord; it would

have been like her. Father Parsons told me then that he had
been anxious to obtain my services for *America*. This was a
total surprise to me. It would have been not unpleasant to
accept at once but conditions in Maryland seemed to make
it impossible to leave abruptly without upsetting my plans
for the schools and for the Institute. Rightly or wrongly, I
begged Superiors for a bit of a postponement. A year later,
on July 22, 1926, I received word that I was appointed to
the staff of *America*, and departed for New York on August 16.

For many reasons my leaving was heavyhearted. It was one
of those cases encountered in the life of every Jesuit and every
priest where one has to leave one's own will to God. I had
announced on June 6 at St. James the transfer of St. David's
School pupils to Great Mills and to St. Michael's. Many of the
children had been withdrawn, there were difficulties of revenue, and the road was still impassable for cars. This was a
bitter blow to Mrs. David McCarthy and, in a way that I can
hardly explain to anyone who did not know the circumstances,
an intense grief to me; but it was the will of the good Lord
and had to be. I left then to take up my work at Campion
House on West 108th Street in New York, which the Society
had acquired for *America* the year previous.

I had never cared for the city and it took time to get used
to it. For some fifteen years I had lived in a community where
I could speak to everybody; even if they happened to be stran-
gers, I immediately made their acquaintance. To walk through
the streets and see attractive, appealing children, just like the
children for whom I had worked in the country, and yet realize that I was totally unknown to them, and had no relation
to them—that was difficult. There was no more strolling along
the street or road and passing the time of day with everybody
whom you met.

It is not easy to recount in any narrative form the long years
I spent as one of the associate editors of *America*, from 1926
until I became executive editor in 1942. The printed pages
themselves are the obvious record of a journalist's week-by-

week, all-the-year-round routine. They look impressive as they pile up into a row of volumes, but are wearying if you try to recount them in any detail. The meanest job of those years was the weekly news chronicle, which was apportioned among the various members of the staff, each of whom was supposed to collect information about the important week's doings in a specific geographical area from any current sources he could tap. I did my best with France, Russia, and the countries of eastern Europe. The weekly chronicle was abandoned, to everyone's relief, in 1941. The pleasant task, of my regular routine, was that of composing the weekly column, "With Scrip and Staff," of which I shall speak later. It brought plenty of unexpected response, in the form of correspondence, and one had the sense of a continued conversation with friends. And the life itself at Campion House brought unusually stimulating fellowship with my associates on the review.

In point of fact, the story of the various activities with which I have been connected—rural life, interracial justice, liturgy and liturgical art, etc., etc., covers much of the doings of this period. These activities, in my case and in the case of the other staff members, were not something just tacked on to our literary work on the review. Father Richard H. Tierney, S.J., *America*'s third and highly enterprising editor-in-chief, was insistent that *America*—and by inference, Campion House, its home—should be no ivory tower, but the center of such priestly activities as would place its writers in immediate contact with the issues of the day. In like manner, he wanted the general public to benefit by whatever knowledge, talent, and experience the staff could offer. This meant for each of us a certain quota of lecturing, outside writing, participating in various organizations, or even initiating them. The Catholic Poetry Society, and the Catholic Book Club, founded by Father Francis X. Talbot, S.J., belong in the latter category.

One of my first thoughts, in my new surroundings, was to fulfill a long-cherished desire, and cultivate a closer acquaintance with the new and dynamic Catholic Rural Life Move-

ment in the United States; and Father Parsons, my new
Superior, encouraged me in this ambition. Indeed, the rural
life was a link, and a very helpful one, between the completely
bucolic life which I had quit and the new urban world into
which I was plunged.

CHAPTER FOURTEEN

The "Green Revolution"

※》《※

In the course of my life I have met with complete optimists and complete pessimists. I would classify as a complete optimist the good Father in Hot Springs, North Carolina, who undertook during a vacation to teach me how to play billiards. As an example of the pessimist, I recall meeting Mr. Mart Jones on the road near Leonardtown and remarking that it was beautiful weather. "I hate fine weather," replied Mart. "Fine weather breeds bad weather."

Both types of thinking occurred in the Catholic Rural Life Movement in America: some thought the movement useless and a waste of time; others saw in it a panacea for all difficulties, economic, political, and spiritual as well. My experience in southern Maryland had put me in contact with persons and agencies connected with the promotion of better rural life. The pessimists looked on their activities as hopeless: the only practical future for rural youth was in the cities. In fact, a fellow country-parish priest addressing my own school children insisted that the only practical and sensible thing for a bright young boy or girl was to get out of the country as quickly as possible, although he himself was country-born and -bred with a fine agrarian tradition extending back for generations. That type of attitude often arises from sheer ignorance. The optimistic attitude, on the other hand, was undiscriminating enthusiasm for the back-to-the-land movement, for the Green Revolution, as Michael Williams entitled it. Both notions were false. Nobody, however well meaning, can stop a certain process of urbanization; yet certain rural facts remain stubborn.

The work in St. Mary's County had helped me to realize how closely the life of families and thereby the salvation of souls was affected by welfare and adjustment within the rural community. I became painfully aware of the gap between the city and the country, which in many respects is greater in the United States than it is abroad.

The rural question was particularly important in the case of the Negroes, and confronted me in working for the development of the Cardinal Gibbons Institute. A generally depressed state of rural life made the special problem of the Negro all the more difficult, as he contended not only against purely racial obstacles but obstacles which he shared with the entire white rural population.

I was also aware of how much a rural-minded priest could do to help matters, if he put his people in touch with government and state aid and encouraged efforts on the part of the parishioners to better their own condition.

For this reason I became interested in the work of my brother priests in the United States who had recently organized the National Catholic Rural Life Conference. The Conference laid great stress upon the dignity and basic importance of the rural parish. Its leaders recalled that the Church itself was built in this country on the personnel contributed by rural parishes to her priesthood and to her religious Orders. Too long had the rural parish been regarded in Catholic circles as a place of exile, a sort of disgrace. Through the Conference I found that I could be in contact with other priests over the country who had been facing similar situations. I believed, too, that the nation as a whole would welcome any contribution the church might make toward solving the problem of rural life.

An instance occurred in 1933, when Henry A. Wallace was appointed Secretary of Agriculture. Mr. Wallace's name was a household word among farmers of the Middle West, chiefly through the Wallace family organ *Wallace's Farmer*. The boundless optimism that accompanied the beginnings of the great Russian agricultural experiment appealed peculiarly to a man of Wallace's background and temperament.

One day, before Mr. Wallace made his famous trip to the Soviet Union, I received an invitation to visit the Secretary of Agriculture in his office in Washington. He wished, he said, to consult me with regard to some plan he had in mind. Mr. Wallace received me graciously and kept me in conversation for a couple of hours. He had followed the work of the National Catholic Rural Life Conference, as well as some of my own writings on rural life topics, and was convinced that it was feasible to start some kind of a pioneer settlement project in the United States. His idea was to find a group of men and women endowed with the religious spirit of the early pioneers, with their sense of idealism and self-abnegation. In that way, he thought, there might be a complete renewal of agrarian life. Catholics, he believed, knew the secret. The Catholic Church had a rural life philosophy and, moreover, had provided the great examples of pioneering in the past, the work of St. Benedict and his monks, St. Bruno and his Carthusians, the great Jesuit Missions of Paraguay, and so on, about all of which he had made a study. He wondered if it would not be possible for such a project to be started in some way under Catholic auspices. I offered no objection to the plan, though it was not clear to me how it was actually going to be executed. In the course of his conversation he mentioned his own religious spirit and told me that he spent half an hour a day reading the *Imitation of Christ*, the works of St. Theresa of Avila, and of St. John of the Cross. Nothing to my knowledge ever came of the conversation, but our Rural Life Conference seemed to have made more impression on the public mind than I had suspected.

When the Conference met in Springfield, Illinois, in August 1930, several items of good news were announced. We learned that our president and founder, the Rev. Dr. Edwin

V. O'Hara, had been appointed Bishop of Great Falls, Montana. One of the rural pastors present, a son of the old sod, waggled his head and remarked that so small a man wouldn't be able to fill the bishop's robes. However, the future disproved the prophecy, and Bishop O'Hara's very distinguished career has continued to give luster to his robes. At this conference we also learned that one thousand vacation schools were already running in the dioceses of the country. Word was received that the Confraternity of Christian Doctrine was now launched as an organized means of instruction enjoined by the canon law of the Church and was recommended to all the dioceses of the United States as a means of preaching religious enlightenment.

The *Fellowship Forum,* a vicious anti-Catholic sheet and successor to the famous or infamous *Menace,* published an article when I was still in Maryland warning the public against the writings and speeches of two, as they called them, foreign papistical priests. One of these was called John LaFarge; the other one was Luigi Ligutti. The name Ligutti was enough to brand him. How could any decent Anglo-Saxon, any person with red American blood in his veins tolerate the language of an Italian called Ligutti? As for this LaFarge, you could see from his name that he was a foreigner and unable to talk English except with a flannel-mouthed accent. I had never met Father Ligutti, now Monsignor Ligutti, but this called my attention to him.

He did an extraordinary job at Granger, Iowa, a little village off on the prairie not so very far from Des Moines. There he had completely transformed the lives of a group of miners who could work only three or four days in the week, which meant about 180 days a year. The rest of the time they were idle and lived in miserable shacks amid loneliness and poverty. Their pastor conceived the idea of starting a part-time farming community. He worked out a housing plan; they could pay for their homes by long-term loans, and the houses

were provided with gardens which they worked themselves
and could make financially profitable. Father Ligutti built
for them a fine school and the pastor at Granger, his successor,
Father John J. Gorman, showed me the place when I visited
there. The boys and girls were instructed by competent teachers in practical arts; the boys in various types of carpentry,
woodwork, and machinework, and the girls in domestic economy. The parish became more or less a rural show-place and
a model of what could be done in the way of part-time farming.

Father Ligutti was a man of boundless energy, imagination,
and resourcefulness, and profited by valuable experiences obtained in his younger days in his homeland of northern Italy.
He took an active part in the life of the Conference, and in
1939 he became our first full-time secretary. He appealed for
my help in reaching the important decision whether or not
to quit his active pastoral life, which he loved, and devote
himself to the rather ungrateful task of working full time for
an organization which commanded only such funds as were
provided for it by the charity of the bishops and a few small
contributions. Deciding to do so, he jumped bravely into the
task, opened the Rural Life Center at Des Moines, Iowa, and
has since made the Conference a success. At present it counts
some ten thousand members drawn from every phase of the
Church, both clergy and lay and different professions and
occupations. In later years Monsignor Ligutti developed into
a really great rural ambassador for the Holy See itself.

Three visits I made to the prairie country remain particularly
vivid in my mind. One was in 1936 when the annual Conven-
tion of the National Catholic Rural Life Conference was held
in Fargo, North Dakota. The trip began in Saint Paul where
I had been visiting Father Francis J. Gilligan, Professor of
Sociology at Saint Paul Seminary. Dr. Gilligan was and is one
of the great apostles of the social teaching of the Church in
the Northwest. In later years he was chairman of the Minnesota State Interracial Conference. I had always felt close to

the Minnesota city, for the former Archbishop of Saint Paul, the Most Rev. John J. Dowling, as a child had been a next-door neighbor of ours in Newport. Archbishop Dowling took a great interest in my brother Bancel, the mural painter, and invited him out to Saint Paul where he did some work, along with his son Tom, on the Cathedral and on the chapel of Saint Paul Seminary. Bancel became extremely fond of Archbishop Dowling, and the Archbishop's influence had much to do in strengthening Bancel's faith and enlightening him as to the liturgical program of the Church.

My old friend, the late Father George Esterguard, a Bayonne, New Jersey, priest who was a pastor in South Dakota, met me in Saint Paul. We drove down through southern Minnesota and ran into a bona fide dust storm, happily of no very long duration, but it was the dust storm period and it gave me an unpleasant experience of that strangest of phenomena. Certainly, one rarely feels so helpless as when sunlight is blotted out and a tightly closed auto is filled with pestiferous, dusty fog. I then spent a few pleasant days at Father George's flourishing rural parish of Big Stone City, close to the Minnesota border.

More than five thousand persons gathered for the four-day session in Fargo, with its riot of displays and visual material.

Another, earlier, experience that brought me close to the heart of the prairie country was a visit in 1929 to Shelby County, Iowa, where I spent a few days with one of the Conference officials, Father (now Monsignor) Martin A. Schiltz, at his open-country parish of Panama, Iowa. Shelby County and vicinity had been settled by German Catholic farmers in 1872 with, as Father Schiltz explained, just enough Irish among them to keep it sweet. The little hamlets of Panama, Earling, Defiance, Portsmouth, Harlan, and Westphalia were centers of a uniformly Catholic rural population, well integrated and progressive. I admired the handsome churches that these German-descended people had built right in the midst of the prairie. In the sacristy Father Schiltz showed me a set of vestments costing $1,700, which was the straight gift to the church from the parishioners. Panama parish was an instructive example of how ingenuity and taste could transform a monotonous countryside. An enthusiastic gardener and tree lover, Father Schiltz had established a parish park, reforesting the church property and the park itself with Japanese junipers, hard maples, Lombardy poplars, decorative shrubs, etc.

In the community of Westphalia, Iowa, Father Duren (now Monsignor) had built up a co-operative plan by which the whole parish became an integrated economic unit. Father Duren's parishioners were as eager to explain to me about their co-operative organization as was the pastor himself, a cultivated gentleman with artistic and literary tastes. The Shelby County communities were examples of independent, self-contained, rural, religiously centered communities; yet the question was in my mind how far they could serve as models for the rest of the country, for the conditions under which they functioned were, after all, particularly favorable.

A more far-reaching answer was provided by a visit to the Omar experimental farm, otherwise known as the Rural Life Institute, at Omar, Nebraska, not far from Omaha and adjacent to Monsignor Flanagan's famous Boys Town which, incidentally, I had the satisfaction of glimpsing. The Creighton University Rural Life Institute was the creation of one whom I might truly call an agricultural genius, the late and lamented Father John C. Rawe, S.J. Father Rawe had taken up the rural life work well-equipped with long experience both of agriculture in his youth and of legal study—he was a member of the Bar—and a knowledge of sociological and economic questions. His plan was to take a small number of pupils, not more than ten—eight would be a convenient number—all of college age, and give them one or two years' training on the college level with college credits. He believed in intensive training, both in the actual technique of agriculture, food production itself, as well as in rural economy, sociology, and human relationships. For all this he had worked out a completely detailed integrated program. Through the co-operation of Omaha businessmen he had obtained the use of the Omar Farm, a magnificent tract of several hundred acres with a fine residence. There he was able to work out his plans with eight carefully selected students. Father Rawe was a born pedagogue, one of those fortunate Socratic beings who impart knowledge continually and easily in such a way as to captivate his pupils with apparently no effort.

When I arrived at Omar four of his eight pupils had been lost to the draft. As we sat by the big open fire in the evening the four young men still remaining recited to me the details of their work and, like Father Duren's parishioners, they were as eager to explain and illustrate as was their leader himself. One of these lads rose every morning around three or four o'clock and drove a milk truck into Omaha where he ran a route of hospitals and other institutions. The farm was a combined poultry and dairy farm. The former owners had run a tremendous, elaborate sort of poultry scheme with thousands of chickens bred in wire cages. From a biological standpoint the breeding process was perfectly successful. The hens grew large and fat and toothsome. The only disadvantage was they developed neuroses and at the slightest noise would bump their heads against the cages. Father Rawe liberated the neurotic hens and had equal success without the disastrous consequences. The most striking feature of the Omar Farm was an earthworm ranch, a big wooden barrel filled with countless squirming earthworms. These were Father Rawe's pets, for he was an enthusiastic believer in organic agriculture. A disciple of the famous Dr. Ehrenfried Pfyffer of Switzerland, his starting-point was the all-necessary compost heap.

Life at Omar Farm centered around the chapel with its daily Holy Sacrifice, as would the ideal farming community, in Father John's conception. He had taken everything into account, the whole scope of public relations with Catholics and non-Catholics alike, the farmer as a citizen, as a consumer and distributor, the farmer as part of the whole social, religious, and political organism.

Alas, the project came to a speedy end. Immediately after I left two more of the young men were drafted. With only two left the experiment obviously could not be carried on any more and Omar was closed. Father Rawe was transferred to the Arapahoe Indian Mission in Wyoming, where he labored a while on the Mission farms and unfortunately contracted an infection which later brought about his death. In the hope that he might recover, he was transferred a second time to my old parish of Ridge in St. Mary's County, Maryland, where he labored in conjunction with Father Horace B. McKenna for a couple of years attempting to teach his methods to the colored children at the Cardinal Gibbons Institute. But Father Rawe's strength had failed and the conditions under which he labored at Ridge were too remote from those which he needed to carry out his educational program. His death was a great loss to the rural life cause and it also left unanswered the enigmatic question: How far is a completely self-subsistent co-operative farming community possible under the conditions we have in the United States? Just how far can farming as a distinct way of life remain an economically viable and practical venture, something that can offer a career to the man of small means and can permanently hold his young?

It was a revelation to me to discover that the Jewish people of the United States had in some ways come closer to a successful answer to the farm problem than had their non-Jewish neighbors. Once on a Southern trip a young Jewish lawyer from Atlanta, Georgia, was seated opposite me in the dining car of the train. The talk turned on farming and he was astonished to learn that there were some 100,000 prosperous Jewish farmers in the United States. If a Jew himself did not know of this fact, how much was it known to the rest of Americans?

In Maryland, in St. Mary's County, I had happened upon a pitiful instance of a misplaced Jewish farmer. This unfortunate old fellow had been sold a bill of goods by some local

sharpers and tried to eke out a living on a desolate, eroded
place some two or three miles out of Leonardtown near the
Glebe schoolhouse. He lasted a couple of years and then pulled
up stakes and left, an example of the helpless, uninformed
immigrant. The majority of Jewish farmers, however, have
been well provided for by the Jewish Agricultural Society,
which was in large part the creation of a real agricultural
genius, Dr. Gabriel P. Davidson. I came in contact with the
Jewish farmers on various occasions and noticed the simple
and efficient ways with which they had bridged the gap between the city and the country. Most of them were centered
either in New Jersey or Connecticut or else in the Chicago
area, as a rule engaged in poultry farming. The Jewish Agricultural College at Doylestown, Pennsylvania, is said to be
one of the most efficient and practical agricultural schools in
the United States.

In April 1937 I met with a group of Catholic Rural Life leaders in Saint Louis to discuss the scope and contents of the
proposed Manifesto on rural life, which appeared in 1939.
Out of this group committees were appointed to draw up
statements on various phases of rural life. These statements
furnished materials for a tentative draft of a Manifesto. The
sixteen chapters of the Manifesto, forming a 213-page book,
including the ample annotations, were issued by the Bruce
Publishing Company in Milwaukee, and made a sort of bible
of the Catholic Rural Life Conference movement.

I worked with the late Father Virgil Michel, O.S.B., of Col-
legeville, Minnesota, on the chapter dealing with farmer co-
operatives. Father Michel was a pioneer in the rural life field
as in the field of liturgy and was one of the first to see the
connection between Catholic social science and the social worship of the Church in the United States. We held that "while
co-operatives are not proposed as a panacea for all conceivable
economic and social ills, nevertheless soundly established co-

operatives will be potent agencies for the protection of the farming group."

The general aims of the Rural Life Conference were re-stated in later years, as:

1. To care for the underprivileged Catholics living on the land.

2. To keep on the land Catholics now living there.

3. To increase the number of Catholics living on the land, not as a back-to-the-land movement, but to offset a false ur-banization and encourage the practical rural indoctrination of country youth.

4. To convert the non-Catholics living on the land.

The fourth of these statements, on converting the non-Cath-olics living on the land, never seemed to raise any objection among the many non-Catholics, both clergy and lay, who have attended our meetings and generously co-operated with us.

At the meeting at LaCrosse, Wisconsin, in October 1948 the Conference bestowed for the first time in its history an annual award or medal upon some person who had taken consider-able part in its work. They were most gracious in conferring upon me through the hands of the Most Rev. Bishop Treacy of LaCrosse the first of these annual rural life medals, though I contributed only a small addition to the pioneer work of the Conference's originators.

After some twenty-five years of the Conference's existence its leaders once more assembled and issued a new statement completing and in some ways revising the pronouncements of earlier years. It is interesting to compare this latest mani-festo with the earlier ones. The work of the Conference had taken on a most dynamic aspect. It was now concerned with technical aid to the undeveloped countries of the world, espe-cially in connection with the work of the Missions. Questions of international trade and of migratory labor and of food production for the world came up on the floor of the meeting, and the Conference was linked with similar programs in

other countries that were striving in their own way to meet
the agonizing problem of food production and distribution.
At the same time, the Conference has joined forces with the
Catholic Rural Life Movement first in Mexico, through the
mediation of the late Archbishop Diaz, and later in Colombia
and other Latin-American countries.

The question of land ownership—its distribution, its title,
its use—which three modern Popes have treated but which
seemed to be the affair of only a few country pastors like myself and friends meeting in St. Louis or Baltimore—has today
become the great social problem of our time, in the words of
Archbishop Antoniutti, Apostolic Delegate of the Holy See
to Canada (Sept. 8, 1952, at St. Boniface, Manitoba). Land-
hungry millions in Latin America, other millions of migrants,
legal and illegal, to the United States, look to the clergy and
lay leaders and the teachings of the National Catholic Rural
Life Conference, for their aid, guidance, and protection. The
idealistic seed of our home-grown rural life plans fell on many
an acre of stony soil here in the 80 per cent industrialized
United States. But it is beginning to bear a harvest of aid
to families in the 70 per cent agrarian remainder of the world.

In conjunction with the work of the American bishops and
that of Pope Pius XII, as well as with the agencies of the
United States government and the United Nations, the Conference became a vehicle for working out the intricate problems of resettlement, and Conference experts served as
consultants to the World Health Organization and FAO.

CHAPTER FIFTEEN

Man's World and God's House

≫≪

Only once did I see Al Smith. My brother Grant, the architect, had made the Governor's acquaintance in connection
with some government work that he had undertaken, and
called on him in his office in Albany. After the professional
talk was finished, the Governor said to Grant: "Mr. LaFarge,
do you really know anything about the way the state of New
York is governed?" Grant professed his ignorance, whereupon
the Governor volunteered: "Let me explain it to you briefly.
I think you will find it interesting." Then followed a half-
hour's description of the machinery of New York state government. My brother was dumbfounded at the clarity and
ease with which so complex a question could be reduced to
a few simple ideas and presented to a layman. From that time
on nothing was too good, in his estimation, for Al Smith.

When I visited Al Smith, he was close to the end of his
life. I wanted his name for a committee of sponsors for some
work I was interested in. Raising his hands in despair, he exclaimed: "Good Lord, I belong to some three thousand committees, according to my secretary, and don't know the names
of one-tenth of them. I couldn't possibly take on anything
more." However, he offered to make me a gift of the Empire
State Building, where offices were not renting so well at the
time. "If that will be any help to you," he said, "it is yours,
provided you can take it away."

In the course of my brief petition, I mentioned Communism. Mr. Smith bridled at once. "Communism," he said,

"that's just a bunch of crackpots. It's not worth bothering about. I have seen those fellows down at Union Square and they are just a lot of lunatics. It isn't worthwhile giving any attention to the thing."

For some years previously, in giving serious thought to the nature of Communism and how it could be dealt with, I had encountered precisely the attitude that Governor Smith represented. Most Catholics thought it a mere crackpot idea and the vast majority could not begin to grasp the extent, the malice, and the perverted intelligence which had seized power through the Bolshevik revolution and was guiding the destinies of a large part of the human race. Communism was foreign; it was crazy and odd; it was something that you might study speculatively as you would Bali dancers or the food habits of the people of Arabia. After all, people as a rule are more concerned with what is nearby and affects them personally than they are with something explained in terms of a completely different land, language, and habits, and an alien mentality.

On one occasion I lectured at the old Catholic Club on Central Park South in New York, on the cruelties wrought by the Soviet government upon the Russian peasants and the Ukrainians. I described the origin of the Russian famine and told of the millions of Ukrainian people who starved to death because of the deliberate Soviet policy. The audience appeared moved, but in the back of the room I noticed an old Irish lady who shook her head all through the lecture. On my way out I asked her why she seemed to express a disagreement. "What's all this talk," she said, "about the people in Russia and their troubles? Nothing they do to them over there can compare with what the Irish in New York City have suffered under a Fusion Administration!" I suppose her brother or son or nephew had lost a job in the city government.

The more I studied the question of Communism, the more I was convinced that one could never grasp its nature unless one kept always in mind two main aspects, one of them negative and the other positive. The negative aspect was the revolution against God: the Bolshevik revolution was essentially a politically organized atheism. Atheism, the formal denial of God and the formal opposition to God and rebellion against Him, was not a mere corollary to an otherwise interesting theory but was of its very essence and contributed to its dynamism, appealing to certain demonic recesses of the human heart. On the positive side I saw Communism as a caricature of Christianity, or rather of the whole Judaeo-Christian concept of man and of time and destiny.

The world has now become so disillusioned over the great myth of Russia's material, cultural, and intellectual progress that it is hard to reconstruct the aura of novelty and excitement which surrounded the beginnings of the Bolshevik transformation of Russia's natural resources. My years in rural life work had made me conscious of the strong appeal to humble but naturally intelligent rural people of modern machinery and technology. A little book published in 1931, *New Russia's Primer: the Story of the Five Year Plan* by M. Ilin, though ostensibly written for children, vividly dramatized this mechanical gospel. As Dr. George S. Counts of Teachers College, who translated it from the Russian, remarked: "Gigantic tasks of social reconstruction are brought into intimate relation with the interests of boys and girls. The lifting of their country out of a condition of severe cultural and technical backwardness is made to appear in the guise of a thrilling adventure." Says the primer:

The Five Year Plan is a project: not of one factory but of 2,400 factories and not only factories but also cities, of electric stations, of bridges, of ships, of railroads, of mines and state farms, of rural communes, of schools, of libraries. It is a project for the rebuilding of our whole country and was prepared not by one man or by two men but by thousands of trained persons. To the work of building came not tens but millions of workers. All of us will help to build the Five Year Plan.

While the *mystique* of Communism, its subtler and deeper psychological aspects, eluded most Americans, mechanical skill, especially on a huge, dynamic, highly planned basis, made a simple bold appeal to the American mind. Thus supposedly hard-headed American businessmen went overboard for Soviet planning. American railroad men helped to reconstruct the Russian railroads, and I was rebuked on one occasion by one of our prominent and most pious Catholic industrialists in New Jersey for having even suggested that Soviet Russia might be reprehensible. The same man severely criticized Father Edmund A. Walsh, S.J., founder of the Foreign Service School at Georgetown University, for his exposé of the Bolshevik revolution and the harm it had done.

The evil repute which the Communist world has earned through the record of the last twenty years or so, particularly the postwar years, rather obscures for us the difficulties encountered by anybody who a quarter of a century ago wanted to explain the facts to the public. One had to contend against the simplified attitude expressed by Al Smith about "crackpots." A columnist in one of the popular Negro papers, the *Afro-American* of Baltimore, quoted a remark of Mr. Smith contrasting the foul air of Communist Russia with the free air of America. The Negro columnist immediately retorted that he himself had been in Moscow, was lodged there in a magnificent hotel of three hundred rooms with every possible convenience, and received, with his wife and family, the greatest possible courtesy from all the management and help, whereas he couldn't get a place to sleep in any Southern city. The great disillusionment had not yet taken place, in the mind of the Negro or in the mind of the admirers of Russia. Embittered and rebellious spirits in this country were happy to find something that might seem to reflect on our own way of life. But also plain, somewhat materialistic Americans thought that anything producing results and making the wheels turn around must be pretty good, especially if it would help American trade. One of our ultra-conservative contemporary columnists ought to re-read one of his old paragraphs in which he violently denounced critics of Russia, saying they did not know what they were doing. Russian trade and Russian friendship were necessary for the United States, and those who tried to make hard feelings between Russia and this country were trouble-makers and not realists.

There was no use, I felt in those early days, in indulging in a mere policy of drifting and waiting for events to take shape, or for people, in the recent words of Henry Wallace, to "have more sense." An armed crusade was impracticable; it had been tried and found disastrous. There was need, I was convinced, of a planned and definite policy to meet the challenge of Communism intelligently and with full recognition of its unusual and profoundly historic nature.

I was convinced that the problem of social disorder which had betrayed the Old World would, if neglected, prove an abundant seed-ground for Communism even here in the United States.

The labor movement in this country for the most part was sound and patriotic. It was moved by practical, professional considerations, only infrequently by ideology and class hatred. Inequalities between the rich and the poor were not so glaring as in Europe. However large might be the proportion of those who professed no religion and were affiliated with no church, the American people manifested a fundamental respect for religious matters, a fundamental sense of decency and tradition of morality, of law and order.

On the other hand, the Second World War had projected its shadow far in advance. Thirty years ago, in 1922, Pope Pius XI issued his encyclical *Ubi Arcano Dei* in which he prophetically warned against the tragedies that were to come. The idea of a world revolution would appeal, I felt, to certain elements in the American mind: to those who felt themselves disinherited, and particularly to the discontented minority groups, the American proletariat, whether they were rural workers or racial and religious minorities. It would appeal again to a certain type of liberal believer and social idealist. Some of our fine conservative Protestants took up with enthusiasm the revolutionary bandits in Mexico. I was particularly bewildered that younger and more sophisticated members of our old and socially prominent conservative families, young folks who by breeding would despise people on the other side of the tracks and shudder at the idea of being associated with Catholics, were ready at the drop of a hat to throw over the whole content of Christian revelation, proclaim themselves devotees of pure experimental science and thoroughgoing pragmatists, and praise without restriction the marvels of the Soviet experiment.

The task, as I saw it, was one of getting to work early on the problem of social reconstruction. That meant a fundamental renewal of religious life in its totality, and particularly in its communal aspect, the renewal of communal religious worship as it was practiced in the earlier ages of the Church and was recommended by the leading liturgical scholars of the present time. Furthermore, it meant putting our shoulders to the wheel in working out the remedy for some of our grave domestic social disorders whether in the economic or the racial area. At the same time we had an obligation to study the causes of international conflict and the obstacles to world peace.

It is easy after all these years to register these convictions, in now commonplace phrases, but before the year 1931, when Pope Pius XI issued his famous encyclical "On the Reconstruction of the Social Order" (*Quadragesimo Anno*), the warnings of Pope Leo XIII in his "On the Condition of the Workingman" (*Rerum Novarum*) had been largely forgotten. Those who were *Rerum Novarum*-minded were in a distinct minority among Catholics in this country, and Catholics themselves were a minority. Archbishop Curley of Baltimore told me he had heard the late Monsignor John A. Ryan, Professor of Moral Theology at the Catholic University of America, publicly denounced as a socialist at a meeting in Florida.

From the very beginning two difficulties confronted any religious journalist who wished to discuss questions of social disorder. The first was the objection that you were dealing with temporal or material matters, whereas the office of the Church or the office of a priest as a spokesman of the Church was to deal with spiritual things, with prayer and individual moral reform, but not with human livelihood and social and political institutions. A Catholic, clerical or lay, could talk all he wanted about purely local politics and temporal matters concerning the country of his own or his parents' national origin. But when it came to serious discussion of the morality of certain economic practices he was accused of dealing with merely earthly affairs.

It was always easy to swing into the old lines. In preaching the Gospel week after week and month after month, one could always avoid over-obvious social conclusions of some of the discourses of our Lord Jesus Christ. Social reform was avoided in retreats and in mission sermons, and those who treated these matters were suspected of a certain degree of socialism.

The criticism that falls on the apostle of a better social order in this day fell upon the ears of St. Vincent de Paul, the great father of modern organized charity, in the seventeenth century. His most outstanding lay disciple, the founder of the Conferences of St. Vincent de Paul, Frédéric Ozanam, was under no such illusion. To use the happy expression of Pope Pius XI, he was solicitous not only for remedial charity but also for preventive charity, for such organizational methods, for such institutional improvements as would prevent the need of relief in later times.

The alternative to an active social program on the part of the clergy and the Church always was and always will be the curse of anti-clericalism. Neglect of St. Vincent's lessons contributed to the growth of anti-clericalism in France. Looking but a few hundred miles across our own border into Canada, I was encouraged from the very start by the ideas and publications of the Ecole Populaire of Montreal, founded and di-

rected by my colleague Father Joseph P. Archambault, S.J.
I think it is safe to say that the work of this Ecole Populaire
and its comprehensive social program have been a great preventive of violent anti-clericalism in French Canada.

The great difficulty was the plain, hard work such a program involved. In the mountains around Innsbruck there
were two ways to climb the slopes. One was to rush up, leap-
ing over crags and grasping at trees, gasping oneself out of
breath and finally collapsing. The other was to tramp the
good old path that the cows followed, the *Kuhpfad* in the
German expression. It was slow and less picturesque, but it
got you there.

As the great spiritual leader and historian of the life of
Christ, Father Moritz Meschler, S.J., used to tell the Jesuit
scholastics, by the *Kuhpfad,* the ordinary way, numberless souls
reached the heights of great sanctity. The path downward to
Bolshevism and later to Fascism and Nazism had taken, in
point of fact, hundreds of years. The climb upward to the
heights of spiritual liberation would also take time and would
mean thousands of footsteps and the collaboration of hundreds of minds thinking and working and toiling. It was
necessary to discover the truth, to study the truth in its totality, in all its aspects, historical, social, psychological, religious,
etc. It was necessary, above all, to *do the truth* in all sincerity,
as St. Paul says.

As a mere journalist, obviously I had to confine my research
to a limited area, the fields in which I had personal experience. As for other areas, I had to accept for the most part
what others had handed down and see what body of doctrine
was available. This task became easier after the appearance
of *Quadragesimo Anno* in 1931. After that had dispelled the
clouds more light began to appear on the scene and it was
easier to discuss the application of social teaching to the
American situation as well as to the organization of the international community.

My own thinking on these matters was reflected in articles

that I wrote for *America* regularly, and from time to time for other publications. Along with these more formal expressions of opinion I conducted in *America* for twelve years, as I have mentioned, a weekly column entitled "With Scrip and Staff," which for the first few years I signed "The Pilgrim," but later signed with my own name. The Pilgrim specialized in trying to keep track of the more important organized movements—religious, cultural, and social—in the life of the Catholic Church in this country and, to some extent, in other countries. Where it was feasible, the Pilgrim attempted to enrich his store of information by direct personal contact, either as a participant in some of these movements or at least by attending some of the more important annual conventions.

For the same reason, I associated myself with the small group which started the Catholic Association for International Peace in November 1927. It was organized in a series of meetings during 1926-1927—the first following the Eucharistic Congress in Chicago, the second in Cleveland that autumn to form an organizing committee, and the third during Easter Week, 1927, in Washington where the permanent organization was established. The CAIP was started and has continued to operate under the wing, as it were, of the National Catholic Welfare Conference, though it is not an organic part of the Conference. The Association works largely through the preparation of Committee reports and through national and regional conferences.

The discussions of the CAIP and the study of similar groups, such as the Catholic Committee on International Peace in England, and other groups in Germany, Italy, Spain, and France, as well as the leading non-Catholic organizations interested in peace and international organization, led me to reach a number of decisions.

Catholics for the most part, even Catholic scholars, were remarkably unfamiliar with the important body of doctrine that already existed in the Church on the subject of peace and international relations. It was the work of the CAIP, following the plan of its secretary, Father R. A. McGowan, to acquaint the Catholic public with some of this material and at the same time to stimulate the colleges and universities to research and to encourage discussion.

Indeed the very idea of discussing peace and international order seemed strange. One of the early meetings of the CAIP was held at the now defunct Catholic Club in New York City. The distinguished leader of Tammany, the late John F. Curry, happened into the Club while the deliberations were occurring upstairs.

"What's going on up there?" Mr. Curry asked me, in somewhat agitated fashion.

"Why," I said, "they are holding a meeting of the Catholic Association for International Peace."

"The Catholic Association for *what?*" groaned Mr. Curry. "My Lord, what are we coming to!"

Well, there can be a certain amount of pedantry, of *snobisme* in these matters, but the solid fruit continued to appear. Through the agency of the CAIP a splendid collection of pamphlets has been issued treating of such topics as international ethics, the ethics of war, tariffs and world peace, peace action of the Popes, peace agenda of the United Nations, etc.

All these questions became enormously sharpened with the advent of the Second World War. But even in the earliest stage of the CAIP certain fundamental positions became clear from the study of sources. Witness, for instance, our definite disapproval of the policy of aggression. We were for peace but not for pacifism. We were not in favor of neutrality where the defense of an invaded country was involved. We believed that there were certain conditions ascertainable for a just war. We discussed the problems of the conscientious objector. We held that charity, as well as justice, obtained between nations —a rather abstract doctrine in 1928 but an enormously practical one today with many hundreds of thousands of desperate refugees seeking admission to our country, and other dispossessed and wandering millions whose welfare is the obligation in charity of the United States. The CAIP held out for the admissibility of intervention, and even the duty of intervention where natural rights are violated in a foreign country, basing our stand on sound pronouncements of Christian authority.

It was lucidly clear from Catholic teaching that no nation could enjoy unlimited and absolute sovereignty, just as in the social order no person can rightly claim absolute possession of material goods. Though man has a right to private property, a right given to him by God, this right is not absolute but is in the form of a stewardship and implies certain definite obligations to one's neighbor and to the community, and indeed to the entire human race. In the same way no nation can exist entirely for itself. The common good of all mankind imposes a limit upon the natural right of sovereignty. Yet unrestrained internationalism, the abolition of all sovereignty, one-worldism in the bad sense, is contrary to Catholic teaching, but a certain limitation of national sovereignty becomes more and more necessary in the complicated conditions of the modern world, so much so that in 1953 this principle was embodied in the Constitution itself of the Netherlands.*

And from that teaching flows a very practical consequence. The more we appreciate the precious gifts of order and freedom at home, the more seriously we shall wish to guarantee them for the entire community of human beings. The most far-reaching of such guarantees, humanly speaking, is that of the "organization of international society according to the demands of natural law and Christian order." †

Criticizing the original Dumbarton Oaks proposals that

* Catholic doctrine on this topic is discussed in detail with references and documentation in *National Patriotism and Papal Teaching,* by John J. Wright (now the Most Rev. John J. Wright, Bishop of Worcester, Massachusetts), Newman Bookshop, Westminster, Maryland, 1943.

† *Code of International Ethics:* Second Edition, Newman Press, Westminster, Maryland, 1947.

preceded the adoption at San Francisco of the present United Nations Charter, the American Catholic Bishops declared on November 19, 1944, that "an international institution, based on the recognition of an objective moral obligation and not on the binding force of a covenant alone, is needed" for such a purpose, and called for a discussion of the proposals "in the spirit of constructive effort." It is not, they said, "a question of creating an international community but of organizing it."

I know no more challenging opportunity, before it is tragically too late, for all those who like myself see the need of an adequately juridic and morally based world organization, than to take an active part in the present world-wide deliberations for the proposed revision of the United Nations Charter in 1955. I see it as a challenge to American Catholics, and to all intelligent and God-fearing citizens of the United States.

CHAPTER SIXTEEN
The Gathering Storm

➤➤➤ ◄◄◄

In April 1938 Father Talbot, editor of *America,* decided to send me to the International Eucharistic Congress at Budapest. The decision was extremely welcome because a visit to Hungary would include a visit to other parts of Eastern Europe, Bohemia and Slovakia in Czechoslovakia, Yugoslavia, Hungary itself, and an opportunity to learn at first hand of conditions that I had read and heard about for many years, beginning with my contact with the Slovak people in Maryland. It would also enable me to become more closely acquainted with our companion Jesuit magazines, such as *The Month, Etudes, Action Populaire, Stimmen der Zeit* in Munich, the Croatian magazine *Život,* and, if I were privileged to go to Rome, the *Civiltà Cattolica,* as well as many non-Jesuit publications.

In the event of a visit to Rome, which would depend on the good will of higher Superiors, I would have the opportunity to become more closely acquainted with the Papal and Roman point of view on public issues, as treated for instance in the social encyclicals of Leo XIII and Pius XI, and I could retrace ground I had covered in my youth. From an editorial standpoint I considered it extremely important to learn at first hand of Hitler's Germany. Personally I was convinced that the situation under Hitler was just as deplorable as commonly reported. Nevertheless, plenty of skepticism was current on that matter, especially in Catholic circles where German influence was prominent, and one could only be satisfied if one could see and test for oneself. The same applied to the situation in Mussolini's Italy. I wished to examine Fascism at first hand and learn more of the attitude of the Church. I hoped in addition to take a flyer to Spain, though unfortunately developments prevented my carrying out that part of the program. Finally, I thought such a trip would enable me to come in contact with many currents of thought in the different countries of Europe.

When our ship arrived in the late afternoon at Plymouth, the customs officer merely waved a card at my nose, bade me welcome to old England, and pushed me into a thoroughly British taxi with a solemn, bearded driver and right-hand drive, directing him to take me to the station and put me on the 6:15 P.M. train to Bristol.

As we sped through the darkened landscape I was struck with the almost total absence of any lights, such a contrast to an American train ride. At Bristol we took an autocar for Bath, where I was headed at the invitation of Mr. Robert Wilberforce, husband of my cousin Hope Warren. Robert met me at the station and drove me along the sodium-lighted boulevard to the Spa Hotel.

The following day with the Wilberforces I inspected the beauties of Bath, including the cathedral. The next day we visited Bradford-on-Avon, with its eighth-century Saxon church, and Downside Abbey of the Benedictines. There Brother Kevin (Carroll Horsey), a young American monk, met us, and after lunch showed us the Abbey and the school. At Glastonbury, where the sinking sun lighted the ruins, I said a prayer to Joseph of Arimathea that he might bless the rest of my journey.

In my youth I had spent one day at Oxford and on this occasion I balanced it by one perfect day in Cambridge with an ideal guide, the late Father Demetrius Zema of the New York Jesuit Province, who seemed to know everybody worth knowing, including that delightful logician Father Thomas Gilby, O.P., who welcomed us at his hospitable fireside.

I was particularly interested in meeting vivacious and

knowledgeable Miss Annie O'Brien Christitch, a Serbian-Irish Catholic correspondent for *America*. After conversing with her I wrote to Father Wilfrid Parsons that the British seemed to be showing a more friendly attitude toward Italy, as well as to Ireland: "People here do not seem anxious about war, as in the U.S. Rather a general idea that happy days are coming, and that Hitler can somehow be handled. I hope they are right." Alas, it was only a hope. The "somehow" for "handling Hitler" was never discovered, if it ever existed.

Since I was headed for Czechoslovakia, Miss Christitch had arranged for me to take lunch with Jan Masaryk, son of the famous former Prime Minister of Czechoslovakia. Mr. Masaryk received me alone in his apartment and poured out his soul in emotional fashion for a couple of hours. He began at once to talk about Hitler, unspeakably disturbed and terrified at the thought of what Hitler was going to do to his native country. If only, he kept repeating, the British would do something. "I have argued for hours and hours with Lord Halifax," he exclaimed, "saying to him that if only he would let us know where my country stands with Great Britain, I should then know how to act. If they said they couldn't help us we'd find some kind of way out. If Great Britain is not going to support us, then I shall simply pack my valise, take a trip to Berlin, and lay all the cards on the table before Hitler. The game will be up, and I shall simply accept what Hitler chooses to leave us. On the other hand, if Great Britain intends to support us, we shall keep up the fight. But they refuse to say that they will and refuse to say that they won't. I could get nowhere with the Foreign Office."

I needled Mr. Masaryk, as far as I could politely do so, on the treatment of the Slovaks by the Czechs. On that point I found him extremely on the defensive, and uneasily so. "I am," he said himself, "a Slovak. My father was a Slovak," which was one-half or one-quarter true. Czechs, he said, were being badly misrepresented, all of which was quite natural under the circumstances. He would gladly arrange, he said, for me to see Mr. Benes in Prague but I would find him in a state of utter alarm and dejection. It was a depressing experience, and the depression was increased by what seemed to me the troubled condition of Jan Masaryk himself.

My own impression is more or less in accord with the opinion expressed by Alexander Sachs, economic consultant, in a paper he contributed to the symposium, *Moral Principles of Action.** Mr. Sachs believes that the death of Jan Masaryk, whose body was found under an open window on March 10, 1948, was not at the hands of Soviet assassins but was a voluntary act on Masaryk's part, a sort of symbolic protest against the complete anonymity which totalitarians impose upon their victims. During 1941, the Nazi period, Dr. Sachs was the recipient of Jan Masaryk's confidences and worries about developments. Masaryk told him he was haunted by the type of persecution that the Nazis were imposing upon prominent personalities taken as hostages in reprisal for any form of resistance. Says Sachs:

In its impact upon our civilization the Communist totalitarianism, like the Nazi, has consistently striven to deprive the objects of its persecution of that integral confrontation of personality with fate that permits the expression of and the right to tragedy and martyrdom. The procedure and the method are degradation and atomization of the individual in the setting of rightlessness.

There is evidence, in Sachs's theory, that "definitely points to Masaryk's efforts to surmount the threat of historical erasure that confronted him." An indication of this was an exceptional fact connected with his death that did "manage to break through the curtain of silence": that on his bed was found a Bible opened at the fifth chapter of St. Paul's Epistle to the Galatians, verses 22 and 23. From previous experiences and items of conversation it seemed evident that the text of this entire chapter was deeply associated in the mind of Jan Masaryk and his father with the idea of a spiritual protest

* Harper, 1952.

against tyranny and persecution, and was used in this case
to indicate his protest against an anonymous martyrdom.

Splendid work was being done by the Church at Oxford and
Cambridge under conditions vastly more congenial than those
I had experienced at Harvard or which exist at the average
American secular institution. Both of England's great universities were originally established by Catholics, of course, and
were distinctly church schools. The Catholic Church present
today within their walls is a living representative of those days
when Oxford and Cambridge achieved their greatest glory
and moved in the most international sphere. Nevertheless,
talking in London to scholarly men like Father Philip Hughes,
and Richard O'Sullivan, K.C. (now Q.C.), who hospitably
welcomed me to the Inns of Court, I found a distinct regret
that Britain lacked a Catholic college or a Catholic university.
With such a nucleus and rallying point, they thought, the
position of the Church today in Britain would be considerably
stronger.

After a week in Paris with my Jesuit brethren, I took the
train to Germany via Thiancourt. Considerable time on the
trip was consumed by an international meal, served by an international waiter in an international dining car. The meal,
with an indefinite supply of fried potatoes, was the sort that
stays with you; something that, in view of later developments,
I did not regret.

The passengers grew fewer as we reached the German border, and my spirits at the same time sank correspondingly at
the ever-nearing prospect of Hitlerland. When we reached
Perl on the German frontier only one passenger was left on
the train, a sad-looking Polish lady who was returning to her
home country. I have often wondered whatever became of
her. I was told to remain in the station waiting room until
notice should come to board the train. The waiting room was
cheerful enough, with a restaurant counter and a pleasant-
looking person in charge. But there was nothing to eat. A

handsome portrait of the Fuehrer hung on the wall with elaborate decorations. Two ladies from the countryside around
dropped by and discussed their vegetable sets for the garden.
Finally, the customs was ready in the person of a stout, red-
headed, elderly official who was terribly embarrassed because
I paid him ten pfennigs too much, and almost weepingly exclaimed: "I'll have to go through *all* my forms and make everything out again to correct the error." A couple of other
gentlemen then appeared who viewed with suspicion a copy
of *Portugal,* by Gonzague de Reynold, but returned it to me
after careful inspection. They then confiscated a little French
travel book I had picked up on a walk and were disturbed
because I carried an Italian grammar. They took it as evidence
that I had been in Rome at the time Hitler was there. I explained that I was not *from* Rome but was *going to* Rome,
and they let me pass. Only after I was again safely on the train
did I recall that happily they had not spied the map of Czechoslovakia I had absent-mindedly taken with me in the satchel,
the last thing you'd want to carry in visiting Hitler's Germany.
Oddly enough, they paid no attention at all to my typewriter,
which I had been lugging around.

My destiny was Coblenz, where I was to spend a few days
with my old Innsbruck classmate Dr. Heinrich Chardon, pastor of the venerable Liebfrauenkirche. A solitary and silent
young German huddled at the other end of the compartment
and looked terrified when I addressed a word to him. Changing at Trier, I was greeted with a most welcome *Hochwürden*
("Your Reverence") and hustled kindly with all my bundles
into the wrong train, a *Personenzug* (whistle-stop local), by a
buxom young red-headed lady with the railroad mission or
Bahnhofsmission white armband on her sleeve. After the
tenth stop in the rain, the international dinner and the fried
potatoes had become as remote in history as Dr. Samuel Johnson's cups of tea. I had memorized every province, river, and
town in Portugal, as well as twenty-five Italian adverbs; and
anticipated every daily spiritual exercise.

Lovelier and grander grew the country; quainter and neater the delightful little villages; colder and darker the evening in the long twilight of northern Europe. Then appeared the *Mutter Gottes:* blue-robed and gold-braided, newly carved out of wood, Our Lady stood in a little niche, with a vigil light or two burning before her. Her countenance radiated that grave sweetness which seemed to me the reflection of all that was finest in old Catholic Germany; that wonderful mixture of the matron and the maid. An old refrain I had heard years before in the little country churches on the Rhine, turned in my mind as the train rattled along:

> *Maria zu lieben ist Allzeit mein Sinn!*
> *In Freuden und Leiden Dein Diener ich bin.*

At the last visible station an old Franciscan nun, with thick beads, made her way from the train. Did Our Lady send her, as she sent the girl who said *Hochwürden,* so as to remind me that there was still someone in Heaven whatever might be rampant on earth?

The clouds had lifted by the time I reached Coblenz and the people were streaming out of the church after late May devotions. The pastor stood chatting with the flock and introduced me at once to some of his leading parishioners. All were full of sympathy and most anxious to know where I had come from and when I had left. I explained that I had left Paris at 9 A.M. that morning. "From Paris," they exclaimed. "Incredible! You came right straight through from Paris?" I said yes. "And you are still safe?" I assured them that I was whole in body and limb. "But how fortunate," they exclaimed, "to escape. We understand that in Paris the streets are running with blood; there is a terrible revolution and people are being murdered by the Jews and Bolsheviks." I assured them that I had crossed the Place de la Concorde in a taxi on my way to the station and had seen nothing except a few delivery boys on bicycles, no signs of blood or revolution. One of the men let out an indiscreet yell. *"Potztausend!"* he said. "Look at the stuff they have been handing out to us here."

I soon learned that one of the weirdest features of the Hitler regime was the total ignorance in which people were kept not only about the outside world but even about their own world. In Coblenz you could not learn what was happening in Bonn or in Cologne. You could not write. Obviously you could not telephone, and it was dangerous to send messages. As for the papers, they were devoid of information.

We sat until 2 A.M. at the presbytery talking about Hitler. I soon found the Hitler atmosphere was nothing imaginary, but thick enough to cut with a knife. In the parlor of the presbytery was an enormous oaken table about twelve feet long covered with innumerable documents. The unfortunate pastor and curates had to fill out these documents every day, every week, or every month as the occasion might be. The movement of every person in the parish had to be accounted for. The curates took it philosophically. After all, they said, we are all going to Dachau sooner or later so what's the use of bothering.

When I woke the next morning, all traces of rain had disappeared, and the great bells were booming from a dozen churches, mostly Catholic, the others Lutheran. At lunch that day we entertained a nice old lady who had come down the Rhine on a steamer on the trip to Coblenz. It was pleasant May weather and she was enjoying her holiday. I told her I was from America and from New York. "America!" she exclaimed. "And are you going back to America?" I said yes. "And are you going back to New York?" I said yes, I expected to. With tears in her voice she begged me not to return. "You are so safe here and America is so terrible. In New York, I understand, the people are hung from every lamppost; it is filled with gangsters and lynchers and your life is in danger every moment. You can't even go out on the street." It was again the same story of propaganda.

Out in the country that afternoon we watched the Hitler Jugend, little kids marching in a listless, wooden fashion up and down in front of one of the old village churches, in charge of a pasty-faced young man who looked even more depressed. There the dismal spiritual situation contrasted incredibly with the glory of the countryside. This was Germany as yet untouched by war's frightful devastation, incredibly beautiful. We took our coffee on the Heights of Ehrenbreitstein, looking over the Deutscher Eck, the confluence of the Rhine and Moselle. Every speck of land was cultivated, and every human being was working diligently. Yet it was shot through with a nameless fear and uncertainty.

"Sure," said my companion, "we are still free to hold our beautiful pilgrimage and Corpus Christi processions. In fact, the government promotes them for propaganda use abroad so that people may see how much Hitler loves the Church. But woe to any government official or employee who is filmed in the procession. He gets a note a couple of days later saying that he has lost his job. They don't use physical violence on you, but they use economic violence, especially if you have a home and children to support." I was so used to the Germany of old, where you always engaged in conversation with your neighbor, that I could not get used to the averted glances and the silence that you met on any kind of conveyance, or to the tight-lipped, dead-pan SS guards on the city streets.

The May devotions that evening were crowded, even for that immense church. The statue of Our Lady, brilliantly illuminated, is famous through all that region for its graciousness and compelling beauty; again the Heavenly Maiden of the Rhineland. The congregation sang the old Latin hymns to Gregorian melodies; and at the close all joined in the traditional *Maria zu lieben* . . .

Here was a church where but a few years before thousands of Catholic youth, from every part of the Rhineland, had gathered in complete freedom to proclaim their fealty to the great cause of Catholic Action; of bringing the Gospel teaching to bear upon the social and religious problems of their country. Here had flourished the center of a great organized campaign of intensive Catholic living, of charitable works, of religious instruction, of apostolic works for all classes, of social reform, of liturgical realization. Here the banner of Christ the King had been unfurled before vast multitudes in public squares. Here the clouds of godless Marxism had been rolled away, while Germany's great Catholic traditions were preserved or revived. Here non-Catholics and Catholics joined in fellowship for a new order and a peaceful and happy land. The inspiration for all this revival was the ineffably lovely old Rhenish statue of Our Lady.

When things are definitely past, they seem like dreams. The troubling thought drifted into my mind: will our Catholic churches in the United States some day seem like a dream? Will our thousands of parochial schools, our glorious college and university campuses, our hospitals and institutions and national organizations seem to us, even a few years distant, as remote as do today the Knights Templars of the Middle Ages? This could happen, if we relax an eternal vigilance for the Faith, or if we betray that Faith by lives that contradict its fundamental teachings. The Church of the future lies in the hands of the Church of the present. In England at the beginning of the sixteenth century, who would have dreamed that in a few decades the people of that most pious of Catholic countries would have been robbed of their faith? Nothing was more alien than Nazism to the spirit of Catholic Germany; yet that spirit did not succeed in resisting its outward conquests. The Church is never secure in a too complacent society.

Around the corner from the presbytery was a tumbledown store-front arrangement, with broken panes in the window, which Father Heinrich pointed out to me as the parish recreation hall. He answered my unspoken question by saying

that they kept the place looking as shabby as possible so
the Nazis wouldn't take it: "If we painted it and put in the
window glass, they would send the Gauleiter around in a
moment and appropriate it."

Also in the vicinity was the chapel of the Franciscan Brothers
of the Sick. The chapel was officially closed by the government, but once a week, on Saturday morning, Mass was said
there privately. Father Heinrich could not take me there
himself, but merely pointed out the spot and gave me a mas-
sive key with which I was to let myself in the back door. I
was to speak to nobody, merely celebrate Mass and depart.
They came to Mass, he said, in order to pray for liberation
from Hitler. The following morning, therefore, I unlocked
the sacristy door, found the altar boy waiting, went out on the
altar and found the chapel filled with a silent congregation.
Not a sound was uttered except the murmured responses of
the server. I never felt so close to any congregation in my life.
Holding their missals in their hands, they recited with their
lips every word of the Mass as if their life depended on it.
All of them received Communion. And when I turned to them
and said "Dominus vobiscum," I put all the heart into it that
I could. After locking the door I departed in silence.

Not so far from us in the province of Westphalia, to the
north, our old classmate Count Clemens von Galen, now a
bishop, was preaching in his cathedral against Hitler's assaults
on the aged and feeble-minded, so-called useless members of
society. Other Innsbruckers were standing up too against the
enemy all over Germany and the present satellite countries
as they had, of course, in Bolshevik Russia. I could not foresee
when the fate that had struck them might strike my friends at
Coblenz, and it was with a heavy heart that I purchased my
ticket to Prague and said good-by to Dr. Chardon on that
May morning.

Traveling a few weeks later, I read: "The *Katholische
Bahnhofsmission,* those girls who wear the white bands on
their sleeves, have been suppressed throughout Germany;

though they are still permitted to function in a few places, such as Trier . . ."

At Prague you call for a porter (*nositel*) by saying *nosit'* (pronounced *nossitch*), which means literally "to carry." When I arrived there on May 21, in the midst of the general fear of an immediate German invasion, the din of *"Nosit', nosit'"* brought to the windows and into the train a dozen brisk, burly little fat men, slightly comical and painfully anxious to please. Too anxious, in the case of my *nositel;* for he had lugged out on the sidewalk, in the driving rain where I was waiting for a taxi, two enormous brand-new valises belonging to a high German official who had come with us on the train. *"Hineintun! HINEINTUN!"* ("Put them inside the station!") roared the high Nordic. Half paralyzed with fear, the porter dropped my things on the sidewalk and lugged the big valises inside under an ever-pointing finger. Behind that threatening voice was the voice of Hitler, and that voice spoke not Czech but imperious German.

The invasion-threat crisis had already passed, when that night I lay to rest in the Archbishop's Gymnasium (minor seminary) in Prague, where I was greeted by my old acquaintance and correspondent, Father Ovečka, S.J. Guest rooms were scarce, so the Fathers had kindly prepared a bed in a room appropriately labeled "Geographical Museum." I slept amid maps, globes, and charts. Czechoslovakia was still upon the map that night, but only because the British Ambassador in Berlin but a few hours before had made his reservation on the train for home. The Republic remained upon the map that spring and summer, but fell from it like an autumn leaf when September blew its political gale. I am thankful that I saw Czechoslovakia at least once, before it passed from history as a free country.

At breakfast the next morning everybody read the newspapers, something I had never seen at breakfast in any other Jesuit house, and scrutinized the electoral lists. It was a day of tremendous excitement. There were some thirty or forty political parties, as far as I could make out, all in the race.

The German-language paper carried a passionate appeal from Prime Minister Benes urging everybody to keep calm under the threat of Hitler's mobilization. The streets were filled with trucks of soldiers being hurried to the front, and that was the cause of much of the hubbub that I had noticed at the border. In all this excitement I did not have the heart to visit either Mr. Benes or Mr. Masaryk, for to them I would be simply a clerical bore. The few days in Prague, however, were an unmitigated delight and I was particularly pleased to be able to talk to everybody I met, feeling much more at home than I had anticipated.

At Bratislava, on my way to Budapest, I was at last in the homeland of my St. Mary's County Slovaks. My rural life interests came vigorously to life and I paid a visit to the land office director, who showed us the reforms they were trying to make in the matter of land division. Particularly interesting were the enormous unincorporated villages of four thousand to five thousand souls.

At the crossing of the border into Hungary, the letters SZOB (the frontier station) stood out in blue neon lights against the darkness, and the yellow-and-white papal flag between them. The pilgrims who entered the country were greeted by children carrying flowers. When the delegation from Ireland arrived a Hungarian official made a nice little speech to them in Magyar, which, unfortunately, few of the Irish understood. In the kindness of their hearts they burst out with *For He's a Jolly Good Fellow* and the Magyars stood at reverent attention, thinking, no doubt, that it was one of Ireland's ancient and sacred hymns.*

In Budapest, crowded to the brim with pilgrims, I was fortunate in finding a haven in the villa home of my old friends the Baron and Baroness de Hédry. Mme. de Hédry's sister,

* *America,* June 25, 1938, pp. 268-270.

Miss Frances Coleman, had been one of my chief benefactors
with the Ridge schools.

In view of the frightful events that followed in all eastern
Europe, one can only look back with terrible nostalgia to
those few magic days of the Budapest Congress. A city and a
nation, and delegates from many lands, poured out their
hearts in solemn adoration to the Eucharistic King, with all the
dignity and splendor they could muster. Ominous presage of
the future was Hitler's forbidding all Germans and Austrians
to attend. One sensed the gathering background of totalitarian
hate during the mysterious night procession, when the papal
Legate, Cardinal Pacelli—later Pope Pius XII—carried the Sacred Host in a spot-lighted glass chamber at the prow of a
steamer swiftly moving down the dark Danube and symboli-
cally limned against the huge mass of Buda's mighty rock.

On May 31 in fine summer weather, after mailing my article
on the Congress to Father Talbot in New York, I took the
train from Budapest to Zagreb in Croatia. Father Poglajen,
S.J., met me at the station and took me to No. 33 Palmotic
Street, the Jesuit residence. Father Tomislav Poglajen, a
native Croatian, was Superior and editor of the Jesuit monthly
Život (Life) which was one of the chain of Jesuit journals of
opinion. He had made tertianship at Tronchiennes, in Belgium with Father Harold C. Gardiner, S.J., literary editor of
America, and was a man of extraordinary cultivation, speaking
a half-dozen languages fluently, gifted with a striking personality and a vast amount of information. In fact, he seemed
to know everything about the trends in the changing political
scene of Europe. For some unexplained reason, at that moment the people of Zagreb seemed to have gone goofy over
tennis. Everybody was playing tennis, he told me.

Father Poglajen was insistent that I should meet the Archbishop, the Most Rev. Aloysius Stepinac, who kindly invited
us to dine with him in his archepiscopal palace. He was young,
tall, of athletic build, with a fine direct open manner and

apparently delighted to talk to somebody from the outside world. After dinner the Archbishop complained of the Serbs who, he said, were running the country then known not as Yugoslavia but as the Kingdom of the Serbs and Croats and Slovenes. Like the Czechs in Czechoslovakia, the Serbs were put in all the key positions and the old bitter enmity between the Serbs and Croats had taken drastic shapes. Out of the drawer of his desk he pulled a horrible-looking sort of scourge made of a piece of automobile chain and some metal hooks which he said was used by Serbs to torment their Croatian victims. Particularly gruesome was a slip of paper, a signed receipt for a trifling sum of money, about $1.10, expended by the government in shooting the father of the signer of the receipt. The father, it appears, was a Croatian peasant whose farm lay on both sides of the River Drava. For months he had crossed from one side of the border to the other, always showing a little pass and getting a wave or a nod from the Serbian guards at the border. On one occasion he had neglected to bring his pass. He waved at them the usual way, but as he did not carry it they shot him dead. The government then charged the son for the expense of shooting his own parent.

The Archbishop, now a Cardinal, spoke with abhorrence of the Nazis and struck me as a thoroughly Christian, enlightened person and certainly a promoter of religion, culture, and piety in his diocese. When fourteen and a half years later the Archbishop, tyrannically exiled from his see, was honored by Pope Pius XII with the sacred purple, I recalled the language he spoke in the face of the Nazi conquerors of Yugoslavia and their Ustashi allies:

We assert that every people and every race which has been formed on earth today has the right to life and to treatment worthy of man. All of them without distinction, be they members of the gypsy race or of another, be they Negroes or Europeans, be they Jews or Aryans, all of them have equal right to say: "Our Father, who art in Heaven." If God has granted this right to all

human beings, what worldly power could deny it? Therefore the
Catholic Church has always condemned and will always condemn
every injustice and compulsion perpetrated in the name of social,
racial, and national theories.

The man who in the name of God uttered these powerful
words for right and justice was shortly afterward imprisoned
by an atheist ruler who hated the name of God and has never
ceased to try to erase it from the hearts and minds of the
people of Yugoslavia.

It was impossible to visit Zagreb and not view some of the
masterworks of the greatest religious sculptor since the Renaissance, Ivan Mestrovic, who later deemed it wiser to take refuge in this country before it should be too late. At this time
of writing he is director of the Department of Sculpture at
the University of Syracuse, New York. I came in contact with
Mr. Mestrovic the day of his arrival in New York through his
admirer and staunch friend, the talented American sculptress
Malvina Hoffman. Tito, said Mr. Mestrovic, moved heaven
and earth to induce him to return to Yugoslavia, offering to
place all his works in a great national museum, and so on.
But the fiery modern Michelangelo stood fast. "I could never
return," he repeatedly said to me, "when my dearest friends
are still in prison." He was particularly adamant for the restoration of complete freedom to his friend and patron, Cardinal Stepinac. The Cardinal's voice and the artist's hand
are making a greater impression on the world at large than all
the noise of Tito's propaganda. It was gratifying to see American recognition for the art of Mestrovic in the award of May
1953 by the American Academy of Arts and Letters.

From Zagreb I took the train to Ljubjana through the valley of the Sava River, then through high mountains, passing
picturesque castles on the way. In Ljubjana the next morning we walked up the hill to the citadel and my guide, Father
Berkovic, pointed out the magnificent view of the whole city
and the river Sava. Much of the planning of the city of

Ljubjana was carried out by a scientific-minded Jesuit in the seventeenth century, Father Guba.

The Slovenians had been a subject people and were first aroused to national consciousness by Napoleon with his famous slogan "Awake, Illyria!" In recent times their great Catholic leader, Dr. Korošec, had aroused a sense of national dignity and destiny. Of all the Slavic peoples the Slovenians possibly are or were the most Westernized, due to their long incorporation in the Austro-Hungarian empire and their close relation with Styria and Corinthia. How little I dreamed at that moment that only a few years later I would be recording in *America* the unspeakable outrages committed during and after World War II in that lovely country, first by the Nazis and then by the Communists. Ljubjana was historically one of the great crossroads of Europe. The Argonauts, I believe, had made their way there, sailing up from Colchis on the Black Sea. The great Bishop Baraga, one of the pioneer missionary bishops in the United States, came from Slovenia.

From Ljubjana I took the morning train to Trieste. The outlook gradually changed, as the Slovenian type of dwelling gave way to the Italian. As we approached the Adriatic the blue sea was spread in magnificent panorama beyond the roofs of the houses. We arrived at Trieste at half past one, and I broke a tooth over Mussolini's hard bread in the restaurant. From Trieste I took the train to Venice. Once more I was on territory which I had visited thirty-four years ago and enjoyed exploring Venice in the company of a friendly cicerone, Brother Fini, S.J. The Italian good humor was cheering after the rather austere experiences of the last few weeks.

On the way to Rome the Fascist regime was soon in evidence by the innumerable W's plastered on the walls—for *Viva*. Magnificent slogans exhorted the people to morality, industry, loyalty, and other virtues, signed in each case with the mysterious letter M. Asking an Italian friend what the M stood for—it might stand for morality or Machiavelli or something else—I received only a shocked glance as a reply.

As I had studied Hitler in operation in Germany, I looked forward to a chance to study Mussolini at first hand in Italy. It was a depressing period. The soldiers were back from Ethiopia, confined, I understood, for two or three weeks to their boxcars so as not to contaminate the people by depressing stories of what had happened in Africa. In the bookstores anti-Semitic material was appearing, translated from the German. I paid a visit to a dismal settlement on the outside of the city nicknamed Shanghai where I saw greater squalor than I had ever seen even in the poorest Negro sections of the South. On the other hand, there were magnificent improvements, a great contrast with 1904 and 1905. The Roman Forum, of course, was the first thing to strike one's eye. I thought that Mussolini might have accomplished his vaunted task as regenerator of Italy if he had not been carried away, as was inevitable, by the desire for military glory, seduced into the Ethiopian war and led into the anti-Semitism and racist ideology by Hitler.

Father Joseph Ledit, S.J., Professor of Slavonic History in the Gregorian University, had kindly arranged for me to spend two or three days doing some rather high-class sightseeing. Like myself, he was interested in social questions and in rural development. A member of the Gran Consiglio itself offered to take us around and show us the sights. He was somewhat late for the appointment and I had my vanity flattered when he excused himself and said: "You know, we were having the Council meeting and I told Mussolini that I had an appointment at eleven o'clock with Father LaFarge. But the Duce said, let Father LaFarge wait. The affairs of state are more important." This could probably be credited, in *New Yorker* language, to the Department of Remarks About LaFarge that were never remarked.

In the city we were treated to an elaborate view of Dopo Lavoro, the system of workers' welfare which contrasted oddly with the misery I had seen on the outskirts of town. The other great sight, and considerably more authentic and interesting, was the Agro Pontino, the transformation of the Roman Campagna, the gigantic process of drainage, rural reconstruction, and development. It was a magnificent show. Popes and emperors and kings—Napoleon III was one of them—had schemed and planned. Engineers had dreamed of redeeming the Campagna's vast, swampy, malarious regions. But their plans had been doomed to failure. Mussolini's dynamism was to accomplish this ponderous task, to turn the swamps into acres of well-drained farms, with modern residences and good roads. A prize exhibit was a spotlessly shining sugar beet factory, on which a plaque was attached, "A Reply to Sanctions," indicating that it had been erected as a protest against Great Britain's threat of sanctions against Italy for her invasion of Ethiopia.

A curious feature of the trip was the sight of the new towns, Sabaudia, Littoria, Aprilia, etc., named after famous Fascist military victories. Here in one of the oldest countries of Western civilization were cities or towns in which not a single building was more than three years old. Nothing that I had seen in the United States, even in the far West, was as new as these extraordinary constructions; splendidly built, all Italian style, with broad streets, immense squares, imposing municipal buildings and elaborate churches, one of which, in good medieval spirit, included Mussolini as a toiling harvest-worker in the mosaic representing the Assumption of the Blessed Virgin. On one of Mussolini's visits, when he addressed the populace from the public square, he was extremely annoyed at noticing mosquito screens on some of the houses. He asked what those things were doing there and it was explained they were still left as a precaution. "Mosquitoes have been abolished," shouted the Duce, and they were hastily removed.

Again, as in lovely Ljubjana, the horrors that were to come in this very region cast no shadow in advance. Anzio Beach and Nettuno were simply cheerful rural districts with blossoming fields, elaborately drained and cultivated. We passed through the region where the little martyr of purity, St. Maria Goretti, met her fate and her glory, but nobody there at the time recalled the event of some twenty years before. With all the fanfare, painful foreboding remained in my mind as to how it would all turn out. The impressive superstructure rested on the lavish expenditure of government money. Probe and examine as I would, I could find no solid economic basis for the Fascist social program. Perhaps the Duce's wild foreign-policy escapades were partly stimulated by his inner sense of the uncertain conditions at home. I had witnessed a magnificent show, but was it really more than a show?

Father Vincent A. McCormick, S.J., the Rector at the Gregorian University, arranged for us to attend a general audience where we could see the Holy Father Pope Pius XI. We drove out to Castelgandolfo where the Pope was spending the summer in his residence. After the audience we paid a visit to Father Stein, S.J., papal astronomer, who occupied the room directly above the papal apartments, and advised me to walk softly. From there we looked out over Lake Albano which did resemble Maria Laach, as my friend Dr. Chardon had remarked.

A few days later a message from the Vatican was delivered to me in the well-known yellow and white envelope, saying that His Holiness would like to see me privately and appointing a time for the visit. I was mystified, wondering what it could be, and again took the long drive to Castelgandolfo, followed by an apprehensive wait in the papal antechamber. As I stepped into the elevator to go up to the antechamber, the Papal Secretary of State, Cardinal Pacelli, stepped out, but I was in no position to ask him for an explanation.

The Holy Father received me graciously. Apparently he had just returned from a walk and his white cane rested on a ledge behind him. I found he wished to talk to me on the question of racialism, which had now become a burning issue in Italy and in Germany. He said he was continually revolving the matter in his mind, and was deeply impressed by the fact that racialism and nationalism were fundamentally the same. He had read my book *Interracial Justice* and liked the title of it. " 'Interracial Justice,' *c'est bon!*" he said, pronouncing the title as if it were French. He said he thought my book was the best thing written on the topic, comparing it with some European literature. Naturally, this was a big lift to me. Apparently what appealed to him in my little effort was the spiritual and moral treatment of the topic, and the fact that I did bring into synthesis the Catholic doctrine and the natural law and the pertinent facts, as well as some practical methods for dealing with the question.*

He questioned me about my own work and was much interested to hear of the work of the Catholic Interracial Council and told me to keep going ahead and not be discouraged by obstacles. He also suggested to me that I should pursue the subject further from the standpoint of science and study, collect material on it and go into the whole question very thoroughly. If I were in Rome again, he said in conclusion, I should be sure to drop in to see him. He might like to talk to me again on the question and might have some further ideas.

Though the Pope conversed with me in French, I had a curious sensation that I was talking to my own father. His gestures were singularly like those of my father, particularly the characteristic one of the joined index and middle finger raised and waved paternally in the air. Little turns of expression reminded me of Father, and there was the same atmosphere, as it were, of conversation. Apparently somebody had told him that I spoke both French and German. Although, as I had heard, Pius XI was not given to pleasantries, he enjoyed causing me a bit of confusion. Smilingly he addressed

* The book was published by the America Press in 1937, and was followed by a revised and greatly enlarged edition, entitled *The Race Question and the Negro* (Longmans 1943). *No Postponement* (Longmans 1951) deals with the history and some of the techniques of the Catholic Interracial Council, as well as with the challenge to Americans of the Point Four program for foreign aid.

me in both languages at once until he finally slipped into French.

This conversation was indeed a great turning-point in my life, especially as it was totally unexpected. I had never thought of a private audience, much less of any interest the Holy Father might take in my work, although in routine fashion I had sent him a copy when the little book was published. It gave me no small encouragement and impetus.

My visit to the Pope was followed by a visit to Very Rev. Father Vladimir Ledóchowski, the Superior General of our Society. His wiry, vivacious person reminded me oddly of my Philadelphia friend, Mother Katharine Drexel, Foundress and Superior General of the Sisters of the Blessed Sacrament for Indians and Negroes. He spoke of his own experiences as a young Jesuit when editor of the Polish Jesuit monthly *Przeglond Powszechny,* and insisted on the following points: first, that *America*'s writing should strive to reflect the mind of the Church rather than the notions of a mere individual; secondly, that it should be an interpretation of events, a key, as he said, to understanding them, rather than a mere exposition of facts which at the present time people have from other sources. People, he said, want to know not only *what* has happened but *why* things are so. In the third place he urged that the interests of religion should be authoritatively explained so that our writings could be referred to.

The General was deeply concerned, as was obvious, over the Communist issue, and grasped it with great clarity as a world revolution. He had already written to the entire Society alerting its members to the danger and urging their prayers as well as deep analytic study of the situation. As a Pole, he was particularly aware of what was happening in Russia. At the same time, he held nothing could be accomplished by a purely negative approach. His view was in accord with the broad position taken by Pope Pius XI in the famous encyclical on "Atheistic Communism" entitled *Divini Redemptoris.* In

that encyclical the Pope insists on the revival of social studies
and an active, effective correction of grave social evils.

Many of the Italian Fathers were deeply concerned over the
religious ignorance of the people in the environs of Rome,
particularly, Father Del Giudice of the Church of San Andrea.
Italians, he said, are a good people and they are not vicious:
"*È un buon populo, non è furbo.*" I was queried about the
interracial problem in American parishes and told of the work
of the Clergy Conference on Negro Welfare. To Father Eu-
genio Pellegrino's student group I described our missionary
situation in the United States. Everywhere I found, as always
in Europe, an intense interest in what we were doing in this
country to alleviate the racial problem.

It would be hardly possible for an American editor to visit
Rome without a glance at the Vatican radio. So Father Killeen
of our own Province took me there by auto. A twenty-minute
period was free for an American broadcast, and I used a talk
on the interracial problem that I had given in the United
States, and it fitted in nicely. I watched the hand of the clock
mark the minutes and even the seconds as Father Soccorsi, S.J.,
director of the radio station, looked on.

With a sigh of relief I saw my time had expired and started
to rise when the director cheerfully remarked, "Well, there is
nothing more going on at present. You can talk another twenty
minutes." The broadcast, I understood, was being beamed to
Ceylon. What I then knew about Ceylon I could write on a
sheet of note-paper. However, I improvised as best I could.
Six or seven months later I heard from a passing missionary
that people in Ceylon were pleased by the fine broadcast they
had heard telling them of the good will of the Vatican, and
how much good the words had done. If I had known more
about my audience I might have been less facile.

The full import of what I had witnessed in Germany and
Czechoslovakia burst upon me when, during my stay at the

Jesuit Curia, I heard the speech of Hitler at the Sportspalast
on that fateful September evening. The circumstances were
dramatic. Father Ledóchowski invited all the Fathers to attend toward the close of the recreation period which custom-
arily follows the evening meal in Jesuit houses. Father General
seated himself in his usual alert fashion close to the instrument, while the others were grouped around. The transmis-
sion was perfect, as if we were seated in the vast hall itself.
The speech was a rhythm of passion. Starting in a quiet, reasoning voice as if he were taking the great audience into his
confidence, Hitler rose rapidly to frantic screams of fanati-
cism, followed by the terrific rumbling roar from the audience:
"Sieg Heil! Sieg Heil! Sieg Heil!" My own bones quaked at
each of these recurrent episodes. Over and over the voice died
down and rose again, but Father General's attentive face and
eager form remained impassive. Benes was the main object of
all this oratory. Benes the aggressor. Benes the tyrant. Benes
the betrayer of civilization. Benes the enemy of the German
people. Benes in whom Hitler had put his childlike trust only
to be betrayed. Benes the tool of foreign perfidy.

The shouting in the Sportspalast was the voice of impend-
ing war; it was furthermore the voice of a blind, dark passion
which might erupt anywhere in the world. Echoes of it even
appeared in the United States; the voice of the mob, of hate,
of hysteria. Trotsky and Lenin had shouted in that voice yet
those who opposed them could be stirred up to the same degree of insanity. Curiously enough with all his denunciations
Hitler still had a kind word to say of the French and the
British. They might understand him or sympathize with him.

The oratory went on. The bell rang for the evening's spiritual exercises at the close of recreation, but Father General
remained at the radio. Again the bell rang fifteen minutes
later for the examination of conscience, customary at the close
of a Jesuit's day, but he still remained. I could not avoid wondering what would have passed in Hitler's mind if he had re-

alized that on that night he was upsetting the inflexible time-order of Jesuit headquarters in Rome and making us all stay up and listen to the radio when we should have been quietly saying our prayers. Finally with a last effort the Fuehrer screeched to a finish. Father General rose abruptly, darted to the door, then turning back, simply said: "Don't worry, there will be no war." And sure enough there wasn't—not then.

I made my trip to Paris via Geneva, leaving Rome on the evening of June 27. At Geneva my host was my friend Father Albert LeRoy, S.J., who had been for some time a Vatican delegate to the International Labor Office.

Arriving in Paris, I settled myself down for three months of hard work. *Études* was distinguished among Catholic periodicals by having built its own home. Père de Scoraille erected the present edifice in 1890 on the rue Monsieur, a quiet little street on the Left Bank, not far from the Invalides.

I found my French friends in a state of political optimism. As for Hitler, they explained to me, there was really nothing to worry about. France, I learned, was amply protected by that wonderful institution called the Maginot Line. If perchance the Fuehrer did undertake to cross the boundary, a half-hour of telephoning would summon all France's might and main to the frontier and that would be the end of Hitler. The militarily knowledgeable members of the community repeated to me how calm they were: *"Nous sommes si calmes."* But when you have heard people tell you four or five times a day how calm they are, you wonder just how deep is the tranquillity.

Any lurking anxieties seemed to have been removed by the visit of the King and Queen of England on July 19, 1938. Fathers Doncoeur and Poidebard invited me to see the show with them as the royal couple passed down the Champs Elysées. We had a splendid view of the procession from the fifth floor of an apartment. It was a wonderful sight, the Spahis magnifi-

cently mounted, those from Tunis being dressed in red, and
those from Morocco in black. The Garde Mobile, we were
informed, kept the Army out of politics and, furthermore, no
riots were possible. The Communists, according to my friends,
were now quite tamed. They realized the people didn't want
colère but *épanouissement,* smiles rather than frowns. Youth
was bade by the Reds to be joyful, and girls were invited to
enroll in the Daughters of France. The Army was idolized by
the people and the crowd was cheerful and in good humor.
Periscopes were on sale everywhere. The President of the Republic passed by and was applauded but there were no vivas.
He was said to be not so popular. We were treated to an impressive sight of old General Pétain on his horse. A man called
DeGaulle, I was told, had smart ideas but he was not to be
taken too seriously. With Great Britain at France's side, what
further ground was there for worry? And as for Mussolini,
or Mussolin, as they contemptuously referred to him, he was
a mere mountebank or crackpot. Such was the official military
view, but the more reflective members of the community were
by no means so optimistic.

At the time the Communists were making every effort to
develop some kind of intellectual fraternity in the United
Front. It was the time of *la main tendue,* the "outstretched
hand," and it was difficult for Catholic intellectuals to avoid
the idea that somehow or other a complete unanimity could
be reached on certain basic principles, provided the objec-
tionable obstacles could be ignored, or placed in parentheses,
as the French said. Father Gaston Fessard of the *Études* staff
took the challenge head-on. He engaged in prolonged, cau-
tious debate with the leading Communist intellectual, Vaillant
Couturier, always reverting to the point that no truce could
be reached unless the Communists would yield on the capital
issue of atheism. Not that they were expected to deny their
atheism, but Father Fessard urged that at least they admit the
possibility of agreement on fundamental principles taking

honest religious belief into account. Just as politely and stubbornly the Communists refused to budge.

The threatening international situation aroused extreme
concern as to the idea of peace itself. Father Fessard in 1926
had published a long and careful study, an examination of
conscience, as he called it, of the situation of the Christian conscience in view of the international crisis. It was entitled *Pax
Nostra,* reference being to the central theme of the book,
that Jesus Christ, as St. Paul says, had broken down in his own
person the wall of enmity between the divisions of mankind
and thereby had become "our Peace," *pax nostra.* So the work
brought into contrast and conciliation at the same time the
concepts of the love of peace claimed by the pacifists and conscientious objectors, the love of one's country, which was
claimed by the nationalists and the racists. He raised the question of capitalism and internationalism and thereby faced
the anti-Semitic question.

Joseph Folliet, one of the leading Catholic publicists of the
younger generation, pointed out how paradoxically the theme
of peace was being urged by those who were naturally belli-
cose, such as the nationalists, and the theme of warfare, violent
and savage warfare, was being advocated by the supposed pacifists and internationalists, namely, the Leftist groups. They
were clamoring for intervention in Spain to stop Franco from
resistance, and for intervention in Germany with no regard
for the possible consequences to France itself.

As for the Spanish situation, I found that sympathy for
the situation of the Spanish nationalists was not confined to
extreme Rightists as much as I had expected. The French
were eager to give asylum to the refugee Loyalists and the
exiled Basques, and nothing could be too good for them. But
at the same time there was considerably more understanding
of the agonized situation than I anticipated. After all, if the
Reds would carry on as they were doing in the country of
Spain it was evident that if they had the chance, despite their

soothing words, they might be undertaking similar projects in France itself.

When Father Superior at the rue Monsieur learned I had relatives in Brittany whom I had visited in my younger days, he recommended I should pay them a little visit and obtain a bit of much-needed holiday at the same time. Yvonne de Nanteuil, my contemporary, was now living with her husband Baron du Halgouët at Ploujean, a little village near Morlaix in the "dream house" that they had constructed, the manor of Roz'Avel. The old castle of Nec'hoat was now in the hands of other members of the family. Her younger daughter Généviève, aged seventeen, was head over heels in Catholic Action and was also, to use the expression, *très sportive,* which meant that she liked out-of-doors and driving a car. Not long after my visit Généviève entered the religious life, joining the modern and very active community of the Helpers of the Holy Souls, whose New York house is on East Eighty-sixth Street. At this writing, she is Mother M. Vianney, Superior of the Helpers' Holy Rood House in London.

My brother Grant had visited Ploujean three years previous and both of us had experienced the same emotion at suddenly finding a hundred reminders of home in such a remote part of the world. The guest room was, as it still is, on the third floor of the house, and they laid on my table a big box of family papers and documents. In the shimmering summer evening I read them until long after midnight. I found Father's old sketchbook made in Brittany the year before he came back to the United States and became acquainted with Mother.

The village curé at the time was a delightful Alsatian abbé who had been a chaplain: one of the seven official chaplains in the French Navy. The church, he said, was so full of curiosities, of old mortuaries and dim and dark corners, so cold and uncomfortable in winter and so stuffy in summer, that he would like to have turned it into a pilgrimage shrine and build a brand-new church where, he said, "everybody would be at least as comfortable as in a motion-picture theater." His unorthodox ideas were symptomatic of a constant preoccupation that I found with so many of the more thoughtful French clergy. They had difficulty in reconciling the tremendously institutional and traditional outward trappings of the Church with the attractions of modern life. Tradition is inspiring when it does not weigh too heavily, but if it becomes a ponderous shroud it can extinguish rather than inspire spiritual life.

Back in Paris I began taking afternoon tea in a neighboring restaurant where the waiter, a grumpy individual, seemed to resent my appearance; I assumed he was anti-clerical. One day Francis M. Hammond turned up, an American Negro intellectual who was pursuing his studies at Louvain. His photogenic New Orleans wife had joined him, coming over from the States, and I had the job of showing them around Paris and trying to persuade Mrs. Hammond that it didn't mean anything when French people stared at her. It was just their absent-minded way, I explained. This seemed to reassure her and they had really a very pleasant time. We stopped in at the same restaurant for a bit of refreshment and to my astonishment I found the grumpy waiter had turned cordial; nothing was too good for us. From that day on, when I went there he was all smiles. Perhaps he thought that the abbé who had the good sense to hobnob with a Negro couple must be a real guy.

On the 13th of August, just two days before the Feast of the Assumption, the Brother Porter handed me a telegram telling me of the death of my brother Bancel at his home in Mount Carmel, Connecticut. The story of his last hours came to me later by mail and they were a worthy conclusion to his long and innocent career. He had completed the panel of the Transfiguration for St. Aidan's Church in New Haven. His last hours were of great peace and really all that was most fitting for such a life. He was laid out in his artist's smock, as befitted one who had given the best of his talents to his chosen profession. At his death I reproached myself, as I have done before and since, that I never had really expressed, as I should, all my indebtedness to Bancel, for if it had not been for him I should never have obtained my education, possibly not at college and certainly not abroad. He himself had enjoyed but a minimum of opportunity; only a fragmentary schooling and a life broken up by various hazards in his earlier years. His marriage to Mabel Hooper of Boston, however, proved to be extraordinarily happy and the two of them had a gift for friendship.

One of the last times I had seen Bancel was in the company of Paul Claudel who, like so many others, had been charmed by the peace and simplicity of the Mount Carmel home just outside New Haven. I accompanied Paul Claudel to New York but found the trip not very satisfactory since he was pretty completely deaf and the conversation was unilateral. "I am working," he said, "on a commentary on the Apocalypse and have a trunkful of notes." He discovered that the locusts mentioned in the Apocalypse really were meant to be journalists, about whom he used uncomplimentary expressions. This was discouraging for a person engaged in religious journalism, and since he explained to me that he thought all modern journalistic writing was not only a waste of time but was the curse of the earth, it was difficult to establish much intellectual contact save to express a few—very heartfelt—appreciations of his literary wonders.

I had so hoped to be with Bancel during his last hours that it was a bitter disappointment to find myself on the other side of the ocean. Yet I could meet his soul at the altar. My own brethren in Paris offered generously their sympathy and Masses, and I also learned of the comforts he had received from the clergy at home in New Haven at the time of his death. He was buried near my mother in St. Columba's cemetery in Newport, in a lot he had reserved for himself, his wife, and sons, and had planned with his usual originality and taste.

In September, Father General expressed the desire that I should return to Rome and discuss with him some of the social and political developments I had investigated. Mails were uncertain, and from Paris I carried to Father General a message from the Spanish Jesuit community beleaguered in Barcelona. Returning to Paris from this second trip, and with the Roman episode finally concluded, I faced the question of getting back home. War clouds were shaping up and I anxiously scanned the news. One afternoon, after lunch, when we were sitting in the Fathers' recreation room in the rue Monsieur, the telephone rang in the adjoining office of the Superior. Returning in a few minutes he informed us that there would be no war. "M. Daladier and M. Chamberlain have conferred with Hitler and Mussolini in Munich and all will be well." My passage home was now assured.

The steerage trip back to New York was anything but comfortable, especially as I was not a good sailor; but this was made up for by the greetings on my return. Shortly after my arrival in New York I attended a welcome dinner where I prophesied that Hitler and Stalin would get together in the not too distant future. All my studies that summer and my conversations had convinced me of the complete compatibility of Nazism and Communism, and the prophecy was thoroughly borne out by the Ribbentrop-Molotov pact. My trip to Europe had cost me thirty pounds in weight, which probably I could miss, and a rich harvest of experience. It afforded me a copious background for the understanding of the years that were to become a tragic part of the world's history.

Immediately upon my arrival I heard of the illness of my oldest brother, Grant, at his home in Saunderstown, Rhode Island. I prepared to visit him at the earliest opportunity but,

alas, just as I was about to leave I received news of his death
and had to content myself with the sad consolation of officiat-
ing at his funeral Mass in the Church of St. Joseph in Wick-
ford, Rhode Island.*

* See Appendix III.

CHAPTER SEVENTEEN

Eggshells in the Sanctuary

※》》《《※

Not long after my return from Europe in the fall of 1938, I gave a talk to a group of Quakers in the parlor of the Friends' Meeting House of Stuyvesant Square, in New York. The topic was the Catholic idea of mysticism, and I dwelt considerably upon the Catholic concept of the use of material things—such as water, wine, oil, candlelight, and so on—in divine worship and particularly in the sacraments of the Church. I told, too, how certain acts or gestures took on a sacramental character, such as the pouring of water, gestures of reverence, the sign of the Cross, breathing of air, etc. My audience kept two minutes' silence before and after my talk, in accordance with the Quaker custom, and silence, I noted, is one of the tangible outward acts enlisted in the service of the Catholic Church, as are "plain clothes," in the form of the habits worn by certain religious orders.

The Catholic mystic, I explained, does not despise the material world, nor fly from it. He is a man, not an angel, and knows that Christ Himself honored the humble materials that make up man's world. The real materialist is not the person who uses and reverences the material, as God's gift to man, but the proud preacher of dialectic materialism, who teaches that man, of his own strength alone, can utterly conquer and subdue all the forces of nature, which is the Marxian godless and impossible boast.

Silence has its place in the program of Catholic worship, but why should we observe a stony silence at Mass, even at a

285

Low Mass with no choir singing? Song is sacramental, and is one of the finest functions of corporate worship. It is a strange experience, one to which I can never quite reconcile myself, to celebrate Mass before a totally silent congregation on, say, a lovely summer's day. In the church itself you can hear the proverbial pin drop: no sound but an occasional cough or the rustling of a prayerbook. And sometimes through the open windows comes the faint echo of singing at a Protestant service a few blocks away. They sing, in some cases, old Catholic hymns, which they have incorporated in their hymnals, or adopted bits of our age-old plain chant, the ritual music of the Church, and I do not begrudge them these treasures. But I certainly see no reason why we should be liturgically or devotionally starved. As Pope Pius XI, whom I had just seen in Rome, put it: "The faithful should not be silent and detached spectators at the sacred ceremonies."

I found myself after the 1938 trip more than ever preoccupied with the two thoughts that were really one: Could we not do more to restore to Catholics the priceless inheritance of their liturgy, their chant, their glorious hymnology, these aids to corporate worship; and again, could we not do more to restore the sense of corporate worship itself? After learning, as I did on my trip to Germany, how Hitler had successfully managed to sweep away the impressive structure of German Catholic church organizations, I was convinced that the Church, if it was to stand up against organized assaults of our times, must encourage its members to return to a deeper source of collective strength. The world situation itself demands of us that we strengthen in every way possible our corporate unity with the Person of Christ our Lord, living and acting in our midst. And that would be powerfully aided by a living, popular, and corporate liturgical revival. In my earlier years I had already become interested in two organizations that we dedicated to such an end, though from different angles: the National Liturgical Conference, and the Liturgical Arts Society, and each ensuing year convinced me increasingly of their importance.

I was once traveling of an autumn evening on the rural trolley car that ran from Tiverton to Newport. Of the two passengers on the car beside myself one was a dour-looking old Yankee farmer; the other a jovial individual apparently of the True Faith. He edged himself closer to the old farmer, who correspondingly withdrew into a corner and tried to look as secluded and forbidding as possible, but to no effect. Pointing to me, the man presumably of my Faith said to the old gentleman: "D'you know what kind of a person that is?" The other man shook his head. "Well, I'll tell you. He's a dominus vobiscum; that's what he is, he's a dominus vobiscum. I have no use for him and he has no use for me."

These remarks, though uncomplimentary in tone, were more exact than they might sound, for indeed I *was* a Dominus Vobiscum. Turning to the people at the altar and passing the Lord to them, as it were, and awaiting their response was an expression of the desire to impart all that could be imparted of that Divine Sacrifice to everyone present. Every Mass I celebrate increases in me the desire to bring every detail of it to the knowledge of everybody. There is nothing recondite nor secluded about the Latin Mass; no iconostasis bars the congregation from the altar. Even in the Greek Church this partition is only symbolic, for in point of fact the people take far more active part in the Greek rite than they do in the rite of Rome. The Mass has a certain communal aspect in which the congregation takes part, according to its own particular function. And people today need more outward helps than they did in earlier times.

To meet this difficulty many rely upon the non-liturgical devotions of the Church. These non-liturgical or semi-liturgical devotions fill their sublime role in the life and worship of the Church of Christ. They are historic and fruitful developments of Christianity, as Pope Pius XII has pointed out, and today are absolutely necessary. We cannot starve people of them. Nevertheless they can be overworked. No matter how beautiful and inspiring, they cannot supply the place of a full participation in the official worship of the Church. Restoration of liturgical worship, therefore, appealed to me as one of the great problems of our religious life at the present day. It was strange to see how this idea was stirring even among non-Catholics.

Thoughts like this that ran through my mind as I attended the National Liturgical Conference, which had been initiated by the late Father Virgil Michel, O.S.B., and Father Michael Ducey, O.S.B. One encountered some opposition in the popular and sometimes in the clerical mind.

Liturgy was often confused with rubrics. If you objected to the cut-and-dried form of the vestments and asked that they might be restored to their earlier, rather ample form, you were accused of favoring "Gothic" vestments. Of course certain eccentrics would exaggerate, and it was easy, as in all such movements, to make fun or misunderstand. For example, a professor of chant in the seminary explained that when you use the Italian pronunciation of Latin the word *"excelsis,"* which occurs in the Gloria, should be pronounced with the soft *g,* thus: *egg shel sis.* I heard one angry anti-liturgist exclaim: "I want no eggshells in my sanctuary!" But nobody wanted to scatter eggshells in his sanctuary. If he didn't care to pronounce the Gloria chant in this or that way, it made little difference. Many real advantages attend the Italian pronunciation, but no scandal occurs if you don't use it, as long as the vowels are correct and pronunciation is dignified and melodious.

In spite of all these difficulties, however, I made a few starts. Shortly after the arrival of the Sisters of St. Joseph at Ridge I suggested that every morning in the chapel they should recite in a group the Latin responses to my Mass, and they have preserved the custom. The Catholic Laymen's Union, a group of largely Negro professional and businessmen, about whom I shall speak later, adopted the idea of the dialogue Mass during their annual retreat and their inter-racial Mass several times during the year.

In my pastoral days I had experimented considerably with the chant with both white and colored children. I had found the Negro children were particularly proficient in learning it and they seemed to find the chant sympathetic. I had observed that we often forget the distinction between the easier and the more complex features of the chant. The highly figured forms are used in the Gradual and other changing parts of the Mass. But the simple forms run with only one note to each syllable, such as the forms of the Gloria and the Credo, the Sanctus, etc. The idea kept turning in my mind that there was no reason why an ordinary group of laymen could not learn to sing the chant of the Church. The intervals are simple: no chromatics or half-notes. Moreover, the chant officially author-ized by the Church, that of the monastery of Solesmes in France, requires no great musical proficiency or vocal range. Any person who can make some sort of a musical sound, even of a very obscure character, can fit into a choir or group sing-ing the Gregorian. The requirements are much less strenuous than they are for any form of polyphony or part singing and of course for solos. I had experimented from time to time quite a bit along this line. As I have already mentioned, dur-ing my early days at Leonardtown I had taught the altar boys there the chant of Holy Week, and it was a surprise to see how readily they could pick it up. At the same time I nurtured the the idea that such a group of laymen might find spiritual strength and solace in the very simple task of praising God.

Lady Vivian Gabriel of Mount Kisco, New York, a recent convert to the Faith, suggested that I meet Dr. Becket Gibbs, the former English choir director, at that time in New York. As an Anglican Dr. Gibbs had had experience in choir work and later was director in England of the choir in the Catholic cathedral at Leeds. Coming to this country he had continued his work, and when I met him through Lady Gabriel's kind

introduction he revealed an encyclopedic knowledge of choirs
and chant and everything else musical. He followed, in a
word, the great tradition of the choir of Westminster Cathedral
in London.

Dr. Gibbs's ardent soul caught fire at my idea. We solved
the problem of personnel through my cousin Harry Lorin
Binsse, who was at that time secretary of the newly formed
Liturgical Arts Society, of which, incidentally, I was chaplain.
Harry was also the first editor of *Liturgical Arts,* the quarterly
organ of the Society. He suggested that we form a group, the
Liturgical Arts Schola, among our members. We assembled
them without difficulty and began a program in 1933 which
has continued to the present day.

This program consisted of preparing for a certain number
of Gregorian chant services during the course of each season.
We would sing the Mass, very frequently the Requiem Mass
but sometimes some of the other Masses, say to the number
of four or five in the season, and then perform Vespers from
time to time in any church or chapel where we could get a
hospitable reception. The purpose of the Schola was simple,
as I said, just to praise God, but also to give some example to
the Catholic people as to how the chant could be performed,
and to try to bring out some of the beauties which had been
neglected. The rehearsals have always been weekly, every
Monday night; first, a supper, a pleasant get-together, and
afterward a rehearsal. In the year 1946 Dr. Gibbs, quite advanced in years but still sturdy and active, moved to Philadelphia. His place was taken by the distinguished choir
director, Father Joseph Foley, director of the Paulist boys'
choir of the Church of St. Paul the Apostle (the Paulist
Fathers), in New York. Though the group was and is officially known as Liturgical Arts Schola, we adopted the title
Quilisma Club, after the *quilisma,* a melodic sign used in the
chant.

The Liturgical Arts Society, a national, non-profit organization under the patronage of His Eminence Francis Cardinal

Spellman, Archbishop of New York, was founded in 1928 by a group of laymen, the majority of them professionally interested in the arts. Among these were my brother Bancel, and his son L. Bancel LaFarge, the architect; Charles D. Maginnis of Boston, and J. Sanford Shanley of New York, both prominent in the field of architecture. The membership today includes a number of members of the American hierarchy, several foreign prelates, members of the clergy, both secular and religious, nuns and laity.

After Harry Binsse found himself unable to continue the editorship of *Liturgical Arts*, the Society's organ, the job was taken over by Maurice Lavanoux, who had been an assistant in the architectural office of Charles D. Maginnis. Neither the initiation of the Society nor the magazine itself were my doings: they were started by the group that I mentioned. But I was glad to be identified with them as a not very active or useful chaplain, but one deeply convinced of the value and importance of the work itself.

Correct performance of the liturgy, in point of fact, has never been my strong point. In any elaborate ceremony, I have always had to fall back upon the principle which I inculcated among the children in the country: if you find you are doing the wrong thing, do it with grace and dignity. In fact, on the one occasion on which the utmost effort was expected, when I sang a High Mass as chaplain of the Society in the presence of our patron, Cardinal Spellman, I succeeded in omitting the solemn *Dominus Vobiscum* after the *Credo*. But calm deportment usually helps to compensate for defect of rubrical exactitude.

The Society was naturally concerned about mass-produced devotional art, such as is prevalent in our churches, schools, and other institutions. If a generation of Christians are familiar with none but a naturalistic representation of the Saviour of mankind, their concept of His sacred Humanity will correspond in the long run to what meets their eyes in nearly every church, convent, or rectory parlor. And this idea or

concept can affect the very substance of their religious practice. One such producer, whose works are widely diffused
over the scene of American Catholicism—and pious Protestantism as well—once lamented in my parlor to the verge
of tears that I should express such a sentiment; he was alarmed
lest it should affect his extremely lucrative business.

The troubled world will not explode tomorrow because
such substandard pictures or statues prevail; nonetheless there
is no reason why the world should be more troubled than
need be. Much argument has centered on the type of artistic
production that should supplant spurious church art. Should
reform be satisfied with purifying more or less conventional
treatment or with popularizing the masterpieces of the past?
Or should it strike out along bold, new lines, not fearing to
appropriate highly "modern" techniques—which are often
very ancient?

As in most such discussions, time, good sense and the facts
of artistic give-and-take are apt to iron out the extremes. Enjoying no special competence of my own, I have tried to guide
my judgment by the utterances of the Holy Father; and the
same is the policy of our Liturgical Arts Society. These utterances sharply condemn cheap and mawkishly sentimental devotional art. They emphasize, as is natural, the importance of
tradition, of reverence, and of a reasonable degree of popular
appeal. At the same time, the Holy Father vigorously insists
upon a living art; one that will absorb and transform into the
service of divine worship all that is of permanent value in
modern artistic creation.

Whatever be ultimately the right formula, I cannot attach
to it much meaning unless it is joined to a creative spirit and
truly genuine, artistic workmanship. If these essentials are
absent, it makes little difference whether the formula is con-
templatively Thomistic, comfortably pious bourgeois, or
radically *avant-garde*. A great weakness of our times is the
decay, one could say the disease, of the imagination. Until

that is restored to its proper and active function, cure for the ills of liturgical art remains slow and difficult, and it is hard to avoid some touch of the extreme as a reaction against sheer mass vulgarity. The final answer will much depend upon the type of humanistic education provided in our schools.

CHAPTER EIGHTEEN

Hoisting a Visible Sign

※ ※

On July 12, 1942, Father Francis X. Talbot, editor-in-chief of *America,* asked me to take the job of executive editor. He wished to devote himself to promotion work for the magazine and believed that its direction would be helped by a division of editorial work.

America was unique among religious periodicals of its type. The magazine first saw the light in 1909 at 32 Washington Square West, and its first editor was Father John J. Wynne, S.J., renowned organizer and editor of the *Catholic Encyclopedia.* Jesuit students and priests were canvassed for a name for the new periodical and suggested the usual quota of Reviews, Journals, Proceedings, etc. Then a former Provincial, the Rev. Thomas Gannon, S.J., proposed the name *America.* It was immediately adopted.

The press which issued the magazine was exceptional in possessing a constitution, or *Ordinatio,* provided for it by the General of the Society, Very Rev. Father F. X. Wernz. The *Ordinatio* provided that the ultimate responsibility for the magazine should be vested in a Board of Governors consisting of the heads of the several Jesuit Provinces in the United States. These were five in 1909; there are eight at the present day. The staff was to be drawn as far as possible from each of the American Provinces, as well as from the English-speaking Province of Canada.

The Constitution provided that once a year the Governors should assemble to consider the problems of the America

Press: a deliberation which later was expanded to other works of the Society in the United States. The editor at the same time was summoned to appear before this plenary session in order to render an account of his year's stewardship, receive advice, and ask for what he needed in the way of additional help, materials, and whatnot. Two of the meetings I attended as executive editor; the other four as editor-in-chief (except that at one of the four, being prevented by illness, I was represented by our treasurer, Father Joseph Carroll of the California Province).

Before each of these appearances I felt much the same sinking of heart as that experienced by a pastor when he receives notice to come down to the Bishop's office and explain what is happening in his parish and why. Anything can happen in a magazine, and if one dignitary can make you feel uncomfortable, how about eight at once? However, the anticipation always proved far worse than the reality. Since I wrote to the Fathers Provincial once a month during the year, I found they were pretty well posted and were ready to support the work and sustain it against objections and criticism. Moreover, I was urged to speak out and state my views, needs, and objections. The treasurer took care of the bad news, if any, in the financial report.

In October of 1944 Father Talbot called me into his office on the ground floor and notified me, in his own inimitably gracious, encouraging manner, that I was appointed editor-in-chief.

I was therefore called on to direct a national religious weekly magazine at an unusually difficult time, the climax of World War II. The problems of any war are appalling, but none were ever as vexatious as at that catastrophic time. For the first time in history, our country was engaged in war against an armed ideology quite as much as against a nation in arms. In fighting for our country the situation was enormously complicated by the fact that we were allied with a great and powerful nation whose ideas, aims, and ultimate

policies we were obliged in conscience to combat to the very
end. Communism was not simply an excess, or a distortion
of the truth; it was, in the words of Pope Pius XI, intrinsically
wrong. It was wrong beyond the possibility of any conciliation, as Father Gaston Fessard had so clearly demonstrated
in his discussions with the Parisian Communist leaders. As he
said, the first condition of discussion is that the Communist
will be ready to grant that there is a *possibility* of other opinions besides his own in the matter of religion. But no orthodox Marxist could grant any possibility of an error in dogma
on his part. And this dogmatic intransigence in the field of
anti-religious propaganda applied to the whole field of social
and political action.

The Nazi ideology was inflamed with hatred of Christ the
God-Man and His Church, as I had seen on my visit to Germany in 1938. Yet in the United States some religious people
were deceived and confused by the fact that Hitler was pro-
fessedly an enemy of Stalin. The fact that Hitler was warring
on the Mystical Body of Christ itself was ignored or was even
attributed to Jewish or British propaganda. Yet the war between Hitler and Stalin was ideologically unreal, as was shown
by the Nazi-Soviet pact. On November 5, 1938, I had already
written that Nazism might salvage for its own purposes the
irreligious tyranny of Communism—"in short, that Brown and
Red Bolshevism may come to terms more easily and more readily than we dared suspect." A similar opinion was expressed
a month later in the *Saturday Evening Post* by Demaree Bess.
Denunciations of Bolshevism in Nazi Germany had given
place very largely to attacks on democracy and the "democratic powers." The most basic sign of all, as I observed, was
the evident fact that Nazism did not oppose Bolshevism on
religious grounds. I looked to the "ultimate union of the two
greatest anti-Christian forces of the world."

I was convinced that a Catholic weekly needed to tackle the
ideological question more thoroughly than was the case with
the usual organs of current news. Communism was not just

an instance of ordinary political ambition or greed. A vast
difference separated the ideas of the thoroughgoing Marxist
from the simple power-philosophy of the anarchistic free-
booter, such as a Calles, or a Carranza, who had initiated revolution in Mexico and paved the way for the spread of Communist influence.

Such a philosophical approach was somewhat unpopular
and open to considerable misunderstanding. Typical was a
banquet in one of our New England cities when some one
thousand Catholic laymen were told by the reverend director
of a retreat, as reported: "Don't worry about the spirit of the
modern age; don't worry about Communism. Communism
can never touch the United States; Communism can never
take over its government or desecrate its homes or its churches,
as long as there are men filled with the spirit of Jesus Christ."
A prominent citizen of the aforesaid city quoted the editorial
with the remark, "How sensible!"

Men, including pious men, naturally follow the line of least
resistance; and considerable mental effort and spiritual energy
is needed to follow up the devious windings of Communist
propaganda through daily study and effective action, particularly when such following up is frowned upon by local Catholic politicians.

It has taken a long time for our American thought to dis-
engage itself from the notion that the problem of Communism
is wholly a matter of economics. This was the type of thinking
that was bedazzled by the Soviet industrial development and
by its vast agricultural co-operative and state farms, the type
of thinking that made Senator Borah in 1933 urge recognition
of Russia, and made Senator Brookhart exclaim, "Never was
there such industrial development and so little indebtedness"
as in Soviet Russia. It was against that mentality that Joseph
Motta, the President of Switzerland, argued when he opposed
vainly the admission of Soviet Russia to the League of Nations. "We cannot believe in the peaceful evolution of the
Bolshevist regime, which we hope for as you do. We cannot

sacrifice, even to the principle of universality, the idea of a necessary minimum of moral and political conformity between states." Until bitter experience drove them home to unwilling minds, those were hard words to express to a reluctant world. They were truths that had to be expressed on grounds that could be accepted by those to whom they were addressed. An editor could not rely too much on the authoritarian language of dogma.

American liberals regarded anyone who spoke against the Communists or Stalin or compared his conduct to that of Hitler as betraying the Resistance, as in league with Nazism and Vichy. I willingly recognized the honesty of those liberals who finally expressed their disillusionment with the Communists and Communism. They had been taken in by a naive idealism, and they have shown great courage in finally acknowledging the truth. Yet it is hard for one like myself, who has suffered a painfully clear vision of the perversity of organized political atheism ever since the very beginning of its operations at the close of the First World War, to avoid a certain touch of bitterness. If I were of the brooding type—which, thank God, I am not—I would be tempted to brood over the quiet assumptions of my stupidity expressed by intelligent, cultivated people when I was disturbed and shocked at flagrant violations of basic human rights and ordinary justice by the anarchist elements.

It is still a mystery to me how the great top-flight intellectual and literary leaders in this country and abroad could have been blind to the savagery of the Leftist Spanish revolution, to such scenes of savagery as occurred when Barcelona was seized on Red Sunday, July 9, 1936, when the Anarcho-Syndicalists were then in power. Those were the days when the American friends of Spanish "Loyalists" demonstrated in Madison Square Garden. It took a long time for them to learn what George Orwell, who had fought courageously for these same Anarcho-Syndicalists, finally discovered—"about this being a 'war for Democracy,' it was plain eyewash" (*Homage to Catalonia*, p. 180).

Yet the very difficulty of adopting a philosophical approach to these problems was itself a challenge. The function of the magazine, which I believed to be in line with *America*'s tradition, was first to rectify consciences as to the matter of the defense of our country. I rejected pacifist doctrine. "No Christian," I held, "can maintain consistently that all war, all use of military force, is invariably and necessarily wrong." As Cardinal della Costa, Archbishop of Florence, said after that city had been liberated by the Allies in October 1944, if the Allies had not constructed their great armaments, "we don't know what would have happened to Christian civilization, human civilization."

On the other hand, our task was to make every effort to point out the foundations of a just and durable peace, looking to the postwar world. Our philosophy was summed up in the famous statement, the seven-point *Pattern for Peace*. Originated in 1943 by Father Edward A. Conway, S.J., who became an associate editor of *America* in 1948, the *Pattern* was issued separately but in identical form by outstanding representative organizations of the three major faiths, namely, the National Catholic Welfare Conference, the Synagogue Council of America, and the Federal Council of the Churches of Christ in America. The points, in summary, were as follows: (1) the moral law must govern world society; (2) the rights of the individual must be asserted; (3) the rights of the oppressed, weak, or colonial peoples must be protected; (4) the rights of minorities must be secured; (5) international institutions to maintain peace with justice must be organized; (6) international economic co-operation must be developed; (7) a just social order within each state must be developed. These conclusions represented the indispensable minimum of moral law which Pope Pius XII had urged in his appeal to the Christian conscience in his Christmas discourse of 1943.

Moreover, we felt that a religious periodical was obligated

to devote its attention to specific postwar problems of human welfare, of refugees, of migration, of religious persecution, of the treatment of war criminals, and so on, as well as discuss the complete disruption of the social order.

It was clear to me that any defense of human freedom against totalitarianism as a total assault on man—on the human race—was doomed to failure unless it defended the totality of man. Issues back in 1928, in my first years with the Review, were fewer and in general simpler and easier to handle than those of 1942 and after. And yet those later issues were somehow blended into one great issue, which shaped up with startling clarity. In the words of President Truman to Pope Pius XII, it was "the preservation and support of the principles of freedom, morality, and justice"; the issue of the Christian concept of liberty as opposed to totalitarianism. We see now that what looked to us in those earlier years as trifling or transitory was pregnant with the horrors of the future.

Such a defense of the totality of man implied on the one hand the defense of his religious and moral being and dignity, and on the other hand regard for the concrete conditions, earthly and temporal, under which he worked out his destiny. The mere proclaiming of generalities without ever reducing them to deeds brought the doctrine itself into contempt and was apt to gain more enemies than disciples for the truth. Both of these ideas I had seen stressed by Pope Pius XI and his successor Pius XII. Father Ledóchowski, with whom I had conversed in Rome in 1938, expressly encouraged in the United States the formation of the Institute of Social Order among the American Jesuits for the purpose of coming to grips with the concrete problems of the social order in view of our time, our country, and our Faith.

One of the strongest statements to this effect that I know of was made in *America* by the former Secretary General of the Communist organization of Spain, Don Enrique Matorras, in an article describing his disillusionment with Communism:

We cannot escape the truth; we Catholics must face it and may not evade the issues. We who know and have the remedy must also fight in order to master the situation. We who are fortunately acquainted with the full teachings of Christ have the moral obligation even at the risk of our position, prejudice, and persecution to raise our voices in protest against social injustice and to command once more reverence for the dignity of the workingman.

Convinced as I was on this point I regretted that I was not equipped with the specialized study to enable me to handle it adequately. I had spent many years in practical pastoral work when theoretically I should have been working for degrees in sociology, social ethics, or political science. When stationed at Leonardtown I did borrow a case of books on some of these topics from the Congressional Library in Washington, through the kindness of its librarian Mr. Herbert Putnam, and did a little exploring in spare moments. But without guidance one could not get very far. However, I had the advantage of having already probed into a number of problems of our time.

All this made me desire to keep the line entirely clear on two cardinal points: First, the complete integrity of personal responsibility before God; for we cannot fob off on society or circumstances what in the last analysis is an affair of our own personal conscience. Second, the scope of that claim on our integrity; for the burden on our conscience is not confined to purely personal matters.

Man's social nature affects controversial questions like those of sexual morality, such as birth control, or the indissolubility of matrimony. The Catholic Church stubbornly refuses to look upon the exercise of the sexual function and conduct in the marriage relation as matters to be guided by one's own personal choices alone, but insists that these functions carry a wide social implication. No matter how secretly and privately they may be exercised, they invariably affect the entire structure of society. It is as guardian of the principles of decency, justice, and order on which our society rests that the Church preaches certain standards of sexual and family morality.

With equally controversial insistence, the Church preaches the morality of the marketplace. The pursuit of gain cannot be the affair of the individual alone, but is always subject to the responsibilities which rest upon him as a consequence of his place in society. This frequently leads the editor of a Church organ into highly unpopular positions, first with one group, then with another. Yet his position is fundamentally reasonable, and it is his task to see that it should be expounded as far as possible in a manner acceptable to the general public.

If anyone asked me what were the issues that most threatened the poise of my editorial chair during the years I was in charge of the Review I would be at a loss to choose, since every issue dealing with concrete affairs starts a controversy, even if you merely discuss the weather. However, the following items particularly stand out. They reflect the positions *America* took as a journal of opinion in line with its long tradition, and still holds to, as far as I know. They may be summed up as follows: (1) our duties toward the international community and its organization; (2) our obligation of charity toward the war-stricken peoples of the world; (3) the issue of morality in the marketplace and the consequent reform of certain economic institutions; and (4) the question of civil rights of minority groups—whether religious, as in the case of Catholics and the public school question, or racial minorities, as in the case of the Negroes, the Jews, and others in our community. All of these issues were explosive; each touched some neuralgic point in one reader or another.

The policies of the magazine were easy to state, but difficult to execute. I inherited from my predecessor an imposing and ample rosewood desk, which was the chief adornment of the editorial office at Campion House. The office opens pleasantly on a little garden or patio in the rear and is adorned with rosewood woodwork that belonged in former times to the quondam dining room on the floor above. With the desk I also inherited an upholstered editorial swivel chair which afforded a certain sense of dignity, except that one of the casters periodically slipped off. This happened at inopportune moments and always produced a sense of total futility. The only remedy for the situation was to crawl around on the floor on all fours until, temporarily and precariously, the missing caster was restored. It finally occurred to me that an editor was better off in an ordinary kitchen chair.

Homely as was the incident of the missing caster, it symbolized the very first problem that an editor has to face, namely, that of making himself understood. If we are to influence the thought of those who make the policies of the times, we must speak to them at the level of thought and argument which is their own, and we must propose to them that which they can accept, in order that they may also adopt this reasoning which is ours. This, however, is particularly difficult when one deals with the deeper or more ultimate causes—what Lionel Trilling refers to as the "bitter erudition of our times." On the one hand you displease the avoiders—those who would like to escape the whole discussion and take refuge in a purely but falsely posed spiritual solution, and stop short of anything beyond a purely individual conversion. They are the type of persons whom Pope Pius XII severely reprimanded when he talked to the women of Italy on their civic duties prior to the fateful elections of 1948. Then there are the extremists, the extreme right and the extreme left, both of whom have become all too familiar to us in recent years. They would throw all the blame on some group or individual and thereby escape the serious task of probing the real sources of our present difficulties.

There are, I suppose, some fortunate people who find the editor's job an unmitigated joy. I was not one of them. For me, as (I imagine) for most normal editors, it was a source of innumerable worries. Yet these worries were in themselves interesting. They were the editor's occupational hazards— somewhat like the caster on the editorial swivel chair. They opened a perspective on human nature which one must have lived through in order to appreciate. Anthropologists are kindly people as a rule, if not by nature at least by experience, for otherwise their judgment would be warped. It might be interesting for one of their profession to make a study of the anthropology of readers as seen from the editorial sanctum.

First there are the readers, if I may be pardoned for the paradox, who tell you they don't read the magazine. They completely disagree with it, regard it as a nuisance, would like to see it suppressed, or put in entirely different hands—but they haven't looked at a copy for the last five, seven, eight, or ten years, though they continue to subscribe. There are others who do read it, with a magnifying glass, and express their opinion to you very frankly. As long as readers express their views, and their views are based upon something they have read in the magazine, we are always grateful, even if they abuse us. Better abuse than silence.

Some, of course, just are not interested in a journal of opinion. R. L. Duffus—I believe in the *Atlantic Monthly*—once discussed the reader-appetite of the United States. Out of some 150 million people, he calculated, there were about 200,000 who were really interested in issues as such, in discussing questions, in finding out the pros and cons. For the rest the appeal was confined to five or six primary topics, such as romance, religion, mystery, adventure, and a couple of others. Mr. Duffus wrote before World War II; things have sharpened up a bit since then and people are now interested in questions of ideology, if they are made sufficiently simple. But by and large his classification would seem to hold good. *America* frankly was designed for those who were interested in the issues and were willing to do at least a little thinking with some possibility of reaching thought-out conclusions. You could never read through *America* standing on one foot, in Lucullus' graphic phrase.

The editor discovers the many and interesting ways in which readers take offense, all of which is normal enough but occasionally a bit upsetting. I found, for instance, that some of the sharpest protests, whether in this country or abroad, would be aroused by some incidental remark, some editorial *obiter dictum,* when lengthy expositions of one's stand were ignored. This was particularly true wherever Spain was concerned.

America protested repeatedly against irresponsible attacks on Franco Spain which ignored the atrocities of the Loyalists. We pointed out the evident insincerity of those who attacked Franco Spain, yet were completely silent as to the suppression of human liberties in eastern Europe. We protested against the war of nerves being conducted against Spain and reproached Secretary of State Byrnes for refusing to see the threat. We warned against this type of propaganda and remarked: "The swing of these internal conflicting tendencies is a small matter in comparison with the terrible disruption created by the totalitarian forces which made Spain their colony." Again, we quoted Ambassador Carlton J. H. Hayes to the effect that any attempt to put this group in power would certainly result in bloody revolution, which the majority of Spaniards, both Right and Left, wanted at all costs to avoid. We did acknowledge that there were certain political problems in Spain but were optimistic that the Spaniards would find the solution, and urgently looked for a "broad and generous cultural interchange between the United States and Spain, particularly on the university level." And we repeatedly praised the splendid pronouncements of some of the Spanish bishops calling for speedy social reform. Yet all this would be forgotten and subscriptions canceled if we made a slight query as to the details of certain electoral procedures as reported by Spanish correspondents. As I said, these were part of the occupational hazards.

It was somewhat mystifying for an editor to notice how many religious-minded people were earnestly praying for peace but were, nevertheless, unwilling to face obvious realities in organizing it or to acknowledge the patent fact of the existence of a natural international community. They were always ready with objections against the United Nations and complaints as to the defects in its organization, yet when one undertook to propose concrete action to overcome these defects, they refused to go along. It was difficult to see why there was comparatively little reaction among Catholics to the 1944 statement of the American bishops, cited in Chapter Fifteen, calling for a discussion of the Dumbarton Oaks proposals for an international organization.

Among the readers some would delight in stating or quoting broad generalities but were disturbed when these were applied to concrete questions. As the French say, they were *débrayés,* uncoupled, like a locomotive that rolls on its course leaving the rest of the train sitting on the tracks. This was particularly the case in the matter of human rights. Everybody was ready to praise the *notion* of human rights and to demand rights for their own group or interests, but they became alarmed and suspicious if such rights were vindicated for others. Free-born American citizens were ready to demand the full protection for their rights at home and abroad, yet were reluctant to see these embodied in any form of international declaration no matter how carefully safeguarded it might be. They were unwilling to see the rights which they regarded as sacred for themselves and their children extended to minority groups in the United States. On the other hand, persecuted minorities were intolerant when others were concerned.

People of all faiths were unspeakably shocked in this country by the brutal deportation of vast masses of population in Europe, such as the people of the Baltic nations, Lithuania, Estonia, and Latvia. Soviet conduct was denounced, and rightly so, as an unspeakable crime against humanity without parallel in all history. Yet when it was proposed, by Professor Raphael Lemkin of Yale, to define this crime as genocide and stigmatize it as an offense against humanity and the law of nations, this was denounced as a covert attempt to subvert the Constitution of the United States.

When it came to domestic problems, another attitude was common. I was reproached once by one of our clerical readers for making any distinctions at all. "When I pick up a magazine like *America,*" he said, "and see it discuss the issues of the day, I want to know whether things are right or wrong, and I'm not interested in anything in between. If a bill is before Congress, I want to know whether that bill is backed by Christ or backed by the devil. If it is backed by Christ, I'm for it; if it is backed by the devil, I'm against it. But I don't want to be told anything in between."

I had to reassure my friend that a great deal of legislation could not be assigned either to Christ or the devil. Politics, in great measure, is an approximation. Though unprincipled politics are from the devil, there is nevertheless a capacious area left to the ordinary ingenuity of men. The interests of Christ are often better safeguarded by things which work and are legitimate, than by theories which are perfect but still theories. This is not Machiavellianism but simple political common sense. As St. Thomas More remarked in his *Utopia,* we should not desert the ship of state just because we cannot stop the gales from blowing. "For we cannot have everything good unless everybody is good, which I don't expect to happen for a number of years."

This was particularly true in the field of industrial relations where a considerable number of our readers could see only two alternatives, socialism or statism on the one side, and complete laissez-faire enterprise, unlimited free competition in the marketplace, on the other. They were disturbed when they found that the Church taught that God had something to say about the marketplace, that there were certain principles that applied to human conduct even in the field of production, selling, and the hiring of labor.

Among our readers were inevitably a certain number who clung passionately to their own professional prerogatives. For them rugged individualism had brought certain social and economic advantages, and any attempt to weaken it was a betrayal. Hence the editor had the strange experience—or it would have been strange if he had not become familiar with

it over the years—of finding that devout but ill-informed
Catholics were alarmed and disconcerted when current legis-
lation was judged by perfectly obvious and highly authentic
Christian principles of economic and social morality.

We took the position that the right to private property
must at all costs be defended, but that it is not an unlimited
right; there is also a right of free association for all economic
groups whether they be employers, consumers, or workers.
We held that the State has the right to intervene positively
when it was necessary, as Father Blakely himself had held in
criticizing certain propositions of the National Association of
Manufacturers in 1935.

I felt a deep sense of indebtedness to Father Benjamin L.
Masse, S.J., of our staff, for carrying the ball as he did for
America's social and industrial relations policy. He defended
positions somewhat at variance with those held by Father
Blakely in recent years, though in accordance with Blakely's
positions prior to 1936. Masse's priestly reminders to employers, as well as his exposures of leftist intrigues in the critical union area, subjected him to contrasting criticisms. He
condemned labor racketeers and championed small business;
defended the Wagner Act in the face of noisy attacks upon his
personal integrity, and analyzed impartially the merits and de-
merits of its Taft-Hartley successor. When the CIO convened
at Atlantic City in 1946, Father Masse warned President Murray and his followers that the CIO must decide whether to
"renew a citadel of American unionism and a tower of democracy, or be the chief base of operations in the United
States for an alien totalitarian power." His words struck home,
precisely because they came from a sincere and sympathetic
friend. Thenceforth the CIO waged steady warfare against
the Communists in their ranks. At the outset of my editorship
I had placed my bet on Father Masse's competence and sound
principles. This initial judgment was amply justified by the
matured development of his thought and language in subsequent years.

Some of the foregoing may sound like a discouraging story, but it was not so in reality. Reason, the editor found out, does win despite all the storms that it arouses. Reviewing the experience of "2,000 weeks of *America*," on September 13, 1947, I wrote as follows:

We should not confuse the various levels at which the issue is posed. It is all too easy to shift from one level to another and try to make religion do the work of politics, or make politics do the work of religion: to make government undertake the job that falls upon society locally organized; to confuse the function of military defense and that of international peace organization.

It is in a sense true to say—and it cannot be too strongly emphasized—that the issue of totalitarianism *vs.* freedom can only be solved at the level of religion. But it must also be solved at the level of politics and political knowledge; at the level of international organization and at that of social reform and economic cooperation; of public morals and the cultural level. It requires conjoint action at every level. But to conceive of such joint action demands a certain concentration of thought which does not always make for the easiest kind of reading.

Mere analysis, however, will not do the work. As the scientist Lecomte du Noüy says in his *Human Destiny:* "The more deeply man analyzes, the farther away he gets from the principal problem which he meant to solve." The whole must not be lost through over-occupation with the parts; yet the parts must not be neglected through our absorption into the vision of the whole.

The question of party politics was also one of the casters that would work loose and upset the editor's chair if he was not wary. Yet the issue in this matter was clear enough. By our constitution as well as by the whole tenor of the ideals of religious journalism, *America* was to keep out of mere party politics and we did. Yet we urged Christians to participate in public life and suggest ideas and principles. As an experienced Navy chaplain remarked to me on one occasion, "The boys want some sort of a visible sign." Not the visible sign of a political leader is wanted, but the visible sign of Christian principles, of ethics and religion in their application to concrete situations. Where a political party espoused sound, moral reforms or the interest of religion itself we would praise their action. It was not an endorsement of the party, but an endorsement of the act. This again was an occupational hazard, as it would expose one to the reproach of being a Democrat or a Republican, as the case might be. Yet it was better for Christians to participate in public life, and make a few mistakes, than to hold themselves aloof and leave its conduct to the forces of evil.

Moreover, political wisdom itself is a virtue. Pope Pius XII did not hesitate in his Christmas discourse of 1944 to praise the value of democracy as a system particularly well adapted to the situation of modern times.

The editor was supposed to be continually on the job, but during my four years or so of editorial chieftainship I managed some ten months away from my desk in the hospital or during convalescence. As part of my bodily habitation started coming apart in the spring of 1945, I enjoyed a nice repair operation with subsequent repose from August to November of that year. When some of the screws again came loose, I embarked on a similar hospital safari around May 1946. I had managed a trip to Cuba after the first operation, and one to Europe in the spring of 1947 after the second, hoping things might hold together. But by September of that year I realized that something finally must be done. As my physician told me, "Get the best man you can." I couldn't think of anyone better than Dr. William F. MacFee of St. Luke's Hospital in New York City. In October of 1947 he did really take me apart and put me together again. Only the Lord and Dr. MacFee know with what competence and miraculously successful treatment. This time, to my surprise, I might say to my bewilderment I did, thanks to the same two personages, actually stay repaired.

These adventures gave the editor a chance in more comfortable moments to catch up on some of his reading. The leisure time also brought me close to *America*'s literary editor, Father

Harold C. Gardiner, for I could read and ponder over *A Tree Grows in Brooklyn,* about which Father Gardiner was conducting no end of controversy—quite to his own liking—with a certain type of morally rigoristic reviewer.

So this reminds me of the glory that the editor borrows from the literary editor, without whom the cultural part of the magazine, its department of art and literature, its special departments, such as drama, motion picture, and the complex mechanism of book reviews, would be stalled. I could dilate a bit on the sheer number—some 600 or 700 a year—of books Father Gardiner succeeds in having reviewed and the tranquillity with which he works. As for the tree in Brooklyn, it was a symbol of the whole question of moral standards for reviewers which Father Gardiner tackled head-on with his usual directness and quiet efficiency as well. His booklet *Tenets for Reviewers* epitomized his findings in this ticklish area: findings that he painstakingly confirmed with the best theological moralists at hand. It boiled down pretty much to this—if you are going to call every book immoral which depicts the whole of man's conduct, including his sinful conduct—depicts it, that is to say, not in a way that is seductive or demoralizing for the normal adult reader—you will find yourself blacklisting many of the most vivid and profoundly moral creative works that the world has ever seen. Father Gardiner's blows hit in all directions: against the rigorists who, like all rigorists, achieve results precisely the opposite of those which they intend, and against the hedonists and secularists as well.

In the last analysis the philosophy underlying Father Gardiner's theory of literature was closely akin to that which inspires our own editorial philosophy of the social order: a conviction that the genuine Christian point of view—the Christian anthropology, if you will—does not deny but affirms the natural good that is man. It affirms that good which sin vitiates but does not destroy, that good which if left to itself will poison itself, but which grows richer and grander if watered by God's grace and illuminated by His truth. Its assertion is a paradox but not a contradiction. In fact, the only ultimates that do not turn into contradictions appear to us as paradoxes.

I must pay tribute in passing to the editorship of the *Catholic Mind, America*'s twin publication and older sister, which dates from January 1903. The *Catholic Mind* is a monthly reprint publication in the digest format, but different from digests in that its reprints are given in full. Although as editor of *America* I was designated as editor of the *Catholic Mind,* the actual work was carried on by the executive editor, Father Benjamin L. Masse, S.J. The magazine, partly neglected for many years, finally found in him a friend, and a powerful one, who built it up into a distinguished and influential publication. It was only when its impressive Golden Jubilee volume appeared, *The Catholic Mind through Fifty Years,* that the public became conscious of the vast amount of interesting, valuable, and historic information stored within its pages over the years. My old Innsbruck classmate, the late Bishop Joseph H. Schlarman of Peoria, had built into his episcopal residence a special niche for the bound volumes of the *Catholic Mind.*

The editor-in-chief derived also a sort of extraneous credit from another source. One was praised for what one's betters had said or written some thirty years ago, as if a magazine had a kind of continuing personality of its own. It was equally disconcerting to be blamed for the deeds of the past, to be told that *America* was forever banned from this or that parish because some article had appeared at the time of the Sinn Féin troubles in Ireland which did not meet with the approbation of the pastor.

To me it is a source of wonder each week to see the magazine reborn out of nothing, as it were, a whole new venture launched out of the conversation of a group of men seated around the conference table at the weekly editorial meeting on Monday morning asking themselves what is really most significant in the news, what is of greatest interest, what is mere politics and out of our sphere, what are the burning issues, what will be the clear and straight appraisal of the week's events, what will the public expect of us, what will the Church expect of us, what will God Himself approve, what writers possess the required knowledge, what resources have we in our carefully husbanded reference library, our notes, our sister periodicals? How much can we gather together in a short time? How shall the work be assigned? Whom shall we consult? To whom shall we telephone? Each editor has his little sphere of interests polarized, as it were, around a principal specialty. Yet we all share our knowledge with one another besides drawing on our personal contacts in other fields. As I say, it was an ever-renewed venture and the marvel of it remains today as much as it did on the first morning that I sat at that editorial table.

On August 6, 1945, the atom bomb burst into my life as an editor. The atom bomb was a messenger of fear. I immediately asked myself, what can that fear accomplish? How far can it arouse the public to the deepest realization of our present danger?

The New Yorker in its "Talk of the Town" for August 1948 and Hanson Baldwin of the New York *Times* poked some fun at the fact that *Charm,* a New York magazine, had sent a reporter to Bikini to witness the explosion of the atom bomb. The reporter happened to be my nephew, Oliver Claxton, who was doing a job for *Charm* at that time. After his return he told me that he himself was shaken and appalled beyond anything he could express by the horror that the event inspired in him. At the same time he was disgusted with the incompetents whom the United States Navy sent out to report on the affair; disgusted, too, at the levity with which they tried to make capital out of the fact that the animals poisoned by irradiation lasted a couple of weeks longer than they were expected to. Again it was an example of the sterility of mere terror.

Certainly the editor must do his share of scaring, and from time to time play the unwelcome role of a Jeremias. But his job does not end there. His main task is to inspire confidence, to show where the ground is solid and where you can walk. If one reads the utterances of the Holy See, one will notice that the Popes never leave you panting with alarm. As Archbishop Lucey of San Antonio remarked, the papal messages are not just formative, they are creative. They always follow up a warning or a denunciation with words of hope, with some plan for reconstruction, with a vision of something greater, with a reminder of remedies that have worked in the past, and plans that may materialize in the future. And if we sift the spiritual and doctrinal literature of the Church, from the New Testament to the present day, we will find that is one of the touchstones of orthodoxy as contrasted with heresy. Fear and alarm, whether expressed about the individual's salvation or the state of the world, should always be a prelude or a channel to some element of lasting hope. The goal of the best spiritual literature is—confidence. The same applies to journalism which deals with the religious and moral evaluation of world events. It is slower work, and it doesn't sell the paper so fast for the time being, but in the long run it is what people want.

If I had any hesitation as to whether I had helped to chart the right course, it was removed when I received from the Holy Father himself a hand-written letter. It was issued from the Vatican on the feast of St. Robert Bellarmine, May 13, 1946, addressed to "Our Beloved Son John LaFarge, S.J., Editor-in-Chief of the Catholic Review *America*."

The Holy Father praised the "policy of your Review in analyzing in a careful and scholarly manner the complex issues of the day, and pointing to the solution offered for them by the principles of Christian philosophy." He called attention—mentioning that he had done the same on more than one previous occasion—to "the cankers that weaken the body politic in its national and international life." He singled out for particular mention State Absolutism that recognizes no superior law obliging in conscience and imposing even on the State respect for every person's natural rights; an exaggerated nationalism that would close its eyes to the unity of the human family, and the moral necessity of man's social development reaching its perfection in a world-family comprising all free and sovereign peoples. He likewise stigmatized "racial injustices that often brand the guilty with the sin akin to fratricide," and "economic selfishness" with its disastrous effects on family life. "We have denounced them," said the Pope, "as did Our predecessors before Us."

"The Catholic press," he added, "will bring Our teaching into the home, into the circles of labor and management and to the knowledge of those who write and execute the laws of the land, and we are pleased to observe that your Review has been attaining no little success in this noble Apostolic mission."

Touching more closely on the editorial function itself, the Pope remarked: "Some problems pressing for solution today, especially in the social and economic sphere, are delicate ones, indeed; they cannot be solved precipitately. But the good of society demands that they be faced with candor, be discussed frankly though with moderation and charity, and the solution which is dictated by right reason and Christian principles be accepted with resolute courage."

As for the editor's own conscience, the Holy Father laid the personal problem frankly before me: "A Catholic Review carries a grave responsibility to God and His Church. Its judgment on moral questions, whether they arise in conduct or in the written or spoken word, will be received, and rightly, as a sure and safe guide. It is hailed as a herald of truth, and it will present truths with prudence and reserve, it is true, but always in perfect focus." The Holy Father pledged his prayers to the Holy Spirit and his blessing for "this arduous and extremely important work for Church and State," a blessing for myself and for each member of our staff.

Though addressed to me personally, these words contained an inspiration and a program for the Catholic press throughout the world—indeed, not for the Catholic press alone, but for the entire religious press wherever it was striving to treat the problems of the day in the light of basic religious and moral truths.

Our own separate efforts would have been in vain if the religious forces of our time were to confine themselves merely to expressing their fears of one another and emphasizing their differences. In the face of a monolithic Marxism already entrenched over a period of nearly two human generations, and in the face of an almost equally monolithic, "sacral" secularism that would like to take over the direction of our American cultural and social life, religious forces of our time cannot swing their weight if they are unable to move together.

Among the experiences of my editorship I treasure particularly the assurances of a spirit kindred to my own ideals on the part of religious leaders of other beliefs. The simultaneous endorsement of the *Pattern of Peace* back in 1943 was a striking instance of the efficacy of such an approach. My experience in the long contest for a religious and ethical formulation of the issue of civil rights, and the response to it among persons of different beliefs, was another instance of the same. Moreover, I have found that if Catholics take part, wherever basic co-operation exists, their own personal faith is strengthened. Instead of weakening the force and integrity of their faith, such action makes them understand and grasp it more clearly. My hope is that confidence in what we as Catholics say about man may lead to confidence in us as prophets and bearers of a Divine message.

Back in the days while I was still running my "Scrip and Staff" column in *America*, signed The Pilgrim, I missed one warm summer's day my briefcase containing a couple of articles of clothing and a few other odds and ends. I was under the impression that I had left it at Father Blakely's door when visiting him, but when I inquired of Father Blakely he told me he had just received a telephone call from the Third Avenue Elevated Railroad office saying that they had discovered a briefcase containing such and such on one of their trains and would someone come and claim it at their lost property office. I did then absently remember that I had left some object the day previous on a cross-seat of an Elevated car. How they had identified it and got our number I do not recall.

The Pilgrim, therefore, pilgrimaged to the lost property office at Third Avenue and East 130th Street. The address is simple enough, but it is an odd corner of Manhattan Island and took a bit of searching. I finally located the office and found the lost property clerk sitting peacefully at an open window enjoying the cool breezes from the East River. After I had identified my property, I asked him what he did all day sitting there.

"I read," he said, "I read plenty."

"And what do you read?" I asked.

"Well," he said, "I read a lot of magazines."

"Which one do you like best?" I said.

"There is one called *America*," he said. "It's away ahead of all the rest of them. I read the Scrip and Staff," he said, "the one that is signed by The Pilgrim."

"And what do you like about The Pilgrim?" I persisted.

"The fact that he gives you something to think about and something to hold on to," said the property clerk, and with that he handed over the bag.

Well, this was a homely remark, and it led to a homely reflection. It takes no great talent to spread suspicion, fear, and hate. The tools are always at hand, the audience is ready, and a halo of holy zeal is easily adjusted to any ambitious writer's brow. On the other hand, it is tough going to fight with two arms at once: with the negative arm calling for a militant defense against the deadly enemies of God and country, and the positive arm, striving always to build up the full

strength, spiritual and temporal, of the total man according
to the image of his Creator. It is hard to offer no panaceas; to
challenge to laborious thought, patient forbearance, and the
conquering of one's personal and racial prejudices.

The long run wins when the short runs are forgotten. I still
think of that property clerk who thanked God he could find
something he could hang on to.

CHAPTER NINETEEN
Europe, 1947

⇥⇤

The year 1947 was one of the most interesting as well as one of the most difficult of my life. It began with the discovery that I would need a second major operation. After I left the hospital, I felt vigorous enough to avail myself of an opportunity generously offered me by Superiors, with the aid of kind benefactors, an experience which would be very valuable for an editor. This was to make a postwar trip to Europe. Again I would learn at first hand of conditions abroad. I would resume contacts with my intellectual, spiritual friends and colleagues and would possibly be able to present in person to the Holy Father my thanks for his gracious letter.

Before my departure on May 13, I managed with considerable difficulty to squeeze in a couple of engagements. The first of these was to deliver the Dudleian Lecture for the academic year 1947 in the School of Divinity at Harvard University. This lecture is, I believe, the oldest established lecture in the United States, dating from 1740. Its founder, Rev. Samuel Dudley, specified four topics to be taken each year in rotation, one of which was the exposure of the errors and iniquities of Rome. The embarrassment created by this assignment weighed upon the University authorities in latter days, and even in my undergraduate years, so much so that it was dropped altogether around 1917. Of the three remaining topics that entitled "Natural Theology" fell to my lot.

Using the title "Two Concepts," I made a plea for juridic

wholeness, a complete organic view of man's obligation as opposed to an eclectic choosing of one human right in preference to another. I noted the difficulties that an eclectic spirit had produced in the minds of some of Harvard's earlier intellectuals and declared: "For unless the whole of man in a juridic sense is asserted for *the whole of mankind*—that is, for all men without exception—the assertion is meaningless. The assertion of human rights or of any scale or gamut of human rights is easy when it touches only some limited group, when it is for your own advantage; but when it is for all men, then a completely new set of moral factors come into play."

America's Board of Governors met that year, most inconveniently for me, in St. Michael's College, near Spokane, Washington. This meant a hurried plane trip to Spokane and an equally hasty return to New York with just time to take the plane to Paris and Rome on May 13. I arrived in Rome on May 16. I found Europe without milk and almost without meat, without beer, without wine, without butter, and without bread except for a wretched sandy substitute. In Paris the elevators were out of order, so that you walked up four, five, or six very lengthy flights of stairs.

At the Littoria airport in Rome the young customs clerk was visibly affected on reading my passport. "My name," he remarked, "is Lafargio and I am sure we are cousins. Did any of your family come to Italy?" Perhaps they did, I said. We shook hands and promised to remain life-long brothers.

In Rome I visited a relative for the second time: the elderly Marchesa Morelli di Stellara, née Wight. She was the daughter of Louisa LaFarge, my father's much married sister. I had rather expected to find nothing left of Cousin Lena, since during the war the papers reported that the gentleman who lived next door but one to her on the Via Guattani, the truculent Fascist journalist Virginio Gayda, had been blown to bits along with his house by an American bomb. But, she said, the good Lord protected her and all that she suffered was a broken plate-glass door. Some of Father's paintings

adorned the walls of the villa, giving it for me a home-like
aspect. Her two devoted servants, the maid Velma and the
cook Ascenzio, had been with her some twenty-five or thirty
years. Ascenzio, she confided to me rather plaintively, was
now on strike, something she never thought him capable of.
"But," she said, "how can the dear old man resist the spirit
of the age?" Cousin Lena seemed like the last remnant of a
past existence. Since she was pretty nearly stone deaf, conversation was difficult, but I told Velma to send me word if
and when the Signora should pass away. The Signora did die
shortly after and I received a fine letter from her nephew,
the Avvocato Morelli.

The political atmosphere in Rome did not seem any too
bright. By far the most vivid propaganda was that emanating
from the headquarters of *Unità,* the Communist organ situ-
ated only a block or so from the Gregorian University. Barrett
McGurn, Rome correspondent for the New York *Herald Tribune,* and his wife Mary were as hospitable as ever and they
themselves were considerably troubled over the outlook. What
I saw of the Christian Democrats at their headquarters did
not greatly reassure me. Things looked at loose ends, the
headquarters themselves were shabby, and the propaganda
literature looked flyblown and out of date. Nevertheless, a
mere foreigner is in no position to judge, as later events
showed. I had quite a long talk with two of the top Christian
Democrat leaders, Signori Piccioni and Gronchi, Piccioni
leaning more to the Right, and Gronchi to the Left. Both of
these men were hopeful but complained of the difficulty of
getting really trained leaders. Party unity was difficult to
achieve owing to the varying traditions of different parts of
the country, and of course there was always the problem of
Sicily.

I deeply regretted that Luigi Sturzo, the great patriarch of
the Christian Democrats, was no longer a young man. I had
a couple of conferences with him during his exile in the States
at his home in Brooklyn. Two or three times I understood

that he had started to return to Italy, but each time his health had forced him to cancel his trip. Finally, he made a supreme effort and went home. His spiritual power quite as much as his political sagacity was a dynamic factor, and has been right along, in the extraordinary development of Christian Democracy in Italy and other countries of Europe.

On May 19, through the kindness of the Very Rev. Vincent A. McCormick, S.J., who was American Assistant for the Society of Jesus, I was favored with a private audience with Pope Pius XII, scheduled for 11:45 A.M., this time at the Vatican itself and not at Castelgandolfo.

When I arrived, a moment or so before 11:30, I was ushered through one large waiting room after another. In the final waiting room I wondered what happened next and, looking around, saw a person dressed in white writing at his desk. I saw him smile at me, it was the Pope.

Like everybody else, I enjoyed his marvelous faculty of putting one at ease. I thanked him for the splendid letter he had written and spoke with him briefly about some of the points it contained. From him, as from his predecessor, I received a confirmation of the interracial program and particularly the work of the Catholic interracial councils in the United States, about whose work I shall write in the following chapter.

I took the liberty of asking him if the Holy See could not give greater clarification to the thorny question of co-operation between Catholics and non-Catholics, people "of good will," on strictly moral issues, issues that transcended merely civil matters and were concerned with fundamental points of morality which we can agree on, at least to some extent, in combating atheism, totalitarianism, and secularistic materialism. The Holy Father seemed greatly interested and explained his views on a couple of points to me, then suggested that I might work out some of my ideas a little bit more in detail for his future consideration.

The bell rang at 12:15 for the anthem to the Blessed Virgin, which according to Catholic custom is recited during the Easter season instead of the usual Angelus. The Holy Father knelt and recited the prayers, and I answered them. I had learned these prayers as a child when they had installed the Angelus chimes in the old St. Mary's Church in Newport. To me it was inexpressibly touching to be privileged to recite them there alone with the Vicar of Christ Himself. I thought the audience was ended as we stood up, but he beckoned to me to stay a little longer and asked me what was my hurry. He inquired a while about the religious situation in the United States, the relations of Catholics and Protestants, etc., and I learned thereby some of the ways by which he accumulates for his own use his marvelous store of information. The blessing he gave me to carry back home was not for myself alone but for all the works in which I was engaged. Having seen and spoken to four popes, beginning with Pope Leo XIII, as well as to a future Pope, the late Pope Benedict XV, I felt that they had been generous with their blessings on a life desperately in need of them.

As I was staying this time at the Curia, or Jesuit headquarters at Borgo Santo Spirito 5, Rev. Father McCormick arranged for my interview with the new Father General of the Society, Very Rev. John Baptist Janssens. I found his room even plainer, if that were possible, than it was in the days of his predecessor. All I remember is a plain rolltop desk, a couple of chairs, and a picture on the wall, with the usual bare floor. Father General talked frankly about the timeliness and need of journalistic handling of social problems, to be done courageously, he said, though not in a needlessly provocative fashion. He laid great stress on the intercourse between the various Jesuit periodicals; they should know each other, understand each other's point of view and correspond. His method of talking was more relaxed and informal than that of Father Ledóchowski, which made it easier to present one's own ideas.

On May 31 I reached Paris, where I had an extremely busy

time trying to get permission to enter Germany. I had applied
for the requisite formalities before leaving New York and
had been provided with the necessary inoculations, photos,
etc. But it seemed in Paris there were many more formalities
to be gone through. Time was short and I was extremely anxious to get at least two weeks in Germany. The matter was complicated by the railroad strike. Even when I did get the
necessary papers it was a question how I could reach Strasbourg, whence I expected to cross the border.

An American army plane left at regular intervals for Strasbourg. You joined a waiting line at the Gare des Invalides,
the air terminal in Paris, and I was agreeably surprised at the
courtesy of the people waiting in line. The gentleman in
front of me, noticing that I was rather tired of standing, insisted that I should leave the line, take a little walk and come
back and he would see that the place was kept. The plane was
provided with bucket seats; it was a. two-hour trip with the
minimum of comfort. Balancing himself uncomfortably on a
half a seat next to me was a Strasbourg businessman, a stout
red-faced anxious individual who had never before been in
the air. At the same time the plane door next to me didn't
look any too secure and they had had some trouble closing it.
I was glad when I reached Strasbourg and was greeted by my
old friend Father Minéry who had visited us at Campion
House in New York.

On June 12 Father Minéry kindly sent me by auto to Offenburg in Germany. I was surprised at the informal way the
guard waved us through and the absence, apparently, of any
difference either of language or appearance or anything else
as we passed from Alsace into Baden. It made me realize how
pitifully artificial are so many of our national units of the
present day. The burden of this rigid framework, this grille
of national divisions, weighed upon me throughout my entire
visit to Europe. At Offenburg I was greeted by Father Du
Rivau, S.J., at the newly established cultural center where
German and French students met for the first time since the

war. He described amusingly the astonishment of the young Germans in finding that they could speak their minds without contradiction and their enjoyment of the atmosphere of free discussion. Father Du Rivau had established a monthly magazine entitled *Documents-Dokumente* which provides German articles translated into French for French readers and French articles in German translation for German readers.

I deeply regretted that my time was so short but had to hurry on, fortified by a plain but appetizing meat-loaf sandwich, to catch the train to Frankfurt. The German passengers in the compartment were all eagerly discussing a topic of absorbing interest: the recent arrival of potatoes in carload or shipload in Austria and the possibility that they could share them in Germany. The price of potatoes, the possibility of obtaining potatoes was canvassed, the discussion indicating plainly enough the conditions resulting from the war. Suddenly an intellectual-looking youth exclaimed: "We have said all we can about potatoes, let's change the subject and talk about Beethoven." For the rest of the trip to Frankfurt conversation turned upon orchestra leaders. I joined in with reminiscences of the New York Philharmonic, the Boston Symphony, and so on. Old themes were hummed over and our artists were compared. At a way station one young fellow purchased a little sprig of strawberries, tiny strawberries like the wild kind that grow in New England meadows, and presented them to one of the young ladies who was utterly *entzückt*, moved almost to tears, by the lusciousness and generosity of the gift.

A talk with Jim Norris at NCWC War Relief at Frankfurt was my introduction to the great epic of Catholic war relief parallel to that of the other religious bodies, some of which I had heard about already in Rome from Monsignor Landi and Douglas Woodruff, the editor of the London *Tablet*. I was to hear more of this a few days later in Munich. On Sunday I drove to Heddernheim where I heard confessions in the sacristy and preached at two Masses to a military congregation. I felt quite as if I were back in my old haunts in Maryland.

I could not leave Germany without a trip to Coblenz to see once more my old friend Dr. Heinrich Chardon, whom I visited in 1938. From his letters I gathered that things were pretty well shot up there, and he himself had suffered in the war and lost one of his feet.

The trip to Coblenz, contrary to my expectations, was most delightful. It was a glorious June afternoon, the train left on time, I had the compartment and most of the car to myself for the four-hour ride along the Rhine and, as I passed the famous Lorelei, the words of the old song came to my mind, *"Was soll es bedeuten?—What did it all mean?"* To which I never yet have been able to obtain a complete answer.

I found the streets in Coblenz piled high with rubble, with a narrow pathway through it something like the path through a northern snowdrift. Arriving at the church I found that the magnificent old presbytery simply had disappeared save for a few walls, and the basement which was inhabited by the assistant, Dr. Fassbender. Dr. Chardon resided in the sacristan's quarters, a sort of gate house. The courtyard of the church was filled with busy youngsters eagerly carrying away the rubble in wheelbarrows. Pointing to the standing wall, Heinrich remarked: "Look up there! That's where we sat that May evening in 1938 and talked about Hitler."

I spent the night in the curate's quarters, and the next morning, after my own Mass, attended the High Mass in the partly restored Liebfrauenkirche, the Church of Our Lady. The chapel where I had said Mass in secret on my previous visit was closed at the moment, so I could not revisit it. But hard by was the chapel of St. Michael where on Wednesday morning the pastor said a Mass for a youth group, facing the congregation. Evening Mass was celebrated at the Church of Our Lady and, according to all accounts, was extremely popular and reached many souls who could otherwise not attend services. It was the last time I would see Dr. Chardon in the church where he labored so many years. His bishop, the saintly Bishop Bornewasser, had judged that his health was not strong enough to continue and he was relieved of his arduous task and appointed to the congenial post of Spiritual Father at the seminary in the diocesan city of Trier, where he is at time of writing.

The train trip back to Frankfurt was as crowded as the trip to Coblenz had been solitary. The good lady who sat opposite me, a refined, intelligent-looking person, was beside herself with excitement over the political situation, as excited as the male population seemed to be unexcited. She talked so rapidly and vehemently as to be hardly intelligible. Her companion, a motherly-looking matron, tried ineffectively from time to time to calm her down but without success. As the passenger next to me remarked: "Look what politics does to our women. German women are not made for politics and when they go into it they lose their heads." I did not agree with this uncharitable remark, but it was an agonizing spectacle. In Munich I found my old friends of the *Stimmen* still at their place only under considerably more restricted circumstances.

I could not shake off the sense of paradox which pervaded every aspect of American travel in postwar Europe and was most acute in Germany. On all sides there was evidence of the destruction that we had caused, and yet we were there now to take stock of all we could do to bring life and order and peace to these ruins. And all the time great, glowering Russia breathed down our necks.

Some relief to this paradox and to the inner distress that it caused was the consciousness of what voluntary charity in the United States could do for the relief of people abroad. A testimony to that were the War Relief Services of our own Church and the parallel services of the Protestants and the Jews. All these postwar contacts, fumbling as they were, and painful as were the circumstances, did enable us Americans to present to the European mind the spiritual validity and integrity of our religious life in the United States. The secular world saw people of different religious faiths, Catholics, Protestants, and Jews, banded together and working harmoniously for the defense of civilization and for certain great moral and spiritual ends, people who in the Old World were frequently divided by inveterate and bitter enmities. Our Catholic brethren learned to realize that after all there is an American Catholic church in the best sense of the word, a church which has developed its own tradition, its own saints, its own richness of individual and communal life. The American Catholic church, true, is not concentrated and not symbolized by great historic works of art as in Europe, but nevertheless its three hundred years of existence have given it a dignity and validity which we at home perhaps do not always appreciate. There *is* an American Catholic tradition, and the spirit of the great saints and missionaries and pioneers has not been lost but has broadened out into countless channels through our history.

Some of these thoughts passed through my mind as, after my return to Paris on June 20, I met various luminaries of the French Church at a luncheon at the American Embassy. The Ambassador, Mr. T. J. Caffery, had made some of his early acquaintance with the Catholic Church at Campion House in New York. The Archbishop of Paris, His Eminence Cardinal Suhard, was the guest of honor and suggested to me that I should drop over to the *archévéché* and pay him a visit before I left. I found myself in his study with its great casement windows opening out on one of those flourishing hidden gardens which are the perpetual surprise and glory of Paris.

From his vigorous appearance and his equally vigorous speech, I would never have gathered that the Cardinal had so short a time to live. Three people, he said, were in charge of the spiritual welfare of the people in the Archdiocese of Paris—the Pope, the Archbishop, and the pastor or curé. "Under my care and responsibility are five million souls," said the Cardinal. "Yet the greater number of these five mil-

lion are completely inaccessible to the ministrations and even
to the approach of the Church." He then told of some of the
enterprises he had set in motion which have created somewhat
of a sensation both in France and other countries; such as
the priest workmen, for instance, who while keeping their
priestly character and fulfilling the essential liturgical obligations of the priesthood work during the daytime as ordinary
factory hands. I had met a couple of these apostles.

"I have experienced," he said, "quite a bit of criticism, but
the criticism would be beside the point if they understood
what is my aim. The idea is not immediately to convert these
people with whom they come in contact, but to form the very
first and indispensable step, which is simply to make the contact itself. The truth is, we have a vast, completely paganized
population for whom not only Catholicism but religion itself
is completely dead. All they know of it are a few half-civic
observances. The first and necessary step is to know the priest
as a human being, one whom they can speak to, confide in
and respect."

The situation which existed in such tragic acuteness in
France did appear after all in a greater or lesser degree in
other parts of Catholic Europe. In Belgium Canon Cardijn
and his Young Christian Workers were valiantly working to
close the social gap. In Catholic Bavaria, rich in ancient Catholic traditions and practices, young people abandoned their
habits of religious practice when transferred to the city, unless they received special care.

The American Church by its very origin and traditions has
always stood close to the people. But a sobering thought came
to me after my talk with Cardinal Suhard. You never can be
too sure, and human nature everywhere is pretty much the
same. We priests at home can also become careless or can take
refuge in that disastrous formalism that has so plagued and
hampered the Church in the Latin countries. The throne and
the altar will never be united in the United States; but the
pocketbook and the altar can make, if we do not watch out, a

quite unholy alliance. A wealthy Catholic with high political influence—be it local or national—can drive some surprisingly hard bargains.

As I had not time to travel to Finistère, Finistère graciously came to me. Mother M. Vianney, the former Généviève du Halgouët, arranged a bit of a family party at the headquarters of the Helpers of the Holy Souls on the rue Coëtlogon with its oddly contrived chapel that was erected as a memorial to the dreadful holocaust of the Charity Bazaar fire in the '90s. Cousin Jobik and Yvonne were present with the junior members of the family and the third generation, and I learned first hand of the bitter hardships the older folks had experienced during the war. They were right in the line of fire. By almost a miracle their home was not bombed. Yvonne had pedaled or walked day after day into Morlaix, a two-mile trip, to work twelve hours sewing and making bandages, only to find herself accused and vilified by some of the local Communist agitators.

My last few days in Paris were those when the Big Three, Messrs. Bevin, Bidault, and Molotov were discussing the administration of the Marshall Plan. The plan put the last-mentioned gentleman in a tough spot, for the objections he raised to the other two Foreign Ministers showed how conscious he was of the blow the Plan would deal to Soviet prestige in Europe. Julien Green and his sister Ann invited me to lunch at their apartment in the rue de Sèvres. From the room of their apartment the window looked out on the leafy garden of the Russian Embassy where all looked peaceful while a shirt-sleeved gentleman was somberly pacing to and fro. "That," said Mr. Green, "is Mr. Molotov." He was doubtlessly pondering over his reply to Bevin and Bidault.

Two old acquaintances, I found, were absent from Paris at this postwar visit, one dead and the other in prison, both of them examples of the blunders and disillusionments of the Vichy regime. The former, Dr. Alexis Carrel, author of *Man the Unknown,* an expert on nutrition, had returned to France during the war with the sole purpose of trying to do something to save the health and lives of the war-stricken children.

Dr. Carrel had confided to me on one occasion that he had never met Jacques Maritain but was extremely curious about him. "You know," he said, "I wonder how Maritain's mind operates. I have never been able to understand anything abstract. I never think in general concepts. With me everything is concrete. I am a peasant by origin from Auvergne and see everything as something I can see and touch and verify."

I myself knew pretty much how Carrel's mind operated, for he used to quiz me as to the effects of preaching in the churches. He wondered if pastors of souls ever made any real study of the effect, immediate or long distance, of preaching on the individual young people who heard their sermons. Accordingly, I proposed to Mr. Maritain that there might be a meeting. He, on his part, had been curious about Dr. Carrel's mentality. So we spent a long interesting evening at the Century Club in New York City.

After the meeting Dr. Carrel remarked to me: "Monsieur Maritain is a perfectly wonderful man, a delightful character and I am so charmed to have met him. I feel like loving him, but I still don't understand how his mind operates." If my memory does not fail me, Mr. Maritain made somewhat the same remark about Dr. Carrel. At any rate they were so mutually interested that they decided to get together on a future occasion, and so spent several hours in mutual mental exploration.

Both Carrel and his wife were in great distress during their Paris stay. He took ill and his long and useful life soon came to a close.

The other person I missed was the historian and novelist Bernard Faÿ who had frequently visited me in New York and used to come of a morning and serve Mass at Campion House. Faÿ was considerably more political-minded than poor Carrel and had got himself into no end of hot water by associating with Vichy leaders and compromising himself, according to

popular report, by giving a certain amount of information
concerning people with Masonic affiliations. I never ascer-
tained whether these charges were true or not. Certainly, if
anything serious were the case it seemed to be out of keeping
with the man's charitable character. However, he landed in
jail, from whence within the past few months, after long years
of suffering, he has been liberated. His friends in Paris be-
sieged me with requests to obtain some intercession on his
behalf, but I saw nothing that I personally could accomplish.

Squeezing in a press conference at the Quai d'Orsay at the
very last moment, where Mr. Bidault's secretaries handed out
statements on the Marshall Plan, I finally took the plane for
New York. We stopped for luncheon at Shannon Airport in
Ireland, at which luncheon beer was served, the first real beer
I had seen on my entire trip, for even in Munich all they
poured out for you was some kind of herbaceous product.

"Would Your Reverence like a glass of beer?" said the
neatly uniformed waiter.

"And sure," I said, "I would."

"And it will be twenty-five cents," he said.

"But I have no twenty-five cents," I replied. "I have no
American money on me."

"Then it will be a shilling, Your Reverence," he said. But
my only bit of English money, three shillings sixpence, was
locked up in my bag in the plane.

"Then you have no money at all," said the waiter.

"Certainly," I said, "that's just the trouble."

"Then in that case," said the waiter, "the only thing is for
the Government of Ireland to provide you with the beer,
which we shall be most happy to do because we want to make
everybody joyful and contented who passes through the Shannon Airport."

A kindly Jewish gentleman opposite me at the table passed
the waiter a rather nice tip. In the lobby after luncheon a
little newspaper man came up to me and said that he repre-

sented the Dublin press. "May I ask," he said, "where Your
Reverence has been traveling? I understand you have been
moving about quite a bit." I explained to him I had been in
Rome and Paris, not to speak of Germany. "And did you see
the Pope?" he asked.

"Certainly," I said, "I saw the Pope."

"And I understand also," he said, "that you had a glass of
beer at the expense of our government."

"All of this," I said, "is on the historical record." He said,
"We like to know those things because they are of interest
to the general public." By that time I felt as if I had drunk a
gallon of beer.

I forgot about the incident until I met Tom Doyle of the
Religious News Service three or four days later.

"Did you enjoy your trip, Father?" said Tom.

"I had a wonderful time," said I. "I saw everybody from the
Pope down."

"It was nice," he said, "to know you were in the Shannon
Airport and that our Irish government treated you to a glass
of beer. It's in the Dublin papers and they wired it over here."
There is no particular moral to this story except to warn trav-
elers that when they pass through the Shannon Airport it is
best to have a few shillings or quarters in their pocket. And
that was the end of my 1947 trip.

Three days later I received a phone call that in a way was a
sequel to my reflections in Paris about Dr. Carrel. Madame
Lecomte du Noüy, wife of the distinguished physicist, called
to tell me that her husband was fatally ill with cancer at the
Roosevelt Hospital. I had heard of Lecomte du Noüy and
had been much impressed by some of his writing. Ill as he
was, he told me the story of his latest work, *Human Destiny,*
which apparently had an extraordinary effect on the most
unlike types of reader. It had converted a cowboy who was
on the point of committing suicide. It had totally changed the
life and character of a desperate inmate of Dannemora Prison
in New York. It had been read in the interior of China, and

the fan mail poured in day after day from all over the world. Some of his propositions were completely erroneous, from the point of view of Catholic theology, but the work nonetheless was a vigorous defense of the existence of God and the moral law, and its defects were due not to ill will but to the simple fact that Du Noüy in the course of his long life had drifted away from the Church and from the knowledge of his early faith. During his last illness the scientist became completely reconciled with the Church, made his humble profession of faith, and died fortified by the sacraments. May he rest in peace.

Though I was rewarded by lasting health after three operations, the burden of editorship was none too easy and I was relieved when, at the beginning of 1948, the Superiors told me that it might be possible for me to have a successor. Father Robert C. Hartnett, S.J., head of the Department of Political Science of the University of Detroit, had contributed considerably to the pages of *America*. I felt that he could do an excellent job and was happy when in November of that year Father Hartnett was appointed to take over the editor's burden. With that I stepped back to the position of associate editor which I had filled all through the years since my arrival at Campion House in August 1926, and which I am still filling at the present day.

With the laying down of the editorial burden, the summer phase of my life closed and the autumnal aspect began. A completely disproportionate amount of time had been spent during those four years that I was editor-in-chief in the hospital or in convalescence. It might have seemed a waste, and yet those in reality were my most valuable months. Many others have learned, like myself, that you only come down to a sense of two great elemental facts in our lives—one's own littleness and the might of God's aid—when the props are removed for a time and you leave yourself totally in His hands.

PARS AUTUMNALIS

⇒≫ ≪⇐

Autumn merges time with eternity. November is the month of prayer for the faithful departed; living and dead engage in a dialogue of prayer and gratitude. The church-year's end fuses with the end of all time: with the great Feasts of apotheosis, such as Christ the King (end of October), All Saints (November 1), and the Gospel vision of the final judgment calling all men to account for many things that honest, good citizens do not imagine they will be called to account for. Being the season of harvesting, it invites us to reassemble and appraise memories of experiences separated by long intervals of time. No season is more suited for summarizing a complex series of events; for some fresh observations on the passing scene, and for bringing one's own tale to an end.

CHAPTER TWENTY

Venture at Pentecost

God's medicine for the human race, says Saint Augustine, surpasses our human understanding. We need light from above in order consistently and universally to see all men as Christ our Lord saw them, transcending outward appearances. I myself had to learn my lessons through long observation and experience, not from anybody's say-so. It needs more than unaided human strength to translate such an understanding into practical deeds, such as the defense of basic human rights, when you are personally not inconvenienced. From the French Revolution to the present day, the cause of human rights has been compromised so often by those who have made it a vehicle for their own political schemes that it is not easy to steer a straight course between a doctrinaire spirit and a spirit of compromise. It is very hard to keep the motive of love uppermost, rather than that of expediency or mere "enthusiasm." Yet that course can be steered.

On Pentecost Sunday, 1934, leaders in the interracial movement gathered in New York's Town Hall and uttered a powerful appeal to the public for a thoroughgoing policy of Christian justice and Christian charity toward the Negro race. The meeting was sponsored by the Catholic Laymen's Union, a group of Negro business and professional men from the New York metropolitan district, who for the past six years had been following under my direction a program of prayer, study, and Catholic social action. The speakers included Mr. Elmo M. Anderson, the Catholic Laymen's Union president; Father

337

James M. Gillis, C.S.P., editor of the *Catholic World;* Michael
Williams, editor of the *Commonweal;* and Mrs. E. P. Roberts
of the Urban League, whose husband, a graduate of Lincoln
University and prominent Negro physician of New York City,
was a member of the Cardinal Gibbons Institute Board. His
Eminence, Cardinal Hayes, Archbishop of New York, was rep-
resented by his Vicar General, Rt. Rev. Monsignor Michael
J. Lavelle, P.A. Dr. Hudson J. Oliver, vice-president of the
CLU, was chairman.

At the close of the meeting, Monsignor Lavelle voiced the
interest of His Eminence in the spiritual and temporal welfare of the colored race and gave encouragement both in
behalf of the Cardinal and in his own name to the work for
a better race relationship that was being fostered by the Catholic Laymen's Union. The large auditorium in Town Hall
was well filled, both races being about equally represented.
The Honorable James J. Hoey, K.S.G., Collector of Revenue
of the Second District of New York, offered a set of resolu-
tions, enthusiastically adopted, proposing the establishment
of the New York Catholic Interracial Council, as a joint co-
operative venture by both white and colored leaders for the
promotion of a consistently Christian attitude in race relations. Mr. Elmo Anderson had much to do with Mr. Hoey's
proposal. When the Council was formed, Mr. Anderson became its first president. Shortly before the close of his life he,
along with other pioneers in the movement, M. A. Thomas
and Emmanuel A. Romero, and George K. Hunton, the
Council's executive secretary, received through the hands of
His Eminence, Cardinal Spellman, a papal decoration from
the Holy Father in Rome. Later on two other officials of
the Council also received papal decorations—the Honorable
Harold A. Stevens, a Judge of General Sessions, and Gerard
L. Carroll, general counsel for the Grace Line steamship company.

The Catholic Laymen's Union, parent of the Council, con-

tinued to be its spiritual laboratory. Its three-day annual retreat, held for the twenty-fifth time in July 1953, was made
possible for eighteen years by the hospitality of the Fathers of
the Society of the African Missions at their mother-house in
Tenafly, New Jersey, and later by the Rev. Stephen J. Meany,
S.J., who welcomed us in 1948 to the new Jesuit laymen's retreat house at Glenmont, New Jersey.

The first act of the newly organized Council was to come to
the rescue of the *Interracial Review*, a monthly published in
St. Louis and founded by the Rev. William M. Markoe, S.J.,
former pastor of St. Elizabeth's Church for Negroes in that
city. Having had considerable difficulty in carrying on the *Review* along with his other occupations, Father Markoe was glad
to have it transferred to New York. Accordingly, beginning
with October 1934, the publication of the *Review* was completely taken over by the newly formed Council. From a lowly
parish chronicle, it had developed into a monthly magazine
of distinctive character and general national interest.

Those clergy who work among the Negroes often felt themselves isolated. Even their ordinary ministry was looked upon
askance. For the year previous to the pentecostal gathering I
had been identified with a fine group of Catholic clergymen
who were deeply concerned about the welfare of such work.
They were from several dioceses and various religious Orders
and took the name, Northeastern Clergy Conference on Negro
Welfare. Its formation was due to two great-souled men who
decided to attack the problem directly and see if organized
effort would not accomplish what individual approach failed
to achieve. These were the Rev. Harold Purcell, then a
member of the Passionist Order and editor of *Sign* magazine,
and Rev. Cornelius J. Ahern, pastor of Queen of Angels
Church in Newark, New Jersey. Fathers Ahern and Purcell
talked the matter over with two or three besides myself, and
called our first meeting in Newark, New Jersey, on November 12, 1933.

Our deliberations extended from 1933 to 1942 over some thirty sessions, of which I acted as secretary. The meetings were "off the record" and discussion was free and frank. The participants became, as they reported, convinced of two things, "first, that *public opinion is a capital factor in the Negro's spiritual welfare and in the material circumstances that affect that welfare;* and, second, that *the combating of false opinion and the building up of a sound one cannot be left to mere chance.* It cannot be left, as has been so often falsely said, to the good works *merely* to speak for themselves. There must be set on foot a *systematically and intelligently organized propaganda for the spiritual welfare of the Negro and its material implications* and the clergy themselves should be leaders in such an undertaking."

At a meeting in St. Elizabeth's Convent, Cornwells Heights, Pennsylvania, on May 7, 1935, a general program of race relations was proposed which could be offered to both clergy and laity at future meetings. The formula adopted was: "Full Catholic life for the Negro, and a full equality of opportunity in fulfillment of the Negro's duties toward God and his fellowman." It was, in other words, a program of integral justice and charity.

The Northeastern Clergy Conference on Negro Welfare came to an end in 1942. War conditions and the death of Father Ahern, Bishop Joseph M. Corrigan, and other prominent members of the Conference made it difficult to carry on its work. It had given great impetus to a serious consideration of the racial question in relation to the Catholic Church in the United States. But a much more fundamental task awaited us. We had to attack the whole question of interracial justice directly and systematically, as a major phase of religious and Christian action in the contemporary world. This was to be the job of the Catholic Interracial Council.

The Clergy Conference on Negro Welfare had co-operated with the Catholic Interracial Council in starting (May 1939) a permanent center which would serve the Council and the publication office of the *Review* and the Clergy Conference as well. We discovered a large, comfortable office with windows on three sides conveniently located at 20 Vesey Street, in the lower downtown section of the city, to the rear of Old St. Peter's Church on Barclay Street, and a couple of blocks from the Woolworth Building and the old City Hall.

Once the center was set up, requests for information on racial problems and the organization of groups to treat of them started to pour in, and have continued ever since. A precious windfall was the gift of an unusual bibliographical apparatus, some 39,000 cards on every phase of the race question, particularly as it touched the Catholic Church, that I received from the late Father Arnold Garvy, S.J., in Chicago. We baptized it the Claver Index, and placed it at the disposal of the public.

We began holding meetings at the Catholic Interracial Center in 1941. I was a bit taken aback when a Paris journalist was mildly scandalized by the respectability of the Vesey Street gatherings. To his mind they could only be authentic Catholic social action if they gathered in a proletarian atmosphere —as a protest not only against prejudice, but against the economically corrupt situation of the modern, industrialized world. Instead he found at Vesey Street a sort of cross-section of normal New York existence, often with representatives of large and fairly influential elements in the community—of industry, business, labor organizations, city and state government, social work, private and public schools, colleges and youth organizations, parish organizations, and so on. They met for an hour or so, exchanged views and wishes, and then parted to their several ways resolving simply to behave like decent citizens in their contacts with various ethnic groups.

The meetings became a regular weekly affair, every Thursday afternoon from 6 to 7, winter and summer, with a short talk by some competent speaker and a brief question period.

A carefully prepared news release, sometimes with pictures, giving the main points of interest in the talk, has always met with cordial reception in the press. The work has been made possible through the years by various friends to whom I wish to express a deep and heartfelt appreciation. If it had not been for them, and the high patronage, patience, and encouragment of the Archbishops of New York and Brooklyn, it could not have been carried on. In some of our most difficult moments, we were tremendously heartened by the cordial friendship and experienced counsel of such national leaders as Elmer A. Carter of the New York State Commission Against Discrimination; Dr. Peter Marshall Murray, vice-president of the New York County Medical Society; Dr. Channing H. Tobias, chairman of the board of the National Association for the Advancement of Colored People and Roy Wilkins, its administrator; Julius A. Thomas, industrial relations secretary of the National Urban League, and very many others.

The Catholic Interracial Council was a "venture," just as the Cardinal Gibbons Institute was, but it was of vastly greater scope. As I look back over the twenty-five and odd years, I naturally ask myself: What has been the balance of my experience? Where does it all come out? The recital of its many activities I spare the reader, who will find much about them as well as a good part of my theory, in my two books, *The Race Question and the Negro* and *No Postponement*.

I could never see why we cannot talk reasonably upon the matters that divide various racial groups. The facts about racial difference and their meaning, or lack of meaning, for our American life, are now pretty generally known, and certainly there is no shortage of literature on the subject. The difficulties arise not from determining the principles, but from applying them to the countless situations in our rapidly changing life.

Three elements are principally required, I believe, for

reaching unity and harmony among the various conflicting groups in this country. These are intelligent publicity; honest co-operation; and the grace of God.

By intelligent publicity I mean presenting to the public all that is pertinent in the case, not just a partial or distorted view, and doing this in a manner free from passion and exaggeration. The presentation must appeal to intelligent listeners. Naturally it is not easy to keep a balance between precision and strength. People who suffer real grievances become fed up and embittered with mere optimistic double-talk. They are naturally annoyed when slick magazines tell the world of the wonderful progress their race is making, but are silent over grave obstacles that still confront their efforts to attain an equal status. Any recently liberated Negro POW who has faced torture by Communist brutalitarians and has resisted attempted brain-washing after being taken captive in the service of his country is embittered beyond measure when he is denied the ordinary courtesies and decencies of citizenship on coming back to his native town. On the other hand, perpetual harping on grievances meets with diminishing returns. If you have made little impression by telling your story once, you may fail to make any impression when you relate it for the second time, and encounter more stubborn resistance from then on.

Vigorous and pointed protests need to be made, in private and in public, but they are chiefly effective in so far as they appeal to some cherished belief or principle which we accept in common: such as a common religious faith; the spirit and aims of the Catholic Church; the duties, privileges, and traditions of American citizenship or the honor of our country at home and abroad.

Utterly stupid publicity from any useful point of view—the type that only exasperates and perplexes—may be highly effective as a means to further a certain type of subversive propaganda. Now that Stalin is dead, the Communist Party in the United States presumably is freed—or soon will be—from the dead hand of the uncouth slogan to which Stalin stubbornly committed it: that of setting up a segregated Soviet republic in the Black Belt of the Southern states. Communist propaganda can now concentrate upon the other and more plausible prong of their traditional two-tined program for the American Negro, that of agitation for civil rights. Communist civil-rights agitation is a perfect means for capitalizing upon certain types of human misery; but its goal is not to secure civil rights for the Negro or for anyone else. It aims simply at exciting greater and greater bitterness and confusion, until a situation is created where the Communist Party can step in and take charge.

The perfect example of such procedure was the famous Scottsboro case, where the Communists in 1931 edged in upon the legal defense of nine Negro youths who were falsely accused of raping two white women. Large sums of money were raised for which no clear accounting was given and the Comrades carried on provocation for provocation's sake, so that the case could be used as a powerful instrument for world-revolutionary propaganda. From my old friend of Cardinal Gibbons Institute days, Dr. James Hardy Dillard, of Charlottesville, Virginia, who as a liberal-minded Southerner was deeply concerned over the Scottsboro case, I learned how the Communists had deliberately sabotaged the efforts of the distinguished Birmingham, Alabama, lawyer, Roderick Beddow, to come to the boys' rescue. So on December 13, 1935, I wrote to the Rev. L. J. King, chairman of the non-Communist American Scottsboro Committee—which the Communists were trying to pull into their own orbit:

Despite what professions may be made, I do not believe that any organization controlled by the Communists will abstain from using the case, if they are connected with it, for the purpose of radical propaganda. Furthermore, all available sources of information confirm my belief that the temper of the Alabama courts, juries, and people is such that the boys' chances of freedom is utterly destroyed if those sponsoring them are suspected to be in any way affiliated with the Communists, or sympathetic to the Communist cause.

Since my only interest was to see the boys liberated, in the belief that they were innocent, I said I would resign from the Committee if it should enter into such an alliance, and in point of fact I did. Those who continued to work with the Communists suffered an exceedingly bitter and disillusioning experience, for once more the party-liners followed the old pattern of wanton provocation. Though, after nineteen years, the last of the nine boys was eventually freed, the case had served to reveal to the American public once and for all the vanity of hoping to accomplish anything for interracial justice, or any other type of justice, by going along with a Communist Party front.

Though the American public is little impressed by repeated drum-beating of the Communist variety, it affords a wide and ever-increasing welcome to honest reporting of any and all of the elements that enter into the drama of the racial groups in this country. One of the first Catholic newsmen to share our own conviction in this respect was—and still is—Mr. Frank A. Hall, director of the National Catholic Welfare Conference News Service in Washington, D. C. Mr. Hall's example was speedily followed by other agencies, and by the Catholic press. On the other hand, the same principle of impartial and intelligent reporting brought a quick response from the editors of the various national Negro periodicals, which at present reach some four to five million readers per week in the United States, and are widely circulated abroad. These periodicals discovered that the Catholic Church, through her work for the colored race and her efforts on behalf of interracial justice, through her striking events and her outstanding personalities of all groups, had a big story to tell, one of absorbing interest to their readers. The result has been to present to the great non-Catholic Negro public a fair picture of the Church—her teachings, her bishops and clergy, her rites and institutions— where formerly only grotesque caricatures or bitter diatribes prevailed. It was amazing to discover that a few words spoken at any one of our weekly forums at 20 Vesey Street reached, through these various agencies, the hearts and minds of literally millions of people of all races and many nationalities week after week throughout the year. In the favorite expression of one of the founders of our Council and one of Harlem's best-known residents, Capt. M. V. Boutté, "You'd be surprised."

It was surprising, too, to observe how much interest—again of the steadily increasing variety—has been stirred up by the various periodical events that have taken place under the auspices of the Council: such as the annual award for interracial justice given each year, on the Feast of Christ the King, in memory of the late Mr. James J. Hoey; a periodical interracial Mass and communion breakfast; and the organization of a special group of American citizens of Irish descent, the John Boyle O'Reilly Committee for Interracial Justice, on behalf of the American Negro. The point of all this is that the mass of the American public are not deeply prejudiced, but are confused by current notions and hoary stereotypes which are accepted about the Negro, just as the idea is widely current that our American Indians are still "wards" of the United States Government. In the South itself, intelligent publicity is having its results. Notable changes of sentiment can be credited to the alert and capable organized Catholic Committee of the South.

Only a fraction of the New York Council's publicity could have been accomplished without the indefatigable efforts of its devoted secretary, Mr. Hunton, who has made the interracial cause his life work, combining Irish idealism with the canny caution of a New Hampshire-born New York lawyer. Widely current today are the slogans in which he habitually crystallizes his declaration of thought and policy. Largely through his efforts the number of Catholic Interracial Councils in the United States has risen—to date—to twenty-three, four of which are in the Southern states; with others in process of formation. Under his guidance flourishing college and university groups of Catholic college students, undergraduate and alumni, are now working in the same field for the same cause.

Whenever I hear the remark: "But where I live we have no racial problem," I feel skeptical because I have heard this said of so many genuinely problematic places. However, even granting there may be nothing serious to worry about in a given community at the present time, how about the future?

Conflicts and riots are not inevitable, even under great provocation, if steps are taken in time to forestall them. But the time for preparation is in advance, not after the storm has broken. If people, or families, live only for themselves, or for those naturally nearest and dearest to them, they are more or less bound to come in conflict with neighbors of different origin and interests. But a shared interest and devotion to a common good in the community can overcome many a rooted prejudice or antagonism.

As far as the races are concerned, I see the focus of their co-operation directed to the good of the local community, even the local neighborhood. There is no more effective action toward this end than people of different faiths, as well as different racial or national groups, uniting for the common welfare. If the children of light—all those who acknowledge a sovereign moral law—do not join forces, the children of darkness will take over and exploit their apathy and division.

Crowding is an evil in itself. The continual migrations are usually painful and upsetting, and it is highly unpleasant to a community to wake up and find so many new people in their midst—whether it be city or suburb or countryside. But out of these evils and annoyances determined efforts can pluck a precious flower of fellowship and social peace, which is all the stronger because it was tested in the crucible of human hearts. Hence I do not look upon such presences as necessarily a sort of calamity to which we must perforce resign ourselves. I see them rather as an opportunity sent us by the Creator so that we can fulfill our age-old ideals under new conditions and on a broader and more fruitful scale: as a response—to use the language of Mr. Toynbee—to a new challenge, so that we may turn a time of troubles into a sturdy and lasting civilization.

I have appreciated working with various non-Catholics in connection with the problems of African students in the United States. I first made contact with them in 1941 as a member of the Committee on Africa, organized by officers of the Phelps-Stokes Fund in New York City, probably the only American foundation which refers to work in Africa in its actual incorporation, and one which has shown interest in African problems for over a quarter of a century. In fact, it was reading a Phelps-Stokes survey during my early days as a missionary in Maryland that had started me thinking seriously about the educational phases of the racial problem.

In 1942 the Committee issued a soberly-planned report entitled "The Atlantic Charter and Africa from an American Standpoint." The principal feature of this document was the application of the "Eight Points" of the Charter to the specific problems of Africa, especially to those related to the welfare of the African people living south of the Sahara, with related material on African conditions and needs. As a member of the executive committee I had the privilege of working with such men as Professor Ralph Bunche, Professor Charles S. Johnson, Dr. Thomas Jesse Jones, Dr. Emory Ross, and Dr. Channing H. Tobias.

At the invitation of Dr. Emory Ross, Secretary of the Presbyterian Board of Foreign Missions, I joined in 1948 the executive committee of CASNA, the Committee for African Students in North America, of which organization I was elected vice-president. The Committee was non-denominational, organized for the purpose of advising African students both in their homeland and in this country, and in helping them to solve some of their most urgent problems. At the time I joined, a survey conducted jointly by our State Department and the British Colonial Office registered some four hundred students in the United States, most of them from British West Africa and Liberia, a few from Ethiopia and East Africa.

American Catholicism has had comparatively little contact with Africa as compared to other mission fields such as China, the Philippines and South America and Alaska. Nevertheless, with the development of the Point Four program it has become obvious that we can no longer hold aloof from the great spiritual problems of the Dark Continent.

In my own case in this country, I believe that I struck a straight course when I co-operated with A. Philip Randolph, president of the Brotherhood of Sleeping Car Porters, as in June 1942 he and his associates organized a monster demonstration in Madison Square Garden, New York City, on behalf of equality of Negro employment opportunity. On that occasion I spoke—the only white man on the stage—to the largest human assemblage I have ever directly addressed in my life. "The most significant thing about the rally," I wrote at the time, "was the fact that this historical gathering was genuinely American." Leaders of the March on Washington movement, which was inspired by anxiety over the discrimination in the immense defense industries, were bound by no spiritual, intellectual, or political ties to any foreign land or ideology. Significantly, too, these leaders vigorously rejected the advice and financial support of alien radical parties. The Garden rally was denounced by both Stalinist and Trotskyite factions of the Communist Party. The latter sent Mr. Randolph, leader of the March on Washington movement, a check for $25,000 to help defray expense. Mr. Randolph promptly returned the check. Whatever illusions he had once entertained about the virtues of the Communists were by this time completely dispelled.

Incidentally, it cannot be too strongly emphasized that the MOW movement was not Communist inspired. On the contrary, the Communists bitterly opposed it, once they found

they could not take it over. As Randolph remarked: "We have
no use for Nazis, Communists or Fascists or their work. We
consider them a menace, a nuisance, a danger and a pestilence
to the Negroes and to labor in this country. We believe in the
democratic process, ideals, heritage, faith and values . . . so
strongly that we are ready and determined to fight for them
at home and abroad."

The immediate effect of the Madison Square Garden demonstration was seen, of course, in the policies of President
Franklin D. Roosevelt's Executive Order 8802, on fair employment practices. But the supremely important and permanently lasting effect was the total disassociation then and there
of the civil-rights issue from the manipulation of the Communist Popular Front.

The help of God's grace is also needed in order to speak
plainly on racial issues, yet in doing so not to reflect, or seem
to reflect, upon the life and work of men and women who
have dedicated their whole lives to the total service of the
Negro in the very depth of his greatest humiliations.

Having experienced some of these trials myself, in my
earlier years as a priest in Southern Maryland, I could understand, and could even sympathize with the tone of one of the
finest priests and most learned missionaries I have known, who
referred in irritation to "the vaporings of Father LaFarge." I
suffered similar reproaches from various sources because
Father Gillis, at the Pentecost inauguration of the Catholic
Interracial Council, had used some rather severe language
about the attitudes of some of our Catholic co-religionists.
Both in his instance and in mine, our words were taken as
somehow a reflection upon the noble work of good men, for
whose unselfish work we could entertain nothing but admiration. Father Gillis himself was honored with a baptism of
fire: a radio talk he gave over the weekly "Catholic Hour,"
touching the race question, piled his desk mountain-high with
bigoted protests. But I came to look upon these aspersions as
simply the occupational hazards endured by anybody who dis-

turbs an all-too-complacent public opinion. Petulant griping
and name-calling is completely out of place; but without falling into that extreme, at times one must lay a few unpleasant
facts before the public.

As for the friend who complained of my "vaporings," I was
confident that in time he would change his mind. In point of
fact he did, and before his lamented and untimely death he,
and very many others who had expressed similar sentiments,
expressed full agreement with my thesis. This was, that for
the good of the mission work itself, there comes a point when
direct and concerted effort is needed in order to combat those
perversions of prejudiced thought and conduct which frus-
trate most of one's educational and pastoral work, and which
give scandal to the very souls that one has instructed. I was
particularly comforted to find that a complete agreement of
opinion on this subject came to be manifested by members of
some of the religious communities, men and women, who had
longest borne the heat and burden of the day laboring among
the Negroes in the Deep South.

This depressing aspect, however, is far overbalanced by the
encouraging increase each year of religious vocations among
the Negroes, to the priesthood and to the various religious
orders. In the past one hundred years, 69 Negroes have been
ordained to the priesthood in the United States, and today
they are functioning in every field of standard priestly activity.* Prayers and labors of many a devoted priest and teacher
were fulfilled at the impressive consecration at Bay St. Louis,
Mississippi, of a Negro bishop, the Most Rev. Joseph Oliver
Bowers, S.V.D. The presence of Cardinal Spellman as chief
consecrator at this event, along with Bishop Gerow of Natchez
and Bishop Noser, S.V.D., an American, of Eastern New
Guinea, emphasized the importance of the role of an American Negro Catholic clergy in the future conversion of Africa.

* Albert S. Foley, S.J., *America,* June 13, 1953. Reprinted in *Interracial Review,* July 1953.

Cardinal Spellman recalled on that occasion that the consecration of Bishop Bowers marked the second time that a Negro had been elevated to the episcopacy in the United States—the late Bishop of Portland, Maine, the Most Rev. James A. Healy, was the first. At the present time the archbishops and bishops of the Catholic Church in the United States are lending steadily increasing encouragement to the development among Negro youth of vocations to the priesthood and to religious communities.

The Church's mission work for the Negroes in the United States was, and is, a great affirmation of man's love for his fellowman. It has laid the groundwork for another great affirmation as an answer to the challenge of our changing times and neighborhoods. The very circumstances that so disconcert us offer the opportunity to assert convincingly the unity and catholicity of the Church that Christ founded. They likewise offer us the opportunity to assert the unity of all mankind, as fashioned by the Creator—a unity grievously wounded and disfigured by sin, but still retaining the vestiges of its original grandeur.

I believe that we Americans will make this assertion in our own way, the American way: in the grand line of over three hundred years' tradition and experience. This is emphatically not the un-American and un-Catholic way of racial segregation—a social policy which solves nothing and merely feeds back poison into the very organisms that it pretends to heal; but is the democratic way that integrates individuals and families as responsible human beings into our growing communities.

In point of fact, we have learned certain lessons which the entire world needs today, especially in view of the enormous changes that are occurring in the relative positions of the races in the former colonial regions. These are lessons of practical methods and social techniques; they are also much more vital lessons of spiritual attitudes and spiritual wisdom. Why should we Americans keep these to ourselves? The time is near when we shall no longer need to apologize for our own short-comings. The very fact that we have learned certain lessons the hard way enables us to speak with more authority to those who have not grappled with the question as we have here in the United States.

Every day brings new evidence that a movement has already set in toward the complete integration of all racial groups into our American life. This is a movement of logic and reason; of religious faith and grace. Indeed, much that I have just written may seem after a few years to be merely laboring the obvious. Nevertheless, the movement can be delayed, and many evil consequences can ensue from delay. Minority groups who yesterday suffered persecution can tomorrow become per-secutors themselves; for vice and egotism are contagious, and the poor and humble man who deserts his Creator can become as unjust and mean as his former master. So I still do not see this as an easy task. It calls for study, research, patience and a vast expenditure of honest good will and sincere love of God and man. Ultimately, it must be worked out from within, for out of the heart proceed evil thoughts and passions. Men must learn to know intimately the mind and spirit of Jesus Christ, and those emphases that He placed upon the key fac-tors in human relations. They must make this knowledge their own and acknowledge their dependence upon His grace: must meditate in silence, form their own characters, master the grammar of personal responsibility, and become leaders not in the cause of self-interest but in the cause of justice and charity.

We all speak of what will happen later. But why later, rather than sooner? The position of the United States in a world two-thirds populated by non-white peoples is deter-mined by what its citizens do today, not by their conduct ten years hence. Said Pope Pius XII to the citizens of Rome, on March 18, 1945:

There remains no way to salvation than that of repudiating definitely . . . the price of race and blood . . . and to turn resolutely toward that spirit of sincere fraternity which is founded on the worship of the Divine Father of all.

Since our salvation depends upon our present conduct, not upon our future plans, the time to turn to sincere fraternity would seem to be now. For as Saint Ambrose says, "the grace of the Holy Spirit brooks no slow delays. *Nescit tarda molimina Spiritus Sancti gratia.*"

CHAPTER TWENTY-ONE

Europe, 1951

➤➤➤ ➤➤➤

I had seen the peoples of western Europe just emerging from the abyss in 1947, stunned and bewildered amid ruins but touched by the first rays of hope. In 1951 quite unexpectedly another opportunity arose to take a look at the Old World before it should be too late in my own autumn for such an experience to be pleasant or tolerable. I received, through the State Department, an invitation from the Division of Education and Culture of the United States Government of Occupation in Germany to spend seven weeks in Germany as a visiting consultant.

The trip was arranged largely through the kindness of Dr. George N. Shuster, president of Hunter College, who was also acting as High Commissioner for the United States Government in Bavaria at the time. It was Dr. Shuster's idea that, since I spoke German fluently, it might be worthwhile for me to visit a number of the various theological schools in Bavaria, concerning myself chiefly with their social studies programs, and present the fruits of my observations to the U.S. Occupation Government in order that the latter might better understand some of the really fine work in that line that was being done in Germany by the religious groups. At the same time it would provide a helpful and interesting interchange of ideas between an American scholar and leaders of German thought. My own Superiors looked favorably upon the project and it seemed to me a fine opportunity to answer

numerous queries as to the degree of spiritual reconstruction
in Germany a few years after liberation.

At Frankfurt this time HICOG installed me in the VIP
Hotel Carlton instead of the semi-VIP Excelsior. From rubble,
the scene in Frankfurt had changed to reconstruction. The
Bahnhof, scene of desolation in 1947, was now for the most
part repaired and as cheerful and lively as any large railroad
station in the States. Ruins were giving way to new apartments; the city hummed with activity. I learned later that in
the year 1950 seventy thousand more housing units were put
up in Germany than in the entire United States during that
period. The restaurants were full of food, people looked fairly
cheerful and well-dressed, the children were pink-cheeked,
countless trucks were hurrying building materials to and fro.
When I strolled out in the morning to say Mass at the St.
Antonius Church a few blocks from the hotel, I was struck by
the skill with which a few ideas of modern functional architecture had been used to do a simple, inexpensive reconstruction job for a church building.

Dr. John Riedl, head of the Religious Organizations Department in the Educational and Cultural Division of HICOG,
briefed me rapidly on the religious situation, as did James J.
Norris, head of the War Relief Services of NCWC, on the
refugees and DP's. I asked Mr. Norris about the so-called
hard core element among the DP's and he was quite exultant
at the fact that really a dent was being made in the toughest
part of the problem. Some one thousand of these unfortunate
aged and infirm people had been taken over for charitable
care by nuns in France, and some five hundred by Catholic
nuns in Great Britain.

In my six weeks in Germany I talked in various places to
deans and professors of theological faculties, and to the students at Freising, Eichstätt, Regensburg, Freiburg, Berlin,
Frankfurt, Innsbruck, and also at Neuen-Dettelsau, the famous Lutheran settlement for northern Bavaria, and to the seminarians at Pullach, near Munich. The students were uniformly

interested in the racial situation in the United States. All of them sensed in one way or another its relation to the catastrophic problems they had been wrestling with at home. They contended also with their own difficulties in the social area. The Rev. Dr. Hoeck, Director of the theological seminary at Freising, told me that 90 per cent of his students worked on the land in the summer for their support, and that 10 per cent of them suffered impaired health as a result of former hardships. At Regensburg 20 per cent of the students were refugees. Most of the seminarians lacked cassocks, as the material for them was either not obtainable or too expensive. Yet they were as vigorous and courageous groups of young men as you would find anywhere in the country.

In some of the seminaries the students did heroic social work during their vacation period. Each year's class of novices at the Jesuit college in Pullach did a month's turn working in the factories in the neighborhood, not as paid employees but simply as menial helpers. This was in accordance with St. Ignatius' old prescription for our novices, that they should do a month's experiment, as he called it, outside the novitiate, in hospitals or in roadside begging, to learn at first hand what hardship, poverty, and suffering mean. Father Martin Pies, the Novice Master at Pullach, was enthusiastic about the results of the factory experiment. The lads, he said, soon became good friends with the workers and were looked up to and respected. They made no bones about being clerical students, *Theologen.*

I did not meet the seminarians at Königstein, and their enterprising Rector Dr. Kindermann was out of the house on my visit there. But I did hear the story of how these young men spent *their* summer vacation working in the mines in the Ruhr. They were housed in the "colonies" or rude barracks with a thousand or more other workmen, sharing their life in every respect. These young men were being prepared to return later to the East Zone. This was religious Germany at its strongest: featuring the younger generation's determination to break down once and for all the barriers that separated the clergy from the working classes.

At the Lutheran settlement of Neuen-Dettelsau, where I spent an agreeable day in the company of Dr. Merz, the Rector, Dr. Stählin, Dr. Kinder, and others of the faculty, a somewhat different plan was followed. The seminarians for the Lutheran Church were trained at this famous center to be in contact with the work of the church in all its phases. Neuen-Dettelsau is a sort of oasis of Lutheranism with some twelve or thirteen different institutions, social welfare, charitable, educational, missionary, and so on. The young men did a turn in connection with each of them so that they could be familiar with all the activities of their church. A somewhat similar plan is followed in some of our Jesuit Provinces in France and Belgium, where the young men who have completed their theological course and are undergoing their so-called Third Probation spend three or four weeks visiting the social works of the Church and thus getting a perspective of their future ministerial life.

It was almost terrifying to think of the responsibility for Germany's spiritual future that rested upon the shoulders of these splendid young men, lads who had just escaped the full brunt of the Nazi terror or, among the older ones, who had extricated themselves from its blighting influence. They were enriched by the great accumulation of tradition, art, culture, learning, etc., and at the same time they were hindered by it. As one of their professors remarked to me, "We are shackled by too much cultural tradition."

Much of the old parochial system had broken down as the young folk moved to the cities, for, as Dr. Ehardt, Prime Minister of Bavaria, remarked: "Bavaria is not predominantly an agricultural country." It had been too greatly agricultural. Because young folks flocked to the towns to work in the factories and various utilities and services they were withdrawn from the framework of the parish. My own colleagues Fathers Sieben and Prinz were adopting among the working youth some of the Christian cell program of the Young Catholic Workers that had been succeeding so remarkably in Belgium and Holland.

No sooner had I arrived in Munich than the question of co-management or *Mitbestimmung* was raised. Almost the first person I met was Father John F. Cronin, S.S., of the Social Action Department, NCWC, in Washington, who had traveled through West Germany for two or three months making a study of this topic. He had survived a thorough workout of interviews and was a mine of information, though he found it difficult to reach a precise conclusion.

At a panel discussion which I attended the principal speaker was the Minister President of Bavaria, Dr. Seidl. Out of the welter of talk two or three features seemed to emerge. First the *Mitbestimmung* or co-management plan was projected only for the coal and iron industries, hence for a limited purpose. It was, as they generally say, "a leap in the dark." In the second place, nobody objected to the workers' representatives dealing with social or welfare questions. The difficulty lay in the question of making economic decisions, touching on such matters as price fixing. In the third place there was a strong feeling that soon a gap would open between the workers' repesentatives and the trade unions. The workers' delegate would himself become a manager. Finally, the Minister stated frankly that there was a broad difference between the spirit and practice of United States trade unionism and the German. "We Germans," he said, "go to extremes. We do not have the spirit of bargaining and conciliation that you are blessed with in the United States." Hence the strong political trend, so that the issue became a test of political power. The workers were suspicious of the big industrialists, thinking they wanted to start another war; while the industrialists feared the concentration of economic power in the hands of labor. What struck my amateur mind was that similar notions were discussed here with regard to the Industry Councils in the United States, similar trends and cross currents.

What was the reaction of German youth face to face with Communism? Whenever I put this question, I always received the answer: You must go to Berlin. There you will see the West face to face with the East. Indeed the six days in Berlin offered me a chance to see Communism at work in the eastern sector of the city. Immense posters stressed the interracial appeal, with joyous white and non-white lads and lassies linking hands and marching to the never reachable dawn.

All the slogans were calculated to appeal to German youth: slogans for unity, slogans for all Germans to "eat at the same table," slogans for peace, slogans against rearmament (while they armed their police), slogans shouting "Amis go home!" To young people who from birth had been completely isolated from the rest of the world it was naturally pleasing to be told that in the month of August that year, youth of the whole world would be flocking to Berlin. Gently and gradually, a little bit each day, through the monolithic youth organization —the Freie Deutsche Jugend, Free German Youth, or FDJ— the screws were being turned.

The Bishop of Meissen, Dr. Winken, actually working at the time in the East Zone of Germany, quietly faced up to the Russian officials with apparent success. He insisted that the only way to stand up against the Communist surroundings was to lead a completely Christian life. They would tolerate, he said, charitable work and charitable contributions. And apparently the clergy were able to carry on a certain amount of lecturing outside of the regular pastoral work, provided it was done in complete openness without any appearance of espionage. What you need is toughness, he said, or tenacity, "Zähigkeit," a complete absence of fear, but yet a sufficient amount of caution. I sensed that the Bishop was more than ordinarily skillful in getting along with all kinds of difficult people, and I wondered how far his example could be followed by the clergy in general.

During the six days in Berlin I stayed with Father Wilson Kaiser, Director of CRALOG, in the beautiful and unharmed suburb of Zehlendorf, at a handsome villa with porch and gardens and cherry and apple blossoms. It seemed so out of the world that I had difficulty realizing, as Father Kaiser told me, that you needed only to walk down the street a few blocks to bang up against the edge of the Iron Curtain. Indeed the neighborhood looked like fashionable Bellevue Avenue in Newport. But the stream of refugees that drifted onto Father Kaiser's threshold dispelled any such illusions.

From what I had read and from what I had seen with my own eyes I could hardly believe that religiously-minded German youth would be attracted by Communism. The present generation suffered from an almost morbid dislike of regimentation. I had noticed on my previous visit this violent reaction against Hitler. Again, they were much more conscious of the Soviet menace than they ordinarily cared to acknowledge. The Iron Curtain was right at the border and the ever-increasing stream of refugees added witness after witness to its horrors. I was surprised too to find how tolerant they were of the U.S. Occupation forces. Our own information agencies had at last waked up to some of the realities and were no longer perpetrating the ideological blunders of the first couple of years of the occupation. For the German youth the necessary question was rather one of a long-distance policy of rehabilitation, educational and spiritual.

In Frankfurt, on May 22, I attended an all-day conference on the work of the Catholic layman, arranged by Dr. Urban Fleege of the Department of Religious Affairs, in the HICOG Educational and Cultural Division. An impressive group of active Catholic leaders, clergy, both diocesan and religious Order men, and lay people, both men and women, gathered at short notice. Everybody talked frankly and discussion was long and intelligent. Significant was the stress laid on women's part in Germany's latter-day religious life, and eloquent in this respect was Dr. Paula Regnier of Berlin, who pleaded for a spirit of initiative in German women, too long passive. Incidentally, Dr. Regnier urged, "we need lay theologians." Her views were seconded by another woman representative who praised the initiative of American women. Women, she said, should have official positions in church organizations and girls should be taught responsibility. The personality of the German girl should be respected and developed, and the sense of family responsibility was strongly argued. In talking to mixed student groups I myself had been somewhat taken aback by the reluctance of German girls to speak in group discussion, in contrast with the loquaciousness of the male sex. We need women of strong inner convictions, said Dr. Regnier, and then we need the practical help of study and discussion groups to intensify our inner spiritual life.

In European circles the question was constantly being debated whether or not apostolic work for souls should be based primarily upon the *parish* as the primary unit of church structure, or whether the Church should go out and seek for its members in the particular *environments* of their life, even if it meant the crossing of parish lines. But the discussion at Frankfurt avoided a clash of opinions. "Let us see both types of organization," pleaded one of the participants, Father Wothe, "both the parochial and those based on other types of association. We should recognize as many differences as are necessary. The main thing is to train each man to be a responsible Catholic wherever he is and wherever he lives and works, and at the same time we should do plenty of work with the non-organized folk as well."

I found this same breadth of view when I visited one of the leading Catholic clergymen in the Ruhr district, the Rev. Doctor Schwering, Director of the Männerwerk of the Diocese of Münster. Father Ostermann, S.J., of Cologne, kindly agreed to accompany me on the trip to Duisburg via Dusseldorf so that I might enjoy a moment's glimpse of the troubled Ruhr district, the industrial heart of Europe.

That morning, before leaving Cologne, I had glimpsed something of the Männerwerk. A diocesan group of Bundesbahn, or federal railroad employees, in the Diocese of Münster gathered in the house chapel of the Jesuit residence to the number of some one hundred and fifty for their monthly Mass and Communion. I celebrated the Mass and addressed a few words to them of encouragement or rather of admiration, for they were an inspiring sight. In good German fashion they filled the chapel with their hymn-singing and bravely answered the Mass responses in chorus. After Mass we adjourned to a hall in one of the government buildings, where each treated himself to one lukewarm cup of imitation coffee. Somebody had contributed two sandwiches which, to my confusion but also to my distinct internal relief, they insisted that I should eat. They queried me sharply on my talk and I was invited to address in an adjoining room a similar gathering of Cologne city employees who wanted to know something about the way the City of New York was administered. On the latter topic I felt discretion was the better guide and advised them to take a trip over sometime and call at City Hall Square. The railroad employees, who were *Obleute* or foremen, heard a Dutch-uncle talk from Monsignor Böhler, the Vicar General of the Diocese of Münster, on the Christian use of the vote.

Like Father Wothe, Father Schwering, whom we visited in Duisburg, believed in a strong parish organization. Of his parishioners, he said, 25 per cent were practising Catholics, 50 per cent were nominal, which was not so bad in a region where militant Socialist influence was particularly strong. Labor was represented by the *Einheitsgewerkschaft,* the unified syndicate for Catholics and Protestants, Christians and non-Christians and Socialists alike. Of the seventeen local leaders, thirteen were Socialists, SPD. Father Schwering voiced the complaint that I heard so frequently in Germany, that American and Allied funds were allocated generously to the largely Socialist-controlled *Einheitsgewerkschaft* on the ground that it was non-sectarian and devoid of religious or anti-religious partisanship, while the contrary was quite definitely the case. The tension between the workers and the large industries remained extremely bitter, and was not eased by the strongly political character of the labor movement itself. On the other hand, in the small industries, according to Father Schwering, management was definitely on the workers' side.

I asked him about the Young Christian Workers' effectiveness. He praised the solid training they gave to their members, and added his further view that Europe could not stand alone against Marxism without the aid of America.

After leaving Pastor Schwering's hospitable rectory we passed the fine new housing project in Duisburg which had been erected by the Männerwerk members themselves as a private venture in social justice.

Since we were out to examine the homeliest aspects of the Ruhr, we stopped in Hamborn, said to be the ugliest city in Germany. It would be difficult to find more depressing living quarters than the so-called colonies or immense workers' apartment houses with their gloomy courtyards, some accommodating as many as 6,000 people, a good part of whom were Communists. Yet the Catholic folks were celebrating May Day and the grounds of the hospital were beautifully decorated. Sisters, nurses, and children gathered with altar boys and vested clergy before the beautifully decorated statue of Our Lady, while hundreds of patients looked down from the galleries above.

A little later, in the company of my old friend Dr. Heinrich Chardon, whom I visited at Trier, I joined a day's pilgrimage to the popular shrine of Klausen in the Rhineland, near the Moselle River. In a region as glorious and beautiful as Hamborn was ugly and depressing, some four or five thousand youths were on pilgrimage. The lads walked and bicycled from considerable distances. One group with a curate from a church in Trier had marched for six hours, fasting so they could receive Communion. Like the Cologne workmen, they took part in the Mass: chanted the Gregorian magnificently and responded to the Celebrant who stood at an altar facing them, at the edge of the sanctuary. It was a noble outpouring

of faith, with hymns and banners and all the traditional splendor of an ancient Catholic country. The grand old pastor of
Klausen invited us clergy to his rectory for lunch and regaled
us with stories of Roman studies in former times. Yet lovely
and inspiring as was Klausen it did not move me so deeply as
did that humble illuminated statue in the dark hospital court
on the streets of Hamborn. The Blessed Mother had seemed
to say: where I am there cannot be darkness, and I shall conquer the darkness no matter how mighty and depressive are
its forces.

My visit to the Ruhr brought to mind the Schuman plan
for pooling the resources of the coal and iron industries of Germany, France, and four other countries. Workers, I had heard,
were suspicious of the planners giving power to the great
capitalists. But in Trier Dr. Joseph Hoeffner, Professor of
Social Science at the diocesan seminary and one of modern
Germany's leaders in this field, was of a contrary opinion. He
did not feel that the Schuman plan denoted capitalistic influence. The works, after all, were internationally owned and
only the managers were in direct control. It was chiefly a
question of an understanding between the managers and the
trade union organization.

Incidentally, said Dr. Hoeffner, the old *Volksverein,* the
pre-war popular Catholic workers organization, taught practical politics. In later times, especially during the Hitler
period, it was blamed for its political slant. From the discussion group at Frankfurt, too, I heard expressions of regret that
the practical lessons of the old *Volksverein* were no longer
available.

After the expiration of my seven weeks in Germany, Father
Assistant McCormick invited me to stop in Rome on my way
back where I could attend, on June 3, the beatification of
Pope Pius X. I left Frankfurt for Rome on June 1, by a
KLM plane via Stuttgart and Munich.

In Stuttgart air terminal I struck up a conversation with a

Negro fellow passenger, a bespectacled young man in his thir-
ties. I took him to be probably a HICOG employee. He
seemed to be glad to talk and responded in a foreign accent,
questioning me as to my own nationality, and turned out to
be a Cuban businessman engaged in the lumber export industry in Honduras.

"My name," he said, "is Babún, like the monkey, Ismael
Babún." He was on his way to Israel where his father was in
business. "Señor," I asked, "are you married?" "Not yet," he
replied, "not yet." "But," I objected, "you said you were
thirty-eight years old and you are still single." "Well," he said,
"it is a difficult problem. It is difficult where I live to find the
right kind of woman. Women are not what they should be.
However," he added, speaking slowly and pensively, "to all
rules there may be exceptions. It is quite possible I may have
found the exception. I shall give the matter very careful consideration."

He seemed interested in all I could tell him of my experiences in Germany, and as one usually finds with non-white
people, the racial question is an unfailing topic. As we approached Munich, where there was a three-and-a-half hour
wait, he begged that I should take advantage of the free bus
ride provided by the KLM into town and show him something
of the city, as he had never yet visited Germany.

It was pleasant to revisit the streets that had become so
familiar to me during my four weeks in that city. When I
pointed out the newly restored towers of the cathedral, he
was surprised to learn that there were actually Catholics in
Germany and that Bavaria was a Catholic country. "If you
wish to have some idea of what German Catholicism is like,"
I said, "come with me and visit the tomb of Father Mayer."

We descended to the crypt of St. Michael's Church where
lay buried the remains of Munich's famous Jesuit preacher,
the late Father Rupert Mayer. Day and night a constant stream
of people visited the tomb, some 3,000 every twenty-four
hours. During my stay in the city I had twice offered Mass at

the tomb, where Cardinal Spellman, not too long before, had left his Cardinal's skullcap as a tribute.

Rupert Mayer, though he was an eloquent preacher, was a man of fairly moderate talents; but he had tremendous character, and utilized in selfless fashion every ounce of what God had given him for body and for soul. His boundless personal charity was matched only by his equally limitless courage in facing directly up to Hitler. As early as 1923, he declared publicly that no Catholic could be a National Socialist. During the early Nazi days he attended the beer-hall meetings of Communists and Nazis alike, and challenged their doctrines from the floor.

When the Nazis finally landed him in prison, he informed his jailers that he spoke only from non-political motives, simply as a priest of God who could not be untrue to the teachings of Christ and His Church. And he let them know he would talk in exactly the same way if and when he should be released. To the State Prosecutor he declared in 1940: "I have never been a politician. The only questions that could be at issue were questions of State and Church. My attitude to these was determined only by a religious point of view and I acted from duty to my conscience." At his trial he so bothered the judges that the presiding judge asked him, "Do you think it is pleasant for us to be sitting here carrying on this interrogation?" With dry humor Father Mayer replied: "I'd rather sit here as an accused man than as a judge."

He refused positively to entertain hate against his fellow man. "We must hate evil," he said to the nuns whom he directed. "We should loathe evil with all our hearts, but we should not let hate and aversion to our fellow man creep into our lives. Judge not that ye be not judged." Preaching in the cathedral of Eichstätt on February 28, 1937, he warned against the idea of trying to level out religious differences, deconfessionalizing, as the Germans call it. But he insisted at the same time that this offered no excuse for hatred of men of other faiths. "If we are sincere Christians, sincere

Catholics and sincere Protestants, we could and we must live
in love, as is taught by our respective beliefs."

Yet it was not the big, dramatic things that colored one's
character, he told his spiritual followers; it was the small
affairs of life, the day-by-day thousand-and-one acts of humility and patience, observance of the regulations of one's religious community, the hourly trials born in patience and
silence; the humble duties worked out in all their laborious
details. This and only this in the long run made the genuine
"martyr," the witness for Jesus Christ.

This fiery prophet who could sway thousands to tears,
courage, and even martyrdom by his example and his spoken
word, and who brought hidden consolation to still greater
thousands of helpless sufferers, reached the heights of his
sanctity through the "ordinary way": the simple obedience
which he had pledged to his Superiors as a young novice and
reaffirmed in all the critical stages of his religious career.

The Gestapo took charge of Father Mayer in November
1939, placing him first in one concentration camp, then in
another. They finally decided that the safest course with a
man of such influence and popularity was to confine him
under rigid restrictions to the Benedictine monastery of Ettal,
in Bavaria, where his life could conveniently fade away in
solitude. The Americans found him there when they liberated
Ettal on May 6, 1945, and on May 11 he was driven to Munich,
the scene of his former activities. He plunged at once into the
strenuous life, preaching in 22 parishes on a single mission
tour, but the old strength had vanished, and he died on
November 1 of the same year. His remains were first interred
in the Jesuit cemetery at Pullach, but such throngs came to
venerate them that they were later transferred to their present
resting place in the St. Michael's crypt. The Auxiliary Bishop
of Munich, the Most Rev. Dr. Scharnagel, had told me that
the information had been assembled to send to Rome with a
petition that Father Mayer should be declared by the Holy

See a venerable Servant of God, the first step toward his beatification.

The young Negro and I prayed a few moments before we
picked up a few penny pamphlets and emerged into the busy
street. "That was a man," said Señor Babún, "a real man, the
kind we need for our days."

The Señor had two or three days to spend in Rome before
continuing on to Israel. I briefed him on the forthcoming
beatification ceremonies for Pius X and said good-by.

The ceremonies at St. Peter's were simple, consisting of a
solemn Pontifical Mass celebrated by the Cardinal Vicar of
Rome, at which the brief of beatification was read aloud. The
body of Pope Pius X had been removed from its tomb, placed
in a crystal casket, and clothed in sacred vestments with a
silver mask over the face; at Benediction it lay high above the
altar. To me it was inexpressibly moving to think that there
lay the remains of a man from whom I had received Holy
Communion some forty-six years before, and that he had gazed
into my eyes. A year later, when visiting Leonardtown in the
spring of 1952, I discovered at the rectory of St. Aloysius
Church the signed picture which I described in an earlier
chapter.

The most impressive part of the ceremony was at 6 P.M.
when the Pope imparted the sacramental Benediction to a
vast crowd of some 600,000 people in front of the basilica of
St. Peter's. It was a fine summer day, and the coolness of the
shade contrasted with the heat of the great Piazza as the sun
sank behind the basilica. The Holy Father was clearly in view
and could be heard through the loudspeakers.

Paris, when I arrived there, was in a hub-hub in anticipation
of the June 17 elections. The French multi-party groupings and
combinations were as mystifying for an American as our periodical two-party homeric battle is for them. The Communists
were united; their opponents were externally united but in-

ternally completely divided, and the ordinary people found themselves voting for lists about which they know nothing.

At the Action Populaire Father Serve, S.J., and other experts in the agrarian field discussed the agricultural and peasant situation. Father Serve is a decided realist who recently made a trip through agricultural sections of Canada and the United States. He strongly took the point of view that the all-out peasant economy was no longer practical, that the number of farmers would necessarily have to be reduced if they were to be self-supporting. They must face up to the realities of mechanization and improved methods of distribution and marketing. At the present time altogether too many people were striving to make a subsistence off the land.

I found I had still sufficient time to make a short trip to Finistère and revisit Ploujean and Roz'Avel that I had not seen since 1938, just before the war. In 1947, as I have said, the best we could do was to hold a family gathering at the rue Coëtlogon in Paris.

People who in recent years study the religious map of France are sometimes astonished to find that some of the traditionally most Catholic regions, such as parts of Brittany, have turned anti-clerical and more or less been taken over by the Communists. No region of the world can now dispense with active, grass-roots pastoral methods, as the wisest bishops and priests now acknowledge. The Communists, incidentally, had devised a captivating slogan for the country people of Brittany. Posted everywhere was the admonition: "If you love your private property, if you love an honest day's work, if you love children and enjoy the scent of new-mown hay, vote Communist."

Cousin Yvonne, in the meantime, who seemed much restored since I had last seen her in 1947, was endeavoring to bring out the non-Communist women's vote in Finistère, a useful but complicated project.

I took a long walk Sunday afternoon up to the top of the hill that overlooks the Channel and its tributaries toward the western end of the property, climbing through the densely matted, thorny, fragrant gorse banked on the hillside, the same gorse that I had seen after a dreary sea voyage burning on the hillsides near Plymouth when I landed there in the spring of 1938. The German concrete emplacements were largely overgrown with weeds and bushes and had been left for some twenty-fifth century archaeologist to explain. The clear sunshine, the soft sea air, the mighty sweep of the cliffs and bays, reminded me once more of the southern reaches of the Rhode Island shore and it was difficult to shake the mind back into the familiar categories of space and time. After all, God's Eternity is our real home and when we eventually arrive there, please God and through His grace, we may be surprised not at its strangeness but at its homelikeness and familiarity.

On my way back to Roz'Avel for tea, M. Batiste, one of the tenants, greeted me and invited me to step in and meet his family and the neighboring family in the living room of his ancient, thickly stone-walled farmhouse. The neat, clean interior was a pleasant contrast with the medieval look outside. They were a jolly group and they chatted in Breton while Batiste talked French and told me of his travels. He had served in the Navy, he said, and had knocked around quite a bit in southeast Asia and South America. As a result, mission magazines proved more interesting than any novels, and *Interracial Review* was a favorite.

At the other farm nearby René Portier, a sturdy lad of eighteen, was so interested in the farm work that he was shouldering a good deal of the burden. The farms are naturally small, almost diminutive: artichokes and small dairying. The good soil, the mild climate, the industry of the people, and the proximity of local markets will doubtless carry them along as they do the small farms the Portuguese have developed on Rhode Island and in southern Massachusetts. The Du Halgouëts, the family into which Cousin Yvonne had married, carry an old slogan in the Breton language on their coat of arms, *"Eur Nebent Awalac'h,"* which being interpreted means, "A little, but it suffices." That I imagine is pretty much the keynote of life in Finistère.

On my departure from Paris, Jean-Marie Bressand, ardent young worker for a bilingual world, accompanied me to the terminal, where I took, on a very hot day, the usual hermetically-sealed bus to Orly airport for the non-stop trip to the United States. Once we were in the air the pilot announced that we would stop at Iceland at midnight to refuel, and so we did. Shortly before midnight, out of a murky sky darted a gleam of sunlight; it was the midnight sun, revealing to us in incredibly beautiful soft golden-red light limitless ranges and reaches, swamps, moors, and mountains. We landed at Keflavik airport, spent an hour there and continued to New York.

I had never expected to see Iceland; least of all did I associate it in any way with this (as it were) summer afternoon trip between an editor's desk in Paris and an editor's desk in New York. After all, life really is worthwhile if in your autumn you can see realities which in the springtime would have surpassed all your dreams.

CHAPTER TWENTY-TWO

The Cup of the Covenant

❧❧ ❦❦

On February 26, 1952, my friends honored me with a dinner at New York's Waldorf-Astoria commemorating my twenty-five years on the staff of *America* and my services in the cause of religious journalism. I was astonished at the number who attended, not to speak of their cordiality, which appeared to exceed the usual kindly greetings on a term fulfilled, and I pondered over what it might mean. Despite what was said, it did not seem like a tribute to any one person or achievement, but to refer to the vocation with which I have become identified.

The attendance at the dinner, too, of so many persons of other faiths seemed to register an appreciation—gracefully expressed by Dr. Louis Finkelstein, president of the Jewish Theological Seminary in New York City—of the simple fact that I had taken some time out for discussions with persons of all shades of belief and unbelief concerning those basic moral problems which concern the security and welfare of our democratic order. Much of this intercourse was at the sessions of the Conference on Science, Philosophy and Religion, which were held at Columbia University, following plans of procedure devised and patiently promoted by Dr. Finkelstein, Professor R. M. MacIver, and Dr. Lyman Bryson.

Years before, I told the guests, one of my brethren had referred to me as a "champion of lost causes." The remark, light as it was, inflicted a certain sting, since a priest has no right to waste his time upon unprofitable adventures. Yet

373

practically every enterprise of my career which later seems to have borne some fruit began as a "lost cause."

A Catholic can avoid without much difficulty direct contact with the non-Catholic intellectual world. Such avoidance will spare him many occasions of embarrassment; his course will be considered safe, and he may even be praised for his prudence if he restricts his contacts to those that his official or professional duties require. Whether I was wise or unwise in engaging in such discussions and conferences, I gained by them very precious friendships.

Such conferences, incidentally, are not without their discipline—mental and moral—for all who engage in them, regardless of the highly varied opinions expressed. Persons whose minds are elaborately organized to explore one area of thought profit by a glance not only into other people's ideas but into the very fashion by which they reach their conclusions. Scientists would perhaps be less liable to embark upon amateur philosophizing if philosophers would descend from the clouds and explain to them something of philosophy's proper province and function. Philosophers, on the other hand, and indeed theologians, would learn humility by studying the meticulous procedure observed by genuine scientists and their skill in handling unproved hypotheses. The journalist, even though he can emulate none of these experts in any one of their chosen fields, can do his part in assisting them to emerge from their particular shells.

Time and patience, and good chairmen, can usually succeed in eliminating some of the irritants that plague such intellectual excursions—such as the one-track mind, whose owner is interested only in finding a sounding-board for his own pet theory; or, on the other hand, the scatterbrain who enjoys discoursing on everything but has no concern to reach any definite conclusions. They also help to fish up the rare pearls that cling to the hard shell of stubborn intellectual conflict: those really fruitful items of agreement that offer some hope of a wider basis of understanding.

As for myself, the discussions helped me to clarify my own ideas as to the position of religion and of the Church in the modern world. We may not appreciate the content of religious faith unless we see it outlined against the aridity of a certain prevalent type of contemporary philosophical thinking. One senses then the grip of unilateral or two-dimensional monistic thinking upon the present-day mind; its power of emotional seduction; its chameleon-like ability to shift from the dry narrowness of the logical positivist to wide extremes of hazy humanitarian sentiment or one-sided political passion.

The type of thought which would reduce all *Problematik* to a simple formula—whether of philosophical intuition or of flat sense experience—is practically irrefutable as long as it stays in the realm of pure theory or else abides by purely factual data. The fallacy appears when it attempts to interpret facts through its theory, and especially when it works out in terms of human conduct. One whose pattern of thinking is molded along those lines finds it difficult to conceive that Church and State may be separated, each with its own entirely distinct functions, yet can work together in an atmosphere of harmony and mutual respect.

On the other hand, signs of great weariness with this mentality would present themselves occasionally in our discussions. The difficulty the Christian believer feels in confronting this compact monistic thought-package lies in the very vastness of the Christian humanistic synthesis, which becomes unwieldy if it is ineptly presented. We are tempted to respond with an over-simplified package of our own: seed-material for the fanatic and the anti-intellectual. We must never forget that ours is the humanism and the dualism of the God-Man, who has made all things one.

With regard to the very urgent issue of a spiritual reply to Communism and other errors of our day, I believe that all the guests at the anniversary celebration felt as I did that such a reply lacks weight and power unless it is based on a strong core or *massif* of positive religious and moral teaching.

The genuine yearning of American citizens to reach some working agreement on moral principles basic to the preservation of our liberties is clearly shown by such an event as the memorable Aaronsburg Story celebrations, June 9-22, 1953. They were held for the second time in four years at the tiny village of Aaronsburg, Pennsylvania, commemorating the deeds of Aaron Levy, a Jewish immigrant from Amsterdam, who provided the land for his Lutheran neighbors' churches, schools, and burying grounds, and performed other acts of generosity. Two days of discussion at the sessions of the Aaronsburg Assembly, held on the campus of Pennsylvania State College, preceded the pageant. The Assembly consisted of one hundred prominent Americans, representing various races and creeds from all sections of the country, who met together with another hundred local residents in complete democracy and explored the problem of "living above prejudice" in the present-day world.

It was my privilege to serve as chairman of the national planning committee for the Aaronsburg celebration, and still greater privilege to witness to the spirit shown by all who took part. Their sentiments were summed up in the words of one of the participants, Dr. Luther H. Evans, the Librarian of Congress, and since elected president of UNESCO:

The high goal of America today must be the same as the attained goal of Aaronsburg, the achievement of humility, and serenity in the face of the dangers and temptations of a mixed-up world, and firm dedication to truth, the brotherhood of man, and the enduring spiritual values of all man's great religions.

It is easy to be skeptical about such a venture as Aaronsburg. The finest expressions of sentiment can be emptied of meaning by those who wield words without regard for their full significance. But the men and women who talked and argued together those two long summer days were in dead earnest—however much they differed from one another. They were convinced, and rightly convinced, that out of the present confusion we can build a better America.

One final thought is suggested by the anniversary celebration of 1952. My friends presented me with a chalice, the work of a gifted silversmith, Louis Féron of New York. On the base of the chalice he had engraved, in the Greek text, Saint Paul's words that refer to the sacrifice of Christ, the great High Priest: "Of His own blood, He hath entered the sanctuary once and for all." Carvings in the cup's stem, picturing the Vine and Branches and ears of wheat, symbolized the Eucharistic Sacrifice and Christ's Mystical Body.

From its nature and its sacred function the chalice symbolizes the immensity of God's love, something that all my life I have been trying to understand. Nothing I can say can add to what has already been uttered on this subject, and the sum total of all human language is but a poor thing in comparison with the reality. Saint Paul himself, after talking of the "breadth and length and height and depth," is finally obliged to give up and say it is inexpressible.

My father observed that each artist opens a certain window upon the great world. So where elaborate descriptions and analogies fail, humble events, pain and sorrow, reveal glimpses of God's love. The Saviour Himself rested at the well-side conversing with the Samaritan woman, the stranger, the woman of bad life and many husbands, and revealed to her mysteries of the Kingdom of God. He abhorred her sins, but she was infinitely dear to Him as a human being and a woman in sorrow, trouble, and spiritual exile.

The practical demands of God's love challenge our own comfort. Our Lord is not like the good King of Yvetot, who did nothing save ramble around the country cheering people up. His love is like a devastating fire; it scorches you when you want to be left in peace to enjoy people you like and forget the rest of the world. Since it descended to the utter depths for our sake, one cannot escape carrying one's own splinter of the Cross.

The chalice also symbolizes something else, which is harder to phrase, chiefly because so many people today are only vaguely familiar with the biblical story. This is the "solidity" of God's love.* Our God is not a God of ethical self-righteousness: the benign superintendent of a humanly evolved code of morals. He is totally free, subject to nobody's question, accountable to none but His own infinitely exalted self.

Yet He is not an arbitrary God, capricious, unpredictable. Throughout His historical dealings with mankind, He has bound Himself by rules and covenants. He has sworn and will not repent. The priest is a priest forever. Israel, whatever justified quarrel the Lord may have with it, is still His people. He is a juridical God, a God of law, of promises never violated, of fidelity to all commitments and engagements. And he imparted that character to His Church, which has its own legal structure and lives by God's fidelity as well as God's love.

Every morning, with that chalice in my hand, I renew my own pledge in the name of the seen and the unseen congregation. The Mass itself is a perpetual renewal of God's troth, of the new and eternal testament.

Today, when the Church is placed on trial in the face of an unbelieving and, in some places, militantly atheistic world, every Christian is called to bear witness to these same two great truths in his or her individual life. Nothing will convert the world short of a gospel of limitless love; nothing short of a gospel of scrupulous faithfulness to the rights of the humblest person and to our pledges with man and God. I know no finer test of a man's sincerity than his willingness to work constructively for the world reign of love, justice, and law.

* Collect: Mass for the Sunday after Corpus Christi.

APPENDICES

※※ ※※

The Slav Colony at St. Mary's City

The story of the Slav colony at St. Mary's City, to which I refer in Chapter Nine, is a quite obscure part of Maryland history. Since the background has not been recorded elsewhere, and I have made myself familiar with the facts, they are perhaps worth preserving.

In 1911 the first Slav colonists arrived by boat from Baltimore; they continued to come for three years' time. The plan was simple: the colonists would raise garden produce and market it through a co-operative canning factory. They would also sell vegetables and poultry to an Old Folks Home and orphan asylum to be established for the members of the National Slavonic Society.

Two large pieces of property were purchased, the former Brome property and Snow Hill Manor. The Brome property was located in and around St. Mary's City district. This was the original St. Mary's property chosen by Lord Baltimore's colonists for its fine soil, its level ground, and its agreeable position at a small elevation above the level of the St. Mary's River. It was projected on two planes, one somewhat elevated above the other. An agent named Mr. Humbird had acquired the property from the Bromes through foreclosure. He sold it to the National Slavonic Society for $70,000 and he himself received a commission of $20,000. The other property, Snow Hill Manor, was chosen to be the site of the Old Folks Home. Snow Hill Manor is some 400 acres on an eminence overlooking the upper reaches of the St. Mary's River, with another 400 acres further to the east, mostly woodland. It derived its name from Justinian Snow, one of the original English Catholic burgesses of the early Maryland colony.

From all accounts the advertised plan for the Slavonic colony was practical enough. An unfortunate event, however, occurred after the colony was started. President A. S. Ambrose was defeated in one of the Society's triennial elections, and his place was taken by Albert Mamatey (accent on second syllable, Ma-*mah*-tay). Mamatey, who was consul of Czechoslovakia after World War I, and his secretary, Durish, were opposed to continuing the colony. He regarded it as impractical since there was no railroad to the place, and the only communication was by water. Ambrose did what he could to continue it. A wooden "hotel" was built, only to burn down later. While it lasted, which was for about a year, he conducted in the hotel a store for the colonists. Some of the colonists blamed Ambrose severely. He was accused of having profiteered in farm animals and farm implements but these accusations do not seem to be substantiated and are stoutly denied by some of the surviving colonists. The project dragged on for three conventions, over a space of some ten or twelve years, yet hope always recurred that it might be revived. Finally the ax fell. It was decided to sell the Snow Hill property to a firm in New York which, however, became bankrupt, so that it was restored again to the N.S.S. The Society in turn sold it to its present owners, who have developed some of the property in house lots.

The 2,000 acres themselves were purchased by the colonists on their own. They paid one-fourth in cash, and the rest was obtained in long-term mortgages. The lots were all sizes, most of them being 40 to 100 acres, a great deal of which was woodland. Arable land was sold in small lots of 15 acres and thereabouts. The colonists could buy several lots and combine them. John Balta and Joseph Gursky, two of the leading Catholic colonists, purchased four lots of 15 acres each, amounting to 60 acres in all. Some of the lots were bought by the native Marylanders. Some of the colonists who left sold their lots to those who remained.

I have heard it said that some 60 prospective colonists originally signed up for the plan, but I have never been able to locate more than 25 or 26. All migrated from non-farming occupations in the United States. Some had been mere day laborers in the old country and had had no farm experience at all. These, as I understand, were those who left at the beginning of the colony and are not to be included among the bona fide colonists. All who remained for any time had been coal miners in Pennsylvania, except for five Czechs who had been in the Kansas coal mines.

The only exceptions were Klobushetsky, a cabinet maker; Spaček, a cooper; Gasparec, a Pullman factory worker; and John Murchak, a steel worker. Farm experience in the Old World, however, was comparatively little aid to them under the new circumstances, for they were obliged to practice straight tobacco and corn farming in order to exist. There was no market for garden produce, and dairy farming, which developed successfully in later years, had as yet not been elaborated. The long hot Maryland summer, with tedious tobacco crops requiring 18 months of care was for them a new and unpleasant experience. The poor quality of native cattle and the light soil were a contrast to what they had known in Europe, and farm help was uncertain.

Anti-religious propaganda material was provided through a magazine called *Rovnost Lidu,* or "Equality of the People." *Rovnost Lidu,* which was then a daily of large circulation, in later years became a weekly, and finally a semi-monthly, or monthly, if it has not passed out of existence by this time. *Rovnost Lidu* proclaimed, as early as 1910 or 1911, the straight Communist, atheistic line. Its stock in trade was vituperation of the Church and clergy, scandalmongering stories of priests and nuns, and the whole familiar European anti-clerical propaganda. Exposure to this sort of literature was the price that the colonists paid for joining up with the religiously neutral and secularistic minded National Slavonic Society; a fact frequently pointed out to them by their brethren of the Catholic Slovak and Greek Slovak societies. Czechs subscribed to their own periodical entitled *Svornost* or "Union," which was of the same style. The belligerent tone of these magazines contrasted strangely with the peaceful and unrevolutionary character of the colonists who were all, by and large, model citizens.

Since the Slavs quoted from their literature liberally if they were favorable to it; or deplored it openly if they were opposed, it became known to some of the more observant Marylanders. The sexton of St. James Chapel, Henry Johnson, a pious Negro farmer fisherman and meekest of men, was intensely annoyed by loud talk he heard from some of the Communist-infected leaders at Longmore's general merchandise store, at the St. Mary's City wharf. After listening to their stories and vituperations for some time, he determined on action. He told a couple of the ringleaders that if they persisted they would get into trouble. Henry, on his own, appeared at the residence of one of the Czech leaders and demanded that he should produce copies of *Rovnost Lidu* and *Svornost* and burn them before his eyes. Operations of the left wing of the Slav colony were thenceforth continued only *sub rosa*.

The colonists were somewhat troubled by the seating arrangements in our Maryland churches, where the whole family worshiped together in the family pew. By their custom men and women were seated separately, and boys and girls separately again, and they considered our arrangement as distracting and improper. Consequently, in starting St. James Chapel for them, I had to place the Slav men separately from the Slav women, boys separately from the girls in the congregation, and the native Marylanders and the Negroes in their own part of the church. However, it all worked out peacefully and they became used to our ways and we to theirs. They were eager to sing their melodious hymns, of which they had a wonderful repertory. The robust patriarch of the group, old Mr. Kohut—whom a weary Negro farm-hand once characterized as "no man but just a steam-engine on legs"—claimed he knew by heart 125 hymns. He sang with the fervor of an angel and the voice of a foghorn.

Today the survivors of the original colony and their children are completely integrated in the local community, to which they brought new blood and fine traditions.

APPENDIX II

The Jesuit Manor Farms and the Negroes

In connection with my discussion in Chapter Ten of the slave-days on the Jesuit manor property, I would like to quote from my article in *The Catholic Historical Review,* Vol. XXI, April 1935:

"The manor system placed the clergy in the tragically inconsistent position of owning slaves, and, by that token in participating in the trade of slaves; though in point of fact this participation was a mitigation of the slaves' condition, an escape for them from unsupportable conditions . . . The manor conferred certain very definite benefits. It guaranteed spiritual welfare and consideration for the Negroes as human beings, and even a certain degree of independent economic opportunity; for the manor slaves were free to earn money and to conduct small business on their own account. The sole blot that appears to stand against the long record of humanity and recognition of human worth in the treatment of the Negroes upon the Jesuit manors was when—in good faith, and for economy's sake, but in shortsighted judgment —some of the slaves were sold out of the system into the hands of private persons.

"Looked at from a wider point of view, from the viewpoint of the entire situation of the Negro in this country, the very patriarchal kindness of the system had its drawbacks, as an apparent countenancing of evils which manifested themselves when not restrained by the rule of conscience and humanity which prevailed upon the manors. Slavery and the slave-trade, deprived of the painful and inhuman aspects, did not appear upon the manors as a necessary object of the Church's protest, as it did, for instance, when a Blessed Anthony Claret as Archbishop of

Havana lifted up his voice against the trade. The isolation and simplicity of life upon the manors encouraged a certain complacency of attitude, which did not always make for vigor either in ideas or in enterprise. However, this same peace and stability did make for perpetuity. . . ."

APPENDIX III
Saint Ansgar's League

Catholics from Denmark, Finland, Iceland, Norway, and Sweden were almost unknown in this country fifty years ago, when Mr. and Mrs. Frode W. Rambusch, a Danish Catholic couple in Brooklyn, started a little social group to relieve their loneliness and to provide some Catholic reading material in their various languages for Scandinavian converts around the United States. The Saint Ansgar's League, as the group was called, undertook the publication of an annual Bulletin, which became the principal source of information in this country on the condition of the Church in the Scandinavian homelands and its growth among people of Scandinavian origin or descent in this country. Funds for printing and distribution were raised chiefly by means of an annual Christmas party, amply provided with Danish pastry and other aids to good cheer.

I first learned of the League quite by accident, shortly after it was formed. The Bishop of Brooklyn had sent to me, while I was still a novice at St. Andrew-on-Hudson, a catechism in the Swedish language for the usual *censor librorum* reading. I established contact with the League after I came to New York in 1926, and eventually I became their spiritual director.

After the death of Mr. and Mrs. Rambusch, their son, Viggo F. Rambusch, was chosen president of the League, a position he still holds. Under his devoted leadership the League established units in Fargo, North Dakota, and other cities in the Midwest, and has centered much of its activities on assisting the Church in the homelands through the modest means at its command. With the co-operation of several of the bishops in the United States, the League has been able to arrange for scholarships for

Scandinavian young men studying in this country for the priesthood.

The League's most distinguished member was the late Madame
Sigrid Undset, the famous novelist, who attended its monthly
meetings regularly during her exile here in the Second World
War. Tired as she was, and burdened with sorrow over the loss
of her son and the distressing plight of her own country, Madame
Undset sat up night after night sewing and making up packages
to send abroad for the relief of war sufferers.

C. G. LaFarge and the Cathedral of St. John the Divine

The incidents of my brother Grant's relation to the Episcopal cathedral of St. John the Divine in New York City deserve recording. With his partner George L. Heins, husband of our aunt, Aimée LaFarge, he had been the original architect of the cathedral. Heins's work had been more in the administrative line, and Grant's in that of the designing itself. The understanding was that the contract would expire with the death of either partner, and so when Heins passed away in 1907 the trustees, who were dissatisfied with the original plans, refused to renew the contract and instead placed the work in the hands of Ralph Adams Cram.

Grant's design was one of four chosen in a national competition in the year 1890 and it was later selected from the four. It was to exemplify the ideas of Bishop Potter as to the universality of the Church and was more or less in a Romanesque or pre-Gothic style. One of the factors in the design was the Cathedral of Gerona in Spain which Grant had visited in his youth when abroad with Monsignor Thomas Simms Lee of Washington. Its chief feature was a tremendous four-sided tower over the transept, and the magnificent monoliths flanking the main altar. But Grant always said he refused to be bound down by any particular designations of styles.

Mr. Cram insisted that he had done nothing to encroach upon the domain of the architect as long as it remained in the hands of Heins and LaFarge. As it was, one or two of the original trustees became enamored of the Gothic idea and were convinced that an Anglican cathedral in this country would not be perfect unless it were expressed in Gothic terms. Just how far Mr. Cram used personal influence is, of course, a matter of dispute. It is said, though I have never taken the trouble to confirm it, that he received a severe professional censure for his interference. Cram was a born lecturer, a skillful writer and a persuasive personality. On the other hand, Grant's hasty temper and his absences from the scene at critical moments did not promote his case nor strengthen his moral claim. Yet from the day when he was notified of the non-renewal of the contract until his death, he never discussed the matter, and only very rarely did any of his friends or family realize how severe a blow he had absorbed. From an economic standpoint it was terrific, for the work on the cathedral would have been a lifework, and from a professional point of view it was still more bitter. Discussing the change, a New York *Sun* editorial stated:

The trustees were entirely within their contractual rights in abrogating their agreement with the survivor of the firm of Heins & LaFarge, after the death of the senior partner. But of course the "ethical" question has nothing to do with the "aesthetic." The aesthetic question is whether the modified design promises a more impressive and a more expressive completing of the cathedral than the original design. . . .

Clearly it seems that the business of a consulting architect invoked for advice upon a work which has been going on for twenty years and has cost two millions is to help the original design to "abound in its own sense." There is no trace of this purpose in the modified design. The two towers which are substituted for the single and dominant central tower of the original design have no apparent reason for being. Mr. Potter's design contemplated four towers, which would have had their meaning and their value as abutments of the great central vault which he proposed. [William Appleton Potter was one of the four finalists in the national contest for the cathedral.] But can anybody plausibly pretend that two towers, which might as logically be at the other side of the transepts as where they are, and a square truncated tower between them, slurred as far as possible in treatment, constitute so logical, so expressive or so impressive a crowning feature, or promise from any point of view so effective a silhouette as the original spire, itself of course subject to restudy before execution? Is the modified design, from any point of view excepting possibly that of the hidebound Gothic archaeologist, an improvement upon that which it is intended to displace?

Some years ago the authorities of the cathedral decided to re-move the reredos that for so many years had stood behind the high altar. I believe it was shortly after the reredos had been removed in St. Patrick's Cathedral on Fifth Avenue, where the great improvement was obvious. The removal of the St. John's reredos revealed once more the famous monoliths which stand there as reminders of the original design along with the general features of the structure and many details in the crypt. Those who wish to compare the original plan with that which was followed out under Cram can do so by visiting the Library of Architecture at Princeton University. I am not an architect and am a poor judge of such matters, but yet I cannot help feeling that one day some may wonder whether it would not have been a greater contribution to the beauty of New York City if the original purely creative plan had been carried out.

The Spanish Relief Fund

In the spring of 1937, as a practical exercise of international charity, I assisted Father Talbot in organizing the *America* Spanish Relief Fund, for the purpose of bringing relief to the distressed victims of the Spanish Civil War, particularly to the children, in the territory controlled by the Nationalist troops.

Both Father Talbot and myself believed that where suffering was concerned, there should be no partiality in the work of relief. Large-scale aid to assist the sufferers in the territory largely or wholly under Communist control was already well organized by the North American Committee for Aid to Democracy, which was able to draw upon a large sector of public support. On the other hand, no corresponding organization had been formed in the United States for the victims of the Communist revolution in the Nationalist territory, although a considerable number of people in this country within and without the Catholic Church were willing to help. The North American Committee for Aid to Democracy had already had itself registered with the U.S. State Department as an agent for foreign relief, as was required by the Neutrality Law. So our ASRF made a like application, the fifth under the law, and was duly registered on May 18, 1937.

In planning this campaign, we worked in conjunction with the American Friends (Quakers) Service Committee, of which Mr. John F. Reich was the indefatigable and most competent secretary. The Friends' admirable organization distributed aid to the starving children of both sides, with complete impartiality, in response to the appeal made by the Hon. Claude G. Bowers, U.S. Ambassador to Spain. The Quakers were active in both areas in evacuating child victims of the Spanish war from bombed areas, nursing and feeding them, rehabilitating them and establishing them in homes and colonies in Spain. Mr. Reich and his associates were most co-operative, and we in our turn learned much from their direct, practical methods, the heart of which was the personal devotion of their members right in the most difficult areas.

The ASRF was organized through the co-operation of the U.S. Catholic hierarchy and the editors of American Catholic periodicals; so Mr. Michael Williams, editor of the *Commonweal*, proposed the creation of another distinctly civic organization in the same field, the American Committee on Spanish Relief. With the assistance of Father Talbot and the *America* Staff, the ACSR staged an elaborate mass meeting in Madison Square Garden on May 19, 1937. Chairman of the new ACSR was the late Mr. Basil Harris, and leading citizens, Catholic and Protestant alike, undertook its direction.

Shortly after the project was launched, considerable differences sprang up. Father Talbot became dissatisfied with what he considered confused and varying policies on Mr. Williams' part, and quite a bit of argument, in public as well as in private, ensued. However, the original group, the *America* Spanish Relief Fund, kept on with its campaign and made progress. The Fund expanded its work to a national scale, and placed its funds at the disposal of His Eminence Isidro Cardinal Gomá y Tomás, Archbishop of Toledo, for distribution. On March 31, 1940, one year after the termination of the Civil War, the *America* Spanish Relief Fund reported that it had collected and transmitted to Cardinal Gomá the sum of $92,181.79. This he distributed for the benefit of orphans and children, of the aged and destitute families, of charitable services and impoverished priests. Almost every month Cardinal Gomá expressed his deep gratitude to his benefactors.

One of the most terrible aspects of revolutionary Communism is its diabolical double effect: creating boundless destruction and suffering by its direct action, while indirectly it drives its maddened victims to extremes of violence in response. If those who shaped our policies in this country during the days subsequent to the Spanish Civil War had better understood this—to me, so patent—lesson, we would have been spared some of the griefs from which we are suffering today. At any rate, it is comforting to know that American Catholics were willing and able to do something toward relieving Spain's agony, that so many not of our faith co-operated with us in this work, and that it met with undoubted appreciation from the Spaniards themselves.

INDEX